COMMUNICATING EFFECTIVELY

FOURTH EDITION

Saundra Hybels
Lock Haven University

Richard L. Weaver II
Bowling Green State University

McGraw-Hill, Inc.
New York • St. Louis • San Francisco • Auckland • Bogotá • Caracas • Lisbon
London • Madrid • Mexico City • Milan • Montreal • New Delhi • San Juan • Singapore
Sydney • Tokyo • Toronto

COMMUNICATING EFFECTIVELY

This book is printed on acid-free paper.

1 2 3 4 5 6 7 8 9 0 VNH VNH 9 0 9 8 7 6 5 4

ISBN 0-07-016755-9

This book was set in New Aster by Better Graphics, Inc.
The editors were Hilary Jackson and Scott Amerman;
the designer was Wanda Lubelska;
the production supervisor was Annette Mayeski.
The photo editor was Elyse Rieder.
Von Hoffmann Press, Inc., was printer and binder.

Cover photo: Andre Baranowski

Library of Congress Cataloging-in-Publication Data

Hybels, Saundra.
    Communicating effectively / Saundra Hybels, Richard L. Weaver
  II.—4th ed.
        p.   cm.
    Includes bibliographical references.
    ISBN 0-07-016755-9
    1. Oral communication.   I. Weaver, Richard L., (date).
  II. Title.
  P95.H9   1995
  302.2'242—dc20   94-26789

CONTENTS

■ PART THREE: COMMUNICATING IN GROUPS   213

CHAPTER 8: SMALL GROUPS   215

CHAPTER 9: ROLES RESPONSIBILITIES: LEADING, PARTICIPATING, AND MANAGING CONFLICT   239

CHAPTER 15: THE PERSUASIVE SPEECH 427

PREFACE

Communicating Effectively, Fourth Edition, has been written for the beginning student in a speech communication class. With students as our focus, we have tried to show the theories of interpersonal, group, public communication, and intercultural communication and how they apply to situations students may encounter in their work, recreation, and study. The introductory chapters, Chapters 1 to 5, present a model of communication and show how language and nonverbal communication work in our interactions with others. In Chapters 6 and 7, which deal with interpersonal communication, we discuss relationships, their dynamics, and how they can be improved. Chapters 8 and 9, on small groups, look at decision making in groups and address themselves to how small groups solve problems on the campus, in the workplace, and in the community. Chapters 10 to 15, on public speaking, are designed to help students develop, organize, and present a speech without undue anxiety.

The questions that have given us focus and direction in all of our revisions have been: "How do students learn?" "How can we explain concepts so students can relate them to their own lives?" "What will make this book interesting to students?" "How can this book help the classroom instructor?" In answering these questions, our approach to writing has always been to imagine students sitting in the classroom before us and to write as if we are there in the classroom discussing concepts with them.

We have used many examples of key concepts in this book because this seems to be the best way to get students to relate the theories to their own lives. To help students identify with these examples, we have drawn them from actual experiences on campus, at work, in the family, and in the community.

A strong goal of this book is to get students to see the world beyond their own community and even beyond the nation. Both of us have worked and lived in many places of the world that are completely different from the United States. We have drawn on these experiences in two ways: to give students a chance to see how other people communicate and to show how Americans perceive cultures that are different from their own.

More specifically, we draw the students' attention to race, class, and ethnicity by introducing a definition and discussion of intercultural communication in the first chapter. In the examples throughout the book, we try to use Hispanic, Asian, African, and Eastern European names so that all students will feel that this book applies to them. We also include many multicultural ideas. Chapter 2 describes the process one goes through in getting involved in a new culture. Other chapters deal with bilingualism, dialect, cultural sub-groups, and practical exercises to help students talk to someone different from themselves.

We have tried to create situations in which students can try out theory as they are reading the book. One way we do this is through boxes, most of which have been revised in this edition. In the *Try This* boxes, students are asked to take the theory explained in the text and to apply it to their own lives and experiences through a series of questions. Although these boxes are designed for the reader, they can also serve as the basis for class discussion. Our second set of boxes is labeled *Consider This*. These boxes are based on high-interest reading from current books, magazines, and newspapers. In this edition, most of the *Consider This* boxes focus on themes of gender, multiculturalism, and ethics, and are followed by questions. We have taken advantage of the new full-color design to highlight each of these topics with a different logo in the *Consider This* boxes: ethics ,

gender , critical thinking , and multiculturalism .

Other boxes, called *Another Point of View*, are new to this edition. In these boxes we have presented material on communication issues that might be contrary to what is in the text or are provocative and controversial. The purpose of these boxes is to generate critical thinking and lively discussion. There are four of these boxes discussing such issues as "free speech vs. hate speech" in the text, also followed by questions.

FEATURES OF THE FOURTH EDITION

In this edition, we have incorporated new research, have rewritten many examples, and have changed the material in all the *Consider This* boxes and many of the *Try This* boxes. For those who are new to the book, this is also our first all-color edition. We hope that the use of color will make the book more interesting to students and instructors alike.

The greatest change in the text is in the interpersonal communication chapters, where we have added a section about family communication. In these chapters we have defined family and family communication, and we have described what makes families effective in their communication.

In order to keep the book a reasonable length, we have eliminated the chapter about Interviewing. Most of our reviewers said they did not have time to cover this material. For those who are disappointed with this change, the chapter is still available to students by requesting it from the publisher.

This new edition expands on multiculturalism, which was introduced in the third edition. Most of the chapters have multicultural *Consider This* boxes. With these boxes, whenever it has been possible, we have quoted material from autobiographies and memoirs so that people can speak in their own voices. Some of the voices represented are Chinese, Japanese American, African American and Latino. The gender boxes show the many different ways that women and men differ in their communication, ranging from different styles in male and female comedians to who interrupts whom in conversation. The subject of ethics is particularly strong in the public speaking chapters where students are asked to grapple with some tough ethical issues.

The *Try This* boxes, as in previous editions, ask the students to apply a theory to their own experience. Many of these boxes suggest an approach students may not have thought of. For example, students are asked to come up with a list of questions that they might ask someone from another country without asking consumer-type questions. The occasional boxes, *Another Point of View*, are new to this edition. They ask students to consider a point of view that might be contrary to that presented in the chapter. One of these boxes, for example, questions whether Americans put too much emphasis on self-esteem.

Finally, in the public speaking section, all of the annotated sample speeches are new and the text contains fresh examples and updated research.

ORGANIZATION

Communicating Effectively, Fourth Edition, is organized into four parts.

Part One sets forth the basic principles of communication in five chapters:

Chapter 1 discusses the need for communication skills, introduces and explains a model of communication, and focuses on communication as a process and transaction. New material defines and explains intercultural communication.

Chapter 2 covers intrapersonal communication through a discussion of self-concept and perception and how the two concepts are related. Then we discuss communication in which race and ethnicity are involved. New material describes what makes up self-concept and how gender and self-concept are related.

Chapter 3 explains how the listening process works. Listening habits and attitudes are discussed in detail. Students are given direction on how to listen for information, how to listen critically, how to listen with empathy, and how to enhance listening for enjoyment. New material includes an explanation of cognitive dissonance and a discussion of some of the problems of listening to someone from another culture.

Chapter 4 concentrates on verbal communication. Beginning with a discussion of some theories of language, it emphasizes skill building through a discussion of style, language appropriateness, and language choice. The chapter also discusses how men and women communicate differently. New material discusses sexist language and whether the United States should become bilingual.

Chapter 5 talks about the importance of nonverbal communication. As well as introducing basic principles, the chapter describes various kinds of nonverbal communication. There is an extensive discussion of clothing as nonverbal communication. The chapter has new material about how male-female attraction is communicated nonverbally.

Part Two, which has two chapters, focuses on interpersonal communication:

Chapter 6 covers interpersonal communication as a transaction, focusing on interpersonal needs, attraction to others, and the importance of self-disclosure. Almost half of this chapter is new material about family communication.

Chapter 7 concentrates on relationship stages—how relationships are formed and how they are dissolved. This chapter suggests criteria for evaluating relationships, gives communication strategies to pursue and avoid, and explains a model for resolving conflict. New material includes an expanded discussion of criticism and complaints and a new section on assertiveness.

Part Three has two chapters on small groups and how they work: process and transaction. New material defines and explains intercultural communication.

Chapter 8 begins with the characteristics of small groups and discusses why groups can often solve problems more readily than individuals. It also distinguishes between procedural issues and substantive issues. The new material expands the discussion of norms and rules and makes distinctions between informal and formal groups.

Chapter 9 gives more information on the roles and responsibilities of leaders and participants when they are part of a group. It also discusses how leaders get their power and explains how leaders influence group behavior. A number of suggestions are given for managing conflict in groups. New boxes discuss the effect of gender on leadership roles.

Part Four, which contains six chapters, deals with public communication:

Chapter 10 tells the student how to get started on a speech. It focuses on selecting the topic, narrowing it, and choosing a purpose for the speech. The student is given detailed instructions and examples for selecting a general and specific purpose as well as the central idea. The chapter also has a good deal of information on how to go about audience analysis. New materials discuss demographic analysis in greater depth and give speakers suggestions on how to deal with cultural diversity.

Chapter 11 tells students how to research a topic using personal experience, interviews, and library resources. It describes the various types of supporting material. Updated material is provided about database searches.

Chapter 12 focuses on organizing and outlining a speech. Several patterns of organization are described, many with new examples. Other new material discusses mini outlines for introductions and conclusions. The chapter concludes with a new annotated sample outline for a speech about stage fright.

Chapter 13 tells how to deliver a speech using impromptu, manuscript, memory, and extemporaneous methods. It discusses how a speaker should look and sound and the kinds of visual aids to use during the speech. This chapter emphasizes the importance of practice and the student's evaluation of the speech when it is over. New material discusses the need for careful audience analysis—especially in nonverbal communication. There are also new sections on computer-generated graphics and ideas for reducing anxiety.

Chapter 14 focuses on the informative speech. As well as explaining the goals of the speech, it describes some of the more sophisticated ways of developing supporting material. There are several suggestions of how to handle numbers. A new, annotated sample speech appears at the end of the chapter.

Chapter 15 begins with a definition of persuasion and explains the purposes of persuasion. Discussions of ethics and ethical judgment appear throughout the chapter. There is new material on why persuasion is so difficult and additional material about logical and emotional appeals and credibility. Also new is a complete annotated sample speech at the end of the chapter.

PEDAGOGICAL DEVICES

Since the theory and concepts of speech communication can be difficult to master, we have incorporated a number of pedagogical devices to help the reader. We begin each chapter with a list of objectives and key terms to help students focus on the important ideas contained in the chapter. Within the chapter, the key terms are printed in boldface and are defined the first time they are used. They also appear in the updated glossary at the end of the book. Each chapter concludes with a list of recent, annotated readings that the student can use to follow up on the concepts discussed in each chapter. These readings provide a variety of scholarly and popular materials that students may use for course projects or additional research.

The previously mentioned insert boxes give students a chance to apply their own experience to theory, to become familiar with multicultural, ethical, and gender issues, and to develop skills in critical thinking. Many of the boxes and all the captions on the photographs ask the reader questions that encourage them to think about the material and what they have learned.

Communicating Effectively comes with an Instructor's Manual which includes course outlines for semesters as well as quarters. Each chapter in the manual has an overview, discussion questions, and activities that the instructor can discuss, ask, or do with the class to show how the theories of the chapter work in practice. Each chapter concludes with multiple-choice, true/false, and essay questions for examinations. The essay questions may also be used in the class as discussion questions.

Acknowledgments

No author can acknowledge everyone who contributes to a book. While you are working on the manuscript, many of your classroom encounters, the people you talk to, and the people you work with are likely to end up, lightly veiled, in the book's pages. To all of these sources, who would probably prefer to remain anonymous, I give you my thanks.

Other people are more obvious. My department head, Doug Campbell, uses tact and diplomacy in running our department so we all have a peaceful place to work. Many of the people in my summer study group—particularly Karen Kline, Karen Elias, Janet Irons, and Nina Williams—are always a source of new and interesting ideas. Again, I would like to thank the best reference librarian I have ever known, Esther Jane Carrier. My friend, Jude Montarsi, has also been a great help, as he is always willing to go to the library and track down an errant footnote or an article's title. I would like to thank Cynthia Fostle for her expertise in editing. A good editor creates a better author.

On the practical front, I would like to thank my husband, Joansin, and his sisters, Reyann and Maria, for keeping the household going and for always being willing to pitch in as deadlines approach. They also provide the author with the happy background noise that makes her know she is part of a family.

SAUNDRA HYBELS

I would like to thank the members of the Department of Interpersonal Communication for their continuing support and encouragement. They are: John J. Makay, Chair, and Julie Burke, Don Enholm, Al Gonzalez, Ray Tucker, and Jim Wilcox.

Also, I want to thank my colleague of more than seventeen years, Howard Cotrell. Howard is a faculty facilitator who works with a variety of colleagues to help them improve their teaching and research. Not only have we co-authored more than 40 articles, he has been a contributor to my thoughts, feelings, and ruminations on almost every project I undertake. Even though his name does not appear on all my published works, he is there in spirit.

Finally, thank you to my family. Scott, Jacquie, Anthony, and Joanna have been inspirations to my writing and to my life. And thank you, of course, to Andrea, my wife, for her support, her contributions, and her love. She is always there, willing to help, willing to share, and willing to give.

RICHARD L. WEAVER II

Both of us would like to thank Hilary Jackson for having enough faith in this book to publish it in color and Scott Amerman for guiding it through the production process.

We would also like to thank the following reviewers for their detailed and insightful comments: Deborah Andrews, University of North Carolina at Wilmington; Violet Asmuth, Edison Community College; Maresa Brassil, Auburn University, Montgomery; Virginia Chapman, Anderson University; Mary Ann Cox, San Joaquin Delta College; Mary Forestieri, Lane Community College; Teresa Helmick, Johnson County Community College; Carol Lewandowski, Oral Roberts University; Kim Parker Niemczyk, Palm Beach Community College, South; Frank O'Mara, SUNY, Oneonta; Laurinda Porter, St. Cloud State University; Richard Quianthy, Broward Community College; Richard Rea, University of Arkansas; Vera Sheppard, Salem State College; Paul Westbrook, Northeastern State University; Leonard Wurthman, California State University at Northridge; and Myra Young, Johnson County Community College.

PART

I

BASIC PRINCIPLES OF COMMUNICATION

KEY TERMS

abstract symbol
channel
communication
concrete symbol
culture
ethics
feedback
intercultural
  communication
interpersonal
  communication
intrapersonal
  communication
message
noise
nonverbal
  symbol
public
  communication
roles
sender-receiver
setting
small-group
  communication
subculture
symbol
transactional
  communication
verbal symbol

1

The Communication Process

CHAPTER OBJECTIVES

After reading this chapter, you should be able to:

1 Explain communication needs and relate them to your life.

2 Define communication and explain it as a process.

3 Identify the elements of communication.

4 Explain how communication is a transaction.

5 Explain how seeing communication as a transaction helps us to understand it better.

6 Describe the types of communication.

7 Define and be able to explain intercultural communication.

8 Discuss the ways you can improve your own communication skills.

Barry spends his time going in and out of the bodegas and grocery stores in the Hispanic neighborhoods of New York City. He is trying to persuade grocers to stock coconut, mango, and guava ice creams—some of the favorite flavors of the Hispanic population. Barry has had a particularly good week; he has added three new customers and has persuaded four shopkeepers to increase their orders.

Ming attends college in a wheelchair. All buildings where her classes are held have been modified for wheelchair access, but the student center has not. Whenever Ming wants to go there for a meal or to buy books, she has to ask people to carry her wheelchair up the steps. Ming decides that she will try to change this situation. She goes to the student government, which runs the center, and asks them to install a wheelchair ramp. The senators of the government all agree that a ramp is a good idea, and the president asks Ming to get bids from local contractors. At the next meeting she presents the senators with three bids. They vote to hire a contractor, and by the end of the semester, the ramp is in place.

Karen, a judge, speaks to the Jaycees about the need to prevent crime rather than build more prisons. She believes that crime-prevention messages must begin with 10- to 12-year-olds. Her message is so persuasive that several Jaycees volunteer to form and work with local youth groups.

Seventeen-year-old Tara is struggling to succeed as the mother of a two-month-old. Because her husband works long hours, she spends most of the day alone, and she often feels she will go crazy if she doesn't talk to someone her own age. A former teacher tells her about a teen parents' support group, and Tara decides to go. By the end of the meeting, she discovers several mothers who have similar problems and writes down the phone numbers of three of them.

Barry, Ming, Karen, and Tara all have something in common: they were successful in their endeavors because they used communication skills. Barry was able to persuade store managers to order more ice cream. Ming succeeded because she was able to come up with a plan and present it to a group that could make the change she wanted. Karen was so effective in presenting her message about crime that several people were inspired to help her. And Tara recognized and acted on a need that all of us have: finding people who like us and will support us.

■ EVERYONE NEEDS COMMUNICATION SKILLS

People fulfill a variety of needs through communication, and communicating effectively can provide considerable pleasure. A stimulating conversation with someone from another country, participation in a group discussion that leads to solving a problem, a persuasive speech that gains signatures on a petition: all these are instances of successful communication.

Even though we have been communicating since birth, we are not

TRY THIS

Try to state what you want to accomplish in your communication in each of the following situations:

- Presenting an oral report in a class

- Helping a friend who is feeling depressed

- Persuading a potential employer to hire you

How do your goals differ in each of these situations?

always effective. Sometimes communication doesn't work and we end up frustrated. We get lost by using incomplete directions, insult a friend with what we intended as an innocent comment, or bore an audience with a speech. Effective communication is a problem for many of us; that's why it has spawned an entire industry of books, articles, and seminars telling us how to communicate.

Communication is vital in all areas of our lives. We use it for persuasion; to influence relationships; to inform; to share, discover, and uncover information. We want a friend to stop studying and go to a party; we want our relationships to improve; we want someone to join our club or to vote for a particular candidate.

Many people believe that effective communication is the most important key to success in our work and in our relationships. In a survey sent to 1000 personnel managers, the managers listed oral communication and listening as the most important skills for gaining employment. For people who were on the job, they said that the abilities to work with others and to speak effectively were most important.[1] In another survey, college alumni responded that the most important skills for their jobs were making presentations and handling questions and answers and small-group discussion.[2]

In our private lives our most important need is to maintain and improve relationships. Through communication we discover others' needs and share our own. Any kind of relationship requires open and accurate lines of communication. Only when such lines exist will we feel free to voice important thoughts and feelings.

Communication, then, is vital to our lives. To live is to communicate. To communicate effectively is to enjoy life more fully. On the premise that increased knowledge helps us to do things better, let's begin with a discussion of how communication works.

A Definition of Communication

Communication is any process in which people share information, ideas, and feelings. That process involves not only the spoken and written word but also body language, personal mannerisms and style, the surroundings—anything that adds meaning to a message. To see how this process works, consider this exchange between Jason and Christine at their tenth high school reunion.

Before they even start to speak, they look each other over and form some impressions. Jason thinks to himself that Christine is much prettier than he remembered her in high school. Christine thinks that Jason looks good with a beard. After they form these initial impressions, they begin to talk. Christine asks, "What have you been up to for the past ten years? Are you still a writer? I remember that you were always writing stories in high school."

Jason replies, "I'm still at it. My first book is coming out at the end of the year. What have you been up to?"

Christine says, with a bright smile (ignoring the question about herself), "Wow! That's really impressive. What's the book about?"

Even in this short exchange, a good deal of communication takes place. The communication begins before Christine and Jason even start talking. They start with what they remember about each other in high school, and then they form updated impressions of each other. Christine remembers that Jason used to like to write, so she uses that as a conversation opener. Christine's communication with Jason may also be influenced by her gender. Through social conditioning, she may have been taught to focus more on the male in conversation than on herself. Also, while Christine is talking to Jason, she thinks about whether their relationship might continue in the future. For example, she might decide that it would fun to know the author of a book, so one of these days she will call Jason and suggest lunch.

Although everyone goes to high school reunions to catch up on other's lives, the conversations people have with each other vary greatly. If two men start talking, their conversation may be competitive since many American men are competitive about what they have accomplished in their careers. Often the conversation is aimed at finding out who has the job with the most money or status. If two women are talking at the same reunion, they are certain to compare notes about careers and families, and in some cases their talk might also be competitive.

Let's say that during their senior year, this class had a visiting foreign exchange student, Tong Hee, and that he has also come to the reunion. If he talks to various class members, they will probably be interested in what he is doing now. In this case, whether he talks to men or women, the conversations are not so likely to be competitive: since the class members are probably unaware of what constitutes status or even wealth in his culture, they have no way of judging the life he is living now.

These conversations at the high school reunion illustrate communication as a process. When we talk of communication as a process, we mean that it is always changing.[3] Christine's communication with Jason, for example, changes from her first, casual impression of his beard to strong interest when she discovers he has written a book. This present communication also will influence whether there will be communication in the future.

The Elements of Communication

The communication process is made up of various elements: sender-receivers, messages, channels, noise, feedback, and setting. Figure 1-1 shows how all these elements work together. The amoeba-like shape of the sender-receiver indicates how this person changes—depending on what he or she is hearing or reacting to.

SENDER-RECEIVERS

People get involved in communication because they have information, ideas, and feelings they want to share. This sharing, however, is not a one-way process, where one person sends ideas and the other receives them and then the process is reversed. In most communication situations, people are **sender-receivers**—both sending and receiving at the same time. For example, Janet and Al are discussing a problem their 6-year-old daughter, Rebecca, is having at school. Janet, who has just come from a conference

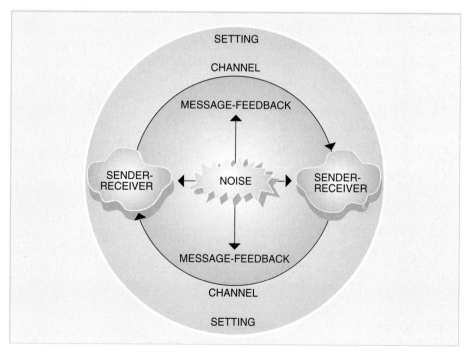

FIGURE 1-1
**The Elements of
Communication**

with Rebecca's teacher, is doing much of the talking. Al is acting as the receiver by listening. However, he is also sending messages that he is concerned: he pays careful attention, he puts his hand on Janet's arm when she starts to get upset, and he puts his arms around her when she starts crying. Through his actions, Al sends as many messages as he gets, even though he doesn't say a word.

MESSAGE

The **message** is made up of the ideas and feelings that a sender-receiver wants to share. In the case of Al and Janet, Janet's message dealt with what had happened and what she was feeling about it while Al's message was one of comfort and support.

Ideas and feelings can be communicated only if they are represented by symbols. A **symbol** is something that stands for something else. All our communication messages are made up of two kinds of symbols: verbal and nonverbal.

Every word in our language is a **verbal symbol** that stands for a particular thing or idea. Verbal symbols are limited and complicated. For example, when we use the word *chair*, we agree we are talking about something we sit on. Thus, *chair* is a **concrete symbol**, a symbol which represents an object. However, when we hear the word *chair*, we all might have a different impression: a chair could be a recliner, an easy chair, a bean bag, a lawn chair—the variety is great.

Even more complicated are **abstract symbols**, which stand for ideas. Consider, for example, the vast differences in our understanding of words such as *home, hungry,* or *hurt*. How we understand these words will be determined by our experience. Since people's experiences differ to some degree, they will assign different meanings to these abstract words.

Nonverbal symbols are anything we communicate without using words, such as facial expressions, gestures, posture, vocal tones, appearance, and so on. As with verbal symbols, we all attach certain meanings to nonverbal symbols. A yawn means we are bored or tired; a furled brow indicates confusion; not looking someone in the eye may mean we have something to hide. Like verbal symbols, nonverbal symbols can be misleading. We cannot control all our nonverbal behavior, and we often send out information of which we are not even aware.

Many nonverbal messages are different from one culture to another. In one culture, showing the sole of your foot when you cross your legs is a terrible insult. In another culture, respectful behavior is shown with a bow, while in still another, deep respect is shown by touching the other person's feet. Whether or not we are aware of nonverbal messages, they are extremely important to all cultures. Albert Mehrabian believes that over 90 percent of the messages sent and received by Americans are nonverbal.[4]

CHANNELS

The **channel** is the route traveled by a message, the means it uses to reach the sender-receivers. In face-to-face communication, the primary channels

What is this couple communicating nonverbally?

are sound and sight: we listen to and look at each other. We are familiar with the channels of radio, television, records, newspapers, and magazines in the mass media. Other channels communicate nonverbal messages. For example, when DeVon goes to apply for a job, she uses several nonverbal signals to send out a positive message: a firm handshake (touch), business clothes (sight), and respectful voice (sound). The senses she is appealing to are the channels.

FEEDBACK

Feedback is the response of the receiver-senders to each other. You tell me a joke and I smile. That's feedback. You make a comment about the weather and I make another one. More feedback.

Feedback is vital to communication because it lets the participants in the communication see whether ideas and feelings have been shared in the way they were intended.

For example, when Deletha and Jordan decide to meet on the corner of 45th and Broadway in New York City, it would be good feedback for one of them to ask, "Which corner?" for these particular corners are among the busiest and most crowded in the city.

Sender-receivers who meet face-to-face have the greatest opportunity for feedback, especially if there are no distractions. In this kind of setting, they have a chance to see whether the other person understands and is following the message. A teacher working with a child, for example, can readily see by the child's face whether he is confused. She can also see when he is getting bored, by the way he fidgets and begins to lose attention. A speaker in a large lecture hall, however, is not as aware of the feedback from his

What kinds of
feedback are these
students giving
each other?

audience. Those listeners he can see might look attentive, but the ones in
the back rows may be having a quiet snooze. In general, the fewer the people involved in the communication event, the greater the opportunity for
feedback.

NOISE

Noise is interference that keeps a message from being understood or accurately interpreted. Noise occurs between the sender-receivers, and it comes
in three forms: external, internal, and semantic.

External noise comes from the environment and keeps the message from
being heard or understood. Your heart-to-heart talk with your roommate
can be interrupted by a group of people yelling in the hall, a helicopter passing overhead, or a power saw outside the window. External noise does not
always come from sound. You could be standing and talking to someone in
the hot sun and become so uncomfortable that you can't concentrate.
Conversation might also falter at a picnic when you discover you are sitting
on an anthill and ants are crawling all over your blanket.

Internal noise occurs in the minds of the sender-receivers when their
thoughts or feelings are focused on something other than the communication at hand. A student doesn't hear the lecture because he is thinking about
lunch; a wife can't pay attention to her husband because she is thinking
about a problem at the office. Internal noise may also stem from beliefs or
prejudices. Doug, for example, doesn't believe that women should be managers, so when his boss asks him to do something, he often misses part of
her message.

Semantic noise is caused by people's emotional reactions to words. Many people tune out a speaker who uses profanity because the words are so offensive to them. Others have negative reactions to people who make ethnic or sexist remarks. Semantic noise, like external noise and internal noise, can interfere with all or part of the message.

SETTING

The **setting** is where the communication occurs. Settings can be a significant influence on communication. Some are formal and lend themselves to formal presentations. An auditorium, for example, is good for giving speeches and presentations but not very good for conversation. If people want to converse on a more intimate basis, they will be better off in a smaller, more comfortable room where they can sit and face each other.

Setting is made up of many components, which can range from the way a place is lighted to the colors used for decoration. Your local discount store is illuminated with fluorescent lights. These lights communicate a message: you are not there to relax but to do business and move on. On the other hand, if you are going to buy designer clothing in a department store, you are not likely to find fluorescent lighting. The lighting will be subdued, and the showroom will probably look more like your living room than like a store.

Setting often influences power relationships. The question "Your place or mine?" implies an equal relationship. However, when the dean asks a faculty member to come to her office, it shows that the dean has more power

How does the setting of this food court discourage people from lingering or engaging in intimate conversation?

than the faculty member. When a couple meets to work out a divorce agreement, they meet in a lawyer's office, a place that provides a somewhat neutral setting.

The arrangement of furniture in a setting can also affect the communication that takes place. For example, at one college, the library was one of the noisiest places on campus. The problem was solved by rearranging the furniture. Instead of sofas and chairs arranged so that students could sit and talk, the library used study desks—thus creating a quiet place to concentrate.

All communication is made up of sender-receivers, messages, channels, feedback, noise, and setting. Every time people communicate, these elements are somewhat different. They are not the only factors that influence communication, however. Communication is also influenced by what we bring to it. That is the subject of our next section.

COMMUNICATION IS A TRANSACTION

A communication transaction involves not only the physical act of communicating but also a psychological one: impressions are being formed in the minds of the people who are communicating.[5] What people think and know about one another directly affects their communication.

The Three Principles of Transactional Communication

Communication as a transaction—**transactional communication**—involves three important principles. First, people engaged in communication are sending messages continuously and simultaneously. Second, communication events have a past, present, and future. Third, participants in communication play certain roles. Let's consider each of these principles in turn.

PARTICIPATION IS CONTINUOUS AND SIMULTANEOUS

Whether or not you are actually talking in a communication situation, you are actively involved in sending and receiving messages. Let's say you are lost, walking in a big city that is not familiar to you. You show others you are confused when you hesitate, look around you, or pull out a map. When you know you will have to ask for directions, you begin to look for someone who might help you. You dismiss two people because they look like they're in a hurry; you don't ask another one because she looks as though she is from somewhere else, like you. Finally you see a person who looks helpful and you ask for information. As you listen, you give feedback, both through words and body language, as to whether you understand.

As this person talks, you think about how long it will take to walk to your destination, you make note of what landmarks to look for, and you may even create a visual image of what you will see when you get there. You are participating continuously and simultaneously in a complicated situation—one which we all take for granted.

ALL COMMUNICATIONS HAVE A PAST, A PRESENT, AND A FUTURE

We all respond to every situation from our own experiences, our own moods, and our own expectations. Such factors complicate the communication situation. When we know someone well, we can make predictions about what to do in the future on the basis of what we know about the past. For example, without having to ask him, Elanda knows that her husband prefers Mexican food to Chinese food, likes to hike, and hates to sunbathe on beaches. This information helps her make suggestions about where to go for their vacation. Her husband Eric can also make predictions about Elanda. He knows that she hates to get household appliances for gifts, does not like to dance, and prefers gourmet meals to fast food. This knowledge helps him plan where to take her for her birthday.

Even when you are meeting someone for the first time, you respond to that person on the basis of your experience. You might respond to physical traits (short, tall, bearded, bald), to occupation (accountant, gym teacher), or even to a name (remember how a boy named Eugene always tormented you and you've mistrusted all Eugenes ever since?). Any of these things you call up from your past might influence how you respond to someone—at least at the beginning.

The future also influences communication. If you want a relationship to continue, you will say and do things in the present to make sure it does. ("Thanks for dinner. I always enjoy your cooking.") If you think you will never see a person again, this also might affect your communication. You might be more businesslike, leaving the personal aspects of your life out of the communication.

ALL COMMUNICATORS PLAY ROLES

Roles are parts we play or ways we behave with others. Defined by society and affected by individual relationships, roles control everything from word choice to body language. For example, one of the roles you play is that of student. Your teachers may consider you to be bright and serious; your peers, who see you in the same role, may think you are too serious. Outside the classroom you play other roles. Your parents might see you as a considerate daughter or son; your best friend might see the fun-loving side of you; and your boss might see you as hardworking and dependable.

Roles are not always consistent within a relationship. They vary with others' moods or with one's own, with the setting and the noise factor. No two communications are the same. They change to meet the needs of each particular relationship and situation. For example, Rachel is a serious student

Who seems to have the most authority here? How do you know?

but recognizes that not all of her classmates value this quality. When Simon confesses that he hasn't even started his term paper (which is due tomorrow), Rachel shows sympathy but doesn't tell him that her own paper was finished a week ago.

The roles we play—whether established by individual relationships or by society—are also perceived differently by different people. These different perceptions affect the communication that results. For example, Tom, in his role of youth director, is well organized and maintains tight control over the activities he directs. The kids who play games he coaches know they have to behave, or they'll be in big trouble. Therefore they speak to him in a respectful voice and stay quiet when they're supposed to. To other kids, however, Tom's discipline indicates rigidity and inflexibility. These kids avoid the youth center; they choose not to communicate with him at all.

THE PRINCIPLES IN ACTION

Let's see how all three principles of transactional communication work as we listen to a conversation between Terry and Rick

Terry: *Hey, man. I'm a little short this week, and I have to get some gas in my car. Can I borrow $10?*

Rick: *Steps back, slight frown) Well . . .*

Terry: *(Steps forward) I wouldn't ask you if I didn't really need it, but I have to go home this weekend.*

Rick: (Folds his arms in front of him) Last week I loaned you $5, and you haven't paid me back.

Terry: (Looks contrite) I'm sorry. I forgot. Look, I'll get some money from my mom, and I'll pay you back as soon as I get back to school.

Rick: (Sounds unenthusiastic) Well, OK. But don't forget this time.

Terry: Thanks, Rick. You're a good buddy.

We know right away in this scene that Rick does not want to cooperate, even though he never says so. As Terry speaks, Rick simultaneously and continuously sends out signals: he frowns, he steps back, he folds his arms in front of him—all nonverbal symbols of resistance. Terry reinforces his verbal symbols by stepping forward—a nonverbal way of showing assertiveness.

This scene between Terry and Rick would probably take no more than thirty seconds in real life, yet it is filled with symbols—some of which non-participants would be unable to detect. What are the past and future aspects of this communication? How many times has Terry borrowed money from Rick? How willing has Rick been to lend it before? What is Terry and Rick's relationship? Do they get along? Do they respect each other and each other's possessions?

TRY THIS

Take a look at your attitude toward the instructor for your speech communication course. Since you are at the beginning of the course, you probably don't know very much about him or her. (If you do know each other, pick another instructor you don't know so well.) Now, assume you are going to go to this instructor's office to ask questions about your first assignment.

Past

How will your past experience affect your communication with this instructor? What has been your experience with other instructors in the past? Have they been helpful? Interested in students? Have you heard anything through the student grapevine about this instructor? Will this influence your communication? Do you feel comfortable with college teachers? Will this have an influence?

Future

How do you want this instructor to think about you? What do you want from this instructor in the future? If your answer is "a good grade," do you think it's important to create a good impression?

We must also look at the roles Terry and Rick play. They are probably equal, since it appears from their conversation that Terry feels free to borrow from Rick. Rick lets him do it—probably because he wants to be friends with Terry and he's afraid Terry will not like him if he doesn't lend the money.

When we look at this conversation between Terry and Rick, we can see how complicated even a simple conversation can be. Still, we can never really understand what goes on in communication unless we look at it from a transactional perspective. Then we can begin to see the complexity and uniqueness of each communication event. As Heraclitus, the Greek philosopher, once observed, we cannot step into the same river twice: not only are we different, but so is the river. The same is true of communication.

TYPES OF COMMUNICATION

As you can see in Figure 1-2, there are different kinds of communication. The figure shows the kinds most often used: intrapersonal, interpersonal, small-group, public, and intercultural communication.

Intrapersonal Communication

Intrapersonal communication is communication that occurs within us. It involves thoughts, feelings, and the way we look at ourselves. Figure 1-3 shows some of the things that make up the self and, hence, intrapersonal communication.

Because intrapersonal communication is centered in the self, you are the only sender-receiver. The message is made up of your thoughts and feelings. The channel is your brain, which processes what you are thinking and feeling. There is feedback in the sense that as you talk to yourself, you discard certain ideas and replace them with others.

Even though you are not directly communicating with others in intrapersonal communication, the people and the experiences you have had determine how you "talk" to yourself. For example, if you have had a good day, you are likely to look at yourself in a positive way. If a teacher was disappointed with your work, or if you had a fight with a fellow student, you are likely to focus more on your feelings of failure or anger. You can never look at yourself without being influenced by the relationships you have had with others.

Interpersonal Communication

Interpersonal communication occurs when we communicate on a one-to-one basis—usually in an informal, unstructured setting. This kind of communication occurs mostly between two people, though it may include more than two.

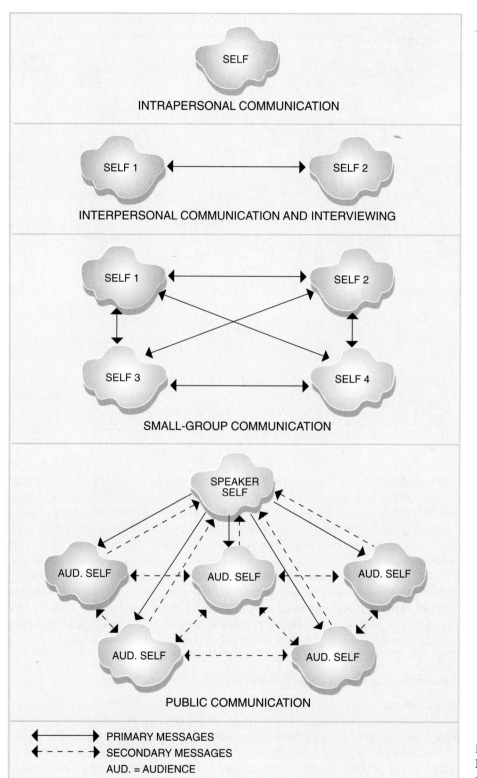

INTRAPERSONAL COMMUNICATION

INTERPERSONAL COMMUNICATION AND INTERVIEWING

SMALL-GROUP COMMUNICATION

PUBLIC COMMUNICATION

PRIMARY MESSAGES
SECONDARY MESSAGES
AUD. = AUDIENCE

FIGURE 1.2
**Kinds of
communication**

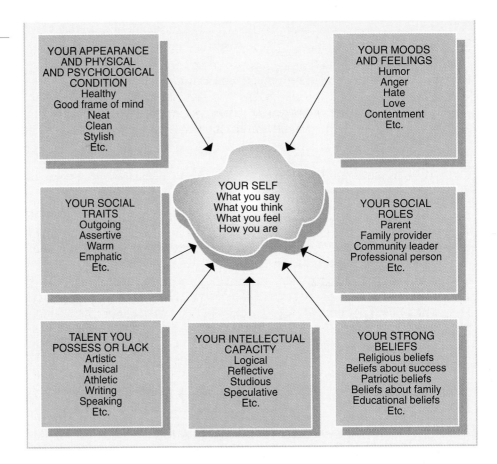

Figure 1.3
Interpersonal
Communication

Interpersonal communication uses all the elements of the communication process. In a conversation between friends, for example, each brings his or her background and experience to the conversation. During the conversation each functions as a sender-receiver. Their messages consist of both verbal and nonverbal symbols. The channels they use the most are sight and sound. Because interpersonal communication is between two (or a few) people, it offers the greatest opportunity for feedback. Internal noise is likely to be minimal because each person can see whether the other is distracted. The persons involved in the conversation have many chances to check that the message is being perceived correctly. Interpersonal communication usually takes place in informal and comfortable settings.

Small-Group Communication

Small-group communication occurs when a small number of people meet to solve a problem. The group must be small enough so that each member in the group has a chance to interact with all the other members.

Because small groups are made up of several sender-receivers, the communication process is more complicated than in interpersonal communication. With so many more people sending messages, there are more chances for confusion. Messages are also more structured in small groups because the group is meeting together for a specific purpose. Small groups use the same channels as interpersonal communication, however, and there is also a good deal of opportunity for feedback. In view of their problem-solving nature, small groups usually meet in a more formal setting than people involved in interpersonal communication.

Public Communication

In **public communication** the sender-receiver (the speaker) sends a message (the speech) to an audience. The speaker usually delivers a highly structured message, using the same channels as in interpersonal and small-group communication. In public communication, however, the channels are more exaggerated than in interpersonal communication. The voice is louder and the gestures are more expansive because the audience is bigger. The speaker might use additional visual channels, such as slides, flip charts, and so on. Generally the opportunity for verbal feedback in public communication is limited. The audience members may have a chance to ask questions at the end of the speech, but usually they are not free to address the speaker during the speech. However, they can send nonverbal feedback. If they like what the speaker is saying, they may interrupt the speech with applause. If they dislike it, they may fidget a lot or simply stop paying attention. In most public communication the setting is formal.

TRY THIS

In each of the communication situations listed below, identify the following: the kind of communication, the participants, the message, the channel, the amount of potential feedback, and the likely setting. What are the possible sources of external and internal noise in each situation?

- You meet on a student government committee to select a band for your school's next concert.
- You go to the writing center to get help on a paper.
- You eat lunch with a good friend.
- You go to the auditorium to listen to a well-known politician make a speech.
- You meet an exchange student from Costa Rica.

Intercultural Communication

Many years ago Marshall McLuhan, a writer about communication, said that someday the whole world will be a global village. That day is here: few of us live in a place where our neighbors, fellow students, and coworkers are all like us. On campus, for example, in a single class we may find students of many nationalities and from a wide range of subcultures within the United States.

When we talk about **culture**, we mean a group of people who share a distinct set of norms, values, and symbols. An example of two cultural groups would be people from Thailand and people from Germany. By **subculture**, we mean people who are part of a larger culture but also belong to a smaller group that has some different values, attitudes, or beliefs. For example, the culture of the United States could be labeled "American." Yet many of us also belong to a subculture in the United States, such as the Cuban Americans who live in Miami or the Polish Americans who live in Chicago.

Although people throughout the world have many characteristics in common, they also have many differences. Thus, if two or more cultural or subcultural groups want to communicate, they must be aware that they may have different norms, values, and ways of behaving. If one group does not realize this, their communication will probably result in misunderstandings. For example, in West Africa, the comment "You've put on weight" is a great compliment—it means that you look healthy and prosperous. If this comment were made to an American, however, it would be perceived as an insult.

What indicators are in this picture that tell us the United States is a multicultural nation?

CONSIDER THIS

People all over the world share some similarities. For example, most people feel joy and sorrow, love and hate at some point in their life. However, day-to-day life and the rules that govern it may differ greatly from one culture to another. Bette Bao Lord, who was born in China but moved to America when she was still a child, feels that she has both a Chinese and an American side. This is what she observes about each side:

My Chinese side wonders why Americans are so uneasy with time on their hands and must busy themselves with activities, the sweatier the better. Why do they keep changing their minds and ways, jobs and towns and spouses; send children packing just because they're able to fend for themselves, and parents just because they're unable to? Why do they toil all year to pay for the costly privilege of diving beneath shark-infested waters or plunging down icy cliffs trussed to greasy planks? . . .

My American side wonders why Chinese are content to warm their seats and sip tea and are so sorely lacking in get-up-and-go. Why do they keep their ancient ways, refuse to pull up stakes to seek a rosier future, yearn to die where they were born, share beds with mothers and kitchens with mothers-in-law, and relish living under the same roof with a mob of relatives constantly in an uproar? Why do they toil all year to put their earnings in the same pot for the humiliating privilege of begging other people's permission to do just about anything?

Source: Bette Bao Lord, *Legacies: A Chinese Mosaic* (New York: Knopf, 1990), p. 215.

QUESTIONS

1. If you are an American, how would you explain to a Chinese student why your family is willing to let you leave home at 18 and live in a dorm or an apartment? How would you explain that is what *you* want to do, too?

2. If you come from a culture in which everyone lives with an extended family, how would you explain that this is a desirable way to live? Also explain what living in an extended family means to *you.*

To help people understand each other better, communication scholars, teachers, and writers have developed the field of **intercultural communication**—the communication that occurs whenever two or more people from different cultures interact. This field studies how differences between people affect their perceptions of the world and, thus, their communication. Of course, there is no way to understand all cultures and subcultures. There are, however, certain characteristics that occur again and again, and the theory of intercultural communication rests on these characteristics.

As long as the people communicating understand that they may have different attitudes and values, intercultural communication works in the same way as interpersonal communication in terms of channels and feedback. Nonverbal communication, however, may be different between the sender-receivers.

COMMUNICATING EFFECTIVELY

Once you understand the process of communication, you can begin to understand why communication does or doesn't work. In an ideal communication situation the message is perceived in the way it was intended. But when messages don't work, it is useful to ask these questions: Was there a problem with the message? Was the best channel used? Did noise occur? Knowing the right questions to ask is essential to building skills in communication.

Most of us already have considerable communication skills. We have been sending and receiving verbal and nonverbal signals all our lives. Nevertheless, we all have had times when we have not communicated as effectively as we should. We got a lower grade on a paper than we expected, we unintentionally hurt somebody's feelings, or the instructor did not understand a question we asked in class.

Where to Begin

The information and research about communication are so vast that most of us could spend a lifetime studying communication and not learn even a fraction of what there is to know. As a beginning student of communication, here are five questions to ask yourself.

WHICH COMMUNICATION SKILLS AM I MOST LIKELY TO NEED?

Find out what communication skills are important to you. What do you intend to do in your life? What kind of work do you expect to do? What communication skills are required in this work? Which of these skills do you already have? Which ones need improvement? Which ones do you need to acquire?

For example, a career in business requires almost every communication skill. You need interpersonal skills to get along with the people you work with, intercultural communication skills if you are going to work with people from other countries, and public speaking skills for making presentations. Although you may use some communication skills more than others, at one time or another you are going to need every one we have discussed in this chapter.

WHICH COMMUNICATION SKILLS AM I MOST LACKING IN?

Which kinds of communication are most difficult for you? Intrapersonal? Interpersonal? Intercultural? Small-group? Public speaking? Why do you have difficulties in these areas? What problems do you have to overcome before you can perform effectively in these areas?

Probably you would prefer *not* to work in the area that gives you the most trouble. For example, if you are anxious about public speaking, you might feel inclined to avoid any circumstance where you have to give a

CONSIDER THIS

Ethics are the moral values you bring to your communication experiences. No communication, however skilled, is acceptable unless it has an ethical foundation. We can ask a number of ethical questions about communication:

- Will my words make someone feel bad?

- Could I harm someone needlessly by what I say?

- Could my words cause embarrassment?

- Is my communication causing damage to some person or some group that is not present?

- Are my words appropriate for the occasion and for the people hearing them?

- Have I spent enough time thinking and planning about what I am going to say?

- Have I been careful to gather evidence that will best support my arguments?

speech. It will be much more to your advantage, however, if you can conquer this fear by plunging in and practicing the thing that gives you the most trouble.

HOW CAN I GET COMMUNICATION PRACTICE?

Are there situations, other than class, where you can practice communication skills that will be useful to you? Are there groups and organizations you can join that will help you develop these skills? It's always a good idea to take what you have learned in class and try it out on the world. Using new skills helps to develop and refine them.

WHERE CAN I GET HELP?

What people do you know who will help you to develop these skills and give you feedback on how you are doing? Are there people you can ask who will give you support when you try to do something new and scary? Are you willing to ask them to support you? We can usually count on this kind of support from our friends. Most of us have at least one friend who would be willing to listen to one of our speeches and tell us whether it works or where we might improve it. Also, don't forget your instructors. Most welcome visits from students during office hours.

WHAT TIMETABLE SHOULD I SET?

Have you set a realistic timetable for improvement? Knowing that it is difficult to learn new skills or break bad habits, are you willing to give yourself that time? Your speech class is going to last for a semester or a quarter. Although you will be making steady progress in your interpersonal communication and public-speaking skills, change will not happen overnight. The act of communicating—whether with a single person or a classroom audience—takes time and effort. We hope your class will be the place where you learn how to communicate more effectively. The most realistic timetable is one where you say, "I'm going to keep working at this until I succeed."

SUMMARY

Everyone needs to communicate effectively. Successful communication helps bring us success and pleasure, helps us to change the way others act and behave, and aids us in maintaining and improving relationships.

Communication is an ongoing process in which people share ideas and feelings. The elements of communication include sender-receivers, messages, channels, feedback, noise, and setting.

All communication is a transaction. Viewing communication as a transaction focuses on the people who are communicating and the changes that take place in them as they are communicating. It also implies that all participants are involved continuously and simultaneously; that communication events have a past, present, and future, and that the roles the participants play will affect the communication.

Five kinds of communication are discussed in this book. Intrapersonal communication is communication with one's self. Interpersonal communication is informal communication with one or more other persons. Small-group communication occurs when a small group of people get together to solve a problem. Public communication is giving a speech to an audience. Intercultural communication is talking to someone from a different culture or subculture.

Communication can be improved if you concentrate on several important areas. You need to find out what communication skills are important to you. You need to discover the kinds of communication that are most difficult for you and work to improve them. You need to seek out people who will help you develop these skills and give you support and feedback, and you need to set a realistic timetable for improvement. In addition to developing these skills, you need to think about the ethics of your communication.

NOTES

[1] Dan B. Curtis, Jerry L. Winsor, and Ronald D. Stephens, "National Preferences in Business and Communication Education," *Communication Education* 38 (1989): 6–14.

[2] John R. Johnson and Nancy Szczupakiewicz, "The Public Speaking Course: Is It Preparing Students with Work-Related Public Speaking Skills?" *Communication Education* 36 (1987): 131–136.

[3] David K. Berlo, *The Process of Communication: An Introduction to Theory and Practice* (New York: Holt, Rinehart & Winston, 1960), p. 24.

[4] Albert Mehrabian, *Silent Messages: Implicit Communication of Emotions and Attitudes,* 2d ed. (Belmont, CA: Wadsworth, 1981), pp. 76–77.

⁵See Carol Wilder, "The Palo Alto Group: Difficulties and Directions of the Transactional View for Human Communication Research," *Human Communication Review* 5 (Winter 1979): 171–186.

■ FURTHER READING

GONZÁLEZ, ALBERTO, MARSHA HOUSTON, AND VICTORIA CHEN. *Our Voices: Essays in Culture, Ethnicity, and Communication*. Los Angeles: Roxbury Publishing Company, 1994. The authors have included twenty-two essays grouped into categories such as "Naming Ourselves," "Negotiating Sexuality and Gender," and "Traversing Cultural Paths." The essays are original and the scholars are outstanding. The authors represent the cultures they write about.

GRIFFIN, EM. *A First Look at Communication Theory*. 2d ed. New York: McGraw-Hill, Inc., 1994 This introductory book describes thirty-four theories that explain a wide range of communication phenomena, including sections on gender and intercultural theories. There is also an excellent reading list following each theory for students who want to do more investigation.

GUDYKUNST, WILLIAM B., AND YOUNG YUN KIM. *Communicating with Strangers*, 2d ed. New York: McGraw-Hill, Inc., 1992. In this text, the authors focus on the theoretical issues necessary both to understand the process of intercultural communication and to improve intercultural effectiveness. Particularly relevant is their Part Four, "Interaction with Strangers," where they includechapters on interpersonal relationships, adapting to new cultures, effectiveness in communicating, and becoming intercultural.

HOWELL, WILLIAM S. *The Empathic Communicator*. Prospect Heights, IL: Waveland Press, 1986. Howell's perspective is that communication is an ever-changing, often unpredictable joint venture. We include this book because of his emphasis on empathy, sending and receiving, and messages. Howell explores competence in spontaneous interactions.

LITTLEJOHN, STEPHEN W. *Theories of Human Communication*, 4th ed. Belmont, CA: Wadsworth, 1992. Littlejohn offers a comprehensive examination of major communication theories. His discussion of the strengths and weaknesses of theories is useful; however, the book is designed for the more serious student of communication.

PETERS, THOMAS J., AND ROBERT H. WATERMAN, JR. *In Search of Excellence: Lessons from America's Best-Run Companies*. New York: Warner Books, 1988. One overwhelming theme in this book is the importance that effective communication skills play in America's best-run companies. An outstanding book full of vital information for anyone seeking a business career.

SAMOVAR, LARRY A., AND RICHARD E. PORTER. *Intercultural Communication: A Reader*, 7th ed. Belmont, CA: Wadsworth, 1994. Many readings explore the various kinds of intercultural communication. The book presents information about people of other nations as well as diverse American subcultures such as deaf people and older people, and it discusses areas such as health and disease.

SPINDEL, CAROL. *In the Shadow of the Sacred Grove*. New York: Vintage Departures, 1989.   This is the personal account of a young woman who goes to live in a village in the Ivory Coast, in West Africa. The book gives a good idea of what it is like to be in a new culture where one does not know the rules and the roles.

TURNER, PATRICIA A. *I Heard It Through The Grapevine*. Berkeley: University of California Press, 1993.   Turner says that rumor is a particularly important form of communication among African Americans. Her thesis is that negative rumors about the white community are started among African Americans to counter oppression and exploitation.

KEY TERMS

ethnicity

ethnocentrism

perception

psychological risk

psychological safety

race

racism

reflected appraisals

scripts

self-concept

self-esteem

self-fulfilling prophecies

self-perception

social comparisons

stereotypes

2

Self and Communication

CHAPTER OBJECTIVES

After reading this chapter, you should be able to:

1 Explain self-concept and how it is formed.

2 Define reflected appraisal, social comparison, and self-perception.

3 Describe some of the ways you can improve your own self-esteem.

4 Describe how perception and self-concept are related.

5 Explain the perceptual steps of selecting, organizing, and interpreting.

6 Define race, ethnicity, and stereotypes.

7 Explain the five steps people might go through when meeting someone from another race or culture.

"Who am I? Am I what other people say I am, or am I who I say I am?" These are some of the most difficult and profound questions we can ask ourselves. The way in which we answer these questions depends on how we see ourselves and also on how others see us. Rabbi Martin Siegel, in his diary, describes some of the conflict between his own idea of himself and others' ideas:

People tend to make me a symbol. They say they know me, but they don't. They know only my roles. To some of them, I am a radical. To some of them, I am a signature on the marriage contract. To some of them I am the man who opposes the indulgence of the psychotic fear of anti-semitism.

People see me only as they care or need to see me.

And poor Judith has to be a wife to all this.

I can't recognize myself in their eyes, so how could she? We both have to live as exhibits in this community. While people are friendly, we have no friends. We have been made into what they want us to be.[1]

In this passage, Rabbi Siegel is distressed that various people see only certain aspects of him. These people in his congregation never communicate to the whole man; instead, they communicate to the person he repre-

---

TRY THIS

Make a list of five things that describe who you are. The list might deal with your looks, your personality, your religious beliefs, your profession, your political beliefs, your affiliations with groups—anything that is important to you. A sample list might read something like this:

I am a woman.

I am a Catholic.

I am a mother.

I am a business executive.

I am tall and thin.

Once you have put your list together, ask yourself why you have chosen these particular items. What influences in your community and your culture lead you to define yourself this way? Are there any things about you that you would like to change? Is it possible to change these things?

sents in their own eyes. For example, if they see him as a highly spiritual man, they may never talk about the ordinary problems of work or even the football game they saw on television. The passage, however, implies that he sees himself differently than the members of his congregation see him. Yet if everyone communicates to him on the basis of who they *think* he is, he (and his wife) have to struggle to maintain a fuller and more rounded self-concept.

 # SELF-CONCEPT

Self-concept, which we will use interchangeably with the term **self-esteem**, is how a person thinks about and values himself or herself. This sense of self comes from our communication with others. They tell us who we are ("You're really a good kid"), they tell us what we look like ("You have your grandfather's nose"), and they tell us how they feel about us ("I really feel that I can talk to you").

Your self-concept is based on the values of the culture and the community you come from. Your culture tells you what is competent and moral by defining attitudes and beliefs; the community you belong to tells you what is expected of you. The extent to which you reflect the attitudes and beliefs of your culture and live up to the expectations of your community will determine how you see yourself. For example, Amelia, who has a good self-concept, is the top female runner at her university. As an athlete, she follows the attitudes and beliefs of American culture by saluting the flag at the beginning of each meet, by encouraging other team members, and by practicing good sportsmanship. Her community, in this instance, is the athletic community (or the team). She follows the expectations of this community when she attends practice, does daily exercises, and listens to the coach. As well as engaging in all of these activities, she does well at her meets, which leads to a positive self-concept. (See Figure 2-1.)

Self-concept is made up of three distinct elements: reflected appraisals, social comparisons, and self-perception.[2] Let's look at each of these in turn.

Reflected Appraisals

Remember the story of Tarzan? Although Tarzan was a human, he believed he was an ape because he was brought up by apes and had no human experience. Tarzan's story reminds us that we are not born with an identity—it is given to us by others. Our parents, our friends, our teachers all tell us who we are through **reflected appraisals**—messages we get about ourselves from others. Most reflected appraisals come from things people say about us. Your college speech instructor may say you are a good speaker, your peers may say you are a good friend, and your coach may tell you that you must work harder. All such messages from others help to create your self-concept.

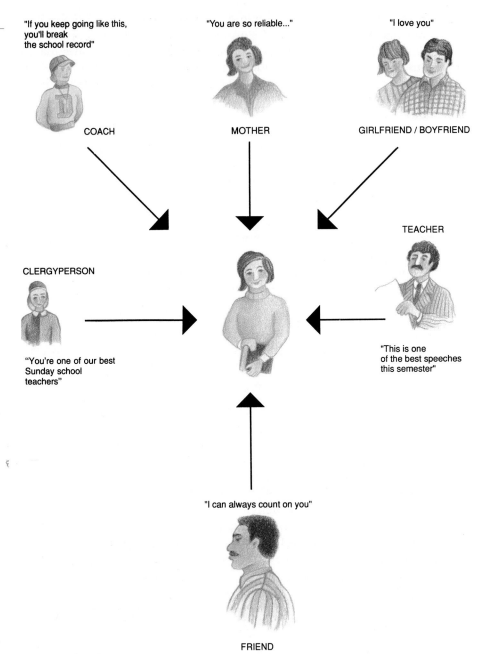

"If you keep going like this, you'll break the school record"

COACH

"You are so reliable..."

MOTHER

"I love you"

GIRLFRIEND / BOYFRIEND

TEACHER

CLERGYPERSON

"You're one of our best Sunday school teachers"

"This is one of the best speeches this semester"

"I can always count on you"

FRIEND

FIGURE 2-1
The Development
of Self-Esteem

Besides being given messages about ourselves, we are also given lines to speak.[3] These lines are often so specific that some people refer to them as **scripts**. Some scripts are given to us by our parents, and they contain directions that are just as explicit as any script intended for the stage. We are given our lines ("Say thank you to the nice lady"), our gestures ("Point to the horsie"), and our characterizations ("You're a good boy"). The scripts tell us how to play future scenes ("Everyone in our family has gone to college") and what is expected of us ("I will be so happy when you make us grandparents"). People outside our family also contribute to our scripts. Teachers, coaches, religious leaders, friends, and the media all tell us what they expect from us, how we should look, how we should behave, and how we should say our lines.

Garrison Keillor, a writer and radio personality, gives a list of scripts we get as we are growing up. Do any of them sound familiar to you?

I. *I don't know what's wrong with you.*
    A. *I never saw a person like you.*
        1. *I wasn't like that.*
        2. *Your cousins don't pull stuff like that.*
    B. *It doesn't make sense.*
        1. *You have no sense of responsibility at all.*
        2. *We've given you everything we possibly could.*
            a. *Food on the table and a roof over your head.*
            b. *Things we never had when we were your age.*
        3. *And you treat us like dirt under your feet.*
    C. *You act as if*
        1. *The world owes you a living.*
        2. *You've got a chip on your shoulder.*
        3. *The rules don't apply to you.*

II. *Something has got to change and change fast.*
    A. *You're driving your mother to a nervous breakdown.*
    B. *I'm not going to put up with this for another minute.*
        1. *You're crazy if you think I am.*
        2. *If you think I am, just try me.*
    C. *You're setting a terrible example for your younger brothers and sisters.*

III. *I'm your father and as long as you live in this house, you'll—*
    A. *Do as you're told, and when I say "now" I mean "now."*
    B. *Pull your own weight.*
        1. *Don't expect other people to pick up after you.*
        2. *Don't expect breakfast when you get up at noon.*
        3. *Don't come around asking your mother for spending money.*
    C. *Do something about your disposition.*

IV. *If you don't change your tune pretty quick, then you're out of here.*
    A. *I mean it.*
    B. *Is that understood?*
        1. *I can't hear you. Don't mumble.*
        2. *Look at me.*
    C. *I'm not going to tell you this again.*[4]

If you were given positive reflected appraisals when you were young, you probably have a good self-concept; if the appraisals were negative, your self-

CONSIDER THIS

Lydia Minatoya grew up as an Asian American, the daughter of Japanese parents. This passage shows how she learned one of America's myths.

When I was four and my sister was eight, Misa regularly used me as a comic foil. She would bring her playmates home from school and query me as I sat amidst the milk bottles on the front step.

"What do you want to be when you grow up?" she would say. She would nudge her audience into attentiveness.

"A mother kitty cat!" I would enthuse. Our cat had just delivered her first litter of kittens and I was enchanted by the rasping tongue and soft mewings of motherhood.

"And what makes you think you can become a cat?" Misa would prompt, gesturing to her howling friends—wait for this; it gets better yet.

"This is America," I stoutly would declare. "I can grow up to be anything that I want!"

Source: Lydia Minatoya, *Talking to High Monks in the Snow* (New York, HarperCollins, 1993), pp. 33–34.

QUESTIONS

1. Many of our scripts define what it is to be an American. What is Minatoya told about being an American?

2. What other scripts do we get that tell us how to be Americans?

3. Do any of these scripts conflict with our understanding of people who come from other countries? For example, what assumptions are made when you ask someone from another country if he or she wants to stay in the United States?

concept is likely to be poor. The messages we receive about ourselves can become **self-fulfilling prophecies**—events or actions that occur because we (and other people) have expected them. For example, at the beginning of the semester Professor Farley said to Kevin, "You're going to be a very good student." In response, Kevin wanted to be a good student and worked hard to live up to Professor Farley's prophecy. Similarly, negative prophecies can have a negative impact. If someone tells a child that he or she will "never amount to much," there is a good chance the child will do just that.

Who is in charge
of this conversa-
tion?

Social Comparisons

When we compare ourselves with others to see how we measure up, we are making **social comparisons**. An obvious example of this occurs in the classroom when the instructor returns test papers. Many students turn to their classmates and ask "What did you get?" in order to make comparisons with their own grades.

We make social comparisons all the time. As a student, you might ask who has the most friends, who dresses the most stylishly, who has the best car, who does the best in school. When you become a parent, you will probably ask how your children compare with those of your friends. In your job, you may ask if you are doing as well as your coworkers. The answers to these questions all contribute to your self-concept.

Self-Perception

In your earliest years, how you think about yourself comes largely from how people react to you. At some point in your life, however, you begin to see yourself in a certain way. The way in which you see yourself is called **self-perception**.

If you gain confidence from successful experiences, your perception of yourself gets better and your self-concept improves. Let's say, for example, that you have a new computer and you get it working without any help from anyone; your success will probably improve your perception of yourself.

For many people, self-perception plays a greater role as they get older. Once they gain some confidence through life experience, reflected appraisals and social comparisons lose significance for them and self-per-

CONSIDER THIS

⚦ American women often have a negative self-perception of their looks, and particularly of their bodies. Gloria Steinem points out that the way we look and the way we *think we look* might be two different things.

I never questioned the way I looked at my body until I was in my 30s and saw myself on television. There was this thin, pretty blondish woman of medium height who spoke in a boring monotone and, through lack of animation, seemed confident, even blasé. It was a shock. What I felt like inside was a plump brunette from Toledo, too tall and much too pudding-faced, with a voice that felt constantly on the verge of some unacceptable emotion. I was amazed. Where had this woman on television come from?

Steinem's experience is not unusual. Women, and even little girls, often have an image of their body that differs from their real body. Various studies have revealed the following statistics about female Americans:

- More than half of a group of 10-year-old schoolgirls rate themselves as the least attractive girl in the class.

- Eighty percent of 10-year-old girls claim to be on a diet.

- Seventy percent of normal-weight women want to be thinner.

- Twenty-three percent of underweight women want to be thinner.

- Fifty-six percent of women aged 24 to 45 are dieting.

- $33 billion is spent yearly on diets and related services.

- 1.5 million Americans undergo cosmetic surgery every year.

Source: Gloria Steinem, "I'm Not the Woman in My Mind," *Parade Magazine* (Jan. 10, 1992), pp. 10–11; "Skin Deep," *Psychology Today* (May/June 1993), p. 96.

QUESTIONS

1. Where do women and girls get these ideas about their bodies?

2. Given society's many messages about thinness and body image, are women and girls being told that they are inferior?

3. Are there any ways to counter these messages?

ception becomes more important. For example, a man in his sixties is probably no longer interested in how he compares with others or what other people think about him. Instead, his self-concept depends on his self-perception of how well he has lived his life.

Gender and Self-Concept

Several research studies show that men and women gain their self-concept in different ways. Schwalbe and Staples found that when forming self-concept, men give the most importance to social comparisons, whereas women attach more importance to reflected appraisals.[5] Men put more value on reflected appraisals from their parents while women give more importance to reflected appraisals from their friends.

Other studies have shown that female self-confidence comes from connections and attachments while male self-confidence comes from achievement.[6] This relates to research findings about gender language (in Chapter 4, we discuss how women's language is tied to social networks while male language is tied to competition and achievement).

Psychological Safety and Risk

Ask some second-semester seniors what they are afraid of. Chances are they will reply that they are very apprehensive about going out into the world. Will they find jobs? Can they survive outside the structure of university life? What is the world like? What is their place in it?

For most of us, **psychological safety**—the approval and support that we get from familiar people, ideas, and situations—is important. However, the late psychologist Abraham Maslow, who worked in the area of self-fulfillment, pointed out that the needs for safety and growth pull us in opposite directions. Maslow believed that in order to grow, people have to abandon some of the safe areas of their lives and take some psychological risks.[7]

A **psychological risk** involves taking a chance on something new. It could be getting to know someone different from us, trying to understand a different point of view, or even moving to a new place. Taking a psychological risk helps to improve self-concept. For example, when students go away to college, they must leave the safety of home, friends, and family. This is such a great risk that some first-year students spend a week or two away from home, decide they can't stand it, and drop out of school. The majority who remain, however, discover that they can cope on their own. This new knowledge helps to improve their self-concept.

New college students take risks not only in leaving home but also in being exposed to new ideas. For example, a student who has heard pro-choice ideas at home or in church will take a big risk if he or she tries to really understand a person who is pro-life. Similarly, it's risky for an athlete or a sports fan to try to understand the view that high schools might improve if they dropped competitive sports. The problem with taking the risk of really understanding a different point of view is that you might be changed. If you do change, you face the possibility that your family and friends will probably not change and you won't completely fit in anymore. Inevitably, whenever you take a risk, your circle of safety grows smaller.

Our first response to ideas that conflict with our own is to refuse to even listen to them. If we take this course, we choose psychological safety. When we take a psychological risk, we are ready to test our self-concept by considering ideas from another person's vantage point.

IMPROVING YOUR SELF-CONCEPT

One of the most difficult things any human being can do is to change his or her self-concept for the better. How can you go about doing this? Here are some suggestions that might help.

Decide What You Want to Change about Yourself

Pick one area in which you would like to improve yourself and, hence, your self-concept. See if you can figure out why you have had problems in this area. Were you given a script saying you were inadequate in this area? Are you living out a self-fulfilling prophecy?

Consider Your Circumstances

Are you living in circumstances that are holding you back? Do the people around you support you in risk taking? Sometimes the people we live with try to hold us back—even though they might not be conscious of doing so. For example, one spouse says to the other, "Why do you want to go to Europe? We haven't seen all of the United States yet."

Sometimes we are locked into roles that are uncomfortable for us. Many women feel trapped when their children are small; some people hate their jobs; some students hate school. Are you in a role that you have chosen for yourself, or has someone else chosen it for you? Has someone else defined how you should play this role? Can you play this role in a way that will make it more comfortable for you? Can you change the role so you can be more like the person you want to be?

Take Some Chances

Colleges and universities offer great chances to take some risks. Take a course from a professor who is rumored to be hard but fair. Study a subject you know nothing about. Join a club that sounds interesting—even if you don't know any of its members. Many colleges and universities also offer opportunities to study abroad or to take an internship. Going abroad is especially helpful in building self-confidence.

What kinds of
experiences
require precise
and specific com-
munication?

Set Reasonable Goals

Too often, people decide they are going to change their behavior overnight.
Students who habitually get poor grades will often announce that this
semester they are going to get all A's. This is an unreasonable goal. If you
are going to try to change your behavior, see if you can break the problem
down into steps you can handle. Let's say that you are shy, but you would
like to speak up more in class because you often know the answers. Why not
set a goal to speak up once a week in one class? That is probably a goal you
can manage. Once you feel comfortable with that, you might increase your
goal to speaking up two or even three times a week.

Use a Program of Self-Discipline

The old saying "Nothing succeeds like success" applies to a positive self-
concept: as soon as you succeed, you start feeling better about yourself.
Sometimes people think they are not successful because they are not motivated enough. Typical thinking might be "If only I could motivate myself, I
would get better grades." People who think this way confuse motivation
with discipline. There's no way to motivate yourself to shovel the walk, do
the dishes, or study your class notes. These jobs can be done only through

In this section we present ideas that may contradict information in the text and may or may not reflect the views of the authors. The important thing is that you read the material, discuss it with your class-mates or friends, and make up your own mind.

Are We Too Obsessed with Self-Esteem?

If you have any doubt that we, as a society, are obsessed with self-esteem, look in the self-improvement section of any bookstore or library. Here you will find literally hundreds of books—each guaranteeing that if you read it, you will feel better about yourself and that you can change your self-esteem from negative to positive.

The American passion for improving self-concept has many critics. Helen Katz, a professor of early childhood education, points out that the elementary schools are filled with self-esteem exercises. She observed, for example, a first grade class in which children made a booklet that answered questions about themselves such as what they liked to eat, what they liked to watch on TV, what they wanted as a present, and where they wanted to go for vacation—all questions that centered on the pupil. Posters in schools named the citizen of the week, the best speller, and the best reader.

All of this seems harmless enough until you start to think about it. Katz argues that all these "I" messages make the child look inward and focus on himself or herself rather than making the child an explorer, an instigator, or a problem solver. The questions of what the child likes to eat, watch on TV, and so forth are all questions we ask of consumers—not of producers. If schools try to make every child special, Katz says, then no one is special.

Christopher Lasch considers the implications of what happens when a whole society believes that self-esteem is the answer to all its problems. This focus, he believes, creates the idea that people are not wrong or evil; rather, society is sick, so no one has to take any responsibility for personal actions. This promotes ideas such as "If the powerless people in our society had better self-concepts, it would eliminate many social problems."

Lasch advocates a return to the idea of shame. He believes that some of our actions or beliefs should make us feel ashamed. It's a cop-out, he says, to avoid responsibility by saying, "I have low self-esteem because of the way my parents (or society) treated me."

Katz and Lasch do not disbelieve in self-esteem; rather, they believe that there are better ways of teaching it than by labeling someone with a sign that says "I'm special." Both of them believe that self-esteem comes from risk and challenge: when we master something, we feel better about ourselves. In acquiring skills and knowledge, they believe, it is inevitable that we will have some failures and meet some obstacles, but, they say, this better prepares us for life. Perhaps their most important point is that self-esteem cannot be given to us; we have to earn it.

Source: Lillian G. Katz, "All About Me: Are We Developing Our Children's Self-Esteem or Their Narcissism?" *American Educator* (Summer 1993), pp. 18–23; Christopher Lasch, "For Shame: Why Americans Should Be Wary of Self-Esteem," *The New Republic* (Aug. 10, 1992), pp. 29–35.

QUESTIONS

1. Is Katz correct in saying that too much focus on the self keeps us from becoming explorers or instigators?

2. Should people feel shame for some of their actions?

3. Lasch is a white male. Does he have a right to say that women and African Americans should take responsibility for their actions, or is he ignoring the fact that society creates their low self-esteem?

discipline: you say, "I am going to do this job for one hour—whether or not I want to do it is irrelevant." This sort of discipline is what leads to success, which, in turn, helps you to feel better about yourself.

Pick People Who Will Support You

Whenever we try to bring about a change in ourselves, we need to surround ourselves with people who will support us. These are people who understand how difficult it is to change and who understand our desire to do so. Let's take the example of speaking up in class. If you are very apprehensive about doing this, you might consider discussing the problem with an instructor you like and trust. Tell him or her that you are occasionally going to try to say something, and ask for his or her support. Also tell a couple of friends in your class what you plan to do. Just having other people know what you are trying to accomplish often provides good moral support.

When we want to change, it's important to pick our supporters carefully. Also it is important that we tell them what we want to do and give them some direction on how they can help us.

■ PERCEPTION

Dan and Jean sit next to each other in class. They have several interests in common, including an interest in each other. Each would like to see the other outside of class, but neither has made a move in that direction. Now they find themselves in the student center at the same time. Dan sees Jean sitting alone at a table, so he joins her. As they talk casually about the weather and the assignments they have for their class, thoughts about each other are going through their heads. Dan is thinking, "I really would like to ask her out to the movies. I wonder if she would go with me. I'd feel pretty bad if she turned me down." Jean is thinking along a similar line: "He really is a nice guy. I'd like to get to know him better, but he is so shy. I think he likes me, but I'm really not sure."

Although Dan and Jean's conversation and thoughts seem to be ordinary, each person is going through a complicated perceptual process. On one level, what Dan is saying and thinking reflects how he feels about himself ("In this situation, I am feeling somewhat insecure"). On another level, his thoughts reflect how he feels about Jean ("I like her and I would like to know her better"). On yet a third level, they are influenced by how he thinks Jean sees him ("I wonder if she likes me"). Jean is going through a similar perceptual process. Her thoughts and what she says are influenced by how she sees herself, how she perceives Dan, and how she thinks Dan perceives her.[8]

What is going on in Dan and Jean's interaction is a complicated mixture of self-concept and perception. Self-concept and perception are so closely related that it is often difficult to separate them. While your self-concept is how you see yourself, **perception** is how you look at others and the world around you. How you look at the world depends on what you think of yourself, and what you think of yourself will influence how you look at the world.

The workings of self-confidence and perception make communication a complicated business. As is true in all transactional communication, many factors are occurring continuously and simultaneously. Dan's perception of Jean is influenced by how he sees himself and how he sees his past relationships; Jean is influenced by her sense of self and her experiences with other men. Both of them are also influenced by how they see their roles in a male-female relationship. Jean wants to be more assertive in moving their friendship forward, but because of her idea of the role a woman should play in a relationship, she's worried about being too aggressive. Dan believes that it is his role to move the relationship forward, but he is too shy to do so.

Jean and Dan are having trouble getting to know each other because of the way they see themselves. Like them, the way you view the world and communicate about it is greatly influenced by the way you view yourself.

The Perceptual Process

Your perceptions affect more than your direct interactions with people. They also influence your response to all of the information around you. Whenever you encounter new information, whether it's from a television program, a newspaper, or another person, you go through a three-step perceptual process: you select the information, you organize it, and you interpret it.

We do not all perceive information in the same way. Even when several people have access to the same information, they are likely to select, organize, and interpret it in different ways. Let's say, for example, that three different people read the same newspaper: Omar is a Syrian who is studying in the United States, Caroline is an American who has been on a student exchange to Syria, and Jim is an American who has never traveled.

Omar selects the news about Syria. In his mind he organizes the information on the basis of what he already knows. He may interpret it by asking the meaning of certain government actions or by thinking that the reporter has the wrong slant on the story. Caroline goes through a similar process. She has high interest in stories about Syria because she has been there. She, too, organizes what she reads according to what she knows about the country. However, she may interpret the news stories differently because she doesn't have as much information as Omar. Also, her interpretation will probably be from an American point of view. When Jim reads the newspaper, he skips all the stories about Omar's country. He has never been there and has no immediate plans to go there. In fact, he skips all the news about the world and goes directly to the sports section. These three people are all exposed to the same information, but they all perceive it differently.

Most people find it easier to communicate with members of their own culture. When people live in the same country they are exposed to basically the same institutions. In the United States, for example, most people go to a church or synagogue, watch football games from time to time, and shop in a mall. When the Americans talk to each other about these things, they all have a common point of reference. However, a visiting student from the People's Republic of China is not familiar with any of these institutions. If an American wants to talk to her about any of them, he or she will have to do a good deal of explaining before the Chinese student understands.

Those of us who belong to a subculture will probably find it easier to communicate within this group. African Americans, for example, share a dialect, and Hispanics share a language. Even German Americans use certain words that are not used by other Americans.

Most people communicate best with those who are in their own cultural group and who see people in pretty much the same light that they see themselves. These people talk a kind of "shorthand." They know what each other is thinking and feeling—they speak the same language. This group of people, however, is small in number and is usually made up of close friends and family members. In the rest of their daily life—at work and in social gatherings—they have to communicate with people who do not know them so well. Even if they did know each other, they might not share similar ways of looking at themselves and the world.

RACE, ETHNICITY, AND COMMUNICATION

In recent years, incidents of prejudice against members of racial and ethnic minority groups have occurred on college campuses throughout the country. Since all such incidents involve negative communication by one individual or group toward another, it is useful to try to understand this problem in the context of self-concept and perception.

To discuss racial and ethnic discrimination, we need to start with some definitions. **Race** refers to biological characteristics, such as color of skin, eyes, and hair.[9] Sometimes members of different races share the same culture, but no common culture is found among all members of any racial group. African Americans, for example, do not share a common culture with Africans.

Ethnicity refers to a shared history, tradition, and culture. In an ethnic group, nationality may or may not be shared, but culture is always shared.[10] Cubans, for example, share a common culture even though some may live in Cuba and others in the United States.

For any accurate communication to occur, the sender-receivers must be operating from the same perceptual point of view. This is usually not a problem when we are interacting with people from our own race or culture—we share the same attitudes, values, and beliefs. When we communicate with someone from a different race or background, however, we should realize that this person may be operating from an entirely different point of view.

When a person from one ethnic or racial group tries to communicate with a person from another group, stereotypes may get in the way. **Stereotypes** are oversimplified or distorted views of another race, another ethnic group, or even another culture. Once a stereotype is learned, it is very hard to get rid of. One researcher has found that stereotypes are very persistent and automatically turn on unless we consciously work to suppress them.[11] When people have stereotypes, they react to them rather than to reality. If you doubt this, read the list of stereotypes in Table 2-1 and see if a specific ethnic or racial group pops into your mind. If it does, you can see how persistent stereotypes can be; thus, we have to suppress stereotypes if we are going to communicate, one human to another.

Misunderstanding is also likely to occur is when a person from one culture tries to communicate in a way that is unfamiliar to people in another culture. When Eva Hoffman immigrated from Poland to Canada as a young girl, she discovered many subtle differences in verbal and nonverbal communication:

> *My mother says I'm becoming "English." This hurts me, because I know she means I'm becoming cold. I'm no colder than I've ever been, but I'm learning to be less demonstrative. . . .*
>
> *I learn restraint from Penny, who looks offended when I shake her by the arm in excitement, as if my gesture had been one of aggression instead of friendliness. I learn it from a girl who pulls away when I hook my arm through hers as we walk down the street—this movement of friendly intimacy is an embarrassment to her.*
>
> *I learn also that certain kinds of truth are impolite. One shouldn't criticize the person one is with, at least not directly. You shouldn't say, "You are wrong about that"—though you may say, "On the other hand, there is that to consider." You shouldn't say, "That doesn't look good on you," though you may say, "I like you better in that other outfit."*
>
> *My words often seen to baffle others. They are inappropriate, or forced, or just plain incomprehensible. People look at me with puzzlement: they mumble something in response—something that doesn't hit home.*[12]

The Development of Racism and Ethnocentrism

Racism and ethnocentrism are variations on the same theme: **racism** implies that one's race is superior while **ethnocentrism** implies that one's ethnic group is so special that it occupies the center of the world. Those who are racist or ethnocentric believe that the values and beliefs of their particular group are best and that therefore any other racial or ethnic group must be inferior.

Janet E. Helms has developed a model that shows the process a person goes through when he or she becomes aware of race and racial problems.[13] Although Helms developed this model to explain how racism could develop, it may also apply to any person who is experiencing another culture. In the discussion that follows, we first present Helms's five-step theory and then explain how each step might work in real life. We use sample encounters between a white American and an African because they involve both racial and cross-cultural perceptions. The five stages in the model are contact, disintegration, reintegration, pseudo-independence, and autonomy.

CONTACT

In this first stage an individual discovers that different races exist. Not conscious of an identity as a racial being, the individual usually reacts to

TABLE 2-1
PREJUDICED ATTITUDES

Here is an outline of stereotypes or prejudiced attitudes one group may have about another. The prejudiced person might believe some or all of these items. These stereotypes and attitudes have no geographical boundaries. A German, for example, might believe they are true of Turks while an Iranian believes they are true of Iraqis.

0.   *General*
0.1 I do not like them.
0.2 Others do not like them.

1.   *Origin and appearance*
1.1 We should not have invited them.
1.2 They should be sent back.
1.3 Immigration policies should be stricter.
1.4 They look different (color, clothing).

2.   *Socioeconomic goals/status*
2.1 They take our jobs.
2.2 They do the dirty jobs.
2.3 They take our houses.
2.4 They abuse our social system.

3.   *Sociocultural differences*
3.1 They have a different lifestyle.
3.1.1 They should adapt.
3.2 They treat women badly.
3.3 They have too many children.
3.4 They do not speak our language.
3.5 They are dirty (cause urban decay).
3.6 Their children cause problems at school.

4.   *Personal characteristics*
4.1 They are aggressive (violent).
4.2 They are criminal.
4.3 They are dirty.
4.4 They are lazy (don't want to work).
4.5 They are noisy.

SOURCE: Teun A. van Dijk, *Communicating Racism* (Newbury Park, CA: Sage, 1987), p. 59.

What steps do we go through in developing a close relationshp with someone from another race?

people of a different race with curiosity and interest. A typical reaction to a person of another race might be "Although you are_____, it doesn't make any difference to me. We are all human beings." This, however, is the honeymoon period; sooner or later the person discovers that it does matter to society and that society has definite, sometimes negative, attitudes toward a particular race. Eventually the individual becomes aware that race or ethnocentrism may create conflict and may decide not to become involved and not to have any more contact than necessary.

Bethany sits next to Muthoni, a student from Kenya, in her world history class. At the beginning of the semester they often smile and say hello to each other. Once in a while, when the instructor is late, they talk about the class and how they think they are doing in it, and they speculate about what the next test will be like. Throughout this exchange Bethany thinks, "Kenyan students are just like us. They study, they worry about their grades, and they like a good social life."

One day Bethany and Muthoni get to class and discover it has been canceled. Since the class is just before lunch, they decide to go to lunch together. In the dining room Muthoni leads Bethany to a table where several other African students are sitting. Bethany enjoys talking to them and thinks to herself, "Gee, this is really interesting. If some of those kids I was in high school with could see me now. . . ."

CONSIDER THIS

Kristin Clark Taylor, the first African American woman to hold the post of White House director of media relations, writes about attending a private school, where she was one of the few African Americans:

My entire world changed when I entered Roeper. At five years of age, a pattern was established which would follow me for the rest of my days. It represented the very first of the delicate balancing acts I would have to perform like a skilled high-wire artist in the circus: being the singular black voice in the midst of a white, powerful status-conscious plurality. Even at age five, I tried mightily to integrate my two separate and distinct worlds—the world of Roeper and the world of Woodland Street—into one cohesive movement. It was to be the beginning of a lifelong effort to converge my two worlds—to weave my competing cultures into one whole cloth.

I struggled with feelings of alienation and isolation at being one of the few black children in the entire school. The only other black folks I came into contact with at Roeper besides my few black friends were the cooks, the domestic workers, and the drivers. . . .

But Roeper was an environment completely different from anything I'd ever known. Straddling the trappings of the privileged, powerful upper class by day and the comfortable, familiar ethnicity of my family and neighborhood friends by night began to take on a ring of cultural schizophrenia. The contrasts became dizzying and disorienting—almost surreal. It was hard to keep a solid footing.

Later that afternoon, Bethany is walking across campus and runs into one of her friends. Her friend says, "Bethany, who were all those black people you were having lunch with?" Bethany answers that they were African students. Her friend responds, "Why do you want to eat lunch with them?"

DISINTEGRATION

This stage will occur only if a person decides to continue to try to make friends with people of different races. In this stage the person is forced to acknowledge his or her own race. Now, aware of discrimination, the individual is likely to react with guilt or depression.

Eventually, the ground beneath me began to slip. Being so far removed from my own people at such a young age, and for so many years, began to do strange things to my "blackness," to my racial identity. Perhaps I started Roeper too young, before I was strong enough to sustain pride in who I was and where I came from. I began to find myself daydreaming about what it would feel like to have lighter skin and longer, straighter hair. I wanted to be more like my white friends. I was appalled and horrified at myself for feeling so ashamed, and I knew my family—Mother especially—would have been outraged and unforgiving of my emotional weakness and complete loss of dignity. But I had been drawn into a different world to which none of them could relate. Rather than finding pride in being different, I sought refuge in trying to become the same.

Source: Kristin Clark Taylor, *The First to Speak* (New York: Doubleday, 1993), pp. 27–28.

QUESTIONS

Taylor finally realized that she could resolve her identity crisis by returning to a multiracial public school, so after ten years at Roeper she went to a public high school in downtown Detroit. Her experience in two worlds raises some interesting questions:

1. Have you ever been part of a minority? If not, can you imagine what it might be like to be the only student of a particular racial or ethnic group in a classroom or other group setting?

2. Consider this passage and your own experience. Do you think your own sense of self would suffer if you were always the minority member in your classes?

A person who reaches this point may take any of three routes. One is to overidentify with the racially different people by taking on characteristics of the group, such as clothing, dress, or behavior. Another possibility is to become paternalistic, deciding to protect this group from abuse. Both of these choices will not work: the individual discovers it is not possible to become like other people. Paternalism often produces resentment in the people the individual is trying to protect. As in the contact stage, the individual might decide that the conflict is too great and will take the third route, a retreat back to his own racial group.

Bethany likes Muthoni so much that she accepts when Muthoni invites her to a party that is attended mostly by African students. Many of the stu-

dents are wearing clothes from their own countries, and the food they eat is like nothing Bethany has ever eaten before. Two of the guys suggest they would like to know her a little better, and Bethany begins to feel uncomfortable. Now she realizes that there are some real differences between her and the African students. Nevertheless, she enjoys the party, and when she goes home, she tells her roommate about it. Her roommate tells her, "If you start hanging out with these people, your friends will think you're really weird."

But Bethany gets more and more interested in East Africa. She starts to read articles in the newspaper whenever they appear and begins to borrow some of Muthoni's clothes to wear. She also learns a few words of Swahili and tries to teach them to some of her American friends (who don't seem very interested).

One day there's a letter in the campus newspaper from an American student who is protesting the scholarships that are being given to African rather than American students. Bethany is so annoyed that she writes a letter to the editor and tells why she thinks the university should give scholarships to Africans. Much to her surprise, Muthoni tells her several African students are angry about her letter. They tell Bethany they can speak for themselves—they don't need her as their spokeperson.

REINTEGRATION

Individuals who cannot resolve the problems of the disintegration stage are likely to feel anger or fear and will act with hostility toward the other race. Helms believes that it's at this stage where people feel prejudice and start to stereotype the other race. On the other hand, the individual might decide to accept his race and to understand the implications of living in a racist society. If the feelings of anger and fear eventually dissipate, the person will enter the next stage.

Now Bethany is mad at all her African friends. She thinks, "I was just trying to help them. What right do they have to be upset? If they don't appreciate me, I'm not going to be friends with them anymore."

A couple of days later, she feels calmer about what has happened. She realizes she has become good friends with some of the Africans—Muthoni in particular—and she doesn't want to break off her contact with them.

PSEUDO-INDEPENDENCE

The individual who moves to this stage becomes interested in the similarities and differences between the two groups and is no longer as naive as in the earlier encounters. By trying to understand the problem intellectually, the individual is able to reduce his anger. At this stage the person might choose to remain friends with people from other groups but might choose those members who most resemble his own racial or ethnic group.

Bethany realizes that she doesn't know very much about the political back

TRY THIS

Foreign students in American colleges and universities are often offended by the questions Americans ask them. They commonly hear naive questions such as "Do you have electricity (McDonald's, cars, television, airplanes)?" Perhaps with the exception of McDonald's, all countries have these things. By asking such questions, Americans imply that people from these places are inferior. Another annoying question is "Do you want to stay here?" This question assumes that given the chance, everyone would like to live in the United States.

Come up with five questions that you could ask a student from Nigeria, India, or the People's Republic of China. Rather than asking consumer-type questions or questions that are related to the United States, ask questions that are related to their attitudes, beliefs, and values.

ground of Kenya and decides to begin by reading some books on the subject. In her reading, she discovers that Kenyans once lived in a country that was ruled by the British, and to gain independence they had to reject their British past. From this book, Bethany realizes how sensitive the Kenyans are to the issue of white control, and she begins to understand that her letter to the newspaper might have been perceived as a form of control. Other books about Africa and racism give her even greater insights. She also attends a series of lectures about South Africa and begins to understand more about the relationships between black and white people.

AUTONOMY

In this stage the individual not only understands the differences between the two groups but accepts them, seeing these differences as positive. The person has a secure racial identity and actively seeks opportunities to interact with people who are different, approaching other racial and cultural groups with appreciation and respect.

Bethany now feels more comfortable with her African friends. She realizes that Kenyans regard their own country as the best place to live and that it might be an insult to ask them whether they would prefer living in the United States. She becomes so interested in Kenya that she applies to spend a semester there as an exchange student. Later in the semester, she meets some students from Sri Lanka. She has lots of questions to ask them.

SUMMARY

Self-concept, used interchangeably with the term *self-esteem*, is how a person thinks about and values himself or herself. Self-concept comes from three sources: reflected appraisals, social comparisons, and self-perception. Scripts, roles, and self-fulfilling prophecies also influence our self-concept. If people are willing to give up some of their psychological safety and take some risks, their self-concepts will become more positive.

There are several ways to improve your self-concept. You should decide what you want to change about yourself, consider your circumstances, take some chances, set reasonable goals, use a program of self-discipline, and pick people who will support you.

While self-concept is how we look at ourselves, perception is how we see the world around us. Our perceptions come from interactions with others and from our cultural background. In the perceptual process we select information, organize it, and interpret it. Our education and experience will influence how we carry out this process.

Race refers to biological characteristics, such as color of skin, hair, and eyes. Ethnicity is a shared common history, tradition, and culture. A stereotype is an oversimplified or distorted view of another race or culture. Racism implies that people believe their own race is superior, and ethnocentrism implies that members of an ethnic group believe their group is so special that it occupies the center of the world.

In our first experience of meeting a person from a different race or culture, we are likely to go through a five-step process: contact, disintegration, reintegration, pseudo-independence, and autonomy.

NOTES

[1] Michael Rubin, ed. *Men Without Masks* (Reading, MA: Addison-Wesley, 1980), pp. 187–188.

[2] Michael L. Schwalbe and Clifford L. Staples, "Gender Difference in Self-Esteem," *Social Psychology Quarterly* 54(2) 1991: 158–168.

[3] Muriel James and Dorothy Jongerward, *Born to Win: Transactional Analysis with Gestalt Experiments* (Reading, MA: Addison-Wesley, 1971), pp. 68–100.

[4] Garrison Keillor, *Lake Wobegone Days* (New York: Penguin/Viking Press, 1985), pp. 304–305.

[5] Schwalbe and Stables, op. cit.

[6] Robert A. Josephs, Hazel Rose Markus, and Romin W. Tafarodi, "Gender and Self-Esteem," *Journal of Personality and Social Psychology* 63(3) Sept. 1992: 391–402.

[7] Abraham H. Maslow, *Motivation and Personality*, 2d ed. (New York: Harper & Row, 1970).

[8] Dean C. Barlund, "Toward a Meaning-Centered Philosophy of Communication," *Journal of Communication* 12(1962): 197–211.

[9] Philip E. Lampe, "The Problematic Nature of Interracial and Interethnic Communication," *The Social Studies* (May/June 1988): 116.

[10] Ibid.

[11]Anita M. Meehan, "Gender Stereotypes: Harmful Biases or Efficient Information Processing?" *Scholars* 4(1) Fall/Winter 1992–1993: 30–34.

[12]Eva Hoffman, *Lost in Translation: A Life in a New Language* (New York: Penguin, 1990), p. 146.

[13]Janet E. Helms, "Toward a Theoretical Explanation of the Effects of Race on Counselling: A Black and White Model," *The Counseling Psychologist* 12(3–4) 1984: 153–164.

■ FURTHER READING

BUTLER, PAMELA E. *Talking to Yourself: Learning the Language of Self-Support.* San Francisco: Harper & Row, 1983. In this book, Butler, a clinical psychologist, provides ways for us to examine messages we give to ourselves. She explains how people can change their negative talk to build a language of self-support that can assist in overcoming poor self-image and insecurity.

GLASSER, WILLIAM. *Control Theory: A New Explanation of How We Control Our Lives.* New York: Harper & Row, 1985. Glasser explains how we can control our emotions and actions to live healthier and more productive lives. His theory is that everything we do, think, and feel comes from inside us; thus, our behavior represents our attempts to get our world to conform to the pictures in our heads.

HARRIS, EDDY L. *Native Stranger.* New York: Vintage Departures, 1993. Harris, an African American, sets out for West Africa to discover some of the faraway world he has heard about since his childhood. He looks at Africa as a motherland, as a source of black pride, and as a place of black dignity.

HOFFMAN, EVA. *Lost in Translation: A Life in a New Language.* New York: Penguin, 1989. A fascinating autobiography of a woman who immigrated from Poland to Canada when she was 13 years old. This is an insider's look at what it is like to be caught between two languages and two cultures.

RODRIGUEZ, RICHARD. *Days of Obligation: An Argument with My Mexican Father.* New York: Viking, 1993. Rodriguez, who is Mexican American, asks what it means to share two cultural identities. He also identifies the ways in which Mexican and American philosophies differ.

SELIGMAN, MARTIN E. P. *Learned Optimism.* New York: Knopf, 1991. The author of this book, a psychologist, argues that optimism can be learned—even if one has been a lifelong pessimist. He also points out that optimism is worth learning since pessimists are more likely to suffer from depression and major health problems. Although this book contains a detailed program on how pessimists can change, it has far more depth than the standard self-help book.

SELIGMAN, MARTIN E. *What You Can Change and What You Can't.* New York: Knopf, 1994. This is a clear, simple, realistic book that examines things we can and cannot change, then shows how to unlearn certain damaging behaviors. Seligman discusses biology, emotions, and habits, and ends with two excellent chapters on "Growing Up—At Last."

VISCOTT, DAVID. *Emotionally Free: Letting Go of the Past to Live in the Moment.* Chicago: Contemporary Books, 1992. Much of one's personal progress in life depends on getting rid of the emotional baggage of the past. Viscott tells how to overcome self-limiting doubts, guilt, and anger.

KEY TERMS

active listener

assessment

cognitive dissonance

credibility

critical listening

empathic listening

fact

listening

main idea

opinion

passive listener

prediction

selective attention

supporting points

3

Listening

CHAPTER OBJECTIVES

After reading this chapter, you should be able to:

1 Explain the problems that lead to poor listening.

2 Explain why listening is important.

3 Identify and explain the various parts of the listening process.

4 List the benefits of active listening.

5 Understand the meaning of listening for information and how to improve your skills in listening for information.

6 Understand the meaning of critical listening and how to improve your skills in critical listening.

7 Understand the meaning of empathic listening and how to improve your skills in empathic listening.

8 Understand the meaning of listening for enjoyment and how to improve your skills in listening for enjoyment.

ne of our friends had a chest x-ray as part of an annual medical checkup. She told the technician that she had a small calcium spot on one of her lungs and asked him to attach a note to the x-ray so the doctor would know what the spot was.

Two days later, the doctor called our friend and said the x-ray showed there was a possibility that she had lung cancer, and he was scheduling her for a CAT scan. Our friend, assuming that the technician had attached the note, concluded that the doctor must have seen something besides the calcium deposit, and she agreed to the scan. A few days after the scan, the doctor called her to report on the results: he told her that she had a calcium deposit on her lung.

Because the technician did not listen, he created a good deal of anxiety for his patient, and he also caused her (or her insurance company) to spend hundreds of dollars for additional medical testing.

■ WHY LISTEN?

Like the technician, we all listen to important information every day. It's not enough to merely hear: **listening** involves responding intellectually and emotionally. Some of the information we listen to is critical: fire drills, first aid, safety instructions on an airplane. Even when the information isn't critical, it can be important to our well-being. Few of us can have successful relationships or be effective in our jobs if we don't develop listening skills.

Why Do We Have Problems Listening?

All of us have lapses in listening from time to time. Sometimes we get clues that we are not listening very well. For example, have you ever done a class assignment incorrectly while the rest of the class did it right? Have you asked an instructor to reexplain an assignment he or she gave to the class? Have you had trouble finding something even though someone told you where to look? Have you been lost because you didn't listen carefully enough to the directions someone gave you? Have your classmates laughed at you when you asked a question that had just been answered? Have you asked a question that had nothing to do with what was being discussed? Have you ever realized that you are not listening very well because you are distracted by your own thoughts? Have you ever been accused of not listening?

Probably most of us could answer "yes" to many of these questions. Listening is hard work, and there are many reasons for your attention to go astray. Let's look at some of the problems that cause us to listen less effectively than we should.

Cognitive dissonance, a psychological theory that applies to communication, states that people look for information that will reinforce their beliefs and ignore information that does not. For example, Gloria spends several weeks deciding whether she should buy an IBM computer or a Macintosh. Finally, she decides on the Mac. For many weeks after her purchase, she reads all the ads and listens to all the commercials that extol the Mac, and she ignores all the ads and commercials about the IBM.

When we engage in cognitive dissonance, we don't listen to points of view that differ from our own beliefs. This is not so important if, like Gloria, we ignore something like ads. The danger comes when we ignore all ideas that are contrary to our own. As we pointed out in Chapter 2, listening to new ideas is risky, but it is the only way we can grow. Imagine what might happen, for example, if antiabortion activists really listened to pro-choice activists and vice versa. Although such listening might not change anyone's mind, the act of listening inevitably leads to a new understanding and respect for someone else's ideas.

ANXIETY

Sometimes we don't listen because our anxiety level is too high. For example, imagine you are driving to a new city and you find yourself hopelessly lost. After driving for a long time and not seeing any highway numbers or

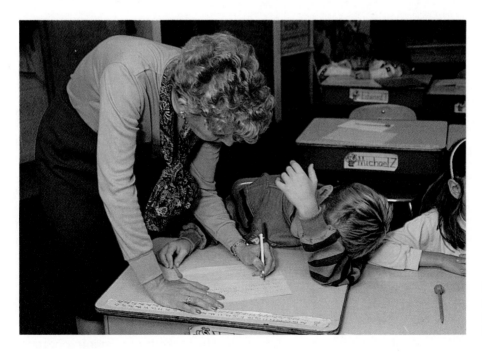

How is this child showing resistance to listening?

CONSIDER THIS

Many students and faculty members in our colleges and universities come from diverse cultural backgrounds. Dr. Renuka Biswas, an Indian in a university department that includes an African American and other faculty members from China, Honduras, and Bangladesh, points out that every student needs to listen more carefully to people from different places—even though their accents may be unfamiliar.

When a student body is largely Euro-American, large groups of the university community are not familiar with accents, modes of expression, and the use of words by African Americans, Asian Americans, Hispanic Americans, and people from different countries. Students and faculty sometimes complain that they do not understand what these non–Euro-Americans are saying. Then they draw the conclusion that these faculty members are not competent, they do not know English, their teaching is below standard, and their behavior is strange.

Many people do not seem to realize that Pennsylvanians, Texans, Brooklynites, and Bostonians also have accents. So do those people from other countries who speak English as a second language.

As an Asian Indian, I have no problem understanding these accents. I understand Pennsylvanians, Texans, Native Americans, and African Americans. I also understand the English of people who come from China, Japan, Poland, and Australia. I am able to under-

signs indicating a nearby city, you probably feel like you are going to jump right out of your skin. That's anxiety. When you finally stop to ask directions, you have completely lost confidence in yourself and your anxiety level is so high that you can't even listen. The result is that once you set out again, you still cannot find your way.

Teachers often complain that students don't listen, not realizing that the students can't listen because their anxiety level is so high. When students fear what they perceive to be difficult material, their anxiety interferes with their ability to respond intellectually. If you're one of those students who has to check and recheck every assignment or if you consistently get your assignments wrong, your listening might be impaired by your anxiety.

THE CONTROLLING LISTENER

Many people don't want to listen at all. They take turns listening because they know it is expected of them, but they would prefer to be talking.

stand these people because of my willing participation in the communication and my interest in what the other person is saying. What I ask is that students take a similar attitude: rather than feeling anxious about other's accents and consequently tuning them out, I would like to ask that they listen carefully and make an attempt to understand other people with accents that might seem strange to them.

Communication has two parties. If both do not cooperate in communication, it cannot take place. Students and faculty alike need to understand that we are living in a culturally diverse society and if we are all going to get along, we must put forth our best effort to understand others.

Source: Dr. Renuka Biswas, "Thoughts about Diversity" *APSCUF Faculty News and Views*, Lock Haven University, Lock Haven, Pennsylvania, April 15, 1993.

QUESTIONS

1. When you hear someone talking with an accent, do you panic and think that you might not be able to understand him or her?
2. Do you think your anxiety might interfere with your ability to listen to this person?
3. If you went into this situation with the attitude that you could understand, do you think that this attitude would help you to understand?

Controlling listeners always look for a way to talk about themselves and what they are thinking about. If someone else talks about an experience, they come up with a bigger and better one. If you say you own a 20-pound cat, they tell you about someone who owns a 25-pound cat. If you say you're going to Spain, they tell you that you really should go to Spain *and* Portugal to make the trip worthwhile.

These people seldom notice the nonverbal cues they get from others. They ignore that their listeners are glassy-eyed and often sneaking looks at their watches. They also ignore cues such as "Well, I had better get going" or "I just noticed how late it is."

THE PASSIVE LISTENER

People often believe that listening involves no work. Their attitude may range from "I don't have to do anything, I can just sit back and listen" to "I'm so bored—see if you can entertain me." These attitudes probably come from all the TV and video watching we do. Entertainment requires little listening ability: a "couch potato" is the ultimate passive listener.

Depending on what we listen to, we need a variety of listening skills. While entertainment listening may be passive, we need to be much more active in listening to classroom lectures or speeches by classmates. This kind of listening requires the attitude that although this might not be the most fascinating subject we have ever heard, we will listen because the information might be useful or important to us and because we have a moral obligation to listen to and understand others.

These attitudes lead to a key point we want to make in this chapter: listening well requires as much skill as speaking and writing well. In the section that follows, we look at the process of listening, the kinds of listening we do, and some of the ways to improve listening skills.

LEARNING TO LISTEN

Listening is a skill that can be learned. In a recent survey of Fortune 500 companies, 59 percent of the respondents said that they provided listening training for their employees. This interest in the development of listening skills makes sense because research shows that employees of major corporations spend about 60 percent of their time listening while executives spend an average of 57 percent.[1] Researchers have found that there is a direct connection between good listening skills and productivity on the job. When employees were given training in listening which was followed by training in computer techniques, they were much more productive than employees who had no listening training.[2]

Figure 3-1 shows the percentage of time we devote to the four communication skills: listening, speaking, reading, and writing. Although we spend the greatest amount of time in listening, it is the skill that is taught the least.[3]

Listening, like any skill, has to be learned and practiced. When researchers polled 450 graduates of business programs as to what kind of communication skills they needed on the job, they responded that listening was the most important skill for success. When they were asked what communication skill they wished they had been taught in college, listening ranked number one.[4]

We must also learn to listen differently in various situations. For example, when you listen to a friend, you probably use only your short-term memory. However, when you listen to a lecture, you are expected to remember what you have heard and, in days or weeks later, be able to write about it on an examination. If students are to benefit from their classes, they have a responsibility to listen. One teacher tells each new class, "Half the responsibility for good communication in this class is yours. Do not go to sleep or talk to your classmates while I am talking. I will assume my responsibilities

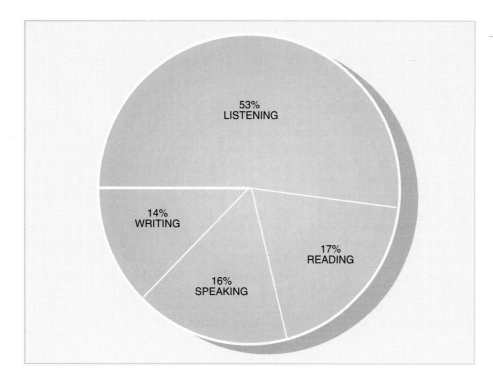

FIGURE 3.1
**Percentage of
Time Devoted to
Various
Communication
Skills**

to be clear, to repeat as necessary, to let you argue with me. You must do your part by listening."[5]

THE PROCESS OF LISTENING

Predictions and Assessment

Listening plays a part in the transactional nature of communication. From our past experience with the person to whom we are going to communicate, we make a **prediction** about how he or she is likely to respond. For example, if you go to an instructor with a paper that is late, you know from past experience that she isn't going to be very happy with you and that you will probably have to listen to complaints about your negligence as a student. You also know that your best strategy is to listen—not to talk back.

When you leave your instructor's office, you engage in **assessment**—an evaluation of what occurred. Although she took your paper, you know from her response that you'd better not try to hand in a late paper again: you predict from this experience that she would be really angry and not accept it.

The listener predicts what will happen *before* the listening event takes place and assesses what has happened *after* the event. The actual listening process has four stages: receiving messages, attending to them, assigning meaning to them, and remembering them. In an ideal listening situation, all these stages will be completed. If listening is ineffective, however, the process might break down at any stage. Let us look at each of these stages.

Receiving Messages

In any one day, all of us receive more messages than we need or can process. Some of these messages we mentioned earlier: commercials, someone shouting in the hallway, an instructor's lecture, a conversation with a friend. We *hear* many of these messages, but we do not *listen* to all of them.

We hear sounds—such as words and the way they are spoken—but when we listen, we respond to far more. It is as if hearing is a mechanical process involving the various parts of the ear, whereas listening is a more composite perceptual process involving our total response to others, with spoken words being just a part of what we respond to.

Thus, receiving messages does not involve hearing alone. Messages come in all forms and from a variety of sources. When we listen, we filter out the irrelevant messages, which brings us to the next step in the listening process—that of attending to what we consider important or interesting.

Attending

We are able to focus our attention on a particular stimulus. For example, if you're in the dorm in the early evening, you hear all kinds of noises: students shouting to each other, music playing, doors slamming. However, when your CD rolls around to your favorite song, you are all attention: the song blots out all the other sounds around you.

The ability to focus perception—called **selective attention**—is quite extraordinary. For decades parents have told their children that it is impossible to study with the television set or stereo blaring away. If you like to study that way too, you will think that these parents are wrong—and research will support you. In one study, listeners were seated in the middle of four loudspeakers, all with different messages, and were told to pay attention to the message coming from only one particular speaker. In all cases, listeners were able to show an almost perfect performance in recalling the message from that speaker.[6]

Although we are able to focus our attention in specific ways, our attention span is very short. Generally, people can give full attention to a message for no more than twenty seconds.[7] Something in the message reminds us of something else, or we disagree with the message and let our minds wander in a completely different direction. Fortunately we are quickly able to refocus our attention on the message, but every listener and speaker should be aware of just how easily attention can go astray.

Attention span is closely tied to boredom. Researchers have found that the best listener is someone who is not easily bored and who has some basic skills in acquiring information.[8] Students who are easily bored, then, must make a special attempt to focus their attention.

How does this child communicate that she is listening carefully?

Assigning Meaning

When we decide to attend to a message, our next step is to *assign it meaning*. This involves assimilating the message—making it part of our knowledge and experience. To assign meaning we must decide what in the message is relevant and how it relates to what we already know. Basically, then, the process of assigning meaning is one of selecting material and trying to relate it to our experience. In assigning meaning we also evaluate. We weigh what the speaker has said against the personal beliefs we hold, we question the speaker's motives, we wonder what has been omitted, and we challenge the validity of the ideas. As well as understanding *what* was said, we also

64

BASIC
PRINCIPLES OF
COMMUNICATION

look at *how* it was said. We assign meaning to the speaker's tone of voice, gestures, and facial expressions as much as we do to his or her words.[9]

Remembering

The final step in the listening process is *remembering*. Again, remembering is a selective process of determining what is important and what is not. As students, few of you record the whole of an instructor's lecture. Instead you take notes that help you remember the important points.

For effective listening to take place, all these stages must be passed through. It is easy, however, to give the appearance of listening without listening at all. Many people master the art of looking attentive and interested without hearing a word that is said. As a student, you probably know that it is possible to take notes without understanding what the instructor is talking about.

The extent to which you complete the steps in the listening process will depend on who and what you are listening to as well as how important the information is to you. Figure 3-2 shows how a student receives stimuli from three places, selects the one that is most important, and acts on it.

ATTITUDES TOWARD LISTENING

Active Listening

The best way to focus on what is being said is to be a good **active listener**. You are an active listener when you make a mental outline of important points and think up questions or challenges to the points that have been made. Even though you might not say anything, you are mentally involved with the person who is talking.

Students have a special need to be active listeners because such listeners generally do better in school than **passive listeners**, who record but do not evaluate what they hear. Most teachers, as they lecture, prefer that students take notes. Although there has not been a great deal of research about note taking, what is known is that passive listeners who merely try to write down as much as they can of what an instructor says will not do particularly well on examinations. (There is also little value in borrowing notes from a friend.) Active listeners, on the other hand, take notes that tie concepts together and that distinguish between main and minor points. Students who take notes in this fashion and review them before the examination are likely to get better grades than students who passively record information.[10]

Active listening extends beyond the classroom. In interpersonal communication, for example, it involves looking for the meaning in what someone is saying as well as showing interest with nonverbal cues such as leaning forward, nodding, smiling, and frowning and using audible cues such as "Uh-huh," "Mmm," and "I see." In interpersonal communication there is

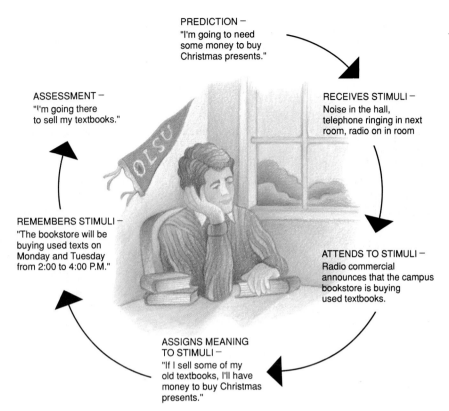

PREDICTION –
"I'm going to need
some money to buy
Christmas presents."

ASSESSMENT –
"I'm going there
to sell my textbooks."

RECEIVES STIMULI –
Noise in the hall,
telephone ringing in next
room, radio on in room

REMEMBERS STIMULI –
"The bookstore will be
buying used texts on
Monday and Tuesday
from 2:00 to 4:00 P.M."

ATTENDS TO STIMULI –
Radio commercial
announces that the campus
bookstore is buying
used textbooks.

ASSIGNS MEANING
TO STIMULI –
"If I sell some of my
old textbooks, I'll have
money to buy Christmas
presents."

FIGURE 3-2
**The Listening
Process**

also ample opportunity to give feedback by asking questions or by commenting on what the person has just said.

Active listening helps to avoid boredom as well. We are more likely to be bored if we are observing rather than participating in an event. Active listening is a way of involving yourself, and once you are involved, you are likely to get interested. If you use active listening techniques when you listen to a lecture, you might be surprised to find how quickly the time passes.

Active listening, then, involves active participation on the part of the listener. An active listener, however, does not listen in the same way in every listening experience. There are four basic listening experiences you can have, and they all involve different listening skills. These experiences are listening for information, listening critically, listening empathically, and listening for enjoyment. Let's consider each of these.

LISTENING FOR INFORMATION

Any college student will find that most of the time in classes is spent in listening, and this listening is primarily for information. Listening to the

What kinds of feedback do you see between the speaker and her audience?

instructor talk about the reasons for the Civil War, the economic structure of the broadcast industry, or the definition of a paranoid individual are all examples of listening for information.

The business world also requires people to listen for information: the company receptionist finds out whom a visitor hopes to see and why; the operator at an 800 number takes orders for computer parts; the mechanic receives information from the boss on how to install a new part. In business, listening can be seen in dollars-and-cents terms. The Sperry Corporation has pointed out that if each of the 100 million U.S. workers made a $10 listening error, the total cost would be $1 billion![11]

Even when it is critical to listen well, some people don't do it. A frequent traveler said that she always used to read magazines while flight attendants explained safety features on the airplane. One day, when her plane had made an emergency landing on the runway and she was crawling on the floor through the smoke toward what she hoped was the nearest exit, she wished she had paid attention to the flight attendant's message.

Identifying the Main Idea

What, then, should be the approach to listening for information? If you are listening to a speech or lecture, your first approach should be to listen for and identify the **main idea**—the central thought that runs through the passage. Then you listen for **supporting points**—the materials that reinforce the main point. It is important to identify the main idea because all the other points will relate to it. Identifying the main idea also aids memory. If you remember the main idea, then the supporting points will follow. If you remember only the latter, you will have unrelated points that make no sense; and because they make no sense, they will be easily forgotten.

With interpersonal communication, the main point is not always evident, and in some cases there might not be one. Main points are most likely to be present when you are having a heated discussion or an argument. A mother, for example, might have a main point when she tells her teenager why he can't have the car that night. Two men who are arguing about the best football team might each come up with a main point to support his side.

When small groups are trying to solve a problem, they will work more effectively when they identify the main point. If you have ever been in a group that didn't accomplish very much, it's probably because the group strayed away from the main point. For example, the food committee meets with the purpose of making suggestions on how the campus food service can improve. If they stick to this point, they will be likely to come up with some useful advice. However, if the group members sit around and swap horror stories about the terrible meals they have had, they won't accomplish much.

Identifying Supporting Material

In listening to a speech or a lecture, once you have identified the main point, your next step is to look for material that supports the main idea. The purpose of supporting points is to build evidence for the main point. Supporting points often consist of illustrations and examples that make the main idea clearer to the listener. Let's suppose a speaker is trying to inform his audience about Americans' impressions of the Japanese. His main point is that the media are unfair in their representation of the Japanese. As a supporting point, he notes that when an English company bought out an American company, there was almost no mention of it in the news, yet when, under similar circumstances, a Japanese company bought out an American company, the purchase made negative headlines throughout the country. As another supporting point, he cites the representation of Japanese as villains in American books and movies. To be more specific, he describes the way the Japanese are portrayed in a particular book and movie.

Supporting material is not really relevant to most interpersonal communication unless you are using it to support an argument. In small groups, however, it's often useful to break down the main topic into smaller, more manageable units. For example, the committee to improve campus food might want to offer supporting material in the form of new recipes that include more fresh fruits and vegetables and use cooking methods other than frying.

Forming a Mental Outline

When you are listening to a speech or a lecture, try to *form a mental outline*. Identify the main idea and then listen for the supporting points. The idea and its supporting points are the information to remember. The illustrations are examples that help you remember the supporting points better. In the overall organization of the speech, however, the examples might be trivia. If, after listening to a lecture about a "nutritional" food pyramid, you remember that you are supposed to eat a lot of fruit but forget the role that fruit plays in the whole nutritional plan, you were not listening very well.

Predicting What Will Come Next

Earlier we discussed the role of prediction in the listening process. When you are listening for information, it helps to focus your attention by *predicting what is coming next*. Once you hear the speaker's main point—that the government has come up with a new nutritional pyramid—you can logically predict that she is going to tell you the foods that are part of this pyramid. Prediction might seem difficult, but you do it all the time. The next time you are listening to a joke, notice how much predicting you are doing—it will continue right up to the punch line.

Relating Points to Your Experience

Another useful way to listen is to try to *relate the points to your own experience*. When a speaker makes the point that professional football is getting too violent, you might try to remember any particularly violent games you have seen. All good listeners attempt to relate material to their own experience—it's part of being an active listener.

Looking for Similarities and Differences

Your understanding of a subject is often aided if you can discover the *similarities* and *differences* in relation to what you already know. Sometimes the similarities and differences are obvious. When you hear that 95 percent of marriages in India are arranged by parents, this is an obvious difference from the American custom. A more subtle difference begins to emerge when you examine the role that parents play in marriage in both countries. You might ask, for example, why Indians of marriageable age permit their parents to arrange their marriages. In turn, this question might lead you to ask whether parents and children relate differently in Indian society than they do in American society.

Questioning and Paraphrasing

Questioning is an important aid to active listening. As you listen, you may ask questions of yourself. If you cannot answer them, then it is important that you ask them of the speaker. Even if you have answers to your questions, you might want to ask them anyway so that you can check your perceptions with those of the speaker. Another useful method for ensuring that your information is correct is *paraphrasing*—simply restating in your own words what you believe the other person has intended. For example, when a person from California says, "In the past five years, the house next door to me was burned during the Los Angeles riots, and we have gone through a major earthquake and numerous small tremors. I've decided I've had enough and I'm going to move to Arizona." A paraphrase might be "Some people think Southern California is a dangerous place to live."

We also listen for information in interpersonal and small-group settings. Many of the methods for active listening outlined above are appropriate for such settings, too; however, relating points to your experience, looking for similarities, and especially questioning and paraphrasing would probably be the most applicable.

CRITICAL LISTENING

Critical listening requires all of the ingredients of informative listening. The listener still should identify the main idea and the supporting points. In **critical listening**, however, the listener should also evaluate and challenge what has been heard. These challenges might take place in the listener's mind or they might be expressed directly to the speaker.

How do you know that this mother and son are paying careful attention to each other?

Ideally, all communication should be listened to critically. When you are receiving new information, however, it is sometimes difficult to evaluate it critically because you do not know very much about the subject—and possibly about the speaker either.

The area of *persuasion* offers the greatest opportunity to use critical listening skills. Products are advertised every day with the promise that they will bring romance, adventure, or success into our lives. It takes no genius to be critical of those sorts of messages! But commercials are not the only persuasive messages that we encounter. A candidate wants our vote; we are asked to sign a petition to impeach the mayor; a friend tries to persuade us to stop studying and go shopping. All these messages require evaluation and questioning.

TRY THIS

Have you ever thought that a class might be giving you difficulty because you are not listening properly? Test this by taking your most difficult class and applying this strategy:

■ *Predictions:* Before you go to class, try to predict what the class will be about. If your instructor follows a syllabus, what will the topic be? Is the subject likely to be connected to an assigned chapter in the text? Have you read it? Review your class notes for the last class period. What were they about, and what do you expect will come next?

■ *Listening:* Rather than take notes on everything your instructor says, concentrate on writing down the main points and listing supporting points below them. Is the instructor writing anything on the board? Does this help you to identify main points?

■ *Interaction:* As you are listening, try to put in your own words what the instructor is saying. Think of some questions about the material he or she is discussing. Even if you don't answer these questions aloud, coming up with them will help you to play a more active role in the class.

■ *Assessment:* After the class is over, look at your notes. Are your main points really the most important information? Do your supporting points really illustrate the main point? Do you need to make improvements in your note taking?

When we use critical listening, our first job is to *question the communicator's motives*. With commercials, it's easy. Someone wants to sell a product. With political candidates, the motive is more complex. Obviously they want to be elected to office. So then the questions are: Why? Are they after money or power? Do they want to bring about social change? Do they want to keep things the way they are?

A petition to impeach the mayor is even more complex and requires more in-depth questions. We need to know what the mayor has done to deserve such drastic treatment. We also might ask whether a petition is the right way to remove the mayor, how a new mayor will be appointed (or elected), and the broader question of whether impeachment will best serve the interests of the community.

Even when a friend tries to persuade us to stop studying and go shopping, we must address a number of questions. What are his or her motives? What are the effects likely to be? When we are involved in persuasive situations, questioning the persuader's motives is a normal, proper response. In public speaking situations we often check the speakers' motives by examining their backgrounds. Some speakers give lengthy introductions that are designed to establish their **credibility**, or believability. Not every speaker has to be an expert; it is enough to have done a sufficient amount of homework to give a credible speech.

Challenging and Questioning Ideas

Critical listening also involves *challenging* ideas and *questioning* the validity of ideas. Where did the speaker get her information? Did it come from a source that is generally regarded as credible? Is the speaker quoting the information accurately, or is she taking it out of context? Does she identify her sources of information so they can be checked later by her audience?

In persuasive situations, speakers sometimes omit information that does not support their cause. If you have information contrary to what a speaker presents, keep it in mind so you can ask questions later. You can assess whether information has been omitted by asking questions about the speaker's sources. In a political speech, for example, is all the supporting material from one particular party or viewpoint—say, liberal or conservative? Does this mean that important information may have been omitted?

Distinguishing Fact from Opinion

Part of challenging ideas and questioning their validity is the ability to *distinguish fact from opinion*. A **fact** is something that can be verified. Everyone who applies the same test should be able to get the same information. Today's temperature is a fact. If we put several thermometers in the same place, they should all show the same temperature. A fact is always true, whereas an **opinion** is someone's belief. During the course of a day, we hear many more opinions than facts, so it is important that you, as the listener, make the distinction. The statement "Women should stay home and take care of children" is an opinion—regardless of how authoritative the speaker may sound.

Although all facts are equal, some opinions are more reliable than others. We are more likely to trust the opinions of speakers who have been right before, who have a high degree of authority or credibility, or whose opinions have been (or are) supported by others.

Recognizing Our Own Biases

Sometimes there are messages we don't want to hear because they contradict our own attitudes and beliefs. If you're a Democrat, you don't go to Republican rallies; if you're a religious liberal, you don't go to revival meetings. If, for some reason, you were forced to go to either of these, you would probably disregard most of what you heard.

In some cases, we might not even be aware that we are blocking out messages. For example, one study found that although jurors had heard instructions about the rules of circumstantial evidence, only 40 percent correctly followed these instructions. The authors concluded that this misunderstanding of the law was not merely a matter of poor listening. They believed that jurors were likely to misinterpret the law when they didn't believe in it. Their interpretation was compatible with the view they held of the law.[12] This tendency to interpret information in the light of our beliefs can lead us to distort the information we hear. As listeners, we have to be aware of our own values and attitudes—especially when we hear information we might resist or disagree with.

Assessing the Message

Earlier in this chapter, we discussed listening as an ongoing process that includes *assessment* of the communication. This assessment can take place while the event is happening and can continue long after the event is over. Assessment is basically a critical process; it is chewing over what you have heard before you swallow it. An idea that may seem acceptable when we first hear it may not be so palatable when we have had time to think about it. This is especially true for important ideas: it is essential to reflect on them before they become part of us and of our thinking. We must learn to *suspend judgment*—delay taking a position—until we receive all the facts and other evidence, until we have had a chance to test the facts in the marketplace of ideas, and until we have chewed everything over sufficiently for digestion.

EMPATHIC LISTENING

When we are involved in interpersonal communication with our friends and families, we engage in both informative and critical listening. In the case of people close to us, we engage in another kind of listening too: *empathic listening*, listening for feelings.

Listening for Feelings

We are often asked or expected to listen for feelings, and we often want to share our feelings with others. We are all upset or happy at one time or another, and if we share these feelings with someone else, it permits us to reveal ourselves. Sharing our feelings also helps us to cope with them. Often when we talk our feelings over with other people, we can gain control of them or deal with them better. Listening to other people's feelings is a way of giving emotional support, and the ability to do this is what creates intimacy with others.

But many of us do not do a very good job of listening for feelings. Because it is one of the most common forms of listening, we assume we can do it easily. You will probably be surprised to learn, however, that you might not be listening as effectively as you could be. Let's look at some of the responses you might make that hamper your effectiveness as a listener.

Negative Listening Responses

To look at negative listening responses, let's assume that your best friend has been feeling depressed for the last few days. You ask her what is wrong and she responds that she is having a terrible time at her job because her boss is picking on her so much. Here are some possible ways you could respond—responses that we all use, but none of which is very helpful.

DENYING FEELINGS

If you respond, "You shouldn't feel that way—everyone knows how hard it is to get along with him," you are focusing on the personality of the boss rather than on what your friend is feeling. When our feelings are very intense, we want them recognized. We don't want them pushed aside while other, less important, items are dealt with.

EVALUATING

If you respond, "Why don't you just stop trying? There are other jobs" or "He really doesn't appreciate all the work you do," you are making an evaluative response—one that passes judgment on and offers an opinion of either your friend or the boss. Often an evaluative response is a way of trying to dispose of another's problems. The listener does not take the time to listen to the problem; he or she just makes some generalizations that are designed to make the problem go away.

BEING PHILOSOPHICAL

The philosophical response is so broad and sweeping that it does nothing to solve the problem. In this kind of response, you might say, "All bosses are hard to get along with; it's the nature of the boss-employee relationship."

Like an evaluative response, this response ignores the problem and the feelings of the person with the problem.

GIVING ADVICE

"Go out and get a new job. Your boss will never get any better." This is concrete and specific advice. When people have problems, however, it is better to let *them* find their own solutions. Your job is not to give advice but to listen in such a way that your friend can solve the problem on her own. Deborah Tannen, a writer on language, points out that men, in particular, are more interested in "fixing" problems than in listening to them.[13]

DEFENDING THE OTHER PERSON

Sometimes we think it might be helpful to present the other person's viewpoint: "Well, you have to understand his side. He has a lot of employees to supervise." But your friend with the problem doesn't want to hear any defense of the boss. If you defend him, she might wonder where your loyalties lie.

EXPRESSING SYMPATHY

Too much sympathy can also be a trap. "I really feel sorry for you. It must be terrible to work for a person who treats you so badly." But with a response like this, your friend may feel even worse. Concern usually works better than sympathy.

QUESTIONING

Sometimes our response to a friend's problem is to ask a series of questions: "What did you do to make him disapprove of you?" "Is there anything you can do to make the situation better?" Question asking can be a valuable interpersonal skill but is less helpful when emotions are very high. Once the *feeling* has lost some of its intensity, questions might be useful to help solve the problem.

All these responses are weak because they do not deal with the problem of feelings. They all, in one way or another, lead the person with the problem away from her feelings. How, then, can we respond in such a way that we focus on feelings?

The Empathic Listening Response

The best way to listen for feelings is through **empathic listening**—where you try to understand what the person is feeling *from his or her point of view* and reflect these feelings back. As the listener, your job is to put aside your own feelings and enter into the feelings of the person who is speaking. To do this you need to recognize what feelings are involved, let the speaker tell you what has happened, and then encourage that person to find the solution to the problem.

IDENTIFY THE EMOTION(S)

First, and this is often the most difficult part, you need to listen to what the person is *really* saying. If, for example, a friend comes over and says, "I am going to kill my boss!" he is obviously not saying that he literally plans to kill him. When you are listening empathically, you first need to identify what the speaker is feeling. In this case, it would be reasonable to assume the speaker is feeling anger, and you respond with, "Boy, you really sound mad." With this kind of response, you open the opportunity for your friend to tell you what has happened.

LISTEN TO THE STORY

The second part of an empathic response is to listen to what the person has to say. As the whole story comes out, there is no need to respond with anything very specific. This is the point where the person just wants to be listened to. You can show your interest by paying attention and looking sympathetic.

Let's go back to your friend and his problem with his boss. What happened to make him so angry? Your friend explains that he was promised a raise with this week's paycheck. Not only did he not get a raise, but someone who has been there a much shorter time did get a raise.

After your friend has told you the whole story, he is not quite so mad, but he is still pretty upset. As you listen, you discover other feelings in addition to anger. Your friend feels betrayed because the boss had told him he would get a raise. He also feels humiliated because his coworkers know that an employee who was hired after him got a raise when he did not. Usually people do not feel just one emotion—they have a whole assortment of them.

If you can let your friend talk through the entire problem, with outmaking judgments but offering support, it is likely that the full range of the problem will be revealed. One way to reach this point, as noted earlier, is through *paraphrasing*—restating the other person's thoughts or feelings in your own words. If your friend says, "I'm going to go in and tell him I quit," an appropriate paraphrased response might be, "You sound too upset to go on working there." This response not only helps to identify the feelings; it also helps to find out whether you have been hearing accurately and shows you are paying attention. A paraphrased response provides a mirror for the other's remarks.

CONSIDER THIS

⚖️ Lloyd Steffen argues that the emphasis in listening should be on focusing on one's partner rather than developing skills or techniques. For this reason, he says, listening is a moral act.

He believes that when people listen carefully, they are likely to find that what the other person is saying is "different," or even strange. Listening to this differentness, he says, means that we might be exposed to another experience that challenges the way we see the world. However, he maintains that if we don't listen, we will never expose ourselves to the mysteries of others or even discover the mystery of ourselves.

Source: Lloyd Steffen, "The Listening Point," *The Christian Century* (Nov. 21–28), 1990, pp. 1087–1088.

QUESTIONS

1. Have you ever had an experience where you chose not to listen because the topic or situation was too threatening?

2. Is it a psychological risk to listen to a different point of view?

3. Is Steffen correct when he says that listening is a moral act?

LET THE PERSON WORK OUT THE PROBLEM

Sometimes just listening for people's feelings and letting them explain what is upsetting them largely solves the problem. We often hear someone say, "I feel better just because I've talked to you." People frequently want to vent their feelings, and once they have done so, they feel better.

But sometimes mere listening is not enough; your friend has a problem, and he or she wants some help in solving it. In such a situation, the best approach is usually to trust in the other person and in his or her ability to work out the problem. This does not mean, however, that you ignore the problem. Empathic listening includes helping the other person find a way to solve the problem.

The last step in empathic listening, then, is to give the person a chance to work out the problem. In the case of your friend, you don't want to say, "You *should* quit!" Let your friend decide what he wants to do. If the emotion in the situation has died down, it might be appropriate to ask some very broad and general questions, such as "What are you going to do now?" It might also be possible to ask some questions that might lead to a solution the other person has not thought of: "Do you think if you talked to your boss, he might change his mind?" or "Do you think he may have made a mistake?"

The important thing to remember at this stage is that you do not have to solve the other person's problem. If you try to solve every problem that people bring you, you put a heavy burden on yourself. Think of the person with the problem as *owning* that problem. This attitude also will help the other person to grow in his or her ability to deal with problems. For example, if parents tried to solve all their children's problems, the children would not learn to live independent lives.

If you are the kind of person who feels burdened because everyone comes to you with problems, you are probably taking on more responsibility than is required. Rather than focusing on solutions, try focusing on feelings and listening empathically. You will be surprised at how well this system works.

Empathic listening can be useful in many situations, but there are times when it might not work well because you, as the listener, are feeling too much stress and conflict. If you are really angry with someone, it is very difficult to use empathic listening because you are not interested in the other person's feelings; you are interested in your own. But if you are not under stress and are able to listen to another person without feeling threatened in any way, empathic listening can work very well.

The important thing to remember is that when strong emotions are involved, people often just need a sounding board. To be there and to utter an occasional "Oh," "Mmm," or "I see" is often enough. Much comfort is derived from just being listened to.

LISTENING FOR ENJOYMENT

Few of us have any difficulty when we listen to things we have chosen for our own enjoyment. We turn on the television or stereo, lean back, and relax. If we like what we hear, we don't even have a problem remembering it. We can often recite, with perfect fidelity, song lyrics from a recording or a dialog from a movie.

You probably find it more challenging, however, when your instructors ask you to enjoy information that is complex and difficult to listen to. When your English teacher puts on a recording of a famous actor reading from *Hamlet*, he hopes that you will both understand and enjoy it. Your theater instructor does not stick to uncomplicated Broadway plays and musical comedies; she also wants you to enjoy George Bernard Shaw and Wendy Wasserstein. As a student, you too are probably interested in increasing your ability to listen with enjoyment to more complex information.

When we want to listen to something for enjoyment but it is too complex to understand, we can try listening in the same way we listened critically for information and listened for feelings. A course in music appreciation is a good example of a place to employ all these skills. Since most of us enjoy music, it is not unreasonable to assume that we will enjoy some of the music we hear in such a class. In addition to enjoying the music, however, we will be asked to use other listening skills. Our informational skills might be tested: Can you identify the theme? What is the rhythm of the piece? What does *allegretto* mean? Our critical skills might be tested if we are asked to listen for the way two different composers treat the same theme or to indicate whether we agree with the way the musician interprets the piece. Since music involves feelings, we are asked to listen for the mood of the piece: Is it solemn or light? How does it make the listener feel? By requiring listening skills other than those needed for enjoyment, the music instructor is hoping to increase the pleasure you find in music—because the more one knows about music, the more one is able to appreciate and savor more complex forms of it.

Listening for enjoyment, then, can be a more sophisticated process than merely sitting back and letting the sounds wash over us. Complex material, even when we enjoy it, involves greater listening skill. In music, for example, if we had not worked on these skills, we would all still be listening to "Twinkle, Twinkle, Little Star."

The same skills can be applied when we listen to a play. Listen for information: What is the play about? What is the plot? Listen critically: Do the scenes flow into one another? Are the characters believable? Listen empathically: What is the character feeling? How does she relate to the other characters?

Listening is often more enjoyable if we can relate what we are hearing to our own experience. Someone who plays the violin can enjoy a violin concerto because he knows what to look for and is aware of the discipline and practice that it takes to play such a piece. Watching a play, we can sometimes think "I have felt that way too."

You will find it worthwhile working to enjoy more complex information. Remember, however, that listening for enjoyment can require skills just as complex as those needed in any other listening situations. The only difference is in the rewards. What could be better than listening to enjoy yourself?

SUMMARY

All of us are surrounded by hundreds of messages every day. Because we are surrounded by so much information, it is often difficult to listen, and many of us become poor listeners.

Listening is a skill, and like any other skill it must be learned and practiced. Obstacles to effective listening include cognitive dissonance, anxiety, a need to control communication, and passivity. Listening is also a process and a transaction. We make predictions about messages before we hear them, we listen to them, and then we assess what we have heard. How well we listen is determined by the attention we give to a message. We are able to tune out unwanted messages through the process of selective attention. Once we hear a message, we must assign meaning to it by selecting and organizing the material we have heard. Our final step in listening is to select what we need to remember.

To be good listeners we must become actively involved in the process of listening. As active listeners we evaluate and criticize material as we listen to it. When we listen actively, we are less likely to become distracted or bored. In many situations we have a responsibility to listen carefully.

There are four kinds of listening: listening for information, critical listening, empathic listening, and listening for enjoyment. Listening for information involves listening for facts. In this kind of listening it is important to identify the main point and distinguish it from the supporting points. Critical listening involves evaluating the material we hear. To listen critically, we listen for the motives of the speaker and mentally challenge the speaker's ideas and information. Critical listening is especially effective when listening to persuasive messages.

Empathic listening is listening for feelings. This kind of listening is most often done in interpersonal communication, and it often has the purpose of helping the speaker to cope with his or her feelings and problems. Listening for enjoyment is the listening that we choose to do. We can learn to enjoy complex material by using all the other listening skills.

■ NOTES

[1] Andrew D. Wolvin and Carolyn Gwynn Coakley, "A Survey of the Status of Listening Training in Some Fortune 500 Corporations," *Communication Education* 40 (1993): pp. 152–153.

[2] Michael J. Papa and Ethel C. Glenn, "Listening Ability and Performance with New Technology: A Case Study," *The Journal of Business Communication* 25 (Fall 1988): 13.

[3] Sperry Corporation, *Your Personal Listening Profile* (Sperry Corporation, 1980), p. 4.

[4] Vincent DiSalvo, David C. Larsen, and William J. Seiler, "Communication Skills Needed by People in Business," *Communication Monographs* 25 (1976): 274.

[5] American Federation of Teachers, "Listen, and Ye Shall Learn," *On Campus* (March 1988): 6.

[6] Neville Moray, *Listening and Attention* (Baltimore: Penguin, 1969), p. 23.

[7] Paul G. Friedman, *Listening Processes: Attention, Understanding, Evaluation* (Washington, DC: National Education Association, 1978), p. 274.

8 Robert N. Bostrom, *Listening Behavior* (New York: Guilford Press, 1990).

9 Rebecca B. Rubin and Charles V. Roberts, "A Comparative Examination and Analysis of Three Listening Tests," *Communication Education* 36 (April 1987): 142–153.

10 Kenneth A. Kiewra and Nelson F. Du Bois, "Note-Taking Functions and Techniques," *Journal of Educational Psychology* 83(2) June 1991: 243.

11 Sperry Corporation, *Your Personal Listening Profile*.

12 Bert K. Pryor, K. Phillip Taylor, Raymond W. Buchanan, and David U. Strawn, "An Affective-Cognitive Consistency Explanation for Comprehension of Standard Jury Instructions," *Communication Monographs* 47 (1980): 69.

13 Deborah Tannen, *You Just Don't Understand* (New York: Morrow, 1990), pp. 49–53.

FURTHER READING

BECHLER, CURT, AND RICHARD L. WEAVER II. *Listen to Win: A Guide to Effective Listening.* New York: MasterMedia, 1994. The authors offer advice about changing listening habits to help readers learn to live with others, connect with them, get the best from them, and empower them. They suggest ways to transform communication situations.

BOSTROM, ROBERT N. *Listening Behavior.* New York: Guilford Press, 1990. This book is a review of most of the studies done about listening plus some new work on listening behavior. It is a useful resource for people who want to know more about how listening works.

FLOYD, JAMES J. *Listening: A Practical Approach.* Glenview, IL: Scott, Foresman, 1985. Floyd presents a skills approach to listening improvement. In a mere 137 pages, he addresses the importance of listening, the nature of the listening process, how to become aware of undesirable listening habits, and how to modify those habits through recognition, refusal, and replacement. Finally, he treats each listening skill area: attention, understanding nonverbal and verbal messages, analysis/evaluation, and feedback.

LORAYNE, HARRY, AND JERRY LUCAS. *The Memory Book.* New York: Dorset Press, 1989. This book is one of the classics on memory techniques. It has many techniques you can use to help you remember items for tests, long lists, concepts, and people's names.

STEIL, LYMAN K., LARRY L. BARKER, AND KITTY W. WATSON. *Effective Listening: Key to Your Success.* New York: Random House, 1983. These authors build awareness, understanding, and appreciation of listening excellence. This book offers a guide for listening improvement for professionals in business and industry. A useful introduction to listening.

WOLFF, FLORENCE I., NADINE C. MARSNIK, WILLIAM S. TACEY, AND RALPH G. NICHOLS. *Perceptive Listening.* New York: Holt, Rinehart and Winston, 1983. This is a comprehensive textbook in listening at the college level. It explains current theory and offers research-based principles. The authors emphasize motivated practice and performance and analyze in detail the entire spectrum of normally experienced listening situations. A fine, well-researched textbook loaded with useful information.

WOLVIN, ANDREW D., AND CAROLYN GWYNN COAKLEY. *Listening*, 3d ed. Dubuque, IA: Brown, 1988.   This complete textbook on listening examines the need for, process of, and types of listening. The authors look at appreciative, discriminative, comprehensive, therapeutic, and critical listening. This is a useful, well-documented resource.

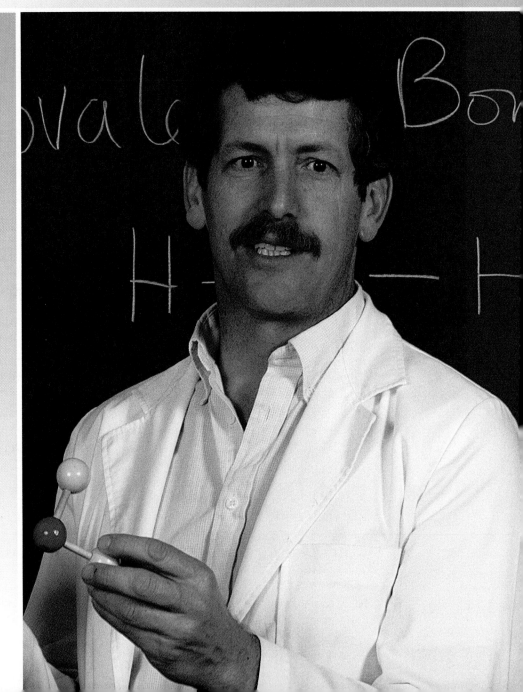

KEY TERMS

bilingualism

*connotative
    meaning*

*denotative
    meaning*

dialect

doublespeak

euphemism

*language
    environment*

metamessage

rapport-talk

report-talk

ritual language

style

Verbal Communication

CHAPTER OBJECTIVES

After reading this chapter you should be able to:

1 Explain how language is symbolic.

2 Explain what is expected of a speaker in a particular language environment.

3 Give examples of the ritual use of language.

4 Explain the function of role in a language environment.

5 Define style.

6 Describe differences between women's and men's language.

7 Define report-talk and rapport-talk.

8 Explain differences between standard English and dialect.

9 Describe the ways in which speaking is more transactional than writing.

10 Describe some of the ways to make your verbal style clearer, more powerful, and more vivid.

11 Define and give examples of metamessages.

From the time you were a small child your memories were connected with language: you couldn't remember until you had the words to describe what you saw and heard. When you began to acquire language you also saw that it was something powerful. You could bring forth a delighted smile when you used the words *ma* or *pa* to your parents. You also found that you could get your own way by saying "no." You were entertained for hours by various word games: "Show me your nose. Show me your mouth. . . ." Through this game and others, you discovered that everything was identified by a word. This made it possible for you to get things by asking for them by name. You probably went through the "terrible twos." At that age you knew the potential of language, but you didn't know the words to ask for what you wanted, so you often felt a lot of frustration and anger.

By the time you were 3 or 4 years old, you probably discovered that you could use words to hurt people. If you were with other children, you picked up words like *poophead* or *fraidy cat*. You might have come home crying because of something someone said to you. This was the age where you also

CONSIDER THIS

Although the exact number of deaf people in the United States is unknown, estimates place the count at about half a million. People who are deaf are completely isolated from those who can hear. For those who are born deaf, learning spoken and written English is extremely difficult. Even deaf people who lip-read usually figure out no more than three or four words in ten. As a result, most deaf people learn English poorly, and the average deaf 16-year-old reads at the level of a hearing 8-year-old.

Rather than remain imprisoned in silence in mainstream America, some members of the deaf community are demanding that they be regarded as a subculture—and not as a handicapped group. They maintain that like any other subculture, such as African Americans or Haitians, they have their own language: American Sign Language (ASL) can express any concept or idea found in spoken or written English.

When deaf people are asked if they would like to hear, many answer "no." They say that if they were to regain hearing, they would be cut off from their community and culture, which is based on ASL. They argue that a deaf child who is "mainstreamed" into a regular class is likely to feel forever lost and isolated. They also oppose new techniques that can help some deaf children to hear. In their opinion, these "advances" cause the deaf child to be taken

tried out newly learned words at home—and found out that some of them were inappropriate.

Through all these early years you learned what language was and what it could do. Even though you may never have thought about it, you needed language to survive. As you progressed through school, much of your education was about language and how to use it. In fact, your success as a student depended on how well you learned these lessons.

Once you have learned how to use language, your words help you to achieve understanding and communication with others. How you use language creates an impression on others: your language lets others know your class and your education. Your success at work may depend on how well you speak and write. It may also depend on learning the special language of the particular job you are doing.

Language is just as important in your personal life. How you use language will affect your relationships with friends and loved ones. Failures in relationships with friends and family are often attributed to a failure of language.

---

away from his or her community—in much the way an African American child could lose contact with the black community if he or she were adopted by white parents.

Those who advocate recognition of the deaf subculture believe that they have a rich cultural life and language. They believe that sending their children to schools where the language is ASL, marrying within the deaf community, and forming relationships within this community gives them their best chance for a fulfilling life.

Source: Edward Dolnick, "Deafness as Culture," *Atlantic Monthly* (Sept. 1993), pp. 37–53.

QUESTIONS

1. Do you find yourself resisting the idea that the deaf should be considered a subculture? If you do, list your objections.

2. If a culture is defined by customs and language, don't the deaf qualify as a subculture?

3. People in the hearing community may find it difficult to accept that deaf adults want deaf children to remain in their own culture rather than being "cured." Is this an unreasonable or a reasonable request? List arguments on both sides.

This chapter is largely concerned with the language behavior of both speakers and listeners and the context within which they operate. To divorce words from how they are spoken and how they are heard is to look at them in isolation—and words are never isolated in oral communication. For this reason, it is impossible to discuss language behavior without discussing the people who are using the language. This applies equally to both speaker and listener. Successful communication depends on the completion of the transaction, and much of the emphasis in this chapter is on how the sender-receiver conveys thoughts and emotions through language.

An understanding of language will help you express what you really want to say in a clear and straightforward way. When a message is misunderstood or has no effect on the listener, it may be that the speaker's language is at fault. And no matter how skillful it may be in other ways, any communication that is not understood cannot be successful.

HOW WORDS WORK

When you say a word, you are vocally representing something—whether that thing is a physical object, such as your biology textbook, or an abstract concept, such as peace.

The word is, as noted in Chapter 1, a symbol: it stands for the object or concept that it names. This is what distinguishes a word from a random sound. The sounds that are represented in our language by the letters *c a t*

Is a wedding toast more likely to have connotative or denotative language?

constitute a word because we have agreed that these sounds will stand for a particular domestic animal. The sounds represented by the letters *z a t* do not make up a word in our language because these sounds do not stand for anything.

A word that stands for a concrete and emotionally neutral thing—such as the word *mailbox*—can usually be interpreted with good fidelity because most people respond primarily to its **denotative meaning**—that is, its dictionary definition.

Other words stand for abstract concepts that evoke strong feelings. Words such as *freedom* and *love* are easily misunderstood because they carry a lot of **connotative meaning**—the feelings or associations each individual has about a word. For example, when we hear the word *love*, we don't just think about the word; we associate it with a person or an experience we have had. The connotative aspect of words may cause problems in communication because a single word may evoke strong and varied feelings in listeners. Think, for example, of the many different reactions people have to the word *abortion*.

Although we need abstract connotative words to express ideas, precise denotative words work better when we want to convey information or get things done. Figure 4-1 shows the usefulness of precise, concrete words.

When you study a language, whether it is your native tongue or a foreign one, you must learn what the words stand for; that is, you have to know both their denotative and their connotative meanings. You must also know how to put the words together to make the phrases and sentences that express relationships between the words. This is the grammar of a language.

Notice, however, that your idea of an object or a concept is never exactly the same as another person's, because each individual has had different experiences. Your notion of what *cat* means comes from all the cats you have ever known, read about, seen on television, heard others talk about, and so on. This composite cat is unique to you, but you can use the sound of the word to refer to cats in general because cats have certain qualities on which we all agree.

A theory of language developed by Edward Sapir and Benjamin L. Whorf suggests that language helps us determine how we see and think about the world. They believe that language restricts the thoughts of people who use it and that the limits of one's language become the limits of one's world.[1]

In Whorf's study of the Hopi language, for example, he discovered that the language has limited tenses and makes no distinction between the concepts of time and space. English, however, has many tenses, and English speakers often discuss events from the point of view of when they happened. One author, commenting on these differences, says that the Hopi language would enable a child to understand the theory of relativity while a native English–speaking child could more easily understand history because history depends on concepts of time and space.[2]

Because the United States has been a one-language nation, many Americans do not understand how language and perception of the world are connected. For example, Americans sometimes complain that immi-

I'd also like a Coke with that, please.

Would you like small, medium, or large? "New" or "Classic" Coke? Regular or Diet? With or without caffeine? Do you want ice with that too?

Never mind—I'll have a milk instead.

We have white, chocolate, whole, 2%, and skim...

FIGURE 4-1
Using Precise, Concrete Words

grants to the United States do not learn and use English. However, if we accept the theory that language defines our world and our perception of it, we see that learning a language is not just a matter of learning a sign system: it is also learning a different way of looking at the world. For example, in Pohnpeian, a Pacific island language, there is no way to ask the question "Are you hungry?" A Pohnpeian who is asked "Are you hungry?" in English cannot answer that question because it would be rude to admit to being hungry.

CONSIDER THIS

Every language has a certain amount of indirectness built into it. For example, in English, instead of saying, "Take these books to the library," we are more likely to ask, "Would you mind taking these books to the library?" The question is still a command, but its indirect form makes it seem more polite.

Nonnative speakers of English might not realize that such questions are really commands. For example, when a teacher asked a Nigerian student, "Would you mind giving your speech first?" he replied, "I would prefer not to."

A native English speaker might have similar problems with indirect language in another culture. For example, an English speaker who knows Japanese may still get in trouble if he or she is not aware of the indirect language of Japan. Robin Tolmach Lakoff, a linguist, points out that Japanese speakers have a more roundabout way of using language. For example, personal pronouns are not used in contexts where Westerners are used to them, and tenses are not explicitly expressed where English speakers expect them.

In summarizing the distinctions between Japanese and Western languages, Lakoff writes: "While most Western cultures are *speaker-based* in their communicative strategies (the job of determining what an utterance is to mean is up to the speaker, who bears the responsibility for the meaning), the Japanese strategy is *hearer-based:* the meaning resides in the hearer's mind, and it's the hearer's job to extract the point of what is said, not the speaker's to be clear about it."

Source: Robin Tolmach Lakoff, *Talking Power* (New York, Basic Books, 1990), p. 174.

QUESTIONS

1. On the basis of what Lakoff says, do you think this textbook, *Communicating Effectively*, is likely to be used in Japan? Why or why not?

2. How would you feel if you always had to figure out the meaning of what someone said to you? If you are from the west, would this be particularly difficult?

Later in this chapter, in the section on gender and language, we will show how male and female language differs to reflect each gender's view of the world.

For the listener to understand what a speaker intends, the speaker should have something definite in mind. If an idea or impression is vague in the speaker's mind, the resulting message will be confused and ambiguous. Understanding is the core of meaning, and understanding is a two-way process; that is, the speaker is responsible for presenting the idea clearly, and the listener is responsible for trying to understand it accurately. Meanings are determined in people, not by words.

When speaking of some subjects, you have to use a very specialized vocabulary. For example, to discuss personal computers, you need to understand such terms as *RAM*, *megabyte*, and *hard drive*. In fact, you probably need to learn these terms before you can even *think* about computers.

Language differences might even occur within a family. For example, the world of adults is different from the worlds of children or adolescents. Parents might wish, for example, that their child were popular. But *popular* to a teenager may mean "being able to stay out late and own a car"—possibly unacceptable conditions to the parents. Because the experiences of the teenager and parent are so different, their values and vocabulary also differ.

New meanings are continually created by all of us as we change our ideas, our feelings, and our activities. As we think, read, travel, make friends, and experience life, the associations and connections that words have for us are changed.

THE LANGUAGE ENVIRONMENT

All language takes place within a particular environment. A minister speaks in the environment of a church; two friends have a conversation in the student center; an instructor gives a lecture in a classroom. Language that is appropriate to one environment might appear meaningless or foolish in another. The language you use in a dormitory, for example, might be completely inappropriate in a classroom.

People, Purposes, and Rules

According to Neil Postman, a writer about language, the **language environment** is made up of four elements: people, their purpose, the rules of communication by which they achieve their purpose, and the actual talk being used in the situation.[3] To illustrate these elements, let's take the simple example of John and Mary seeing each other on the street. Their purpose in communicating is to greet each other.

Mary: Hi. How are you?

John: Fine. How are you?

Mary: Good.

The rules for this sort of conversation are well known to all of us, since we often participate in it ourselves. If John had failed to follow the rules, however, and had stopped to talk for five minutes about how miserable he felt, Mary might have been annoyed. John would have gone beyond the limits of that sort of conversation.

The kind of conversation Mary and John had illustrates language as a ritual. **Ritual language** takes place in environments where a conventionalized response is expected of us.[4] Greetings are a ritual; we briefly respond to each other—usually only half-listening to what the other person has said—and then go about our business.

The rituals we use are determined by the language environment. If we are at a funeral, we are expected to respond in conventional, ritualized ways to the family of the person who has died: "He was a wonderful man, and I will miss him"; "She had a rich and full life"; "It's a blessing he is no longer suffering." At a wedding we wish the couple happiness and tell the bride she looks beautiful.

Every society's language rituals are determined by the cultural values of that society. In rural East Africa, it would be rude to pass a man you know well with a brief "Hello." You are expected to stop and inquire about the person, his home, his livestock, and his health. In some cultures it is appropriate to tell the couple at their wedding that you hope they will have many sons; in American society, such a comment would be considered highly inappropriate.

We learn ritualized language when we are very young, and we learn it from our parents or other adults around us. For example, researchers have found that young children do not automatically make the conventional responses of "Hi," "Good-bye," or "Thanks"—even though they hear adults doing so. If children are going to use conventional terms, they must be taught.[5]

As children grow older, they begin to learn and use ritual language. Anyone who has handed out candy on Halloween can tell you that although the younger children may have to be prompted, this is no longer necessary with the older children; they offer their thanks spontaneously.

Appropriate Language

Through social conditioning, then, children learn appropriate language. Sometime around age 3 or 4 they begin to pick up derogatory and aggressive phrases. They also learn that they can get a reaction from adults not only from their behavior but from their language.[6] At this stage, they typically try out curses or swear words. This is also the point where parents and teachers intercede to let children know that such words are inappropriate. By age 5, a child has a fairly good sense of what is appropriate and inappropriate language.

One common way to avoid inappropriate language is to learn euphemisms. A **euphemism** is an inoffensive word or phrase that is substituted for other words that might be perceived as unpleasant. For example, we ask "Where's your bathroom?" even when we don't intend to take a bath. If somebody has died, we might use the phrase "passed away." In another case, when a restaurant in Taiwan wanted to serve dog meat, the owners knew that it would offend some people, and so rather than admit what it was they called it *fragrant meat*. Closer to home, we call our own meat *beef*, *veal*, and *pork* to veil that it is really dead cow, calf, and pig.

Sometimes government agencies or other institutions create euphemisms to cover up the truth. When euphemisms are created by an institution, they are often referred to as **doublespeak**. For example, if one country accidently dropped a bomb on another country, the offending government would probably use the word *incident* to describe the action. Usually, in English, the word *incident* refers to something small and insignificant: in the case of dropping a bomb, however, *incident* could refer to the killing of hundreds of people.

We learn appropriate language as we become more sophisticated and mature. By the time we reach late adolescence most of us know what language to use for a particular language environment. Whether we want to use the prescribed words is largely irrelevant. The language environment dictates the language that is expected of us. If we violate these expectations, we run the risk of having people respond to us negatively.

Specialization

Language environments can be very specialized. If your plumber tells you that your toilet needs a new sleeve gasket, you probably won't know what that means. You would understand if the plumber told you that the toilet needs a new seal at the bottom to keep the water from leaking out on the floor. Most professions and occupations have a language that only its practitioners understand. Professional cooks make a *roux*, teachers write up their *behavioral objectives*, and contractors install *I-beams*. Not only do occupational groups have their own language, but members must learn it in order to master their field.

Even a highly specialized field may have variations within a language environment. For example, one researcher has discovered that to succeed, social workers must use several languages on the job: the language of the client, the language of the theorist, the language of the researcher, the technical terminology of their field, and the preferential language that conveys values.[7]

Sometimes people create a special language when they feel they don't have as much power as the people around them. Quite often this is a language that those in power do not understand, and it is deliberately used to keep information from them. Students, especially those in high school and

CONSIDER THIS

♀♂ One way to turn a woman into an object is to break her up into small pieces. Advertisers have done this for a long time: if you scan a magazine, you will often see women's legs, arms, and torsos presented as separate images.

A woman can also be turned into an object with words. For example, the world of fertility clinics has created an entire new vocabulary of words coined largely by male doctors and researchers to describe the processes used on women. Here are some of the words used to describe women and their body parts: *uterine environment, surrogate uterus, alternative reproduction vehicle, host womb, gestational mother,* and *nubile young ovaries.*

Some doctors have referred to "harvesting a woman for eggs." Two Australian doctors, in writing about in vitro fertilization, say, "The human female is capable of having substantial litters under certain circumstances."

Source: Robyn Rowland, "Decoding Reprospeak," *Ms.* (May-June, 1991), pp. 38–41.

QUESTIONS

1. What do you think is the effect of using these words to describe women's fertility?

2. If this kind of "dismemberment" language is used to describe women, does it become easier for members of society to treat women violently?

3. The author of this article says that by describing women in this way, researchers and doctors can control their patients. What does the author mean by this?

---

college, are one example of special-language groups. They use slang or a special meaning to exclude outsiders or members of the adult establishment. For example, most adults don't know the meaning of such terms as a *homeslice,* a *crib,* or *fulreal* (for real).

When a group has created a special language, we usually cannot step into that group and use its language unless we have some legitimate claim to membership. Students, for example, might secretly make fun of the teacher who tries to talk as they do. How we are expected to speak in a language environment depends on the role we are playing.

Whenever we shift roles, we shift our language environment and our speech as well. Let's say that in a single day, you talk to your roommate, you go to class, and you speak to your mother on the telephone. Your role has shifted three times: from *peer* relating to peer, to *student* relating to instructor, to *child* relating to parent. Each circumstance has entailed a different language environment, and you have probably changed your speech accordingly—often without realizing it.

The important thing to remember about a language environment is that we must choose language that is appropriate to it. The language used in one environment usually does not work in another. When we think about the environment, we need to ask ourselves with whom we are going to be talking and in what context our language is going to be used. If we don't adapt to the environment, our language will not work, and we will lose the chance for effective communication.

STYLE, ROLES, AND GROUP MEMBERSHIPS

The words you use are determined by all your past experiences, by everything in your individual history. You learn words in order to express thoughts, and thought and language develop together. The way you think and the way you talk are unique; they form a distinctive pattern. In a sense, you *are* what you say because language is the chief means of conveying your thoughts. Neither language nor thought can be viewed in isolation. They are related and constantly growing. Together, they determine your verbal style.

Style is the result of the way we select and arrange words and sentences. People choose different words to express their thoughts, and every individual has a unique verbal style. Not only do styles vary among people, but each person uses different styles to suit different situations. In the pulpit, often a minister has a scholarly and formal style. At a church dinner, however, his or her style is likely to be informal and casual. When a football player signs autographs for fans, he speaks to them in the role of athlete—even though he might drop this role when he is with friends and family.

Sometimes style can negate a communicator's other good qualities. We all know someone who is extremely shy and speaks only in a faltering manner. We also know some people who can never seem to get to the point. Style, because of its power and influence, is as important to the acceptance of ideas as all the other aspects of communication. Even if we have the proper information, the right occasion, and a listener interested in our message, what we have to say may be lost if our style is inappropriate.

Impressions of personality are often related to verbal style. When you characterize a person as formal and aloof, your impression is due in part to the way that person talks. Since your style partially determines whether others accept or reject you, it also influences how others receive your messages. Style is so important that it can influence people's opinion of you, win their friendship, lose their respect, or sway them to your ideas.

Like language environment, verbal style is often connected with the roles we play. Professionals, for example, are expected to speak grammatically correct English—both in private and in professional life. A college student

In the United States, would an interaction of this kind be unusual? Under what circumstances do people touch each other in the United States?

is also expected to use correct grammar. Yet if he takes a factory job during summer vacation, using correct grammar might get him into trouble with his fellow workers, for his verbal style could identify him as a "college kid."

Gender and Language

In recent years there have been numerous studies of the different language styles used by men and women. Deborah Tannen, a sociolinguist, has found that men and women have an almost completely different style of speaking. In fact, she maintains that their languages are so different that they might as well come from different worlds.[8]

According to Tannen, when women have conversations, their goal is the language of **rapport-talk**. This language is designed to lead to intimacy with others, to match experiences, and to establish relationships. Men, however, speak **report-talk**. In this type of speech the speaker's goal is to maintain status, to demonstrate knowledge and skills, and to keep the center-stage position.[9]

Because of their different ways of speaking, men and women often have problems when they try to talk to each other, Tannen says. For example, a stock cartoon shows a man and woman at the breakfast table with the man reading the newspaper and the woman trying to get his attention. The man is using the newspaper as a source of information he needs for future report-talks. The woman, however, is looking for interaction.

Tannen also notes that men are more likely than women to look at problems in terms of "fixing them." A woman, for example, might want to talk

TRY THIS

Analyze the verbal style of one person from the following list. How does the way in which the person selects and arranges words affect your impressions of this person's likability, trustworthiness, and competence? What does the person's speech suggest about age, education, social class, and cultural background? Is there anything in the person's style that gives you a bad impression?

Roseanne Arnold	Jesse Jackson
Beavis or Butthead	David Letterman
Hillary Rodham Clinton	Willie Nelson
Barney the Dinosaur	Bart Simpson
Arsenio Hall	Oprah Winfrey

to her husband about a problem at work. Her husband is likely to respond with a solution: "You should try. . . ." For the woman, this is not a satisfactory answer; she would prefer a statement of understanding or an expression of empathy.[10]

Other researchers have also looked at differences between the way men and women interact. They have found that when men and women talk together, men are more likely to interrupt ("Let's go on to the next topic") and give directives ("Why don't you write this down?"). Women use more personal pronouns and more intensive adverbs ("I really like her"). The researchers also found that women use more questions and more justifiers ("The reason I say this . . .").[11]

Tannen believes that gender differences in language are important considerations in the college classroom. In a typical classroom, she says, male students are likely to say what they know before the whole class and welcome arguments and challenges from their classmates. They are also likely to reject anecdotal information as unimportant. Female students, on the other hand, do not find much pleasure in public opposition and are much more comfortable when they work in small groups and offer personal anecdotes. Since most classrooms are organized on the male model, Tannen believes that many women find the classroom to be a hostile space.[12]

An interesting example of gender differences in language occurred when a teacher asked her students to make up words that described experiences unique to their sex but that did not already exist in English. She found that women's and men's words were in entirely different categories. Women created words that tended to put women in subservient roles, such as *perchaphonic* ("waiting for someone to phone you") and *herdastudaphobia* ("fear when passing a group of strange men"). Men, however, created words that focused on competency and the power to change things, such as *gearheaditis* ("making your car the best on the road") and *beer muscles* ("believing you are tough after you have had something to drink").[13]

Where does gender-specific language come from? Tannen believes that it begins in childhood and that children learn it from their peers. She reports that one researcher who observed preschool children found that when the children wanted to do something, the girls would start with "Let's . . ." while the boys would give direct commands ("Sit down").[14] In looking at videotapes of second graders, Tannen says that in language and behavior, second-grade girls were more similar to adult women than they were to second-grade boys.[15] When the same second graders were put in pairs and asked to talk about "something serious," the girls did so. The boys, however, resisted or mocked authority.[16] Since language behavior starts so young, it's not surprising that it soon becomes automatic.

One encouraging aspect of "gender-appropriate" speech is that women are not locked into it. Once a female plays a role equal to that of a male, her language becomes more similar to male speech. Faye Crosby and Linda Nyquist discovered, for example, that when women are in positions of authority, they use basically the same speech as their male counterparts.[17] Their study indicates that language strongly reflects the role we play in society, and as our role changes, so does our language.

Dialect

Toward the end of the summer in central Pennsylvania, many cooks begin to fry or preserve "mangoes." Outsiders are always surprised that Pennsylvania cooks are so interested in this tropical fruit. What they don't know is that in that part of the country a "mango" isn't a fruit at all; it's what everyone else calls a green pepper or a bell pepper. The central Pennsylvanians' use of the word *mango* is an example of dialect.

A **dialect** is the habitual language of a community. It is distinguished by unique grammatical structures, words, and figures of speech. The community members who use the dialect may be identified by region or by such diverse factors as education, social class, or cultural background.

Linguists refer to dialects as nonstandard forms of language. They generally try to avoid such questions as whether a dialect is a "correct" form of speech or whether one dialect is superior or preferable to another.

For a long time, many people believed that the mass media, particularly radio and television, would lead to standardized speech throughout the country. Among African Americans, the largest dialectal group in the United States, this has not been the case. One recent study shows that the dialect is moving further and further away from standard English. The linguists who conducted the study believe that this has happened because African Americans are becoming increasingly segregated from whites—particularly in urban areas. They point out that African American children often do not meet a white person until they enter school. This segregation has led to a dialect with unique sentence structures and idioms that are not found in standard English.[18]

TRY THIS

An observer of comedy style found that male and female comedians have entirely different styles. Below is a list showing the ways they differ. The next time you watch a comedian, see if you think these observations are accurate.

	Men's Humor	Women's Humor
Attitude	Competitive	Cooperative
Source	Distrust, hostility, envy, jealousy	Caring concern
M.O.	Singles out victims	Brings people together
Effect	Makes some people feel good at the expense of others	Lets everyone feel good
Tone	Negative	Positive
Type	Sarcasm	Kidding
Focus	What one of us did	What any of us might do
Goal	Rhetorical one-upmanship	Spotlighting issues in their lives
Target	The weak	The powerful

SOURCE: "Last Laugh," *Psychology Today.* September/October, 1993, pp. 16–17.

Although there are no clear-cut rules for where and when it is appropriate to use a dialect, it is possible to make some generalizations. A dialect is appropriate in a group with a strong ethnic identity, but it may be inappropriate in situations where standard English is used. Linguistic studies agree that some dialects have more prestige than others and that prestige is determined by both the people who speak the dialect and those who hear it. Thus, if you want to be accepted by and identified with people who use a dialect or who use a standard English different from your own, you might have to adapt to their way of speaking. Many people in America have discovered that it is not difficult to speak two "languages," a dialect and standard English. By so doing, they find it possible to keep their ethnic roots as well as function in a world where expectations are different.

Speaking and Writing

We use language in both speaking and writing, but the transactional nature of speaking makes it much different from writing.

When two people are engaged in conversation, they interact continuously and simultaneously. Both get and give information, form impressions, and respond to each other. On the basis of each other's responses, both can change their comments to explain, backtrack, hurry up, slow down, or do whatever is necessary to be understood.

Sometimes our conversation reflects past knowledge of each other. We can use a kind of shorthand because of the experiences we have had togeth-

TRY THIS

If you look back at some of the textbooks of twenty or so years ago, you will notice that they are written in what we now call sexist language. Characteristics of sexist language are that *man* is used to refer to both men and women; the pronoun *he* is used when the person could be either male or female; and many of the nouns begin or end with *man*, such as *mankind* or *mailman*.

Authors today are trying hard to avoid this language and have come up with some useful strategies. Here are some of the guidelines:

1. Try to find a neutral word that does not imply a particular gender. For example, use *letter carrier* instead of *mailman* and *police officer* instead of *policeman*.
2. When you are using a pronoun to refer to one person, try using *he or she* and *his or her*.
3. If you use *he or she* too many times, see if you can recast the sentence in the plural, making sure that the pronoun is also plural. For example, instead of "The student will be assigned to his room at 7 p.m.," try "The students will be assigned to their rooms at 7 p.m."
4. Don't assume that a role is masculine or feminine. Doctors and principals can be referred to as *she*; nurses and teachers can be referred to as *he*.

How might children benefit from bilingual education? How would it affect a child's self-confidence if everyone were learning his or her language?

In this section we present ideas that may contradict information in the text and may or may not reflect the views of the authors. The important thing is that you read the material, discuss it with your class-mates or friends, and make up your own mind.

Should Americans Be Required to Learn Another Language?

Many people believe that Americans should become bilingual. (**Bilingualism** means to speak two languages.) They argue that the fastest-growing segment of the United States population is Hispanic and that it would ben-efit the nation if every person spoke both English and Spanish. Although the best time (and perhaps the only time) to learn a lan-guage fluently is during childhood, only 5 per-cent of the children in the United States study a foreign language in elementary school.

One plan proposed by those who believe American children should be bilingual calls for total immersion of children from kinder-garten through second grade—meaning that this age group would learn all of their lessons in a second language. For example, English-speaking children would learn in Spanish while Spanish-speaking children would learn in English. This plan is offered as an option in 93 school districts. In some districts, parents can also choose a partial immersion where language and reading are taught in English but all other classes are in the second lan-guage.

Those who favor partial or total language immersion believe that this is the easiest way for the nation to become bilingual. They point out that because young children can easily go from one language to another, elementary school is the place to begin. They argue that Americans are too ethnocentric, that Americans don't realize that other cultures and languages are just as rich as ours, and that use of another language would add a valuable diversity to the American experience. These people would probably agree with Jesse Jackson that America is not so much a melting pot as a mixed salad—a place where separate and distinct elements make up the whole.

Others are opposed to any kind of plan for bilingual education. They maintain that America has a tradition as a melting pot and that for this idea to work, everyone must speak the same language. The English lan-guage is also associated with patriotism: many consider it as American as the flag and the national anthem. Their position is that any ethnic group that wants to live in the United States should learn English. Many also believe that the schools should be under no obligation to offer bilingual education.

Source: Jean Seligmann, "Speaking in Tongues," *Newsweek*, Special Issue (Fall-Winter, 1990), pp. 36–37.

QUESTIONS

1. Can you come up with additional reasons why the United States should be bilingual? Any reasons against bilingualism?

2. Canada is a bilingual nation. What are the arguments for and against bilingualism there?

3. Most language experts agree that language determines the way we look at the world. Would we look at the United States in another way if everyone were bilingual?

er. If we are in a close relationship or desire one, we know that the words we speak may affect our present and future relationship. If the relationship is more impersonal, then the choice of words might not be so important.

Finally, we can change our language to reflect the circumstances. When we get negative feedback, we can change language to appease our listeners. We can use simpler words or concepts if listeners don't seem to understand.

This kind of adaptation occurs in every conversation. Whether you are talking to your father, a professor, or a friend, your language will reflect your impression of this person, the kinds of experiences you have had together, and the role you are playing. In contrast, it's not so easy to change your written language. When you are speaking, people are reacting to you as the message *occurs*. Writers, however, never have an immediate reaction from their audiences. In fact, they usually don't have a reaction at all. The message flows one way—from writer to reader—and the writer has no chance to revise on the basis of the reader's reaction.

Writers have no way of taking the past, present, and future aspects of their words into account. When Salman Rushdie wrote *The Satanic Verses*, he had no way of predicting that his words would be seen as blasphemous and would be condemned by the Ayatollah of Iran, who "gave permission" for any Moslem to kill the author.

A writer can play only one role at a time: he or she is a term-paper writer, a romance-novel writer, or a humorist, for example. Words are then chosen from the point of view of that role.

Writers, however, enjoy one advantage over speakers. They have the time to go over their words, polish their phrases, and check their grammar. The reader has more time too. A reader can always reread the words when the meaning is not clear the first time.

Speech, on the other hand, must be understood as soon as the listener hears it. As a result, speakers must take care with vocabulary and make sure that their train of thought is logical and easy to follow. If they present complex ideas, they must allow time for feedback—that is, for questions from the audience.

■ WORKING ON YOUR COMMUNICATION

When we set out to communicate verbally, we are more likely to be successful if we use words and ideas that have the same meaning to the person with whom we are communicating as they do to us. Unfortunately, although we think we are being clear, the other person often does not perceive what we think we have communicated.

Communication can break down at various stages. Let's look at some of the places where this might happen.

Is the disk jockey likely to get any feedback from her audience? If so, what kind?

What Do You Want to Say?

In 1938 Orson Welles broadcast *The War of the Worlds*, a radio play about Martians invading the United States. We can assume that in writing this play, Welles had the intent of entertaining his audience. Although Welles's intent was clear to him, at least one million people misunderstood it and believed the play was real—they believed that Martians really had landed and that their lives were in peril. By the time the misunderstanding was cleared up, many people had already reacted to the play by leaving their homes and trying to find a place of safety.

Although this is an extreme example of intent going astray, most of us have had times when people's responses were different from those we intended. You intend to tell your roommate to meet you at 7:00, but she thinks you said 7:30. You intend to make a joke, but you end up insulting someone. When you are involved in one-to-one communication, you often have a chance to clear up misunderstandings. You see that the other person looks confused or annoyed, or the response you get indicates that you have not communicated something as precisely as you had intended, and you have a chance to clarify what you said.

When you are talking to an audience, however, it is not so easy to clear up misunderstandings. In a public speaking or mass communication setting, you may not have a chance to respond to feedback—or you may not be able to respond until the communication is over. Therefore, when you are going to communicate to a large audience, you must prepare your words much more carefully than in an interpersonal setting.

The first thing you must consider is: What exactly do you want to say? Students who are new to public speaking often do not think out this step clearly enough. Speakers who do not know precisely what they want to say frequently end up confusing their audience. The same may happen if they have not clearly thought out their words.

How Do You Want to Say It?

Once you have decided on your intent, you must choose the language you are going to use. A speech on writing computer games might entail the use of a highly specialized vocabulary that your audience does not know. To what extent do you have to define and explain your terms? If you have highly technical information to impart, how can you modify the language so that your audience will understand your concepts on the basis of their own experience?

If descriptive and informative language must be carefully chosen, you run into an even greater problem when you are dealing with abstractions. In speaking about justice, for example, you have to consider your language very carefully. *Justice* is not only an abstract word but an emotional one, and it might have as many different meanings as there are members in the audience. One person might think about a low grade she felt she didn't deserve; another might think of prison reform; still another might think about the backlog of cases in the courts. It would therefore be a mistake to think that people know what you are talking about when you use this word. When you use the language of abstraction and emotion, you must be careful to define your language *from your point of view* as it relates to the subject you are talking about.

To Whom Are You Talking?

When you seek a specific response from a listener, your words have to have meaning within the person's experience. If you are talking about snow to a student who has spent his entire life in Puerto Rico, for example, he is likely to have little idea of what it means to live with snow—even though he might understand the concept intellectually. By the same token, a professor lecturing to a beginning psychology class would probably assume that students do not know the words *affective* and *cognitive* and therefore would define them as she lectured. Some knowledge of the listener's (or audience's) interests, experiences, and expectations will help a speaker to choose words and arrange ideas in the way that will be most effective.

Metamessages

You probably choose your words carefully when you are making a public presentation. It might not occur to you, however, to be so careful when you are talking to a friend or conversing with a small group of people. Yet you might occasionally have had a conversation that made you feel uneasy—the words all *sounded* right, but there was something else going on.

In such cases, you need to think about the **metamessage** (or subtext)—the meaning apart from what the actual words express. For example, one friend tells another, "A lot of people say you're cold, but I believe you're acting professionally." This message provides little comfort. Its recipient suddenly imagines everyone talking about her behind her back. She also realizes that the person who told her this is feeling some hostility toward her. The feeling that comes across is a metamessage.

Metamessages take many forms. At a graduation ceremony, the president of the university introduced everyone on the stage except one of the deans. The dean realized this was more than a simple oversight, that he might be in serious trouble. He was right—he was fired the next semester.

Sometimes metamessages don't involve words at all. Deborah Tannen believes that American men refuse to ask directions because it puts them in an inferior position. Asking another person for information puts the possessor of the information in a superior position.[19]

Sometimes metamessages are recognizable to people within a specific culture but not to outsiders. A Polish professor complained that when she was in the United States, one of her American colleagues kept saying, "Let's have lunch sometime." When she tried to pin him down, he looked annoyed. What she didn't realize until much later was that this is an expression that Americans commonly use to terminate a conversation.

Language is filled with metamessages, and you have to listen for this kind of talk and understand its meaning if you are going to have accurate communication. You also should be aware of the metamessages you yourself send. For example, it is not unusual for a student speaker to begin a speech by implying that the speech will not be very good: "I just finished this speech this morning," "I couldn't find any research on this topic," or "You'll have to excuse me because I am feeling sick." If you say anything of this sort, you may be engaging in a metamessage; what you may be saying is, "I am feeling extremely nervous and anxious about giving this speech."

LANGUAGE CHOICES

Although you are often told that you should use clear and precise language, you might not know how to go about it. Command of language requires years of practice and study. Since it is impossible to lay down strict rules that govern the choice of language for all occasions and for all circumstances, the discussion here is limited to four important aspects of language choice: clarity, power, vividness, and morality.

Clarity

Sometimes our meaning is unclear because our sentence structure is faulty. For example, if you say "Having taken his seat, you started asking him questions" and your listeners look baffled, you can try again. There are other times, however, when the need to speak as clearly and precisely as possible is more urgent. If you are saying something of special importance or if you are making a formal speech, clarity is essential since you will probably not get a second opportunity to clarify your point.

Jargon is a language that can be so specialized that it is inappropriate to use outside the field where it originated. *Interface*, for example, is a word from computer science, and it shouldn't be used for human interactions. "I would like to work with you" is certainly better than "I would like to interface with you." Physicians often use a highly specialized language to describe illnesses and injuries. Although doctors can communicate with each other, sometimes they have problems communicating with patients. Many newspapers carry a column in which a physician answers questions from readers who do not understand what their own doctors told them.

Other language that might not be clear to everyone is slang. Slang has its place when you are talking informally with your friends. However, many slang words have such broad and vague meanings that they could apply to almost anything. If you use the word *awesome* in reference to someone's shirt and use it again to describe outstanding scenery, you reduce everything to a common element.

Sometimes people feel that if they have taken the trouble to learn long and complicated words, they should use them whenever they can. On a bottle of fluoride, the consumer is advised to "hold the solution in the mouth for one minute and then expectorate." In case the consumer doesn't understand the word *expectorate*, the phrase *spit it out* follows in parentheses. Since the purpose of this message is to communicate with the consumer, the simpler words, *spit it out*, should have been used in the first place.

Use more complicated words only when they help to make your meaning clearer. For example, if you want your car painted red, you'll be happier with the final results if you use a more precise description than *red*. What shade do you prefer? Burgundy? Crimson? Vermilion?

One of the delights of language is that it offers many subtleties and shades of meaning. Choosing the same words to express all our ideas is like eating a Big Mac for dinner every night. Language is a marvelous banquet providing us with a vast array of choices for anything and everything we want to say.

Powerful Talk

Many communication researchers have been looking into the issue of powerful talk. Powerful talk, they agree, is talk that comes directly to the point—talk that does not use hesitation or qualifications. People who engage in powerful talk are found to be more credible, more attractive, and more persuasive.[20]

To achieve powerful talk, you should avoid certain communication behaviors. First, avoid hedges and qualifiers—expressions such as "I guess" and "kind of"—because they weaken the power of your speech. Next, eliminate hesitation forms such as "uh" and "you know." These words make speakers appear to be less powerful. Third, stay away from tag questions—comments that start out as statements but end as questions ("It would be nice to go on a picnic, wouldn't it?"). Tag questions make the speaker seem less assertive. Finally, do not use disclaimers. These are words and expressions that excuse or ask the listener to bear with the speaker. Examples are "I know you probably don't agree with me, but . . ." and "I'm really not prepared to speak today."[21]

Many of us dilute our conversations and speeches with powerless words and expressions. However, the use of these expressions is mainly a matter of habit. Once you recognize your habits, you can start to break them.

Besides using powerful language, there are several techniques you can use to make your language more lively. A sense of urgency is communicated mainly by verbs—the action words of language. "Judy slapped him" and "The children jumped up and down" are both sentences that sound energetic. Adjectives and adverbs slow the language down, as in "The outraged Judy slapped him soundly." Language is also livelier when you put sentences in the active rather than the passive voice. "The boy hit the ball" is more energetic than "The ball was hit by the boy."

Vividness

Remember those ghost stories you heard when you were a child? The best ones were those that filled you with terror—the ones laced with blood-curdling shrieks, mournful moans, mysterious howling. They were usually set in dark places, with only an occasional eerie light or a streak of lightning. If any smells were mentioned, they were sure to be dank and musty.

The teller of a ghost story usually speaks in the first person. (Remember Edgar Allen Poe?) Any narrative told from the point of view of "I was there" or "It happened to me" is particularly vivid. By re-creating an experience for your listeners, you can often make them feel what you felt, a technique for making your language more vivid.

Vividness also comes from unique forms of speech. Some people would say that a person who talks too much "chatters like a magpie," a phrase that has become a cliché. To one Southern speaker, however, this person "makes a lot of chin music." When we say that language is vivid, we often mean that someone has found a new way of saying old things. Children often charm us with the uniqueness of their language because they are too young to know all the clichés and overused expressions. One of the best places to look for vivid language is poetry and song. Although more words have been written about love than any other subject, many songwriters have given us new expressions and therefore new ways of looking at the experience. Their unique perspectives make an old idea sound original and exciting.

Moral Choices

Ray Penn, a communications professor, points out that "a choice of words is a choice of worlds."[22] He reminds us that we can cause considerable damage to others by choosing the wrong words. For example, if you are asked to remember your most painful moment, the response will most likely be something someone said.

Penn asks us to consider whether "our analogies create a self-fulfilling prophecy that will ultimately keep us from relating to others unless we get our way." For example, how often in life do we talk of "winners" and "losers," condemning the "losers" to permanent failure? On the international scene, does calling Saddam Hussein "another Hitler" create a self-fulfilling prophecy? When political figures in the Middle East refer to the United States as "Satan" or "the devil," does such labeling influence the way we, as a country, react to them?

Penn also reminds us that language choices can influence people's perceptions of themselves. Insulting words, he points out, can reduce an individual to a mere trait ("four eyes," "fatty"); they can reduce someone to less than human status ("pig," "chicken"); or they can tell the person "I know all about you and you have no mystery" by means of labels ("hillbilly," "redneck," "women's libber").[23]

Penn's ideas are a reminder that we make moral choices in our use of language. Many of the choices we make not only determine how we present ourselves to others but also decide the nature of our relationships in the years to come. For this reason, it is important that we choose our words wisely and well.

■ IMPROVING YOUR VERBAL STYLE

Your verbal style says a good deal about you. If you make a favorable impression, do well in a job interview, or make a good grade in a class, some of your success has come about because of your verbal style. Thus it is to your advantage to pay attention to the way you talk and to question whether you can improve.

Three ways to improve your verbal style are by increasing your vocabulary, by adapting your speech to the language environment, and by making a determined effort to break bad verbal habits. You can actively pursue one or all of these goals in the course of daily interactions.

Increasing Your Vocabulary

You hear thousands of words every day, and you can benefit from this continuous access to other people's vocabularies. By becoming more conscious of the words used by telephone or radio advertisers and how skillfully and subtly they try to sell their products, or by politicians and how they present

TRY THIS

When you use the verb *to be* in a sentence, you often introduce vagueness or make the sentence less lively. For example, the sentence "I am sick" would be much more effective if you said, "I have a headache and think I'm going to throw up."

Here are some pictures of people involved in actions that are described with *to be* verbs. See if you can describe the action in a sentence that does not use any form of this verb. The first one is done for you.

PHRASE THAT TELLS

PHRASE THAT SHOWS

The girl jumped into the icy water and saved the drowning child.

The heroic girl

The naughty girls

The accident-prone boy

The tired old man

The vicious dog

their ideas, or by teachers and how they teach a lesson, you can take advantage of a resource that is readily available.

When you hear a new word, try to understand it in its *context*—that is, from the words or actions that precede or follow and that are directly connected with it. Although you may not always be able to stop another person to ask what he or she means by a certain word, do so when possible. People sometimes use words incorrectly, of course, and contexts can be deceiving or misleading. When you hear a word that you do not know or when you hear a word in an unfamiliar context, check its meaning. You can also develop sensitivity to the meanings of words by paying attention to people's feelings as they are revealed in verbal expressions and in nonverbal cues. This will help you become more aware of the emotional content in the messages of others.

Another way to build your vocabulary is by looking up and remembering the meaning of any new words you encounter while reading. When you are reading, just as when you are listening to your friends talk, try to be aware of new words—then find opportunities to fit those words into your own conversation. If you do not actually use a word, you will not remember it for long.

When you increase your vocabulary, you increase your chances of getting your intended meaning across to your listener. The more words you have at your command, the more precise you will be. This does not mean that you should search for big words; on the contrary, familiar words are often the best.

In addition to building your vocabulary, note how the words you read and hear are used in combination. It is the combination of words that makes style effective or ineffective. Thus you should not examine just the individual trees—the words—but the way the trees combine to make up the forest—the sentences, the phrases, and the ideas themselves. Thoughts are expressed in groups of words, seldom as one word alone.

Adapting Your Oral Language

As you talk to people, become conscious of them as particular individuals for whom you need to adapt your message. Note the language environment in which your conversation is taking place, and make the adjustments that are necessary. Also, be aware of the topic you are discussing, since it too can influence your choice of words. Be conscious of what you are saying. This added consciousness will increase your sensitivity to other people as well as your awareness of language choice and use.

Sometimes people confuse personal authenticity with inflexible language usage, and they equate undisciplined speech with spontaneity. "Telling it like it is" becomes an excuse for allowing the first words that come into your head to spill out in a torrent. Such language choices reflect a kind of self-centered indulgence that says to your listener, "Never mind who you are—listen to me." Adapting your language to the individual with whom you are talking can result in a more satisfying exchange.

Breaking Bad Habits

Although someone may tell you that you are making language mistakes, such as using poor grammar or misusing or mispronouncing certain words, you will probably find it hard to correct yourself because you are so accustomed to talking this way. If you live in a language environment where these mistakes are constantly being made, it is even more difficult, because hearing the errors reinforces them. The only way to correct such mistakes is to have someone constantly point them out to you—someone with whom you spend a lot of time. In using this method, it is advisable to tackle only one wrong usage at a time. Once you get that one cleared up, then you can begin to work on the next one. All habits are hard to break, and when you are trying to break one, you need all the help you can get.

SUMMARY

A word is a symbol; it stands for the object or concept it names. For us to understand one another, we must agree on what the particular word symbol stands for—in both its denotative and its connotative meaning.

Language is directly linked to our perception of reality and to our thought processes. Our perceptions and our thought processes begin in our earliest childhood. Each person creates meanings for words as ideas, feelings, and activities change. Because meanings are determined by each person, it is important for the speaker to present ideas as clearly as possible while the listener tries to understand accurately.

For language to be successful, it must be appropriate to the language environment. The language you should use in a particular environment is often determined by the role you are playing in that environment. Certain language rituals, conventionalized responses, are predetermined for us by the values of our society. We learn these and other forms of appropriate language during our childhood. When we become adults and enter the work world, we often must learn a specialized language used by our occupational or professional group.

Style, the way we express ourselves, is an important aspect of language. The style that is expected of us is often determined by the roles we play. If we do not modify our language to fit our role, we may speak in ways that are inappropriate to the occasion.

Language style may differ significantly by gender. Men are more likely to use report-talk, a language that maintains their status, demonstrates their knowledge and skills, and keeps them the center of attention. In contrast, women are more likely to use rapport-talk, a language that leads to intimacy with others, establishes relationships, and compares experiences.

If we belong to an ethnic group, we are likely to use a dialect—the habitual language of our community. The advantage of dialect is that it helps a person to fit into an ethnic community; the disadvantage is that it might not have prestige in a community where standard English is spoken.

Speaking and writing differ in that oral communication is more transactional. In oral communication, people interact continuously and simultaneously, and their conversation reflects their past knowledge of each other.

It is impossible to lay down strict rules for making good language choices. But the most effective language is clear, powerful, and vivid and shows that the speaker has made responsible choices. To speak clearly you must learn how to use and understand metamessages, the hidden messages that lie beneath the surface of what is said.

You can improve your verbal style by increasing your vocabulary, adapting your language to appropriate circumstances, and breaking bad language habits.

 NOTES

[1] Benjamin L. Whorf, "The Relation of Habitual Thought and Behavior to Language," *Language, Thought and Reality* (Cambridge, MA: M.I.T., 1956), pp. 134–159.

[2] Barry Lopez, *Arctic Dreams* (New York: Scribner, 1986), p. 274.

[3] Neil Postman, *Crazy Talk, Stupid Talk* (New York: Delta Books, 1977), p. 9.

[4] Erving Goffman, *Relations in Public* (New York: Basic Books, 1971), p. 62.

[5] Esther Blank Greif and Jane Berko Gleason, "Hi, Thanks, and Goodbye: More Routine Information," *Language in Society* 9 (1980): 159–166.

[6] Lawrence Kutner, "Parent and Child," *The New York Times*, May 20, 1993, p. C12.

[7] Martin Bloom, Katherine Wood, and Adrienne Chambon, "The Six Languages of Social Work," *Social Work* 34(6) May 1991: 530–535.

[8] Deborah Tannen, *You Just Don't Understand* (New York: Morrow, 1990), pp. 42–43.

[9] Ibid., p. 76.

[10] Ibid., pp. 51–52.

[11] Anthony Mulac, John M. Wiemenn, Sally J. Widenmann, and Toni W. Gibson, "Male/Female Language Differences and Effects in Same-Sex and Mixed-Sex Dyads: The Gender-Linked Language Effect," *Communication Monographs* 55 (1988): 316–332.

[12] Deborah Tannen, "How Men and Women Use Language Differently in Their Lives and in the Classroom," *Education Digest* (Feb. 1992), pp. 3–6.

[13] Lynn H. Turner, "An Analysis of Words Coined by Women and Men: Reflections on the Muted Group Theory and Gilligan's Model," *Women and Language* 15 (1992): 21–27.

[14] Tannen, *You Just Don't Understand*, p. 153.

[15] Ibid., p. 245.

[16] Ibid., pp. 255–256.

[17] Faye Crosby and Linda Nyquist, "The Female Register: An Empirical Study of Lakoff's Hypothesis," *Language in Society* 6 (1977): 314.

[18] Marsha Houston Stanback and W. Barnett Pearce, "Talking to the Man: Some Communication Strategies Used by Members of 'Subordinate' Social Groups," *Quarterly Journal of Speech* 67(1981): 24–25.

[19] Tannen, *You Just Don't Understand*, p. 62.

[20] Craig E. Johnson, "An Introduction to Powerful Talk and Powerless Talk in the Classroom," *Communication Education* 36 (April 1987): 167–172.

[21] Ibid.

[22] C. Ray Penn, "A Choice of Words Is a Choice of Worlds," *Vital Speeches of the Day*, Dec. 1, 1990, p. 116.

[23] Ibid., p. 117.

■ FURTHER READINGS

BATE, BARBARA, AND ANITA TAYLOR, EDS. *Women Communicating*. Norwood, NJ: Ablex, 1988. This book has a collection of essays on various aspects of women's talk. The essays all deal with issues important to women—ranging from talk about athletics to talk about victimization.

BAUGH, JOHN. *Black Street Speech: Its History, Structure, and Survival*. Austin: University of Texas Press, 1983. Baugh takes an intriguing look at African American street speech, the nonstandard dialect that thrives within the African American street culture and frequently varies depending on the social context. Baugh's procedures draw on linguistics, ethnography, and sociology. This is an important work for those doing research in spontaneous speech and conversation interaction.

ELGIN, SUZETTE HADEN. *Genderspeak: Men, Women, and the Gentle Art of Self-Defense*. New York: Wiley, 1993. Haden has written several books about defending yourself when you have been verbally attacked. This book deals with the difference between men and women and their use of language and how to avoid conflict when men talk to women and vice versa.

GONZALEZ, ALBERTO, MARSHA HOUSTON, AND VICTORIA CHEN (EDS.) *Our Voices: Essays in Culture, Ethnicity, and Communication*. Los Angeles: Roxbury Publishing, 1994. These original essays aid readers in understanding the language and culture of Asians, Latinos, Native Americans, the Jewish, and Arab Americans. Outstanding scholars offer valuable insights in this useful and readable volume.

HAYAKAWA, S. I. *Language in Thought and Action*, 5th ed. New York: Harcourt Brace Jovanovich, 1989. First published in 1939, this book has become a classic. It is a clear and intelligible introduction to the field of semantics. Written in a lively style, it has numerous examples.

PEARSON, JUDY CORNELIA, AND LYNN H. TURNER. *Gender and Communication*, 2d ed. Dubuque, IA: Wm. C. Brown, 1991. This well-researched textbook focuses on how women communicate and offers both theory and practice.

TANNEN, DEBORAH. *You Just Don't Understand: Women and Men in Conversation*. New York: Morrow, 1990. A fascinating look at the differences in language between men and women. Many examples in the book will sound familiar to the reader. This book is fun to read as well as informative.

VAN HORNE, WINSTON A., AND THOMAS V. TONNESEN, EDS. *Ethnicity and Language*. Madison: University of Wisconsin System Institute on Race and Ethnicity, 1987. A collection of essays about ethnic groups and language. Some essays cover the importance of ethnic language to the group that speaks it.

5

Nonverbal Communication

CHAPTER OBJECTIVES

After reading this chapter, you should be able to:

1 Explain the differences between verbal and nonverbal communication.

2 List the various functions of nonverbal communication.

3 Explain the basic principles that govern nonverbal communication.

4 Describe the various types of nonverbal communication.

5 Be more sensitive to your own use of nonverbal cues.

lmost as soon as we begin school, we note some kids who don't fit in. These kids, labeled with such cruel words as *nerd* or *geek*, always seem to be doing something wrong. They walk in front of the class when the teacher is talking, they get too close when they talk to other kids, they talk and laugh at inappropriate times. Worst of all, these kids seem to be completely unaware of their behavior and don't seem to pick up cues from others about how they should behave. Basically, the problem with these children is that they do not understand and are not able to use **nonverbal communication**—the information we communicate without using words.

Two psychologists believe that the inability to recognize nonverbal communication cues affects about 10 percent of children.[1] Since as much as 93 percent of communication is nonverbal,[2] with 55 percent sent through facial expression, posture, and gestures and 38 percent through tone of voice,[3] it's not surprising that children and adults who do not understand nonverbal communication are regarded as outsiders.

We believe, as do these psychologists, that nonverbal communication can be learned. We also believe that by understanding nonverbal communication, we can communicate more effectively. We know that our use of voice, body movement (for example, eye contact, facial expression, gesture, and posture), clothing and body appearance, space, touch, and time are essential parts of every message we send.

THE IMPORTANCE OF NONVERBAL COMMUNICATION

Nonverbal Communication as a Transaction

The transactional nature of communication is very evident in nonverbal communication. Without saying a word, you could be communicating by your choice of clothing, your facial expressions, your posture, or any other number of nonverbal signals. In just the simple act of walking across campus, you are giving and getting signals from passersby you might not even know. You think, "Nice coat—wonder where he got it," "She's in my dorm—I'd like to know her better," "He's really tall—maybe a basketball player." As these people see you, they may be making similar assessments of you.

When you attend a class for the first time, some of the judgments you make of the instructor are based on her nonverbal behavior. She hands out the syllabus and then discusses some of the assignments for the class. As you listen to her, you think, "She sounds tough. I'd better get my work in on time." In making these assessments, you are comparing her with past instructors who may have looked and acted the way she does. You are also predicting what you will have to do to get a good grade. At the same time she may be assessing you—judging you by your posture and clothes, thinking about past students you may resemble, and predicting whether you'll be a good student.

Information about roles is communicated nonverbally as much as it is verbally. When you visit your instructors in their offices, you will probably wait to be asked to sit down. If you're smart, you won't plop your book bag on anyone's desk since that would be an invasion of territory.

Verbal and Nonverbal Differences

Verbal and nonverbal communication differ in seven important ways: environment, feedback, continuity, channel, control, structure, and acquisition. Let us consider each of these differences in turn.

ENVIRONMENT

In contrast to much verbal communication, nonverbal communication can take place when we aren't around for people to get an impression of us. For example, the rooms we live in tell a good deal about us. The pictures of family members show the important people in our lives; the stack of tapes or CDs gives away our musical taste; and the posters on the wall show whether we prefer art, music, or sports.

The environments we choose can also tell about us. Let's say you take a friend out to dinner for his birthday. You will give him one message if you take him to a restaurant with plush seating, indirect lighting, and a French menu. You give him another message if you take him to a place with plastic chairs, fluorescent lighting, and a menu posted on the wall. In addition to telling something about yourself, your choice of restaurants will tell something about how you feel about your relationship.

TRY THIS

In Western culture, personal territory is important. For example, how would you feel about the following invasions of your territory?

- You have been sitting in the same seat all semester. One day when you come to class, someone else is sitting there.

- You go away to college and your mother gives your room to one of your younger brothers or sisters.

- Without asking, your roommate borrows one of your CDs and takes it home for the weekend.

- Your family sells the house in which you grew up.

FEEDBACK

As well as reacting verbally to others, we give a lot of nonverbal feedback. We show we are interested in what someone is saying by smiling or nodding our heads; we show a lack of interest by fidgeting or looking at our watches. Much of our emotional response is expressed by our facial expressions and body positioning.

CONTINUITY

Unlike verbal communication, which begins and ends with words, nonverbal communication is continuous. Imagine yourself as an onlooker in your local convenience store. A woman in the bread section picks up and puts down several items, showing that she can't make up her mind. A customer waiting in line keeps shifting his feet and jiggling the coins in his pocket—he's clearly in a hurry. Several young children are trying to decide what they can afford from the candy jars near the register. From the clerk's face, you can see that she is impatient with them. All these people in the store are giving us nonverbal information and will continue to do so until they are out of our sight.

CHANNEL

Nonverbal communication often uses more than one channel. Imagine, for example, what you communicate about yourself at a football game. Anyone would know which team you favor because you wear the team's colors and

What does this picture tell you about nonverbal communication of young children?

you jump up and down and yell when your team makes a touchdown. Thus, you use the channels of both sight and sound in your nonverbal communication.

If you went to the senior prom, you showed this was an important occasion in mostly nonverbal ways: you wore your best and most expensive clothes, you wore perfume or cologne, you brought (or wore) flowers, and maybe you rode in a limousine. Through several different channels of nonverbal communication, you marked the senior prom as very important.

CONTROL

Most of us have very little control over our nonverbal communication. Unlike verbal communication, where we can choose our words, nonverbal communication is under our control only part of the time. The area where we have the least control is our emotional responses. When we are happy, surprised, hurt, or angry, most of our nonverbal signals are spontaneous, arising out of the occasion.

STRUCTURE

Because so much nonverbal communication occurs unconsciously, it follows no planned sequence. Unlike verbal communication, which has a grammar that determines how we build our sentences, nonverbal communication lacks formal structure. If you are sitting and talking to someone, you don't plan when you will cross your legs, get up out of your chair, or look at the other person. These nonverbal actions occur in response to what happens during the conversation. The only rules that govern nonverbal communication are those which determine whether a behavior is appropriate or permissible. When children are learning manners, for example, they are being taught appropriate behavior for public places.

ACQUISITION

Many of the formal rules for verbal communication, such as grammar, are taught in a structured, formal environment, such as a school. We also learn what style is appropriate to particular situations—that formal English is required for essays, whereas informal English is more suitable for speech. In contrast, much nonverbal communication is not formally taught; we pick it up through imitating others. Young children commonly imitate the nonverbal communication of their parents, siblings, and peers.

The Functions of Nonverbal Communication

Nonverbal communication has four functions. Nonverbal cues *complement* a verbal message by adding to its meaning. When you are talking to someone with a problem, for example, you might say, "I'm really sorry" and complement the message with a pat on the shoulder or a hug.

Nonverbal cues also *regulate* verbal communication. How would your

CONSIDER THIS

When Perri Klass, an American doctor, started practicing medicine in India, she found that she could not read the nonverbal communication of her patients:

But it wasn't just a question of my medical knowledge. In India, I found that my cultural limitations often prevented me from thinking clearly about patients. Everyone looked different, and I was unable to pick up any clues from their appearance, their manner of speech, their clothing. This is a family of Afghan refugees. This family is from the south of India. This child is from a very poor family. This child has a Nepalese name. All the clues I use at home to help me evaluate patients, clues ranging from what neighborhood they live in to what ethnic origin their names suggest, were hidden from me in India.

Source: Perri Klass, *A Not Entirely Benign Procedure* (New York: Signet, 1987), p. 194.

QUESTIONS

1. When you are among people in the United States who belong to a different subculture, can you assume that their nonverbal behavior is the same as yours? If you assume it is the same, what might happen?
2. List the clues that were missing as Klass evaluated her patients. Why were these clues important? What clues does your doctor pick up when he or she is treating you? Why are these clues important?
3. If an American doctor from the suburbs went into practice in a poor urban neighborhood, would he or she have difficulty picking up nonverbal clues from the patients? Why or why not?

boss or one of your teachers tell you that it's time for a conversation to end? He or she might do something obvious, like getting out of the chair, or might do something more subtle, like arranging papers on the desk, in order to communicate to you that the conversation is over.

Nonverbal messages can also *substitute* for verbal messages. The elementary school teacher gives her students a certain look that means they had better be quiet. Your neighbors wave to you as they back out of their driveway; your best friend has balloons delivered to your room on your birthday. All these nonverbal messages substitute for verbal ones.

Often nonverbal messages *accent* what we are saying. The instructor's voice is strong and firm when she tells the class she will accept no late papers; the teenager leans forward while she is trying to persuade her parents that she *needs* a new dress; a man communicates to his family, by his posture, that he is filled with energy and ready for the family outing. Whenever people are communicating something they consider important, they are likely to accent it with a nonverbal message.

THE PRINCIPLES OF NONVERBAL COMMUNICATION

Four fundamental principles underlie the workings of nonverbal communication. The first is that much nonverbal communication is unique to the culture or subculture to which we belong. Second, verbal and nonverbal messages may be in conflict with one another. Third, much nonverbal communication operates at a subconscious level—we are not even aware of it. Fourth, our nonverbal communication shows our feelings and attitudes.

Nonverbal Communication Is Culturally Determined

Much of our nonverbal behavior is learned in childhood, passed on to us by our parents and others with whom we associate. Through the process of growing up in a particular society, we adopt the traits and mannerisms of our cultural group. When meeting people for the first time, Americans put a high value on eye contact and limit their touch to firm handshakes. A Polish man, however, might kiss the hand of a woman when meeting her for the first time. People from the Micronesian islands in the Pacific neither speak nor touch when they meet; instead, they greet another person by raising their eyebrows or giving a nod.

Besides belonging to a broad cultural group, such as a nation, we also belong to cultural subgroups. U.S.-born Hispanics and African American children grow up with broad American cultural conditioning, but they also belong to subgroups that have nonverbal behaviors of their own. For example, when they are with people from their own cultural group, they probably touch each other more. Other groups, formed because their members have something in common other than ethnic or national identity, might have specific nonverbal communication that enables members to identify and communicate with one another. Street gang members wear gang colors and mark their territory with gang symbols; members of a bowling team wear identical bowling shirts to signal their membership. All these nonverbal signals say, "I belong to this group."

In most cultures, the nonverbal behavior of males differs from that of females. In American culture, for example, there is a good deal of difference in the way men and women position their bodies. As Deborah Tannen observed after watching videotapes of communication between males and

Does the way these students are sitting support Tannen's theory of how males and females sit when they are in each other's company?

females of different ages, both girls and women sit closer and look directly into each other's faces. Boys and men, on the other hand, sit at angles to each other and hardly ever look at each other directly.[4] She finds that men usually sit in a relaxed, sprawled-out way—whether they are with groups of men or in mixed groups. In contrast, women sit in ladylike poses when they are in mixed groups, but they also sprawl out and relax when they are in all-female groups.[5]

Nonverbal Messages May Conflict with Verbal Messages

Nonverbal communication is so deeply rooted, so unconscious, that we can express a verbal message and then directly contradict it with a nonverbal message. For example, you go to talk to your economics professor about the low grade you got on your last test. To you, the professor seems like a calm, reasonable man who likes students. What you don't know is that this professor has just gotten off the phone with a mechanic who told him that his car needs $1400 worth of work. When you walk into the office, you find the professor glaring at you, with his arms crossed tightly over his chest and both feet planted firmly on the floor. The professor is giving off the air of someone who can't be questioned about anything.

Now you are confused. You have received a **mixed message**. The professor told his class one thing ("I'm always willing to help students"), but his nonverbal behavior communicates something else ("Don't bother me").

In mixed messages, the nonverbal communication is often more reliable than the verbal content. We learn to manipulate words, but we find it difficult to manipulate our nonverbal communication. Your professor probably was not aware of the negative nonverbal message he was giving. The message, however, was coming through loud and clear.

Nonverbal Messages Are Largely Unconscious

You wake up feeling that you might be getting a cold. It's not yet bad enough to stay home, so you go to work. The minute your coworker sees you, she says, "You look like you aren't feeling very well." She is reading this infor-

---

CONSIDER THIS

Edward T. Hall, an anthropologist, has long studied the nonverbal communication of other cultures. As a young man, one of his first jobs was working with the Navajo. He soon discovered that a Navajo handshake conveyed a good deal of information and feeling:

For white American males the emphasis is on a firm strong handshake with direct and unblinking eye contact. One must demonstrate mutual respect, equality of status (for the moment at least), strength, sincerity, and dependability. With the Navajo the handshake is different. While it is a greeting in the true sense of the word, the emphasis is on proper feelings rather than image. One does not look the other in the eye (to do so signals anger or displeasure). All that is necessary is to hold the other human being in one's peripheral visual field while grasping his hand gently, so as not to disturb the natural flow of feeling between his state of being and yours. These handshakes could be protracted because the Navajo . . . like to ease into things and are jarred by abrupt transitions.

Source: Edward T. Hall, *An Anthropology of Everyday Life* (New York: Bantam Doubleday Dell, 1992), pp. 105–106.

QUESTIONS

1. If you did not know that the Navajo handshake had a specific meaning and style, how would you think about it from your own cultural perspective?
2. If you were to judge a Navajo's handshake by the standards for shaking hands in your own culture, would you judge it negatively?
3. Do you come from a cultural or subcultural group that has its own handshake? How does it differ from the standard American handshake?

mation nonverbally. She can tell from your posture that you're not feeling well, or maybe she can hear it in your voice or see it on your face. She is making a nonverbal assessment: you don't have to say a word for her to know you're feeling low.

Often we don't recognize our own nonverbal behavior. For example, we stand farther away from people we don't like than from people we like. Our body position, such as our crossed arms, might show that we are resisting what is being said. We use our head and eye movements to begin and end conversations with others. When we consider the amount and ordinary-ness of our nonverbal behavior, it is hardly surprising that we are unaware of much of it.

If you doubt the unconscious nature of nonverbal messages, look at Table 5-1. How much of this nonverbal behavior are you aware of?

TABLE 5-1
NONVERBAL CUES THAT INDICATE A WOMAN'S INTEREST IN DATING

Cue	High Amount	Moderate Amount	Low Amount
Eye contact	Looks at him constantly	Looks at him half the time	Looks at him very little
Smiling	Smiles almost constantly	Smiles half the time	Does not smile
Lean	Leans toward	Sits straight up	Leans backward
Shoulder orientation	Faces directly (shoulders parallel)	Partially faces (shoulders at 45 degree angle)	Faces away (shoulders at 90 degree angle)
Distance	18 inches	4 feet	7 feet
Touching	Brief touch above the knee	Brief touch on forearm	No touch
Catches his eye (while hearing joke)	Laughs and catches eye	Laughs, does not catch eye	Does not laugh or catch eye
Attentiveness	Stops what she is doing and looks at him	Looks away while listening, toward while talking	Glances at beginning, but then looks away
Attentiveness (looking at other people)	Does not look at other people	Looks at other women	Looks at other men
Avoids public grooming	Does not groom	Mild grooming	Excessive grooming
Animated speech	Speaks quickly, accentuates, varied facial expressions	Average tone and movement	Slow monotone with little movement

SOURCE: Charlene L. Muehlenhard et al., "Cues That Convey Interest in Dating," in Joseph A. Devito and Michael L. Hecht, Eds., *The Nonverbal Communication Reader* (Prospect Heights, IL: Waveland Press 1990), p. 364.

Facial expressions, gestures, body movements, the way we use our eyes all communicate our feelings and emotions to others. The feelings and emotions others can detect in our faces include happiness, sadness, surprise, fear, anger, and interest.[6] Research has also shown that most people can accurately identify emotions expressed by the voice.[7]

In your work, your attitude counts for more than your ability.[8] According to research, early on the job, bosses pick up negative traits such as hostility or irritability, often shown through facial expressions and body language. Once the boss forms an impression, it's difficult to change it. Ultimately the boss regards each employee as a member of either the "in-group" or the "out-group." The in-group gets to do the most desirable work and is given the most flexible schedules; the out-group gets the drudge work and the least desirable working hours.

■ TYPES OF NONVERBAL COMMUNICATION

Paralanguage

Paralanguage is the way we say something. For example, a father calls his son from another room. From the tone of his father's voice, the child can gauge whether the call is urgent enough to come right away or whether he can watch another minute or so of television. The tone of voice in this example is paralanguage.

A clear distinction exists between a person's use of words (verbal communication) and a person's use of paralanguage (nonverbal communication). Paralanguage includes such vocal characteristics as rate (speed of speaking), pitch (highness or lowness of tone), volume (loudness), and quality (pleasing or unpleasant sound). When any or all of these factors are added to words, they can modify meaning. Albert Mehrabian estimates that 39 percent of the meaning in communication is affected by vocal cues—not the words themselves but the way in which they are said.[9] In languages other than English, this percentage may be even higher.

RATE

The **rate** (speed) at which one speaks can have an effect on the way a message is received.[10] Researchers have studied people speaking at rates varying from 120 words per minute (wpm) to 261 wpm. They discovered that when a speaker uses a faster rate, he or she is seen as more competent.[11] Of course, if you speak too quickly, people won't be able to follow you, and your articulation may also suffer.

PITCH

Pitch refers to the highness or lowness of the voice. Pitch can determine whether a voice sounds pleasant or unpleasant. Some people believe that high-pitched voices are not as pleasant as low-pitched ones. However, the same researchers who studied rate of speaking also found that speakers were judged more competent if they used a higher and varied pitch.[12] Lower pitches are more difficult to hear, and people who have low-pitched voices may be perceived as insecure or shy because they don't seem to speak up. Pitch can be changed, but it requires working with someone who has had professional training in voice modification.

VOLUME

The meaning of a message can also be affected by its **volume**—how loudly we speak. A loud voice is fine if it's appropriate to the speaker's purpose and is not used all the time. The same is true of a soft voice. Expert teachers know at what points to increase or decrease their volume when they want a class to be quiet.

VOCAL FILLERS

Vocal fillers are the sounds we use to fill out our sentences or to cover up when we are searching for words. Nonwords such as *uh, er,* and *um* and phrases such as *you know* are a nonverbal way of indicating that we are temporarily stuck and are searching for the right word. We all use vocal fillers; they become a problem only when we use them excessively or if they are distracting to listeners.

QUALITY

The overall **quality** of a voice is made up of all other vocal characteristics—tempo, resonance, rhythm, pitch, and articulation. Voice quality is important because researchers have found that people with attractive voices are seen as more powerful, more competent, and more honest. However, people with immature voices were seen as less competent and powerful but more honest and warm.[13]

Many of us do not have a very good idea of how we sound. Our classroom experience has been that when students see and hear themselves on videotape, they are almost always more unhappy with how they sound than with how they look. Voices can be changed with hard work and professional assistance.

Body Movement

Body movement, also called *kinesics,* is responsible for a lot of our nonverbal communication. P. Ekman and W. V. Friesen, researchers on nonver-

TRY THIS

In American culture, what emblems might accompany or substitute for the following words or phrases?

Absolutely not.

I don't care.

Maybe . . .

I'm warning you . . .

Get lost!

Ask someone from another culture to say these phrases. Observe the nonverbal gestures he or she uses. Are they the same as the ones used in American culture?

bal communication, divide body movement into five categories: emblems, illustrators, regulators, displays of feeling, and adaptors.[14]

EMBLEMS

Emblems are body movements that have a direct translation into words. The extended thumb of the hitchhiker is an emblem that means "I want a ride." A circle made with the thumb and index finger can be translated into "OK." These emblems are known by most of the people in our society, and they are used to send a specific message. Emblems often cannot be carried from one culture to another. If you shake your head back and forth in southern India, for example, it means "yes."

Emblems are often used when words are inappropriate. It would be impractical for a hitchhiker to stand on the side of the road and shout, "Please give me a ride!" Sometimes emblems can replace talk. We cover our faces with our hands if we are embarrassed, and we hold up our fingers to show how many we want. Also, subgroups in a society often use emblems that members of the group understand but whose meanings are intentionally kept from outsiders—the secret handshake of a fraternity is an example.

ILLUSTRATORS

Illustrators accent, emphasize, or reinforce words. If someone asks how big your suitcase is, you will probably describe it with words and illustrate the dimensions with your hands. If someone is giving you directions, she will probably point down the road and gesture left or right at the appropriate points. Illustrators can help to make communication more exact. If someone tells you he caught a huge fish, you will have an idea of how big the fish was by how far apart he holds his hands. He could tell you the size in inches, but you will get an even better idea if he uses his hands as illustrators. But not all illustrators are gestures. When an instructor underlines something she has written on the blackboard, she is telling you that this point is particularly important. When a car salesperson slams the car door, you can hear how solid it sounds and assume the car is well built.

REGULATORS

Regulators control the back-and-forth flow of speaking and listening. They include the head nods, hand gestures, shifts in posture, and other body movements that signal the beginning and end of interactions. At a very simple level, a teacher uses a regulator when she points to the person she wants to speak next. On a more subtle level, someone might turn away slightly when you are talking—perhaps indicating "I don't like what I'm hearing" or "I don't want to continue this conversation."

DISPLAYS OF FEELINGS

Displays of feelings show, through our faces and our body movements, how intensely we are feeling. If you walk into a professor's office and the professor says, "I can see you are really feeling upset," he or she is responding to nonverbal cues you are giving about your feelings. You could also come in with a body posture indicating "I'm really going to argue about this grade"—with your jutting jaw or stiff body position showing that you are ready for a confrontation.

ADAPTORS

Adaptors are nonverbal ways of adjusting to a communication situation. Because we all use such a wide variety of adaptors, and because they are so specific to our own needs and the individual communication situation, they are difficult to classify or even describe generally. Let's look at how they work in some specific communication situations. You have rented your first apartment and your mother has come to visit. While she is there, she spends a good deal of time moving objects and furniture around. By moving things around, she is using adaptors. What does her nonverbal behavior mean? On a simple level, she might be telling you that you are not very tidy. On a more complicated level, she might be telling you that you are still her child and that she, your mother, is still in charge.

People often use adaptors when they are nervous or uncomfortable in a situation. We might play with jewelry, drum on the table, or move around a lot in our seats. Each of these behaviors is an adaptor—a way of helping us cope with the situation. We all use adaptors, but we are generally not aware of them unless someone points them out.

EYE MESSAGES

We all send many messages with our eyes. Even if we don't feel any eye movement, we use our eyes to indicate a wide range of information, such as our interest in another person, our boredom in a class, or our excitement at getting a gift we want. In American culture, meeting another's eyes is a sign of honesty and credibility.

Never underestimate eye messages. An Israeli army officer was quoted as saying that in battles between Israelis and Palestinians, it was often a "war of the eyes." Some looks were meant to kill, others to intimidate. Some eyes begged for friendship while other eyes showed fear. The most piercing, chilling eyes came from teenagers, according to the officer. "Even if you give them a daring, intimidating look, they stare right back at you with self-confidence. Their parents are different. You feel that you can negotiate with their eyes. The eyes say you can even shake my hand."[15]

ATTRACTIVENESS

Attractiveness in women is usually defined by face and body, whereas in men it's largely defined by face.[16] The media examples we get of attractiveness tell us we should be thin and tall (especially men) and have a lot of hair.

People who are perceived as attractive get a more positive response from others and have an easier time in life than people who are not perceived as attractive. Researchers have discovered that attractive women have more dates, receive higher grades in college, persuade males with greater ease, and receive lighter court sentences.[17] Men or women rated as attractive are also perceived as being more sensitive, kind, strong, sociable, and interesting.[18] In business, attractiveness pays off in several ways, including finding jobs and obtaining higher starting salaries.[19]

Clothing

Because clothing gives such a strong and immediate impression of its wearer, it is enormously important to nonverbal communication. Clothing projects a message and, by choosing particular clothing, the wearer commits himself or herself to the statements the clothing makes.[20] The viewer responds not only to the clothing itself but also to what it says about the wearer in terms of status, affiliation, norms, and conformity. For example, if we see a man walking down the street in a well-tailored suit, we probably assume that he is a white-collar worker and that he might work for a bank or a big company. If we see a young woman on the same street in jeans and a T-shirt and carrying a book bag, we probably assume she is a student.

Clothing falls into four categories: uniforms, occupational dress, leisure clothing, and costumes. Each of these categories conveys a somewhat different meaning.[21]

CONSIDER THIS

According to researcher Karl Grammer, when men and women meet, they use a good deal of nonverbal communication to indicate interest in each other. How much interest a woman can communicate is ambiguous. Too much could attract a man who is interested only in a short-term relationship or one who is physically aggressive. If a woman wants to avoid these problems, she must send out discreet signals that show she is interested only in exploring the possibility of a relationship. Unlike women, men can communicate a direct interest.

How is all of this information communicated nonverbally? Mostly by the positioning of the body, says Grammer. When both parties are in a seated position, a man is likely to show interest by leaning forward with his trunk turned toward the female. His elbows are lifted so that his arms are up and behind his neck. His hands touch his arms and he crosses his legs. A woman being watched by a man shows interest by turning her trunk and head away from him. Her arms and legs are relaxed. Grammer asserts that the higher the interest, the more the man and woman are likely to exhibit all of these body positions.

In another study of courtship displays by women, Monica M. Moore found that women engaged in some very specific nonverbal behavior when they were trying to attract the attention of men. The most common signals were a variety of glances, smiling and laughing, head tosses, and "hair flips" (when a woman runs her hands through her hair or runs her palm along its surface).

All these nonverbal signs say to a man, "I'm interested—come and talk to me."

Source: Karl Grammer, "Strangers Meet: Laughter and Nonverbal Signs of Interest in Opposite-Sex Encounters, *Journal of Nonverbal Behavior* 14 (4) (Winter 1990): 209–236. Monica M. Moore, "Nonverbal Courtship Patterns in Women: Context and Consequences," in Joseph A. DeVito and Michael L. Hecht, Eds., *The Nonverbal Communication Reader* (Prospect Heights, IL: Waveland Press, 1990), p. 365.

QUESTIONS

The best way to understand these theories is to try them out yourself by observing men and women in public settings. The next time you are at a party where the men and women do not know each other, stand aside and watch for awhile. Do they duplicate the body positioning that Grammer describes? Do they give out the cues described by Moore?

UNIFORMS

A uniform is the most specialized form of clothing. It identifies the wearer with a particular organization. There is little freedom of choice in a uniform: its wearers are told when to wear it (daytime, summer) and what they can and cannot wear with it (jewelry, medals, hairstyles).

The most common uniforms are worn in the military. By showing rank, these uniforms tell what positions the users hold in the military hierarchy and what their relationships are to others in the organization. The uniform also implies that its wearer will follow certain norms.[22] For example, we expect someone in military uniform always to be respectful of the flag.

OCCUPATIONAL DRESS

Occupational dress is clothing that employees are expected to wear, but it is not as precise as a uniform. Occupational clothing indicates the performance of a certain kind of job, and it is designed to present a specific image of the employer.[23] In some cases, the clothing is quite specific: letter carriers, airline pilots, and train conductors have little choice about their clothing. In other cases employees have choices: flight attendants are required to wear specific pieces of clothing, but they can mix them according to their own preferences. Nurses might be required to wear white, but they can select the style they like. People who wear business clothing have even more choices. A company might expect its employees to wear suits, but the employee can choose both color and style.

Who has the most power in this picture? How can you tell?

Sometimes in order to be part of the group that has the power and control, you are expected to wear a certain occupational dress. Kristin Clark Taylor writes about the clothing and hairstyles expected in the White House when George Bush was president:

> *For the women: cute bob haircut, preferably one that bounced slightly when the wearer walked. Black velvet headband or bow. Expensive, heavy gold jewelry, simply designed (usually somebody's grandmother's or great-aunt's, passed down as an heirloom). Christian Dior "Alabaster" ultra-sheer hosiery (nude heel, and never, ever flesh-colored; flesh-colored hosiery was the ultimate in tacky). The classic, low-heeled Ferragamo pump with the flat bow in the center (preferably black patent leather), or, for those whose wallets would allow, the Bruno Magli slingback. And never, ever anything higher than an inch-and-a-quarter heel. Lots and lots of crisp linen in the summer. Dark paislies and houndstooth in the fall and winter. No frills, lace, polyester, press-on nails, hair weaves, cornrows, or stiletto heels. . . .*
>
> *For the men: starched, plain white shirts with French cuffs (the better to wear the much-coveted presidential cufflinks on special occasions). Wool pants with a three-quarter-inch break at the cuff. Black tasseled loafers, always spit-shine clean. Lots and lots of expensive black and dark blue suits—never, ever double-breasted. No natty tweeds, Old Spice cologne, dusty shoes, shiny suits, pony tails, pocket protectors, short-sleeve shirts, or rubber galoshes.[24]*

LEISURE CLOTHING

Leisure clothing is used when work is over. Because this kind of clothing is left to choice, individuals sometimes assert their own identity by wearing it.[25] However, some people don't see styles of leisure wear as a choice. Many teenagers will wear only a particular brand of jeans because when their group agrees on a brand, everyone wears it. Skiers might use a certain brand of skis, parkas, and goggles—even though others would work equally well. The mass media have had such a great influence on leisure clothing that it's hard to separate media influence from individual preference.

COSTUMES

Costumes are a form of highly individualized dress. One example of a costume is imitation cowboy dress: boots, bandanna, and hat. By putting on a costume, the wearer announces, "This is who I want to be." Such a costume might have symbolic importance—the cowboy costume, for example, announcing a macho kind of individuality.[26] Few people are interested in wearing costumes. Costumes not only require thought about the image they convey, but they also go against many norms. As one student shrewdly observed as he changed his shoes for a job interview at a supermarket, "I had better not wear my cowboy boots. They look too aggressive."

The study of space and distance, called **proxemics**, concerns the way we use the space around us as well as the distance we stand or sit from others. The minute you enter a classroom, you are faced with a decision that relates to how you use space. You have to decide where to sit. You may choose to sit in the back for a variety of reasons: you do not want to be noticed; you feel it is a "safer" distance from the teacher; you do not want people behind you staring at you; you will have an opportunity to see other students' reactions and thus give yourself confidence. On the other hand, you might select a front-row seat because you have a lot of confidence, because you want to be noticed, or because you want to be sure to hear everything the teacher says.

What is interesting about your choice of seating is that you might be sending your instructor a message. If you sit in the far corner of the back row, your instructor might decide you are not very interested in the subject and are looking for a place to go to sleep. If you are in the front row, he might conclude that you are an unusually bright and attentive student and that he should give you special attention. You could also be sending your classmates a message. They might interpret the front-seat choice as a way of trying to win points with the instructor. If you sit toward the back of the room, you are one of them—since that's where most students decide to sit— yet that's where the least interaction with the instructor is likely to take place (see Figure 5-1).

We also map out certain spaces as our territory. **Territory** is the space that we consider as belonging to us—either temporarily or permanently. For example, you would probably be upset if you came into the classroom and found someone sitting in "your" chair. Most of us have territories that we consider our own, and other people can enter them only with our permission. A bedroom, for example, is usually considered the territory of the person who sleeps there.

People who are the victims of burglars and muggers commonly report that not only do they feel distress at losing personal possessions, but they also feel anger at having their personal territory violated by strangers.

We make judgments about how others are thinking and reacting to us on the basis of the way they use space. Edward T. Hall, author of *The Silent Language* and *The Hidden Dimension*, two classic books on nonverbal communication, coined the term **proxemics** for the study of space and distance.[27] From his observations and interviews, Hall discovered that North Americans use four distance zones when they are communicating with others: intimate distance, personal distance, social distance, and public distance.[28]

INTIMATE DISTANCE

In the *intimate distance* range, people are in direct contact with each other or are no more than 18 inches apart. Look at a mother with her baby. She

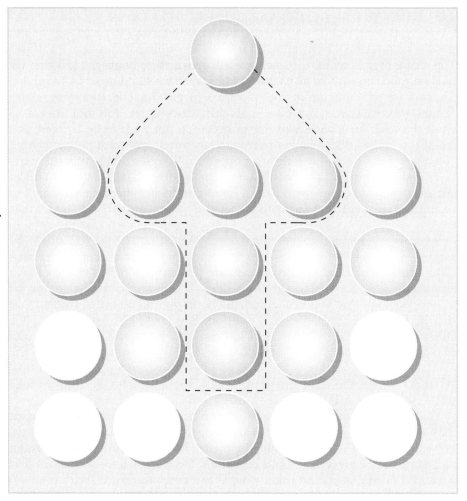

FIGURE 5-1

A traditional classroom arrangement. In such an arrangement, those students occupying the rose seats will account for a large proportion of the total interaction that occurs between teachers and students. Those in the blue seats will interact some; those in the white seats will interact very infrequently. The area enclosed in dotted lines has been called the "action zone."

picks him up, caresses him, kisses him on the cheek, puts him on her lap. All her senses are alert when she is this close to the baby. She can touch him, smell him, and hear every little gurgle he makes. We also maintain an intimate distance in love relationships and with close friends. Intimate distance exists whenever we feel free to touch the other person.

When our intimate distance is violated by people who have no right to be there, we feel apprehensive. If we are on a crowded bus, subway, or elevator and people are pressed against us, they are in our intimate distance. We react by ignoring these people and not making eye contact. In this way we can protect our intimate distance—psychologically if not physically.

PERSONAL DISTANCE

In the range of *personal distance*, people stay anywhere from 18 inches to 4 feet from each other. This is the distance we keep most often when we are in casual and personal conversations. It is close enough to see the other person's reactions but far enough away not to encroach on intimate distance. If we move closer than 18 inches, the person will probably back away. If we move farther away than 4 feet, it will be difficult to carry on a conversation without having the feeling that it can be overheard by others.

SOCIAL DISTANCE

When we do not know people very well, we are most likely to maintain a *social distance* from them—that is, a distance of 4 to 12 feet. Impersonal business, social gatherings, and interviews are examples of situations where we use social distance.

Whenever we use social distance, interaction becomes more formal. Have you ever noticed the size of the desks in the offices of important people? They are large enough to keep visitors at the proper social distance. In a large office with many workers, the desks are placed a social distance apart. This distance makes it possible for each worker to concentrate on his or her work and to use the telephone without affecting others in the office. Sometimes people move back and forth from social distance to personal distance. Two coworkers might, for example, have desks 10 feet apart. When they want to discuss something privately, they move into each other's personal distance.

PUBLIC DISTANCE

Public distance—a distance of more than 12 feet—is typically used for public speaking. At this distance, people speak more loudly and use more exaggerated gestures. Communication at this distance is more formal and permits few opportunities for people to be involved with each other. Figure 5-2 shows the dimensions of the four distance zones.

Space/Distance as an Indicator of Intimacy

When we observe the distances that people maintain between themselves and others, we can tell which people have close relationships and which people have more formal relationships. If you enter the college president's office and she remains behind her desk, you can assume that your conversation is going to be formal. If she invites you to the corner where there are easy chairs and you sit side by side, she has set up a much more intimate situation, and consequently, the conversation is going to be more informal.

As we get to know people better, we are permitted into their more personal space. Remember when you were in junior high and went with a boy or a girl to the movies for the first time? When your hands met in the popcorn box, you were exploring the possibilities of moving from a personal to an intimate distance. The opposite can also happen. A married couple experiences a lot of intimate distance. If there are problems in the marriage, however, the couple's communication is conducted mostly at a personal dis-

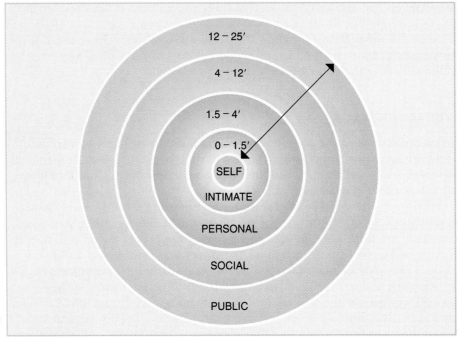

FIGURE 5-2
**The Four Distance
Zones**

tance. If they start to negotiate a divorce, they will probably carry out most
of their negotiations at a social distance.

Space/Distance as an Indicator of Status

Besides degrees of intimacy, degrees of status are communicated through
the use of space. Executives, presidents of colleges, and government officials all have large offices with expansive windows and elaborate furnish-
ings, whereas their secretaries and support staff are in smaller spaces—
often spaces that are used by many people. In a household, children have
the least amount of space. Even if they have their own rooms, that space is
often controlled by adults. It is planned and decorated by an adult, and the
adult sets the rules for how the space will be used. Adults also punish children by depriving them of space. Commands such as "Go to your room" or
"Stay out of my room" limit children's access to space within the household.

Touch

The closer we stand to one another, the more we increase the likelihood of
our touching. We are all familiar with the use of touch in intimate situations. We kiss babies, hold hands with loved ones, and hug family members.
In fact, researchers have found that in order for premature babies to thrive,
they must be touched. When they are touched, brain chemicals are released
that promote growth. Premature infants who were massaged three times a

TRY THIS

Lydia Minatoya (who in Chapter 2 wanted to grow up to be a mother cat) gives us a cross-cultural and nonverbal riddle. Can you figure out the answer?

In Japan, a young man and woman meet and fall in love. They decide they would like to marry. The young man goes to his mother and describes the situation. "I will visit the girl's family," says the mother. "I will seek their approval." After some time, a meeting between mothers is arranged. The boy's mother goes to the girl's ancestral house. The girl's mother has prepared tea. The women talk about the fine spring weather: will this be a good year for cherry blossoms? The girl's mother serves a plate of fruit. Bananas are sliced and displayed in an exquisite design. Marriage never is mentioned. After the tea, the boy's mother goes home. "I am so sorry," she tells her son. "The other family has declined the match."

Source: Lydia Minatoya, *Talking to High Monks in the Snow* (New York: Harper Perennial, 1993), pp. 101–102.

How did the boy's mother know the marriage was unacceptable? Answer: To a Japanese, the answer is obvious. Bananas do not go well with tea.

---

day for 15 minutes gained weight 47 percent faster than those who were left alone in their incubators. They were also able to leave the hospital an average of six days earlier. Eight months later, they still held their advantage in weight and did much better on tests of mental and motor ability than premature infants treated in the usual way.[29]

Touch is certainly important to interpersonal relationships. Researchers found that when people who did not even know each other began interacting, if one person touched the other, he or she was seen as affectionate, relaxed, and informal.[30]

When and where we touch one another is governed by a strict set of societal rules. Richard Heslin has described five different categories of touch behavior.[31] The first is *functional-professional touch*, in which you are touched for a specific reason, as in a physical examination by a doctor or nurse. This kind of touch is impersonal and businesslike. *Social-polite touch* is used to acknowledge someone else. The handshake is the most common form. Although two people move into an intimate distance to shake hands, they move away from each other when the handshake is over. In close relationships people use the *friendship-warmth touch*. This kind of touch

TRY THIS

Imagine that you are in the following situations. How much distance would there be between you and the following people?

- Someone you are romantically involved with

- Your boss when you're discussing business

- Your instructor when you ask a question after class

- Your dentist, who is working on your teeth

- Your best friend as you discuss something private

involves hugs and casual kisses between friends. In more intense relationships the *love-intimacy touch* is common. Parents stroke their children; lovers and spouses kiss each other. The final touch Heslin describes is *sexual arousal touch*—touch used as an expression of physical attraction.[32]

The kind of touch that is used communicates information about the relationship. The more intense the relationship, the more frequent and more intimate the touch. Often we can tell how much others are involved and what kind of relationship they have by how much they touch each other. For example, nurses know that if a mother does not frequently touch her young child, something is wrong in the relationship.

Time

People seem to fall into two categories—those who are always on time and those who are always late. Have you ever noticed that certain students always come late, whereas others are always in their seats when the class begins? From the viewpoint of an instructor, the person who is always late may be communicating considerable negative information: he is really not interested in this class, he doesn't respect the instructor, and so on. By the same token, students might resent an instructor who is always late. They might think he doesn't plan well enough or that he doesn't respect the class.

We all use time for psychological effect. If you have a date with someone you don't know very well, you will probably not arrive too early because this might make you appear too eager. If you dent the family car, you might wait for the right time to tell your parents about it. Our control of time, then, is an important form of nonverbal communication.

Time is often connected with status: the higher our status, the more control we have over our time. Children have little control over time. A higher-status parent can interrupt children's play to have them eat dinner or to make them go to bed far earlier than they want. Professionals in our society often make others wait for them. How long do you wait in the doctor's office before your examination? Students have little say in how their time is spent. If they want a particular class and it is offered only at 8 A.M., they have little choice but to take it then. They also have no choice about when papers are due or when exams are given. If you want to discover who has the most status in society, watch who waits for whom.

■ IMPROVING YOUR NONVERBAL COMMUNICATION

Because our nonverbal behavior is so tied in with our social and cultural conditioning, it is not very easy to change. Fortunately, most of us don't need to make any drastic changes. We should be concerned with nonverbal communication that distracts from what we want to say or that contradicts our verbal messages. If we find that people regularly misunderstand us, we would do well to ask whether this is due to nonverbal cues people are picking up.

We should also check to see if we are correctly picking up the nonverbal communication of others. Nonverbal communication is often ambiguous; to make sure you are picking it up correctly, you might say something like, "You look upset. Are you?"

How does this culture differ from North American culture in terms of standing in line and touching others?

CONSIDER THIS

Even though we might classify a name as a word, it has many nonverbal associations. For example, most people consider *Buck* a more masculine name than *Percy*.

Dr. Albert Mehrabian, who has done a good deal of research in nonverbal communication, has studied the meaning of names as well. He maintains that names are extremely important:

Our names, as well as our physical appearances, have a significant impact on how others react to us in social relationships and at work. The name we sign to a letter, a piece of art, or a piece of writing contributes to the overall impression that letter or work makes on others. The name we mention to a stranger over the phone tells the stranger something about ourselves. Whether we are physically present or not, our names alter the impression we make.

Mehrabian and his researchers have studied hundreds of names and have ranked them by whether they communicate six qualities: success, morality, health, warmth, cheerfulness, and masculinity/femininity. Each quality is broken down into several other qualities. A person who is successful, for example, is also considered ambitious, intelligent, and creative.

Mehrabian deals with hundreds of names in his book. We can't list them all, but here are the top ten women's and men's names for success:

If we want to change our nonverbal behavior, it is important to pay attention to feedback we get from others. Ask, "Why have I been misunderstood?" or "Why do people see me as unfriendly, rigid, unhappy . . . ?" For example, if a number of people tell you that at first they thought you were a snob, you can learn a lot by asking what you did to make them feel that way. Once you have this feedback, you will be able to make concrete plans for changing your behavior.

If you realize that you have distracting mannerisms (playing with your hair, saying "you know" too much), it might be useful to have friends and family members tell you when you are doing these things so that you can break the habit.

Probably the single most important tool for discovering negative nonver-

Female	*Male*
Jacqueline	James
Katherine	Madison
Samantha	Charles
Victoria	Alexander
Lauren	Kenneth
Jessica	Thomas
Pamela	Parker
Diana	Ross
Margaret	Adam
Alexandra	Colby

Dr. Mehrabian suggests that if you do not like the associations that people make with your name, you should change it. You could use your full name instead of your nickname (or vice versa), or you might use your middle name instead. If these ideas do not work, he suggests you make a legal name change.

Source: Albert Mehrabian, *The Name Game* (New York: Signet, 1992).

QUESTIONS

1. Dr. Mehrabian suggests that a name is a self-fulfilling prophecy. Do you agree?
2. Do you know anyone who has a name that would be hard to live with? Why?
3. What does your name say about you? Do you wish you could change it?

bal behavior is videotape. Most people who see themselves on tape know immediately what their bad habits are. If you have access to a videotape recorder, take advantage of it. Have someone tape you giving a speech or in conversation with another person. You will be amazed at what you can learn about yourself. If you have a chance to tape your voice, don't spend all your time reacting to it emotionally; see if you can figure out what you don't like about your voice and how you might be able to change it.

Observe people in the roles they play. How do bosses act? How much of their communication is nonverbal? What nonverbal elements are desirable? Undesirable? When you get to be a boss, which of these behaviors would you want to imitate? Which people *don't* you want to be like? Is it their nonverbal behavior that turns you off? Do you do any of these same things? Can you stop doing them?

Time and space are two forms of nonverbal communication you can control somewhat. What does your room, apartment, or house look like? What will people think of you when they see your space? How about time? Are you sensitive to other people's time, or do you make them wait for you? How do you think they feel about you when they have to wait?

Our greatest problem with nonverbal communication is that we don't think about it enough. When we realize how important the nonverbal component is in our total communication, we are more likely to realize that we should all pay careful attention to it.

SUMMARY

We send more messages through nonverbal communication than we do through verbal communication. Verbal and nonverbal communication often reinforce each other, but there are clear differences between them. Verbal communication begins when a word is uttered, and it requires a single channel. It is under your control; it is structured; and it is formally taught. Noverbal communication is continuous; it is multichanneled; it is mostly habitual and unconscious; it is largely unstructured; and it is learned through imitation.

Nonverbal communication serves important functions. It can complement, regulate, substitute for, or accent a verbal message. Most nonverbal communication takes culturally determined forms. It may conflict with verbal messages. It is sent subtly, perhaps even unconsciously, and it communicates feelings and attitudes.

There are several types of nonverbal communication. They include paralanguage, eye messages, attractiveness, clothing, space/distance, touch, and time. The way we use space and time communicates both status and intimacy.

Much nonverbal communication is difficult to change, but through feedback from others, it is possible to modify some of our nonverbal behavior—particularly if it is distracting to others. Videotape is a valuable tool for discovering the nonverbal cues we are sending to others.

NOTES

[1] Jane Brody, "Personal Health: Helping Children Overcome Rejection," *The New York Times*, Aug. 19, 1992, p. C12.

[2] Albert Mehrabian, *Silent Messages: Implicit Communication of Emotions and Attitudes*, 2d ed. (Belmont, CA: Wadsworth, 1981), pp. 76–77.

[3] Brody, p. C12.

[4] Deborah Tannen, *You Just Don't Understand: Women and Men in Conversation* (New York: Morrow, 1990), p. 246.

[5] Ibid., pp. 235–236.

[6] Loretta A. Malandro and Larry Barker, *Nonverbal Communication* (New York: Random House, 1983), p. 9.

[7] Ibid., p. 280.

[8] "Impressing the Boss: Good Vibes vs. Good Brains," *Psychology Today* (Jan./Feb. 1993): 10.

[9] Mehrabian, *Silent Messages*, pp. 42–47. See also "Communication Without Words," *Psychology Today* 2 (1968): 53.

[10] James MacLachlan, "What People Really Think of Fast Talkers," *Psychology Today* 13 (November 1979): 113–117.

[11] George B. Ray, "Vocally Cued Personality Prototypes: An Implicit Personality Theory Approach," *Communication Monographs* 53 (1986): 272.

[12] Ibid., p. 273.

[13] Diane S. Berry, "Vocal Types and Stereotypes of Vocal Attractiveness and Vocal Maturity on Person Perception," *Journal of Nonverbal Behavior* 16(1) (Spring 1992): 41–54.

[14] Paul Ekman and W. V. Friesen, "The Repertoire of Nonverbal Behavior: Categories, Origins, Usages, and Coding," *Semiotica* 1 (1969): 49–98.

[15] Julius Fast, *Making Body Language Work in the Workplace* (New York: Viking Press, 1991).

[16] Robert S. Raines, Sarah B. Hechtman, and Robert Rosenthal, "Nonverbal Behavior and Gender as Determinants of Physical Attractiveness," *Journal of Nonverbal Behavior* 14(4), Winter 1990: 253–278.

[17] Mark L. Knapp, *Nonverbal Communication in Human Interaction*, 2d ed. (New York: Holt, Rinehart and Winston, 1978), pp. 153–161.

[18] Ellen Berschied and Elaine Hatfield Walster, *Interpersonal Attraction*, 2d ed. (New York: Random House, 1978).

[19] Lawrence B. Rosenfeld, "Beauty and Business: Looking Good Pays Off," *New Mexico Business Journal* (April 1979): 22–26.

[20] Nathan Joseph, *Uniforms and Nonuniforms* (New York: Greenwood Press, 1986), p. 49.

[21] Ibid., p. 50.

[22] bid., pp. 2–3, 15.

[23] Ibid., p. 143.

[24] Kristen Clark Taylor, *The First to Speak* (New York: Doubleday, 1993), p. 56.

[25] Joseph, *Uniforms and Nonuniforms*, pp. 168–169.

[26] Ibid., pp. 124–125.

[27] Edward T. Hall, *The Silent Language* (Greenwich, CT: Fawcett, 1959), and *The Hidden Dimension* (Garden City, NY: Anchor Books, 1969).

[28] Hall, *The Hidden Dimension*, pp. 116–125.

[29] Daniel Goleman, "The Experience of Touch: Research Points to a Critical Role," *The New York Times*, Feb. 2, 1988, p. C1.

[30] Judy K. Burgoon, Joseph B. Walther, and E. James Baesler, "Interpretations, Evaluations, and Consequences of Interpersonal Touch," *Human Communication Research* 19(2), December 1992: 237–263.

[31] As cited in Winter, "How People React to Your Touch," *Science Digest* 84 (March 1976): 46–56.

[32] Ibid., pp. 46–56.

ACKERMAN, DIANE. *A Natural History of the Senses*. New York: Random House, 1990. This is a fascinating book about how we perceive, savor, and experience the world through our senses. Each chapter contains a series of short essays about each sense, so readers who are particularly interested in one sense may choose the most interesting section.

DEVITO, JOSEPH A., AND MICHAEL L. HECHT. *The Nonverbal Communication Reader*. Prospect Heights, IL: Waveland Press, 1990. This is a book of readings about research studies in nonverbal communication. It covers all the areas discussed in this chapter and has additional information on detecting lies, understanding the nonverbal in interpersonal relationships, and researching nonverbal communication.

ELLISON, RALPH. *Invisible Man*. New York: Vintage Books, 1989. This reissue of a classic novel is about a man who, because of his race, seems invisible to those around him. The book illustrates brilliantly how a person's self-concept is defined on the basis of how people react to his or her physical appearance.

HALL, EDWARD T. *Hidden Dimension*. Garden City, NY: Anchor Books, 1969. In this paperback book the author deals with spatial experience as it is dictated by culture. The "hidden dimension" is people's use of space, and the author convincingly presents the idea that virtually everything a person is and does is associated with the experience of space. This is an immensely interesting and exciting book full of examples and illustrations that develop the concepts of social and personal space and how they are perceived.

_____. *The Silent Language*. Westport, CT: Greenwood Press, 1980. This paperback book examines the cultural component of nonverbal communication, especially how Americans' behavior differs from that of people in other cultures. The author, an anthropologist, uses numerous examples and anecdotes to examine the world of nonverbal communication. The book will stimulate you to observe and analyze the nonverbal behavior of others.

HICKSON, MARK L., III, AND DON W. STACKS. *NVC: Nonverbal Communication—Studies and Applications*, 2d ed. Dubuque, IA: Brown, 1989. Although this book contains material found in other nonverbal textbooks, the authors also emphasize the interaction between biological and sociopsychological functions. In addition, they illustrate how research may be used in real-life situations. Well-documented, interesting material.

JOSEPH, NATHAN. *Uniforms and Nonuniforms: Communication through Clothing*. New York: Greenwood Press, 1986. A fascinating account of how our clothing communicates our rank, status, and place in the world. The book covers the meaning of uniforms, nonbureaucratic clothing, occupational, leisure clothing, and costumes. This entertaining book is based on solid scholarship.

LEATHERS, DALE G. *Successful Nonverbal Communication: Principles and Applications*, 2d ed. New York: Macmillan, 1991. This introductory textbook focuses on how knowledge of the informational potential of nonverbal cues can be used to communicate successfully in the real world. A very complete, well-written, and well-researched book.

MALANDRO, LORETTA, LARRY BARKER, AND DEBORAH BARKER. *Nonverbal Communication*, 2d ed. New York: Random House, 1989.   The authors provide examples, applications, research findings, a historical perspective, contemporary information, and complete reference lists. This textbook is enjoyable to read. It is also intellectually and emotionally challenging.

NOWICKI, STEPHEN JR., AND MARSHALL P. DUKE. *Helping the Child Who Doesn't Fit In*. Atlanta, GA: Peachtree, 1992.   The authors, two psychologists, identify why some children do not understand nonverbal communication and therefore break its rules. They suggest several ways of sensitizing children to nonverbal communication. This book is particularly useful for parents and teachers.

RICHMOND, VIRGINIA P., JAMES C. MCCROSKEY, AND STEVEN K. PAYNE. *Nonverbal Behavior in Interpersonal Relations*, 2d ed. Englewood Cliffs, NJ: Prentice-Hall, 1991.   The authors present nonverbal communication as a unique blend of social, scientific, and humanistic study. In the first ten chapters they consider the traditional categories of nonverbal behavior. After a chapter on how these categories relate to immediacy, they consider four essential nonverbal contexts: female-male relationships, superior-subordinate relationships, teacher-student relationships, and intercultural relationships.

PART

II

INTERPERSONAL COMMUNICATION

KEY TERMS

affection

attitudes

beliefs

compatibility

control

control messages

family

inclusion

interpersonal communication

intimacy

Johari Window

proactive

proximity

reactive

regrettable talk

self-disclosure

small talk

support messages

systems theory of family

Interpersonal Relationships

CHAPTER OBJECTIVES

After reading this chapter, you should be able to:

1 Define interpersonal communication.

2 Tell why people are attracted to each other.

3 Define and explain interpersonal needs.

4 Discuss how roles influence interpersonal communication.

5 Give some ways of beginning a conversation.

6 Explain regrettable words and their impact on relationships.

7 Define self-disclosure and tell why it is important.

8 Describe the four panes of the Johari Window.

9 Explain the systems theory of family.

In one of the most interesting experiments of the late twentieth century, eight scientists lived inside a 3.5-acre dome for two years. This experiment, called Biosphere 2, was not without problems. The scientists faced swarms of cockroaches and ants, severe weight loss, and air that was less than pure. All of the participants were separated from people they loved in the outside world—one mother from her 3-year-old child.

When the two years were up and the eight scientists left the dome, they were greeted by a crowd of eager reporters who asked about their experiences. One problem took precedence over all the rest. It wasn't discomfort, it wasn't isolation: all of them agreed their greatest problem was getting along with each other.[1]

This communication that gave the scientists problems is called **interpersonal communication**. It occurs when one person interacts with another—often on a one-to-one basis—in an informal setting. We use interpersonal communication every day: we talk to a friend, we argue with a spouse, we scold a child, or we negotiate a business deal. We use it to get a deeper sense of who we are and to maintain relationships that are important to our lives.

Researchers have found that interpersonal contacts are so important that they even help us live longer. In a study of loneliness and health, researchers at the University of Michigan's Institute for Social Research examined biomedical and survey data collected over two decades and discovered that isolation from others was as detrimental to health as smoking, high cholesterol counts, and lack of physical activity.[2] Polls have shown that Americans put a high value on friendship, an important part of interpersonal communication. In a Harris poll, 97 percent of the 3001 respondents, when asked what they wanted for their children, replied they hoped their children would have lots of friends and would be well-liked. In a Roper poll, eight out of ten persons said it was absolutely essential to have friends who respected them.[3]

ATTRACTION TO OTHERS

In the course of a week, most of us have hundreds of casual encounters with other people. With most of the people we meet, we conduct our business and go on our way. Most of us, for example, do not remember the waitress who served us most recently or the bank teller who cashed our last check. These people recede into a kind of human landscape. Occasionally, however, we have an encounter where we think, "I would like to get to know that person better." Out of all the people we meet, how do we pick some we want to know better? What ingredients make up our attraction to others? What do we have to gain?

Physical Attraction

Often we are attracted to others because of the way they look. We like some-one's appearance and want to get to know the person better. In some cases physical attraction may be sexual attraction. In most cases, however, it goes beyond that. Sometimes we are attracted to people because of the way they dress. They choose a style of clothing that is our own style or is a style we would like to imitate. They have a certain "look" that we like very much.

Physical attraction is particularly important to teenagers. For them, what matters is: "Is he or she cute?" If a high school student is able to date some-one who other teenagers consider desirable, any aspect of that person's per-sonality is irrelevant. For adults, who have had more experience in the world, physical attraction is superficial; it usually recedes into the back-ground as they get to know a person. Physical attraction, then, can be a rea-son for getting to know someone; it is seldom the only basis for a long-term relationship.

Perceived Gain

Sometimes we are attracted to people because we think we have something to gain from associating with them. For example, you join the Spanish club because you know they're planning a members-only trip to Spain. Or you join the ski club to get discounted lift tickets. Someone else joins a business management club because she believes that meeting certain people might give her an advantage in getting a job. Other people like to make friends with those who have status or power, hoping that this association will con-fer status and power on them too.

Similarities

Often we are attracted to people because we like what they say. We are attracted to people when we discover that they share our attitudes and beliefs or they seem knowledgeable about topics we find interesting and sig-nificant. Our **beliefs** are our convictions; our **attitudes** are the deeply felt beliefs that govern how we behave. Although we like to think that opposites attract, when it comes to a strongly felt belief, we look for people who believe as we do. For example, it would be difficult for a Bosnian and a Serb to be close friends—their political beliefs are too different. Although a fun-damentalist Christian and an Orthodox Jew might share similar ideas, they would be so far apart in religious beliefs that they probably would not seek each other out.

As adults grow older and meet more and more people, they become aware of the kinds of people they like and dislike and they recognize the importance of compatibility. **Compatibility** is made up of attitudes, per-sonality, and a liking for the same activities.[4] For example, one couple decides to live in the city and focus on their careers rather than having a family. Their personalities are the same in that they like drama and excite-ment in their life—something the city provides. They also like the same activities: they often attend hockey and basketball games, and they spend their money on trendy clothes and eating out. Because they like the same things, their relationship is likely to last.

Differences

Although two people who have very different beliefs are unlikely to form a strong and lasting relationship, people with different personality characteristics might well be attracted to each other. For example, a person who doesn't like making decisions might be attracted to a strong decision maker. Because these qualities complement each other, they might help to strengthen the relationship.

Sometimes we have a chance to meet people from a different race or culture. In this situation we might expect different attitudes and beliefs. Interests, however, may be so similar that they outweigh anything else. An American who runs the Boston Marathon might have more in common with a runner from Kenya than with someone who spends every Sunday morning reading the newspaper and eating donuts. A white American and an African American may share similar beliefs about child rearing. An association with a group might bring people together. A Rotary member from Indiana would have a different cultural background from a Rotary member from India. However, the fact that they both belong to Rotary will create a common ground for some of their interaction.

Proximity

A quick look through the engagement and wedding notices in the newspaper will show the importance of proximity. **Proximity** is the close contact,

TRY THIS

Think back to the time you met your best friend. Then answer the following questions about your relationship:

1. Did physical attraction have anything to do with your interest in this person?
2. Did you receive any gains from getting to know this person better?
3. How are the two of you similar in attitudes? In personality? In what you like to do?
4. In what ways are you different? Does this ever create a problem?
5. How important is proximity to your relationship? If you are separated by distance, will the relationship continue?
6. How does this person communicate that he or she likes you?

that occurs when people share an experience such as work, play, or school. Through this contact, people meet their friends and often find their mates. Even when people might not otherwise have been attracted to each other, they may begin to know and like each other because they are together so much. For example, being in the same study group for a semester, sharing an office, or standing side by side on an assembly line all place people in close proximity. Once they begin to share their lives on a day-to-day basis, they may find themselves becoming friends or even forming a romantic relationship.

Sometimes people who are attracted to each other form a strong friendship but lose touch when they no longer have proximity. Typically, friends who move to different cities vow to stay in touch. However, if they can't afford telephone calls or if they aren't letter writers, it's not unusual for contact to drop to a yearly holiday card. Proximity, then, is important not just for starting relationships but also for keeping them going.

■ MOTIVES FOR INTERPERSONAL COMMUNICATION

Interpersonal communication is valuable to people because it serves so many important purposes. Our sense of self comes from our communication with others. We all have different interpersonal needs that vary with our personalities and moods. When we seek out others, we are trying to meet one or more of the following needs: pleasure, affection, inclusion, escape, relaxation, and control.[5]

Pleasure

We engage in a lot of interpersonal communication because it's fun. This kind of communication is a form of entertainment. We gossip on the telephone with our best friend; we sit around and argue about sports teams with our buddies. We stop at the student center to have coffee, but also in the hope we will meet someone we know.

Affection

Affection is the feeling of warm emotional attachment we have for people we appreciate and care for. Whether it is expressed nonverbally (hugging, touching) or verbally ("I'm really glad you called me today"), affection is important to human happiness.

Affection is a one-to-one emotion. Unlike inclusion, which can involve many people, affection is a matter of singling out a particular person.

Inclusion

The need for **inclusion**—involvement with others—is one of the most powerful human needs. At one time or another, we have all had the experience

Were you ever excluded from a group? How did you feel when this happened?

of being excluded. In a single week, one of the authors spent time with people who were speaking a language she didn't understand, thereby excluding her from the conversation. On another day a student came to her office who seemed to be depressed. When she asked him what was wrong, he answered that he didn't get a bid from the fraternity he wanted to join. She also noticed, in one of her classes, that there were some class members no one wanted to work with. All of these are examples of not being included.

Although we all have had the experience of being excluded, most of us have had more experiences of being included. Many of us eat with a certain group at the cafeteria, go to parties at friends' houses, or join a club at the university. Belonging in this way is important to our sense of well-being.

Escape

At one time or another, we all engage in interpersonal communication to try to avoid the jobs we are supposed to do. For example, before you begin writing your term paper you decide to wander down the hall of your dorm to talk to a friend.

Relaxation

We often talk to our friends or families to relax and unwind from the activities of the day. We might sit with coworkers during a break, spend a few minutes with our spouses after work, or go out with a group of friends on the weekend.

Control

Control is defined as getting people to do what you want them to do. It could involve something minor such as persuading someone to go shopping or something major such as persuading a spouse to buy a house that he or she really doesn't like. Probably because control involves manipulation, it is seen as the least satisfying of communication motives.[6]

Although control is defined as a negative quality, we all need some control in our lives because it gives us some options and enables us to make the choices that are best for us.

Recent research has found that people who have control over their lives are healthier—both mentally and physically.[7] Students learn better when teachers give them some autonomy, and workers feel better about their jobs and their workplace when they can make some decisions about how their work should be done. Elderly people in nursing homes live longer if they have some say about what they eat and how to arrange the furniture in their rooms.[8]

 ## TALKING TO EACH OTHER

Roles, Relationships, and Communication

All relationships are governed by the roles that the participants expect each other to play. Sometimes these roles are tightly defined; other times the participants have more flexibility in defining them. A conservative boss, for example, might expect his employees never to engage in personal conversations during working hours and never to receive or make personal telephone calls. In this case, the roles of boss and worker are traditionally defined. In another office, the boss might not interpret the roles so rigidly. She might want to be on a first-name basis with the people who work for her, and she might not care about personal conversations and phone calls as long as the work gets done.

Often the roles we know best are those that are the most traditionally defined. We have certain expectations of teachers, coaches, and employers. In families, parents decide what time young children should go to bed and whether they should be permitted to eat junk food. In public schools, the state, the school board, the principals, and the teachers decide what children should learn. Health-care workers recommend what is best for a patient. Even though the people who work in these roles might want more flexibility than that allowed by traditional definitions, they often feel social pressure to conform to traditional roles and thus to traditional behavior.

As roles get farther away from the nuclear family or the institutions of society, they are not so tightly defined. Usually at the beginning of a peer relationship, we can choose the roles we are going to play. Friends, for example, often decide on the role they will play within the friendship.

CONSIDER THIS

Empathy, the ability to share someone's feelings, must be present if people are going to form close relationships. It is the ability to say, "I've been there, too, and I understand what you're feeling." To achieve this kind of empathy, however, we must have some shared experiences and values, most of which come from our culture.

When we try to understand people from another culture, we often talk about how our cultures are different and how they are the same. This is largely an exchange of objective information. However, when someone from another culture tells us how he or she felt in a certain situation, we often don't understand because we haven't had a similar experience. For example, in many countries, only students who pass a competitive examination are admitted to high school. Thus, if someone says, "The day I got into high school was the happiest day of my life," we may not understand what this person is feeling—especially if we come from a country where everyone can go to high school.

Most of our cross-cultural experiences, then, are largely superficial, and we rarely form deep and lasting relationships with people from other cultures because we cannot understand them—especially on an emotional level. Does this mean that we have to give up the idea of having empathy with someone who comes from a different culture? Experts agree that it's difficult, but not impossible, for empathy to work in a cross-cultural setting. One author has suggested that it is necessary for both participants to leave their own cultural reference point and to create a new shared meaning in their interpersonal encounter. Here are the steps of the process:

1. We must move away from a self-centered view of the world and focus on our relationship with the other person. Let's see how this applies to a real situation:

   The city school board has ruled that adults of any age who did not finish high school can return to school to earn their diploma. A white middle-aged teacher who works in a school near a large housing project gets one of these adults, a 30-year-old African American woman, in her class. Trying to make her new student feel comfortable, she talks to her after class and asks her why she has returned to school. The student replies, "Well, I guess I want my degree, but mostly I want to go to the senior prom."

At this point we have two people with widely differing ideas of school. The teacher believes the main reason to go to high school is to get a diploma; the student believes one reason to go to school is to be eligible to attend the senior prom.

2. We must understand how our own prejudices and prior understandings influence how we look at the situation. If the teacher examines her prejudices, she might find her thoughts go something like this:

   I have always believed that education and getting a diploma are the only reasons for going to school. Maybe I don't realize how important social life is to students. If this student is coming back to school because she wants to go to the prom, the prom must have an important emotional meaning for her. Is there a way I can understand what she is feeling?

3. We must focus on building communication by trying to understand how the other person feels about an experience.

   One day, the student stays behind to ask the teacher to explain an assignment. After the teacher answers the question, she takes the opportunity to ask the student, "Have you thought about what you want to wear to the prom?" The student describes her dream dress in great detail and then goes on to talk about riding in a limousine, going to a fancy restaurant afterward—all the experiences connected with a prom. Her description is so vivid that the teacher begins to imagine the experience and to feel what it is like to have it.

4. We must see each party's actions in an appropriate context.

   As the teacher begins to imagine the student's dream, she thinks about how difficult it is to live in the projects. She begins to understand that the prom provides a chance to live a night of fantasy, a chance to be a Cinderella for a while.

5. We must be willing to accept that "truth" is not merely a product of the culture but also a product of the encounter.

   Through dialog, the teacher begins to understand and empathize

*with the feelings of her student. Through her willingness to aban-
don preconceptions, she has been able to reach from her own cultural world into the world of another.*

This example is one-sided in that the teacher has tried to understand the student. If the teacher-student dialog were to continue, the student might try to understand the teacher's perception of education and why it is important to her.

Source: The ideas in this box are influenced by Benjamin J. Broome, "Building Shared Meaning: Implications of a Relational Approach to Empathy for Teaching Intercultural Communication," *Communication Education* 40 (July 1991): 235–302.

QUESTIONS

1. Have you ever had a strong personal relationship with someone from another culture? If so, why do you think this was possible? If you had disagreements about what is important because of your respective cultures, how did you resolve them? Have you ever been able to see one of the differences from the other's point of view?

2. If you come from a Western tradition, talk to someone who comes from a culture where marriages are arranged. See if you can use the above process to engage in dialog that will help you to understand why arranged marriages might be superior to romantic ones. If you come from a culture that arranges marriages, turn this question around and ask why romantic marriages might be superior to arranged ones.

Once the relationship is established and functioning, the role expectations become fixed and friends expect each other to react in certain ways.

Our roles and relationships determine how we communicate. Depending on the role we play, certain communication is expected of us. Teachers expect children to speak in a respectful manner. A boss expects employees to perform their jobs conscientiously. Friends and spouses expect the other person in the relationship to disclose inner thoughts and feelings. We can see, then, that much of our success in playing a role will depend on how we meet others' communication expectations.

Much of the basis for establishing a relationship rests on reducing uncertainty.[9] For example, a new social situation might make you feel uneasy. You may wonder whether you will be able to begin a conversation and whether you will find people you like and people who like you. The uncertainty you are feeling will probably be shared by other people in the room. How do you go about reducing it?

When most people begin conversations, they engage in **small talk**—social conversation about unimportant topics that allows a person to maintain contact with a lot of people without making a deep commitment. Often we are in situations where it would be uncomfortable to stand around without talking. Therefore, there are all sorts of conventions in small talk. Scholars who have studied conversation have found that it follows a routine which varies only slightly. Figure 6-1 shows this conversation pattern.

FIGURE 6-1
How people begin conversations

If you follow this figure from top to bottom, you will see how conversations begin, progress, and end. In the sections that are numbered, there is some variation: people may speak about one or more of these topics.

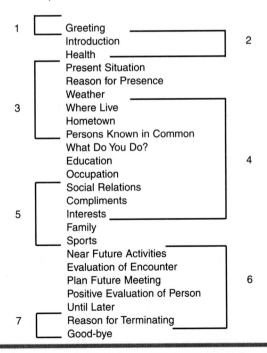

From Kathy Kellerman, "The Conversation MOP," *Human Communication Research*, 17, no. 3 (March 1991), pp. 388–389.

As you can see by the examples in Figure 6-1, many of the conversational routines are based on questions. Some questions are asked to find out information; others are used to find a way of establishing common ground. We also ask questions in certain situations just to fill time or to be sociable. Since most people like answering questions about themselves, they are flattered when someone shows interest in them.

When you are talking to a stranger, you follow certain conventions. The main rule is that questions should be more general than personal: "Where do you live?" "How do you like that instructor?" "What kind of work do you do?" The best response to such questions is to pay attention to the answers. Have you ever had a conversation with someone who paid only half-attention, while looking over your shoulder to see who else was around? This kind of response indicates that the person is just passing time until someone better comes along. It's probably better not to ask questions than to communicate this kind of attitude.

Because small talk and questions are socially sanctioned, they are safe procedures. They provide us with a chance to establish who we are with others. They also permit us to find out more about ourselves through the eyes of others. Although personal information is superficial in small talk, the image we give to others can be reflected in the way others react to us.

Regrettable Talk: Words We Wish We Hadn't Said

All of us, at one time or another, have said something that we regretted. This **regrettable talk** may have been something that embarrassed us or another person, it may have hurt someone, or it may have been a secret we were not supposed to tell. Mark L. Knapp, Laura Stafford, and John A. Daly have studied these "regrettable words" with the aim of finding out (1) whether they fell into certain categories, (2) what people did once they realized the impact their words had on the other person, (3) why they said the words in the first place, (4) how the other person responded, and (5) the short- and long-term effects the words had on the relationship.[10]

The researchers discovered that 75 percent of the regrettable words fell into five categories. The most common was the blunder—forgetting someone's name or getting it wrong, or asking "How's your mother?" and hearing the reply "She died." The next category was direct attack—a generalized criticism of the other person or of his or her family or friends. The third was negative group references, which often contained racial or ethnic slurs. The fourth involved direct and specific criticism, such as "You never clean house" or "You shouldn't go out with that guy." The fifth category—revealing or explaining too much—included telling secrets or reporting hurtful things said by others.

Seventy-seven percent of the people said they immediately realized they had said something regrettable and felt bad, guilty, or embarrassed. Some of them responded nonverbally: they winced or covered their mouths. Commonly the speaker apologized, corrected, or rephrased what he or she had said. Others discounted what they said by covering up their words or denying them.

TRY THIS

From time to time, all of us have conversations in which we aren't able to talk as much as we would like to. Or it might be the reverse: sometimes people complain that when they have a conversation with us, they don't have a chance to "get a word in edgewise."

How does someone dominate a conversation? Research has shown that dominance occurs in a number of ways. First, dominance is determined by *floor management*—who gets to talk and for how long. The longer a person talks, the more dominant he or she is perceived to be. Control also comes from the topic that is discussed. The dominant person is able to keep talking without relating his or her talk to the immediate topic. The dominant person can move the topic in a new direction or change topics at will.

The next time you are having a conversation, try to apply this theory:

> Who changes the subject?
> Who is free to wander away from the topic?
> Does one partner dominate the conversation, or are both participants equal?

Source: Mark Palmer, "Controlling Conversations," *Communication Monographs*, (March 1989), vol. 56, no. 1, pp. 1–18.

When people were asked why they had made the remark in the first place, the most common response was "I was stupid. I just wasn't thinking." Some said their remarks were selfish—they were intended to meet their own needs rather than those of others. Others admitted to having bad intentions: they deliberately set out to harm the other person. On a less negative side, people said they were trying to be nice, but the words just slipped out. Some people said they were trying to be funny or to tease the other person and the words were taken in the wrong way.

How did the people who were the objects of the regrettable words respond? Most often they felt hurt. Many got angry or made a sarcastic reply. Some hung up the phone, walked away, or changed the subject. Others were able to dismiss the statement or to laugh about it. When the speaker acknowledged the error, the listener often helped to "cover" the incident by offering an explanation or justification.

One of the most interesting aspects of this study addressed whether regrettable words had a negative impact on the relationship. Thirty percent of the respondents said that there was a long-term negative change, but thirty-nine percent said there was no change in the relationship at all. Sixteen percent said that the change was positive—for example, "In the long run, I think our relationship is stronger since it happened." In looking at the entire range of regrettable messages, the researchers concluded that regrettable messages seem to be part of our interactions with others and that although they might be hurtful to the other person when they occur, their effects can be overcome and the relationship has a good chance of continuing.

SELF-DISCLOSURE: IMPORTANT TALK

Much interpersonal communication is made up of small talk. We talk to our classmates about a party, we discuss the weather with a stranger, or we talk with a friend about a ball game we saw on TV. Although this kind of talk is important in keeping society functioning, if we used only small talk we would probably end up feeling frustrated. The problem with small talk is that it's not important enough. It doesn't touch on the central issue of who we are and what we need and want from life.

The Importance of Self-Disclosure

In order to communicate who we are to other people, we have to engage in **self-disclosure**—a process in which one person tells another person something he or she would not reveal to just anyone. To see how self-disclosure works, let's look at the case of Natalia and Misha.

One day Natalia comes home from work, and without saying anything to her husband or children, she begins to prepare dinner. When her husband asks her how her day went, she replies "OK" and continues with her work. She pulls pots and pans out of the cupboard with a big bang. When one of her daughters comes in to ask if she can help, Natalia answers, "I've got it under control." After dinner is finished and the dishes are done, Misha says to Natalia, "I know something is wrong. Do you want to talk about it?"

Natalia responds by telling him that her boss had asked her to take part in interviewing candidates for a job. After she had spent hours looking at résumés and talking to candidates, her boss hired the person Natalia believed was the worst candidate. Now she feels angry and betrayed by her boss, who ignored her opinion.

Natalia is able to tell Misha what is bothering her because they are in a close relationship. She trusts him: not only is he her husband, he is her best friend. Her willingness to tell him what is bothering her is part of self-disclosure. She is able to tell him what has happened and, more important, to tell him how she is feeling about it.

Self-disclosure clearly shows the transactional nature of communication. Natalia can tell Misha what is bothering her because she knows from past experience that she can trust him to show concern for her problems. Misha is secure enough in the relationship to realize that Natalia is not mad at him—something else must be the cause of her behavior. Both of them know that when one talks, the other will show concern and understanding. In their conversation, they are communicating continuously and simultaneously. While Misha is wondering what Natalia is thinking, Natalia is sending out verbal and nonverbal signals.

We also rely on our past experience when deciding whether to engage in self-disclosure. Like Natalia and Misha, most of us will disclose things about ourselves to people we trust. Generally, we trust those people whom we predict will react to us in the way we want them to. They are not likely to tell us that we are bad or that we have done a wrong thing. For example, you could confess to a friend that you once flunked out of school because you would expect him to react sympathetically. You can predict his reaction because you know him well and have experienced his reactions to you and to other situations. Self-disclosure, then, occurs when we discover people who believe the way we do and who react to situations and events the way we would. We trust these people enough to tell them about ourselves.[11]

The Process of Self-Disclosure

We all make choices about what to disclose and what to keep to ourselves. One way to look at how this process operates was developed by Joseph Luft and Harry Ingham. Combining their first names, they labeled their model the **Johari Window** (see Figure 6-2).[12]

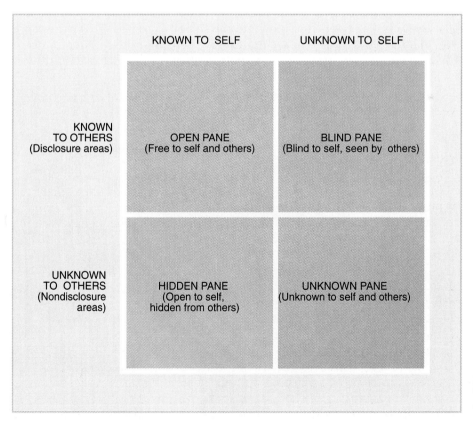

	KNOWN TO SELF	UNKNOWN TO SELF
KNOWN TO OTHERS (Disclosure areas)	OPEN PANE (Free to self and others)	BLIND PANE (Blind to self, seen by others)
UNKNOWN TO OTHERS (Nondisclosure areas)	HIDDEN PANE (Open to self, hidden from others)	UNKNOWN PANE (Unknown to self and others)

FIGURE 6-2
**The Johari
Window**

The "free to self and others" area—the *open pane*—involves information about ourselves that we are willing to communicate as well as information we are unable to hide (such as a blush when we are embarrassed). For example, when a group of students meet for the first time in a classroom, they follow the instructor's suggestion and introduce themselves. Most of them stick to bare essentials: their names, where they come from, and their majors. When people do not know one another very well, the open pane is smaller than when they become better acquainted.

The area labeled "blind to self, seen by others" the *blind pane*—is a kind of accidental disclosure area: there are certain things we do not know about ourselves that others know about us. For example, many of your classmates might say "you know" when they are trying to express themselves, or you might have a friend who always laughs nervously when he feels uncertain about himself.

The *hidden pane*—self-knowledge hidden from others—is a deliberate nondisclosure area; there are certain things you know about yourself that you do not want known, so you deliberately conceal them from others. Most people hide things that might evoke disapproval from those they love and admire: "I was a teenage shoplifter"; "I don't know how to read very well." Others keep certain areas hidden from one person but open to another: a young woman tells her best friend, but not her mother, that her grades are low because she seldom studies.

The *unknown pane* is a nondisclosure area; it provides no possibility of disclosure because it is not known to the self or to others. This pane represents all the parts of us that are not yet revealed. We might think, for example, that we are very brave, but we really don't know how we will react when

How much of self-disclosure is made up of secrets? How many people would you tell your secrets to?

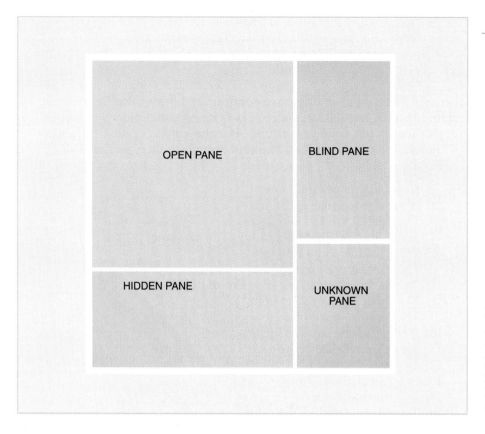

FIGURE 6–3
**This is what
the Johari
Window might
look like after a
relationship has
had a chance to
develop.**

we are faced with personal danger. The unknown area is most likely to be revealed when someone undergoes psychological counseling.

The disclosure and nondisclosure areas vary from one relationship to another; they also change all the time in the same relationship. Figure 6–3 shows how the Johari Window might look in a close relationship. In such a relationship, the open pane becomes much larger because a person is likely to disclose more. When disclosure increases, people not only reveal more information about themselves but also are likely to discover things about themselves that they had not known before. If you apply the Johari Window to each of your relationships, you will find that the sizes of the four panes are different in each relationship. In other words, you are likely to be more self-disclosing in some relationships than you are in others.

Self-Disclosure and Intimacy: Rewards and Fears

Self-disclosure is the most rewarding when it leads to greater intimacy. Only intimate relationships give us a chance to really be ourselves, to share who we are with another person. Although some people find this intimacy in romantic relationships, others find it in relationships with family members or close friends.

Although we take the position in this chapter that self-disclosure is very

TRY THIS

On a sheet of paper, draw two columns and label them Open Pane and Hidden Pane. Read the following items and decide which ones you would tell your best friend. Put the corresponding numbers under Open Pane and put the remaining numbers under Hidden Pane.

1. How I spend my free time
2. What music I like to listen to
3. The kind of job I would like
4. My political affiliation and how I would vote
5. What I think about religion
6. My greatest accomplishment
7. The most embarrassing moment of my life
8. The thing I most regret doing
9. The person I would like to spend my life with
10. How much money I made last year
11. How much I paid for my car
12. The lowest grade I got in college
13. How I feel about the way I look
14. The things I am most afraid of
15. The person I dislike the most

Once you have categorized items for your best friend, go through the list again and do the same thing for a person you don't know very well but think you would like to know better. Now see if you can draw the open and hidden panes for each relationship. How do they differ from each other? In which relationship do you have the biggest open pane? Why?

important if we are going to have deep and satisfying relationships, we also acknowledge that many people fear the consequences of revealing themselves to another. Patricia Noller and Mary Ann Fitzpatrick described fears that cause frustration when we want to form intimate relationships.[13]

FEAR OF HAVING YOUR FAULTS EXPOSED. Self-disclosure in a relationship may lead to communicating that you are not perfect and to exposing faults you would rather keep hidden. For example, some men in American culture will drive miles out of their way rather than admit they are lost or have a very poor sense of direction.

FEAR THAT YOUR PARTNER WILL BECOME YOUR CRITIC. By telling someone you are vulnerable, you open yourself to attack. A wife, for example, tells her husband how bad she felt when she wasn't invited to the senior prom. One day, when they are having a fight, he says, "Don't tell me how much people like you. You didn't even get invited to the prom!"

FEAR OF LOSING YOUR INDIVIDUALITY. Some people feel that if they reveal too much, they lose their sense of self, that there are private things that only they should know. This might be especially true during the years when teenagers are trying to gain autonomy from their families. Part of being autonomous is making decisions on your own and not telling everything to your family.

FEAR OF BEING ABANDONED. Sometimes one partner is afraid that if the other knows something about him, he will be abandoned. For example, someone might not want to tell another about his struggle with alcoholism for fear that the other person will no longer love, accept, or want him.

When Should We Go about Self-Disclosure?

Disclosure should occur only in relationships that are important to you.[14] People who do not know you very well are likely to feel uncomfortable if you tell them too much about yourself too soon. Wait until you have some signs that a relationship has the possibility of developing. For example, if someone seeks you out by inviting you to parties or for coffee, this is a sign that he or she wants the relationship to develop.

For disclosure to work, both parties must do it. If one person does all the disclosing and the other party just sits back and listens, disclosure is not likely to continue. Remember that disclosure means taking a risk. You will never know how another person will respond to your openness until you

CONSIDER THIS

When a friend takes something from the hidden pane and moves it to the open pane, he or she is telling you a secret and is trusting you not to reveal it to anyone else. Some of us (including one of the authors) know that we are not very good at keeping secrets. If we know this about ourselves, when someone else says, "I am going to tell you something, but you must promise not to tell it to anyone else," the only ethical response is, "I really appreciate your willingness to tell me something important about yourself, but I should warn you that I can't keep secrets very well. Maybe you shouldn't tell me."

give it a try. To avoid getting hurt, try testing the water with your toe before you plunge in. One way of doing this is to talk about a subject in general terms and see how the other person reacts before you talk about your own experience with it.

Finally, examine your own motives for self-disclosure. Why do you want the other person to know this information? Will it really enhance the relationship or can it do harm? All of us have some secrets that we should probably keep to ourselves. Sharing them may cause injury or make the other person lose trust in us. Although some secrets are a burden to keep, it may serve the interest of the relationship to do so.

FAMILY COMMUNICATION

What is the single place where you have had the greatest amount of interpersonal communication? Most people would probably say that it is at home, with family members. Families engage in interpersonal communication all the time: they discuss problems with each other, they sit around the dinner table and chat about their day, and they use communication to feel closer to each other.

To understand how interpersonal communication is used within a family, we must start with some definitions. By **family** we mean two or more individuals who are joined together at a particular point in time through the biological or sociological means of genetics, marriage, or adoption.[15] This definition allows for many different kinds of families. For example, one of the authors has a wife and four biological children; the other lives with her husband and two of her husband's teenage sisters. Both of these groups are families. So are a single parent and a child, and so is a couple with no children.

All family communication is transactional. Families engage in continual and simultaneous communication; they have a shared history and future. For children, this shared history may have begun with their birth. The transactional model may be very complex because each family member has a separate relationship with every other family member, and each relationship affects the family as a whole.[16]

The Systems Theory of Family

Because relationships and communication within a family are interconnected, researchers often look at a family as a system. The **systems theory of family** holds that a family is "a dynamic whole composed of constantly shifting interrelationships but still bounded and rule-governed."[17] Systems theory enables us to look at a family as a whole.

THE WHOLE FAMILY IS GREATER THAN THE SUM OF ITS PARTS. Although we may look at individual family members from time to time, our real focus is on how these members affect the whole. For example, if a teenage son has a lot of conflict with his father, this conflict has an impact on the entire family.

A Change in One Member Affects the Whole Family. For example, let's say a new baby is born in the family. Both the parents and the child's siblings will be affected.

We cannot predict whether families that face similar events will react the same way or differently. For example, two families suffer from an earthquake and lose all of their possessions. Members of one family work together by sifting through the rubble and supporting each other emotionally; members of the other family are so frightened and depressed that they are unable to do anything.

Healthy families adapt to outside stress by changing their rules and roles. For example, if a mother loses her job, other family members may react by asking only for essential items, and one of the children may get a part-time job to help with expenses. The mother, in turn, may take on the role of at-home parent.

Family members tend to work to restore household equilibrium, which will reduce household tension. For example, Cindy and Tom are always angry at their children for not doing their chores. They decide that rather than yelling, they will pay for each chore. The children like this system and do their chores, and peace is restored.

Behavior Is More Revealing Than Words. The crucial information in a family can be observed more through how the family members behave than through what they say. A wife, for example, may tell her husband that she loves him, but the real information about her feelings comes from the way she treats him. If she humiliates him in front of their friends or ignores him when he talks, she might be showing that there are serious problems in the relationship.

Family Members Conform to Rules. Families have rules about how individual members should behave and interact. Anyone who has lived in a family is familiar with such rules. Some rules are known even though nobody talks about them. Children know, for example, that there are appropriate ways to speak to their parents; all members know that they are expected to be present for certain meals at certain times; a father knows that he is expected to spend some time with his children and to drop his daughter off at her job. Many of these rules change as circumstances change. For example, the rules about dropping a teenager off at her job and social events change when she gets her driver's license. At this point the family develops new rules about cars and driving behavior.

Intimacy in Couples and Families

Although there are many kinds of families in the United States, the most common one begins with a man and a woman who decide to marry. Once

CONSIDER THIS

When Americans hear that in many other countries, marriages are arranged, their first reaction is usually, "I'm glad that doesn't happen here!" What they might not realize is that at one time in Western countries marriages were also arranged. Many times in Western history a king or other noble married into a powerful family in order to form a political alliance or gain more wealth. The purposes of an arranged marriage, then and now, are to make connections with another family, to increase family wealth through an exchange of gifts and land, and to reinforce class membership. In present-day India, for example, marriages are arranged with a family in the same caste. Much of the negotiation between the prospective families is about the gifts the bride's family will supply to the groom's family. These gifts might be as elaborate as a color television, a car, or money. Because these marriages are arranged on an economic foundation, they are highly stable. Feelings for one's mate are irrelevant: they have nothing to do with the purpose of marriage.

As the concept of romantic love grew in the West, young men and women began to decline arranged marriages and to make their own choices of whom to marry. Under such circumstances, the success of a marriage is not defined by what one family can do for the other; rather, success is defined by how satisfied the man and woman are with each other. Since personal attraction and satisfaction are the glue that holds the marriage together, it is not surprising that when these qualities disappear, the couple divorces.

Someone once said that marriages begin with economic

the couple marries, they become a family. If children are born, the family expands.

To understand how a family functions, it is useful to begin by examining intimacy in couples, since the couple is usually the foundation of the family. Scholars generally agree that **intimacy** is defined by some or all of the following characteristics: spontaneity, self-disclosure, motivation, interdependence, and tension and balance.[18]

SPONTANEITY. In a close personal relationship, a key factor is spontaneity—the ability to be yourself, showing both your good side and your bad. In this relationship, you shouldn't have to play a role that is uncomfortable; when you are with your partner, you should be able to relax.

arrangements in the East and end with them in the West. This remark was based on the observation that a divorcing couple spends a good deal of time negotiating how to divide the property and wealth they have acquired during their marriage.

In some present-day Western marriages, economic negotiations take place before the wedding ceremony. If one partner is wealthy prior to the marriage, he or she might require the other to sign a prenuptial agreement limiting the claims that can be made if the marriage ends in divorce. Prenuptial agreements originated among the wealthy; now they are sometimes signed by middle-class couples, especially if there is a large difference in age between the bride and groom or if there are children from previous marriages.

_____

Source: Some of the ideas in this section came from Patricia Noller and Mary Ann Firzpatrick, *Communication in Family Relationships* (Englewood Cliffs, NJ: Prentice-Hall, 1993), p. 164.

QUESTIONS

1. Can you think of any advantages of having your parents choose a mate for you?
2. Do your parents know things about you that you don't know yourself? Would this aid them in choosing a mate for you?
3. In large cities, many people meet others through computer/matchmaking organizations. What similarities does this have with your parents choosing a mate for you?

Whether you can reach this kind of intimacy during marriage might depend on what went on during your courtship. If you and your mate were on best behavior while you were dating, marriage might be a rude awakening.[19] If a marriage is going to be successful, it is a good idea for you and the person you are dating to risk being who you really are.

SELF-DISCLOSURE. Being yourself requires that you and your mate have the ability to self-disclose with the expectation that your disclosures will be received warmly and sympathetically. This relationship is the one in your life that is likely to have the largest open pane of the Johari Window. Couples in a marriage should be able to say, "I've never told anyone this before. . . ."

What nonverbal
cues indicate that
this family is
enjoying time
together? Do any
members seem less
involved than the
others?

MOTIVATION. Intimacy cannot exist unless both members of the couple are motivated toward it. Intimacy means the willingness to listen to your partner's point of view, share in his or her success and failures, and unite against a world that might sometimes feel hostile. To achieve intimacy, both you and your partner must be motivated to communicate about your feelings.

INTERDEPENDENCE. A couple is considered interdependent when they share activities and have an impact on each other. Interdependence might be seen on a practical level when a partner discusses the possibility of a new job with the other, or on a more abstract level when the two show each other loyalty and respect. Activities are things couples do together, such as sharing meals, going to movies, or taking vacations. The emotional tone of the relationship is also part of interdependence. The tone might be positive or negative or a combination of both. For example, if we look at television couples, the Taylors of *Home Improvement* are high in positive emotion while Marge and Homer of *The Simpsons* have more negative emotions.

TENSION AND BALANCE. The couple in a relationship must work toward both tension and balance. The greatest tension in a couple is likely to come from the need for autonomy (being yourself) and the need for interdependence (being a couple). One of the authors has two colleagues who are completely interdependent. They are married, they teach in the same department, they share an office, and they go everywhere together. The woman has never learned to drive, so her husband drives her everywhere. Other couples may be completely autonomous. The male in the relationship likes sports, but his wife doesn't so he goes to games alone. The wife likes to read, so while her husband watches television, she reads in a different room. Couples who are both autonomous and interdependent do some things together but other things alone. For example, they might try to arrange their schedules so they can eat a meal together every day. They work simultaneously on household chores: she cleans, shops, and runs errands. However, once or twice a week she goes to a movie with a friend, and he spends time on his hobby, building furniture.

The Communication of Intimacy

If we look for the signs, most of us can name some intimate couples we know. They show their intimacy through nonverbal communication, such as by standing close together, occasionally touching each other, and frequently looking into each other's eyes. This has been confirmed by research: studies of proximity among couples have found that happy couples sit closer together and touch each other often, while unhappy couples touch less and are more likely to maintain closed postures by crossing their arms in front of themselves.[20]

Couples also express their intimacy verbally. Many of them show affection with jokes and lighthearted conversation. Often couples have pet names that they call each other when they are together or with close friends. When a couple is with people both partners know well, one will often tell about the accomplishments of the other or cue the other to tell about something he or she has done ("Tell them about the trip you made during that snowstorm last week"). Couples sometimes speak about themselves as a single unit ("We really liked that movie").

Humor is also an important part of communication between couples. This area of communication hasn't been well studied, but it seems that couples often have the same sense of humor and like each other's jokes. Much of the humor between couples comes when they are talking about what has happened that day and about people they both know.

Self-disclosure is one of the most important aspects of communication between couples. However, a relationship is not a place where you tell everything. One researcher has found that when a spouse communicates a negative self-concept, it creates distance rather than intimacy.[21] Young people who are new in a relationship sometimes have to learn that they can't tell their partners everything. For example, it will probably be distressing to one partner if the other partner talks about past relationships. It's also probably unwise to comment negatively about a new haircut or new clothing.

What should and should not be told will probably depend on the relationship. When one wife had a really embarrassing experience, she told her husband about it and they laughed about it together. When another wife had a similar experience, she didn't tell her husband because she knew that he would feel very bad for her.

Communication between Parents and Children

A couple's relationship affects parenting style. Research shows that a couple with a positive marital relationship is more competent in caring for children.[22]

In regard to how parents communicate with their children, there has been much more research on mothers than on fathers. Generally, mothers send support or control messages to their children. **Support messages** make a child feel comfortable and secure in the family relationship. They include praise for the child's competence and reassurance when the child is feeling anxious. Children who get support messages from their mothers have higher self-esteem, engage in less aggressive behavior, and conform more to what their mothers want.[23]

Control messages are designed to get children to behave in ways that are acceptable to the mother. These messages may take different forms. some messages force children to obey. They may be threats, such as "If you don't . . . I will. . . ." These messages may involve physical punishment or take children's privileges away ("You are grounded for a week"; "You can't use the car anymore"). Strong control messages have a negative affect on children. These messages increase aggression and decrease self-esteem, creativity, and academic achievement.[24]

Some mothers also threaten to withdraw their love. They might say they are going to take their children to an orphanage or to the police. The mother may leave the house and not return for several hours or may refuse to speak to the child for several hours or even days. These messages can be very harmful to young children who already have fears of abandonment.

Mothers have two styles of reacting to undesirable behavior. One style is **reactive,** in which the mother punishes the child when the behavior appears. The other style is **proactive**. In this style the mother anticipates that the undesirable behavior is coming and tries to divert the child. For example, children are usually bored in restaurants. The reactive mother spanks the child who misbehaves; the proactive mother brings along some books or toys. Proactive intervention takes more effort from the mother, but the long-term result is better behavior.[25]

Communication between fathers and children is not well documented because until recently, mothers were regarded as the primary caregivers. Fathers have reported distress because work keeps them from spending as much time with their children as they would like. Some cross-cultural studies have shown that men are as good at caretaking as are women. However, it seems that men seldom take total responsibility for the care of a child. Their role is much more likely to be to help out when help is needed.[26]

Adolescent girls and boys have more communication with their mothers than with their fathers. Adolescents see their mothers as more interested in their problems, more open and understanding, and more able to negotiate agreements. Fathers, however, are perceived as more authoritarian, more judgmental, and less willing to listen. Because some adolescents see their fathers as stern and rigid, they are more likely to react defensively to fathers than to mothers.[27]

Step Families

Because of high divorce rates in the United States, many of the children born in the 1980s and 1990s are likely to spend some part of their childhood or adolescence in step families. The most common step family is the biological mother and a stepfather.[28]

Problems in step families are likely to follow a pattern. Discipline is difficult in a "step" relationship, especially if the children are older when the step family forms. Stepparents, for example, have to negotiate the difficult balance of forming a relationship with the stepchild but still being able to discipline him or her.

One of the greatest problems in a step relationship is that children do not want to accept the new stepparent. Many children fantasize that their biological parents will get back together, but a remarriage means that they must give up this fantasy. As a result, children often resent the new partner in a marriage, thinking, "If you hadn't come along, everything would have worked out."

In the new marriage it is inevitable that the natural parent will have less time to spend with the children. Because the children often spent time with the parent between the marriages, they resent the new parent for taking this time away from them.

Perhaps the main problem with step families is that there is no institutionalized set of rules and roles. The stepparent doesn't know how to act, and the children don't understand the role they should play. Although these problems may work out in time, the beginning of a step family is often perilous.[29]

Quality Communication in a Family

Researchers have found that four factors lead to good communication among family members: openness, confirmation, rules for interaction, and adaptability.[30]

OPENNESS. Openness is the ability to disclose feelings in the family. Not only should children be able to tell their parents what they are feeling, but parents should be able to do the same with their children as long as they do not burden them with adult problems.

CONFIRMATION. Family members should be able to be themselves within the family structure. This does not mean that they must always agree; it means that when they disagree, they will still be loved. If children cannot

CONSIDER THIS

In Western societies, most families value their daughters as much as their sons. However, in other parts of the world, especially in agricultural societies, sons are valued over daughters because they can work on the land. Also, where sons don't move away when they get married, they or their wives are available to care for elderly parents.

In a traditional Moslem country such as Saudi Arabia, some families highly prize sons and give daughters little value. In a story given secretly to an American journalist, a Saudi princess compared her life to that of her brother, Ali. In one episode, a servant gave her an apple, and her brother demanded it. She refused and ate the apple as fast as she could—and she was punished severely:

As punishment, Ali was given all my toys. To teach me that men were my masters, my father decreed that Ali would have the exclusive right to fill my plate at mealtimes. The triumphant Ali gave me the tiniest of portions and the worst cuts of meat. Each night, I went to sleep hungry, for Ali placed a guard at my door and ordered him to forbid me to receive food from my mother or my sisters. My brother taunted me by entering my room at midnight laden with plates steaming with the delicious smells of cooked chicken and hot rice.

Finally Ali wearied of his torture, but from that time on, when he was only nine years old, he was my devoted enemy. Although I was only seven years old, as a result of "the apple incident," I first became aware that I was a female who was shackled by males unburdened with consciences.

Source: Jean P. Sasson, *Princess* (New York: Morrow, 1992), p. 26.

QUESTIONS

1. In Western societies, there are often separate roles that boys and girls are expected to play. What are some of these roles in your family?
2. Can you come up with examples of other countries where boys and girls are treated differently?
3. Are special roles designed for girls to keep them from danger? Are these roles necessary?

be themselves at home, they will have problems developing relationships with others, both friends and future partners. Like all members of the family, children play roles, but it is important that these roles not be too confining.

Rules for Interaction. All families have rules for how members interact with each other. A child usually learns these rules while growing up ("Don't talk to me in that tone of voice"; "Don't interrupt your sister"). These rules change as the children get older, since what works for younger children will not work for adolescents.

Adaptability. Children and parents need to adapt their communication to the situation. When parents must decide an issue that affects them as a couple, they are not likely to discuss it with their children. However, children should be consulted when an issue affects them. This may range from "Do you want to take your lunch or buy it in the cafeteria?" to "Do you want to rent a cottage on the lake or go away to summer camp?"

These four principles of communication are equally important if all family members are going to be happy.

 ## SUMMARY

Interpersonal communication, or one-to-one communication, is the kind of communication we use most frequently. Interpersonal communication helps us to build relationships and find out about ourselves and others. Without relationships, we would have no sense of self.

All relationships begin with attraction. Although the basis of attraction might vary greatly from one relationship to another, we are most attracted to people with whom we have similarities and frequent contact. Sometimes we form a relationship because we see something we can gain from it. To form a relationship, we need proximity—frequent contact with the other person.

Our motives for seeking out interpersonal relationships are pleasure, affection (warm emotional attachments with others), inclusion (involvement with others), escape, relaxation, and control (getting others to do as we want them to).

Relationships with others are governed by the roles we are expected to play. Roles that reflect the structure of society are more rigidly defined than roles we establish with friends. Much of the communication we have in relationships depends on the role we are playing.

Our first contacts with others begin with small talk. An important part of small talk is asking questions because doing so helps us discover common ground with others. If we want a relationship to grow beyond superficiality, we must engage in self-disclosure. Self-disclosure is the process of communicating one's self to another person, telling another who we are and what we are feeling. Self-disclosure can be understood through the Johari Window, which has four panes: open, blind, hidden, and unknown. As a relationship develops and disclosure increases, the open pane gets larger.

Much of our interpersonal communication occurs in our family. A family is two or more individuals who are joined together at a particular point in time through the biological or sociological means of genetics, marriage, or adoption. In systems theory, a family is "a dynamic whole composed of constantly shifting interrelationships but still bounded and rule-governed."[31]

The foundation of a family is usually a couple. Intimacy between couples requires spontaneity, self-disclosure, motivation, interdependence, and tension and balance.

Communication between parents and children takes two forms: support messages and control messages. In their relationships with children, mothers are more effective if they are proactive rather than reactive. Most adolescents communicate more with their mothers and see them as more sympathetic than their fathers.

Because divorce is common in America, many children are part of step families. Typical problems in step families include forming a relationship with a stepparent, finding time to spend with the biological parent, and dealing with a lack of institutionalized rules and roles.

Quality communication in a family seems to have four components: openness, confirmation, rules for interaction, and adaptability.

NOTES

[1] Seth Mydans, "8 Bid Farewell to the 'Future,' Musty Air, Roaches and Ants," *The New York Times*, Sept. 27, 1993, pp. A1, 13.

[2] Vincent Bozzi, "Tall, Dark, First Date," *Psychology Today* (July/Aug. 1989): 67.

[3] Roberta Friedman, "Hand Jive," *Psychology Today* (June 1988): 10.

[4] Elaine Hatfield and Richard L. Rapson, "Similarity and Attraction in Close Relationships," *Communication Monographs* 59 (1992): 209–212.

[5] Rebecca B. Rubin, Elizabeth M. Perse, and Carole A. Barbato, "Conceptualization and Measurement of Interpersonal Communication Motives," *Human Communication Research* 14 (Summer 1988): 602–628.

[6] Ibid., p. 618.

[7] Daniel Goleman, "Feeling of Control Viewed as Central in Mental Health," *The New York Times*, Oct. 7, 1988, pp. C1, 11.

[8] Ibid.

[9] Charles R. Berger and Richard J. Calabrese, "Some Explorations in Initial Interaction and Beyond: Toward a Developmental Model of Communication," *Human Communication Research* 1 (1976): pp. 99–112.

[10] Mark L. Knapp, Laura Stafford, and John A. Daly, "Regrettable Messages: Things People Wish They Hadn't Said," *Journal of Communications* 36 (1986): 40–57.

[11] Lawrence R. Wheeless and Janis Grotz, "The Measurement of Trust and Its Relationship to Self-Disclosure," *Human Communication Review* 3 (Spring 1970): 250–257.

[12] Joseph Luft, *Group Process: An Introduction to Group Dynamics*, 2d ed. (Palo Alto, CA: Science and Behavior Books, 1970), pp. 11–12.

[13] Patricia Noller and Mary Ann Fitzpatrick, *Communication in Family Relationships* (Englewood Cliffs, NJ: Prentice-Hall, 1993), pp. 95–96.

[14] John H. Berg and Richard L. Archer, "The Disclosure-Liking Relationship," *Human Communication Research* 10 (Winter 1983): 269–281.

[15] Noller and Fitzpatrick, pp. 2–3.

[16] Ibid., pp. 6–12.

[17] Ibid., pp. 39–40.

[18] Ibid., pp. 76–81.

[19] Ibid., p. 76.

[20] Ibid., p. 90.

[21] Ibid., p. 93.

[22] Ibid., p. 211.

[23] Ibid., p. 201.

[24] Ibid., p. 202.

[25] Ibid., p. 202.

[26] Ibid., pp. 204–205.

[27] Ibid., p. 209.

[28] Ibid., p. 238.

[29] Ibid., pp. 238–240.

[30] Ibid., pp. 17–18.

[31] Ibid., pp. 39–40.

■ FURTHER READINGS

ARLISS, LAURIE P. *Contemporary Family Communication: Messages and Meanings.* New York: St. Martin's Press, 1993. This text about family communication discusses a variety of families. The text is particularly useful in defining the particular words that refer to family communication.

CANARY, DANIEL J., AND LAURA STAFFORD. *Communication and Relational Maintenance.* San Diego: Academic Press, 1993. This book focuses on how people communicate to keep their relationships working. The thesis of this book is that communication and relationships go hand in hand.

DYM, BARRY AND MICHAEL L. GLENN. *Couples: Exploring and Understanding the Cycles of Intimate Relationships.* New York: HarperCollins Publishers, 1993. In this original, engaging, and thoughtful book the authors explore how couples work and what makes them successful or unsuccessful, long-lasting or short-term. Using in-depth examples they identify three recurring stages common to all enduring relationships: expansion and promise; contraction; and resolution.

FOSTER, CAROLYN. *The Family Patterns Workbook: Breaking Free from Your Past and Creating a Life of Your Own.* New York: Jeremy P. Tarcher, 1993. Foster offers strategies for assessing a family's dynamics and shows ways for a family member to make changes. She looks at family patterns, family roots, and how to pattern new growth.

JEFFERS, SUSAN. *Dare to Connect: Reaching Out in Romance, Friendship, and the Workplace.* New York: Fawcett Columbine, 1992. Jeffers first discusses how to get in touch with one's self and how to overcome feelings of inadequacy and loneliness. She presents techniques to make connections in romance, friendship, and business. In concluding, she shows how to participate in the world to avoid alienation.

KNAPP, MARK L., AND ANITA L. VANGELISTI. *Interpersonal Communication and Human Relationships.* 2d ed. Boston, MA: Allyn and Bacon, 1992. This textbook is about the way people communicate in relationships that are either developing or deteriorating. Knapp answers the question of how communication behavior affects our relationships.

NOLLER, PATRICIA, AND MARY ANN FITZPATRICK. *Communication in Family Relationships.* Englewood Cliffs, NJ: Prentice-Hall, 1993. This book contains much of the research that has been done about families and family communication. Although the book focuses on research, it is highly readable.

REARDON, KATHLEEN K. *Interpersonal Communication: Where Minds Meet.* Belmont, CA: Wadsworth, 1987. Reardon examines the ways interpersonal communication scholars use the tools of the social sciences to formulate answers to such questions as "How do children learn to communicate?" "How do we form and maintain relationships?" "How do people interact in various settings?" and "What is competent communication?" Using theory and research, Reardon expands readers' understanding of the interpersonal communication process.

STEWART, LEA P., PAMELA J. COOPER, AND SHERYL A. FRIEDLEY. *Communication between the Sexes: Sex Differences and Sex-Role Stereotypes.* 2d ed. Scottsdale, AZ: Gorsuch Scarisbrick, 1990. This book examines the influence of sex differences and sex-role stereotypes on communication. The authors identify significant sex differences and sex-role stereotypes, explain their implications and consequences, and suggest some strategies for change. Their contexts include friendship and marriage, education, the media, and the organization.

WALKER, VELMA, AND LYNN BROKAW. *Becoming Aware: A Look at Human Relations and Personal Adjustment,* 5th ed. Dubuque, IA: Kendall/Hunt, 1992. In this workbook, the authors discuss self-discovery, self-awareness, self-control, becoming emotional, interpersonal communication, becoming intimate, interpersonal conflict, managing stress, values, and life planning.

WEBER, ANN L., AND JOHN H. HARVEY, EDS. *Perspectives on Close Relationships.* Boston: Allyn and Bacon, 1994. In well-researched chapters several authors look at topics such as attraction, communication, emotion, attachment, love, commitment, resource allocation, sexuality, jealousy, betrayal, abuse, loss, and social support. Designed for students, the authors offer a rich snapshot of the noisy, colorful, and sometimes confusing world of close relationships.

KEY TERMS

aggression

assertiveness

avoidance

commitment

complaint

*conflict
    resolution*

control

*costs and
    rewards*

criticism

*defensive
    communication*

empathy

*evaluative
    statements*

*indirect
    aggression*

7

Evaluating and Improving Relationships

CHAPTER OBJECTIVES

After reading this chapter, you should be able to:

1 Summarize the stages of a relationship in coming together and coming apart.

2 Explain why good relationships need commitment and dialog.

3 Explain how roles and expectations are important to relationships and why you might need to renegotiate them from time to time.

4 Tell how the following can become communication problems: criticism, complaints, avoidance, aggression, and defensive behavior.

5 List the strategies for changing defensive communication.

6 Explain how assertiveness, reflective listening, and "I" messages can help communication.

7 List and explain the steps in conflict resolution.

im and Rich are both sophomores at the university. They are enrolled in the same political science class, and because the class is small, all the members have gotten to know each other. As the class discusses various issues, Kim discovers that Rich says many of the things she is thinking. Rich has also noticed Kim. She often makes interesting remarks in class and she wears a lot of blue— Rich's favorite color.

One day, toward the end of the semester, Rich sees Kim sitting alone at the student union and asks if he can join her. She agrees and they start to talk about their class and the instructor. As they begin to feel more and more comfortable, they talk about what they like to do in their free time, and they discover that they both love movies. Rich asks Kim if she would like to go to see a new film that is opening at the end of the week, and she readily agrees.

Kim and Rich have had an experience that probably occurs in various forms on campuses all over the country. People who don't know each other get together for a variety of reasons. They might be like Kim and Rich, who are attracted to each other. They could be coworkers who want to get to know each other outside of work. They could be people who want to make new friends. On the basis of what they discover when they meet, they decide whether they should explore the possibility of a relationship.

THE STAGES OF A RELATIONSHIP

Most relationships begin with superficial communication; then, if the people like each other, they take steps to see each other again. Mark L. Knapp, a writer and researcher on relationships, has found that relationships develop along rather predictable lines. He describes five stages of how relationships come together and another five of how they fall apart. Each stage is characterized by certain kinds of communication.[1] Let's begin with a relationship that is coming together, using the example of Kim and Rich.

Coming Together

STAGE ONE: INITIATING

When Rich and Kim started talking together, they began the *initiating stage*. As they talked, they probably assessed each other in various areas—such as clothes, physical attractiveness, and beliefs and attitudes. From all these observations each began to make judgments about the other: "He seems like a nice guy." "She sounds like she is very smart."

Rich and Kim were interested enough in each other to begin a conversation, but not all people will begin the initiating stage. On the basis of first impressions, we often decide the other person isn't interesting enough or doesn't seem to want to pursue a relationship with us.

STAGE TWO: EXPERIMENTING

In the *experimenting stage*, people make a conscious effort to seek out common interests and experiences. They experiment by expressing their ideas, attitudes, and values and by seeing how the other person reacts. For example, someone with strong feelings about the equality of all races might express an opinion to see if the other person agrees or disagrees.

Rich and Kim find they have common interests and values, and they both decide that they want to talk even more. They start going for coffee after class. They tell each other about their families and their friends. They meet outside of class to eat a meal or watch a movie. At this stage of a relationship, everything is generally pleasant, relaxed, and uncritical. Many relationships stay at this particular stage—the participants enjoy the level of the relationship but show no desire to pursue it further.

STAGE THREE: INTENSIFYING

Kim and Rich have discovered that they like each other quite a lot. They spend more time with each other. This is the *intensifying stage* of their relationship. They swap cassettes and CDs and spend free time together. Not only do they enjoy each other's company, but they also start to self-disclose. They tell each other private things about their families and friends and introduce each other to them. They also begin to share their frustrations, imperfections, and prejudices.

Other things happen in the relationship. They call each other by nicknames; they develop a "shorthand" way of speaking; they have jokes that no one else understands. Their conversations begin to reveal shared assumptions and expectations. Trust becomes important. They believe that if they tell the other a secret, it stays between them. They start to make expressions of commitment: "Let's go to Ocean City to work next summer." They also start some gentle challenges of each other: "Do you really believe that, or are you just saying it?" Openness has its risks in the intensifying stage. Self-disclosure makes the relationship strong, but it also makes the participants more vulnerable to each other.

STAGE FOUR: INTEGRATING

Kim and Rich have now reached the *integrating stage*—the point at which their individual personalities are beginning to merge. People expect to see them together. If they see just one of them, they ask about the other. The friendship has taken on a specialness. They do most things together. They go to the same parties and have a lot of the same friends; their friends assume that if they invite one, they should invite the other. Each of them is able to predict and explain the behavior of the other.

The integrating stage is reached only when people develop deep and important relationships. Those who reach this stage are usually best friends, couples, or parents and children.

STAGE FIVE: BONDING

The last coming-together stage of a relationship is the *bonding stage*. At this point, the participants make some sort of formal commitment that announces their relationship to those around them. For Kim and Rich, an announcement of their engagement or marriage would be an example of bonding. In other cases, as between friends, the bonding agreement might be less formal, such as signing a lease together. Whatever form it takes, bonding makes it more difficult for either party to break away from the relationship. Therefore it is a step that is taken when the participants have some sort of long-term commitment to their relationship.

CONSIDER THIS

In the Micronesian islands in the Pacific, there is a bonding ritual that is unknown in the West. If a person, usually an adolescent, has a very good friend, he or she might designate this friend as a "promise brother" or "promise sister." This new relationship is announced to the families of both parties. After this announcement, both families consider the promise brother or sister to be a member of the family. This new member has all of the family privileges: he or she can drop in without being invited, eat with the family, stay overnight, or do anything else a member of that family might do.

Promise brothers and sisters have a strong loyalty to each other, and part of their relationship is to look out for each other. Sometimes the relationship crosses sexes: a boy can take on a promise sister or a girl a promise brother. These relationships are strictly brother-sister; they never lead to romance. Once one takes a promise brother or sister, the relationship is for life.

Source: Interview, Reyann Sepety, April, 1994.

QUESTIONS

1. In traditional Micronesian society, family relationships are the only ones that count. Why is it important, then, to recognize promise brothers and sisters?

2. Why is it important that promise brothers and sisters never be romantically involved?

3. In contemporary Western society, friends are often as important as family. Would it be a good idea to have this bonding ritual in the West?

The five coming-together stages build on one another. Whether a relationship will move from one stage to the next depends on both participants. If one wants to move to the next stage, it will not be possible unless the other agrees. Because most of us have only limited time and energy for intense relationships, we are willing to let most of our relationships remain at the second or third stage. The first three stages permit us to become involved in friendships and to carry out normal social activities. The fourth and fifth stages, integrating and bonding, demand much more energy and commitment—they are reserved for very special relationships.

Another point should be made about these stages. People in a new relationship should not try to progress too quickly beyond stage one or two. In all relationships it is important that each participant be sensitive to feedback from the other. It is this feedback that will determine whether it is time to advance to another stage. Since stage three is the first in which there is self-disclosure, moving from stage two to stage three is particularly sensitive. If one person self-discloses too quickly, the other might feel so uncomfortable that he or she will be unwilling to go on to a new stage in the relationship.

Coming Apart

For a relationship to continue, both participants must grow and change together. If they cannot do this in ways that are satisfying to both of them, then the relationship will come apart. Although it is more satisfying to look at relationships coming together, we all know that relationships also fail. Relationships that are failing can also be described in five stages, stages that reverse the process of coming together.

STAGE ONE: DIFFERENTIATING

Time has passed, and Kim and Rich have been married for over a year. The first months were a little rocky, but now serious problems are beginning to emerge. Kim likes to go out several nights each week; Rich wants to stay home. Rich likes to cook new and exotic food; Kim wants to eat meat and potatoes. Even their love for movies is causing conflict: Kim wants to see them as soon as they open; Rich wants to wait until they are released as videos.

Kim and Rich have entered the *differentiating stage*. The interdependence of their courting stage is no longer so attractive. Now they are beginning to focus on how different they are, and much of their conversation is about their differences rather than their similarities.

To some extent, the differentiating stage is a healthy phase that most couples experience. Many couples work out their differences by being autonomous some of the time and interdependent at others. For example, Kim and Rich go together to family gatherings and to parties. However, when Rich goes hunting, Kim goes shopping.

TRY THIS

Look at an important relationship in your life with someone other than an immediate family member. If you choose a more recent relationship, you will have a better chance of remembering the earlier stages. Ask yourself the following questions:

1. *Initiating.* Where did you meet this person? What attracted you to him or her? Do you remember how you started a conversation? What made you think you might be interested in finding out more about him or her?

2. *Experimenting.* How did you get to know this person better? What things did you do and talk about together? What made you think he or she might become more than a casual acquaintance?

3. *Intensifying.* How did you know that you could trust this person? Who was the first to use self-disclosure? How much self-disclosure has occurred by each of you? Has one person been more likely to self-disclose than the other?

4. *Integrating.* How much time do you spend together? When you are apart, do you ever think, "I can hardly wait to tell about this"? Do you have private names? Private jokes? If people see one of you, do they ask about the other?

5. *Bonding.* Have you done anything to show your commitment to each other? Have you made any kind of public commitment? Have you ever refused to do or say something because it would be disloyal to your commitment?

The differentiating stage can be worked out if the differences are not too great. Rich, for example, wants to begin a family right away, but Kim isn't sure that she wants to have children. Since this issue doesn't lend itself to compromise, their conversations begin to take on a quarrelsome tone. Rich says, "I think we should have our children while we are still young." Kim replies, "If I don't work on my career now, I'll be left behind."

The differences the two recognized and tolerated before become focal points for discussion and argument. Kim says, "It's a lot better to watch movies on the big screen than on video. Can't you tell the difference?" On another occasion Rich says, "Didn't your family ever eat anything different? I'm sick of roast beef and potatoes."

The most visible sign of differentiating is conflict. But differentiating can take place without conflict. Even if nothing specific is bothering the couple, they may discover, as they mature and find new interests, that they have less and less to talk about. Kim, for example, reads the newspaper every day and follows world events. Rich, on the other hand, gets his news from television and finds it too depressing to talk about.

STAGE TWO: CIRCUMSCRIBING

When a relationship begins to fall apart, less and less information is exchanged. Since points of conflict exist in the relationship, it seems better to stay away from mentioning them, in order to avoid a full-scale fight. Thus this is called the *circumscribing stage*.

Now conversation is superficial: "Your mail is on the desk." "Did I get any telephone calls?" "Do you want some popcorn?" The number of interactions is decreased, the depth of discussions is reduced, and the duration of each conversation is shortened. Because communication is constricted, the relationship is constricted.

Most people who find themselves in this stage try to resolve their problems by discussing the relationship itself. In response, the negative turn in the relationship might change. For example, Rich could go out to a movie with Kim, and Kim could agree to try some different food. In other cases, discussion about the relationship might reveal even greater differences between the participants. In such cases, discussion about the relationship leads to even more conflict, so the participants limit discussion to "safe" topics. Kim and Rich, for instance, stay away from the topic of children because they know they will fight about it.

Persons who are in this stage often cover up their relationship problems. Although they might reveal problems to very close friends, in social situations they give the appearance of being committed to each other. They create a social or public face—in essence, a mask.

STAGE THREE: STAGNATING

The *stagnating stage* is a time of inactivity. The relationship has no chance to grow, and when the partners communicate, they talk like strangers. The subject of the relationship itself is now off limits. In some cases they may want to talk about the relationship, but then may decide not to. Rather than try to resolve the conflict, they are more likely to take the attitude of "Why bother to talk? We'll just fight, and things will get even worse."

How long this stage lasts depends on many things. If Kim and Rich lead busy lives and just come home to sleep, they might go on in this stage for months or even years. However, if Rich stays home and broods about the relationship, he may look for some kind of resolution to their conflict. Most couples whose relationship reaches this stage feel a lot of pain. They may find it hard to separate and may hold on to the hope that they can still work things out.

STAGE FOUR: AVOIDING

The *avoiding stage* involves physical separation. The parties avoid face-to-face interaction. They are not interested in spending time together, in building any kind of relationship, or in establishing any communication channels.

This stage is usually characterized by unfriendliness, hostility, and antagonism. Sometimes the cues are subtle: "I only have a minute. I have an appointment." They can also be direct and forceful: "Don't call me anymore" or "I'm sorry, I just don't want to see you."

In relationships where physical separation is impossible, the participants may act as if the other person does not exist. Each one carries on his or her work in a separate room and avoids any kind of interaction. In the case of our couple, one might sleep in the bedroom and the other on the living room couch.

STAGE FIVE: TERMINATING

In the *terminating stage*, the participants find a way to bring the relationship to an end. Both parties are preparing themselves for life without the other. Differences are emphasized, and communication is difficult and awkward.

In an article titled "The Rhetoric of Goodbye,"[2] Knapp and his colleagues describe three distinct types of statements that commonly occur in terminating relationships. First, there are the summary statements: "Well, we certainly have tried to make a go of it" or "This isn't the end for either of us; we'll have to go on living." Second are statements that signal the likelihood of decreased access: "It might be better if we didn't see each other quite so often." Finally, there are messages that predict what the future relationship (if any) will be like: "I don't ever want to see you again" or "Just because we aren't going to live together doesn't mean we can't be friends."

Some relationships cannot be entirely terminated. There are cases in which the parties have to have some contact. Couples who have children cannot entirely end their relationship if the children are going to see both parents. In this kind of situation, the parents might terminate their relationship with each other as marriage partners but decide to continue in some kind of relationships as parents to the children. To do so peacefully, they might set down a list of rules that will govern the new relationship.[3]

Sociologist Diane Vaughan has also studied the patterns that occur when a relationship is about to end.[4] She says that one member of the couple, realizing he or she is unhappy, begins the process of ending the relationship. This person typically begins by finding alternatives—often in the form of a transitional person. Although the transitional person might be a romantic interest, it could also be a minister, a therapist, or a good friend. When one partner begins to find satisfaction elsewhere, the couple's relationship becomes less endurable. At this point the dissatisfied person lets the other know of her or his discontent through body language and words.

Finally the time comes when the dissatisfied person lets the partner know that he or she wants to end the relationship. The other partner typically feels betrayed, hurt, and shocked—and is often unprepared. Vaughan says that during the breakup, both partners suffer emotional pain and go through the same stages of disengagement—it just happens at different times for each of them.

ESSENTIAL ELEMENTS OF GOOD RELATIONSHIPS

Most authors who look at the relationships between couples and among family members and friends believe that they have certain elements in common. The most common elements that draw people together seem to be commitment and dialog.

Commitment

All relationships need **commitment**—a strong desire by both parties for the relationship to continue, and a willingness on the part of both parties to take responsibility for the problems that occur in the relationship. Margaret A. Farley, a writer on relationships, says that although commitment is made in the present, it points to the future. It is "a relation of binding and being-bound, giving and being-claimed."[5] She distinguishes among the different kinds of commitments.[6] An unconditional commitment is one in which you commit yourself to another—regardless of what may happen. Marriage vows are often unconditional commitments. A conditional commitment sets forth the conditions of the commitment and carries the impli-

How do people communicate they are committed to each other?

cation of "only if." Examples might be "I will work to resolve our problem only if you will tell me what you're really thinking" and "I will work on this project with you only if you promise to commit ten hours a week to it."

Long-term relationships are usually unconditional commitments. These are commitments that spouses make to each other or that parents make to children. Although friendships may be unconditional, they are more often conditional. For example, if a friend marries, has a child, or moves away, the other friend is likely to expect less from the relationship. Work relationships are usually conditional. A boss expects her employees to do their jobs but not to dedicate their lives and total time to those jobs.

All relationships have some kind of commitment as their foundation, but sometimes the partners in the commitment have different expectations. If these expectations are not fulfilled, the partners must work out changes or compromises if they want the relationship to continue.

Dialog

Partners in good relationships must have ongoing conversations, or dialogs, about the relationship itself. They must be able to search together for ways of reducing conflict, to discuss expectations they have of each other, or discuss anything else that might affect the relationship. What is important is that the partners agree to discuss the relationship periodically. In regard to discussing relationships, Deborah Tannen introduces a cautionary note: "The belief that sitting down and talking will ensure mutual understanding and solve problems is based on the assumption that we can say what we mean, and that what we say will be understood as we mean it."[7]

Discussing points of conflict is particularly important if the relationship is going to be successful. Some of us, however, are conditioned to stay away from conflict. Childhood messages such as "Hold your tongue" and "I don't ever want to hear you talk that way again" lead us to believe that it's wrong to say words that other people do not want to hear. As adults, however, we have to recondition ourselves to discuss areas of conflict: withdrawing from it or avoiding it is too harmful to relationships.

For partners to continue in a relationship, they must find mutually beneficial ways of communicating. We talked about the importance of reflective listening—listening for emotions and acknowledging the feelings of one's partner. Often conflict can be reduced when people engage in this kind of listening.

EVALUATING YOUR RELATIONSHIPS

Roles and Expectations

In successful relationships, the participants have usually worked out their roles and expectations. These roles, however, change through the course of

**Do you feel star-
tled when you
find someone
playing a role
you might not
expect? How can
changes in roles
change people's
lives?**

a relationship. A young couple, for example, might share housekeeping chores. However, if they decide to have a baby, it is important that they discuss how their roles will change once the baby is born. "Who's going to take care of the baby during the day?" and "Who's going to get up at night when the baby cries?" are some of the questions the couple is going to have to answer.

Friends who are in conflict might benefit from looking at their role expectations. Let's say that whenever a man asks her out, Jenn cancels her plans with her friend Beth. Beth feels hurt and angry because, in her opinion, this behavior implies that Jenn thinks a date is more important than their friendship. Jenn indeed does believe that male-female relationships are more important than female-female ones. Unless the two women can decide the roles they will play in regard to each other, their friendship is in jeopardy. To take another example, if a husband expects his wife to cook dinner every night and she does not have the same expectation, then it is time to redefine their roles and expectations. Besides defining their roles, both people in a relationship have to reach agreement on them. Finally, the roles and expectations that people have in a relationship must be satisfying to both parties.

Renegotiating Roles

Sometimes relationships have to be renegotiated when the participants' roles change. Let's say, for example, that a 19-year-old college student marries someone who is 35. In this marriage it is likely that the younger person will depend on the older person to make decisions, to provide reassurance, and so forth. Once the 19-year-old finishes school and takes a job, it is likely that his or her self-confidence will increase and that he or she will no longer depend on the spouse so much. Such change may be threatening to the spouse. To help this relationship, the partners must discuss the roles they have been playing with a view to changing them. How can this be done?

When we have been in a role for a long time, we develop habitual ways of behaving as well as assumptions about how our partner will behave. The young spouse, for example, may have let the older spouse pay the bills, advise on clothes, and make decisions about what social occasions they should attend. If, feeling newly independent, the younger spouse announces a desire to change these things, it will come as a shock to the older spouse.

The best chance for this relationship would be a renegotiation of roles. The younger spouse might say, "I'm feeling more secure now, and I would like to make my own choices about what to wear." Since this is not an unreasonable request, agreement is likely. The older spouse may see this as an opportunity to renegotiate his or her role as well, and may say something like, "Now that you're feeling more comfortable by yourself, I'd like to rejoin my Thursday evening tennis league."

It is much easier to make changes in roles when such changes are seen as being in the best interest of both partners. For example, some parents are willing to give up the role of being on an ambitious career path in order to spend more time with their children. However, if a person sees this change as a loss, it will be very difficult for him or her to agree to it. The ease with

TRY THIS

Are you in a relationship with someone where you are playing a role that is no longer comfortable for you? For example, do you want your parents to treat you more like an adult, or do you want your boss to give you more responsibility on the job? If you are in an uncomfortable role, ask yourself these questions:

1. What circumstances made me play this particular role? Did I ever feel comfortable with it?

2. What is making me feel uncomfortable now?

3. What changes would I like to bring about? (Try to picture what this role would be like if it were changed.)

4. How can I communicate the changes I would like in this role? Are there any changes I could suggest that would be an advantage to the other person?

which role changes are made also depends on the flexibility of the individuals within the relationship. When relationships and roles are rigidly defined, change is very difficult.

Costs and Rewards

In a relationship, the **costs and rewards** need to be weighed against each other. The costs are the problems in the relationship; the rewards are the pleasures. In a work situation, for example, you don't have much choice about your boss or the people you work with. The only way of terminating a relationship at work might be to quit your job. This is a great cost, and it must be balanced with the rewards. You might be worried that you can't find another job, so keeping the job outweighs its costs and you decide not to quit. People sometimes remain in relationships that are not entirely satisfying when the rewards for staying are greater than the costs of getting out.

People may stay in an unsatisfying marriage because the emotional and economic costs of divorce are too great. A middle-aged woman who has never worked, for example, might stay in a marriage because she has no way of supporting herself and can't imagine living alone. Other partners stay together for the sake of the children, or because it is too much of a problem to divide property—or for any number of reasons.

If you are in a relationship that is not very satisfying, you will have to ask yourself questions about the costs and rewards of staying in it. One way to do this is to make a list: on one side list the rewards, on the other the costs. Don't make such a list when you are feeling angry or very upset—your feelings may distort your objectivity. Also, additional costs and rewards sometimes will occur to you later, so give your list time to develop. Once you have listed costs and rewards, take some time to evaluate the results and assess your feelings.

If you are not willing to give up the rewards, it is obvious you will have to stay in the relationship. If the costs are greater than the rewards, your only choices are to terminate the relationship or to try to improve it.

■ COMMUNICATION PROBLEMS IN RELATIONSHIPS

Criticism and Complaints

All couples fight. University of Michigan researchers say that the average couple has one serious fight a month and several small ones.[8] Can too many fights destroy a marriage? It all depends on how you fight, according to the experts.

A typical fight will probably begin with a criticism or a complaint. Whether people are involved in a close relationship, such as marriage, or a more distant relationship, such as boss-employee, how criticism and complaints are handled is important to that relationship. Let's look at criticism first.

We have all probably said at one time or another that we don't mind hearing criticism as long as it is constructive. The question, then, is what is criticism and what do we consider constructive criticism?

Criticism is a negative evaluation of a person for something he or she has done or the way he or she is. In more distant relationships, criticism usually originates with a higher-status person and is directed toward one with lower status.[9] A teacher, for example, criticizes a student; a parent criticizes a child. If the participants are equals, such as friends or a couple, criticism could come from either partner.

Researchers have discovered that criticism has five targets: appearance (body, clothing, smell, posture, and accessories); performance (carrying out a motor, intellectual, or creative skill); personhood (personality, goodness, general ability); relationship style (dealing with others); and decisions and attitudes (opinions, plans, life style). The researchers found that the target of most criticism is performance, followed by relationship style, appearance, and general personhood.[10]

The study also looked at what the recipients perceived as "good" and "bad" criticism. Some criticism was perceived as bad because of the relationship between the criticizer and the person being criticized.[11] Most people believed that someone who did not know them very well didn't have the right to criticize them. They also felt that in the case of an argument, a good friend should side with them—not with the criticizer. Another feature of bad criticism was an inappropriate setting. People were much more likely to identify criticism as "bad" if it was given in front of others rather than privately. Students, for example, felt particularly humiliated if a teacher criticized them in front of their classmates.

The researchers also found that good criticism was distinguished from bad by five stylistic points. First, criticism was labeled "bad" if it contained negative language (profanity or judgmental labels such as "stupid jerk") or if it was stated harshly by screaming or yelling. Second, criticism was better received if it was specific and gave details on how to improve ("Your speech would be more effective if you had eye contact with the members of your audience"). Third, criticism was considered "good" if the person who offered it also offered to assist in making the change ("Pretend I'm a member of the audience and give your speech again. Look me directly in the eyes"). Fourth, criticism was better accepted if its receiver could see how it would be in his or her best interest to change ("If you improve your delivery, you'll get a better grade on your speech"). Fifth, good criticism placed negative remarks in a broader and more positive context ("The content of your speech is really good. All you have to do is work on the delivery").

Good criticism, the researchers found, leads to positive consequences. When the recipients of criticism did not feel threatened, they were able to take the comments seriously and make changes. In contrast, poorly given criticism was likely to evoke negative emotions and to be seen by the recipient as inaccurate.

Research conducted about criticism on the job has found that harsh or inept criticism in the work setting undermines work relationships, increases the likelihood of future conflicts, and prevents people from doing good work. Like the criticism in relationships, the best criticism on the job is specific. It is also important that criticism be timely. The researchers found that people reacted angrily to criticism when the boss stored up grievances and then communicated them all at once. Finally, good criticism at work focuses on what the person has done incorrectly rather than suggesting that poor work is a form of character deficiency, such as laziness or incompetence.[12]

A **complaint** is an expression of dissatisfaction with some behavior, attitude, belief, or characteristic of a partner or of someone else. A complaint differs from criticism in that it is not necessarily directed at any specific person.

In studies of complaints between couples, researchers found that, as with criticism, some responses to complaints were more useful than others.[13] First, when complaints are trivial, they can probably be ignored. "This spaghetti is overcooked" or "Why do I have to be the only one to shovel the snow?" are trivial complaints. Second, a complaint should not be directed at anyone specifically. When you say, "Why doesn't anyone ever close doors?" you are not pointing to any one person, so the guilty party can change his or her behavior without losing face. Third, a complaint should be softened or toned down so that the complainer can express his or her frustration or dissatisfaction without provoking a big argument. Fourth, if the complaint is serious, the partners should discuss it and try to arrive at a solution or a compromise before the complaint turns into a serious conflict.

Complaints were least manageable when the partners were unresponsive or if the conflict escalated. If a partner ignored important complaints, the result was increased anger and dissatisfaction. Also, if the complaint escalated during the exchange, the couple was likely to end up angry with each other. Couples who had the weakest relationships were those who were likely to withdraw from any complaints or to escalate them.[14]

Avoidance

Many people who are in unsatisfying relationships try to dodge any discussion of their problems. Some people use silence; others change the subject if the other partner tries to begin a discussion. People who refrain from discussing relationships are often trying to avoid any kind of conflict. The dilemma of **avoidance**—refusing to deal with conflict or painful issues—is that unless the problem is discussed, it probably will not go away.

Sometimes people refuse to engage in discussion because they believe that nothing is ever resolved or that their partner will not give them a fair hearing. In such cases, discussion can often begin by calling in a third party to listen to both sides. Ideally, this should be a person who is able to listen objectively and not take sides. In the case of roommate conflict, a dorm counselor might be helpful. Partners in marriage often seek out marriage counselors.

Aggression

Aggression is a physical or verbal show of force. Some people resort to physical aggression when they are unhappy in a relationship. Unless the partners can get professional help, these relationships are usually doomed. Other people resort to verbal aggression, such as name-calling or saying hurtful things. This is a very dangerous strategy because it is difficult to recover trust after your partner has said hurtful things about you. People who are tempted to use verbal aggression should be aware that such actions can destroy a relationship.

A more subtle act, and one we are often not aware of committing, is **indirect aggression** (also called *passive aggression*). People who use this form of communication often feel powerless and respond by doing something to thwart the person in power. For example, a teenager whose mother forces him to clean the kitchen might do such a poor job that she never asks him again. A student who is forced to go to college might show indirect aggression by flunking all her courses. One of the authors had a friend whose mother played hymns loudly on the piano whenever her daughter brought home someone she didn't like. All these are acts of indirect aggression.

Sometimes indirect aggression is not a conscious act. The student, for example, might not realize she is failing her classes to thwart her parents. Sometimes the behavior is planned and deliberate—as in the case of the piano player.

When one partner in a relationship commits an act of indirect aggression, it is often useful for the other partner to bring it to his or her atten-

What nonverbal signs tell us there is conflict in this relationship?

tion. This should be done carefully, or it is likely to result in more aggression or a defensive response.

Defensive Communication

Defensive communication occurs when one partner tries to defend himself or herself against the remarks or behavior of the other. If a teacher tells a student, "This is the worst paper I have ever read," the student is likely to think (if not say), "And you are the worst teacher I have ever had." Obviously, this conversation is not off to a good start.

The problem with defensive communication is that we are so busy defending ourselves that we cannot listen to what the other person is saying. Also, defending ourselves is dealing with past behavior, it gives us no chance to think about resolving the problem.

How can we avoid defensive communication? Jack Gibb, in a classic article, came up with six categories of defensive communication and supportive strategies to counter each of them.[15]

EVALUATION VERSUS DESCRIPTION

Evaluative statements involve a judgment. If the judgment is negative, the person you are speaking to is likely to react defensively. If you tell your roommate, "It is inconsiderate of you to slam the door when I am trying to sleep," he might respond, "It's inconsiderate of you to snore every night when I am trying to sleep." Obviously such statements do not lead to solving the problem. On the other hand, a descriptive statement is much more likely to receive a favorable response. If you tell your roommate, "I had trouble sleeping last night because I woke up when I heard the door slam," he is much more likely to do something about the problem. Since you have merely described the problem, the message is not so threatening.

CONTROL VERSUS PROBLEM SOLVING

People who consistently attempt to exert **control** believe that they are always right and that no other opinion (or even fact) is worth listening to. Those who feel they must control communication argue for their point of view, insist their position be accepted, and sometimes even raise their voices to get people to accept what they believe.[16]

Most of us will not choose to be with someone who must always have control. However, when the controlling person has status and power, we may have no choice. Parents have a good deal to say about controlling their children, but once the children reach adolescence, there are often struggles for control. We learn lessons about control from our parents. A boy who has a stern, controlling father is likely to grow up to be a controlling father too.

People tend to respond negatively if they think someone is trying to control them. For example, if you are working on a class project with a classmate, and you begin by taking charge and telling him or her what to do, you will probably be resented. A better approach is to engage in problem solving together. The same applies to close relationships. If conflict arises and you decide what should be done ("I'll take the car and you take the bicycle"), your partner is not likely to respond positively. It is better to discuss your transportation options together.

STRATEGY VERSUS SPONTANEITY

Often strategy is little more than manipulation. Rather than openly ask people to do something, you try to manipulate them into doing it by using strategies such as making them feel guilty or ashamed. A statement that begins "If you love me, you will . . ." is always manipulative. A better approach is to express your honest feelings spontaneously: "I am feeling overwhelmed with all the planning I have to do for the party. Will you help me out today?"

NEUTRALITY VERSUS EMPATHY

Have you ever asked someone "Where shall we go to eat?" or "What movie should we see?" or "What do you want to do tonight?" and heard the person respond, "I don't care"? This kind of neutral response indicates a lack

---

CONSIDER THIS

Researchers have looked at the question of who interrupts whom and why:

- Men interrupt women far more often than they interrupt other men—and more frequently than women interrupt anybody.

- In male-female conversation, when a man introduces a topic, it's more likely to be discussed than a topic the woman introduces.

- Men say they see interruptions as a sign of liking and respecting the conversational partner; women say they see interruptions as showing disrespect, failing to listen, and failing to agree.

Source: Catherine A. Chambliss and Norah Feeny, "Effects of Sex and Subject, Sex of Interrupter, and Topic of Conversation on the Perceptions of Interruptions," *Perceptual and Motor Skills* 75 (1992): 1235–1241.

QUESTIONS

1. The next time you are in a mixed-sex group, ask yourself whether the researchers are correct: Do men interrupt women more? Is the group more likely to discuss a man's topic?

2. Ask women and men how they feel about being interrupted. Is there a difference between the sexes?

of interest, and it is likely to make you feel defensive enough to respond, "Why do I always have to come up with the ideas?" or "If you don't care enough to make a suggestion, then we'll stay home."

On other occasions, we want and expect family members and friends to take our side. If you receive a low grade on a paper and are feeling very bad about it, you don't want your friend to say, "Maybe the teacher was right. Let's look at both sides." When feelings are high, no one wants a neutral, objective response. That can be saved for later. What is really needed in such a situation is for the other person to show **empathy**—the ability to recognize and identify with the other's feelings. An empathic response to a poor grade in a course might be "You must feel bad. You really studied hard for that class."

SUPERIORITY VERSUS EQUALITY

None of us likes people who act as though they think they are superior to us. Feelings of superiority are communicated in a variety of ways. People who always take charge of situations seem to imply that they are the only ones who are qualified to do so. Others feel superior because of their role: "I am the boss and you are the employee, and don't you forget it." It's not uncommon for parents to issue statements of superiority: "I am your father, and I will set the rules." Even if we have a position that is superior to someone else's, people will react less defensively if we do not communicate this superiority. An attitude of equality—"Let's tackle this problem together"— produces much less defensive behavior.

CERTAINTY VERSUS PROVISIONALISM

There are certain people who believe they are always right. Another label for these people is dogmatic. It is important that we don't confuse people who are confident and secure with people who think they are always right. Confident and secure people may hold strong opinions; they are likely, however, to make many more provisional statements—statements that permit another point of view to be expressed. For example, someone might say, "I feel strongly on this subject, but I would be interested in hearing what you have to say." People who are willing to take a more provisional approach are also able to change their own position if a more reasonable position is presented. Table 7-1 shows the categories of defensive and supportive behavior.

TABLE 7-1
CATEGORIES OF DEFENSIVE AND SUPPORTIVE BEHAVIOR

Defensive Climate	Supportive Climate
1. Evaluation	1. Description
2. Control	2. Problem solving
3. Strategy	3. Spontaneity
4. Neutrality	4. Empathy
5. Superiority	5. Equality
6. Certainty	6. Provisionalism

Avoiding Defensive Communication: A Practical Example

Although we have discussed each of Gibb's six categories separately, in most communication situations several of them appear simultaneously. You can see how this works in the following situations.

A Defensive Dialog

> *Boss:* You're an hour late. If you're going to work here, you have to be on time. *(superiority, control)*

> *Employee:* My car wouldn't start.

> *Boss:* That's no reason to be late. *(certainty, evaluation)* You should have called. *(evaluation)*

> *Employee:* I tried, but . . .

> *Boss:* When work starts at 8 A.M., *you* must be here at 8 A.M. *(superiority, control)* If you can't make it, you should look for another job. *(superiority, control, certainty)* If you're late again, don't bother coming to work. *(superiority, control, strategy)*

This dialog leaves the employee feeling defensive, angry, and unable to say anything. Let's take a look at how the dialog might have gone if the boss had been more willing to listen.

A Supportive Dialog

> *Boss:* You're an hour late. What happened? *(description, equality)*

> *Employee:* My car wouldn't start.

> *Boss:* Weren't you near a phone? *(still no evaluation)*

> *Employee:* Every time I tried to call, the line was busy. I finally decided that it would be faster to walk here than to keep trying to call.

> *Boss:* When people don't get here on time, I always worry that we're going to fall behind schedule. *(spontaneity)* Wasn't there *any* way of letting me know what happened? *(problem solving)*

> *Employee:* Yeah. I guess I panicked. I should have asked my sister to keep trying to call to let you know what happened. If it ever happens again, that's what I'll do.

> *Boss:* Good. Now let's get to work. There's a lot of catching up to do . . .

In this conversation, neither boss nor employee is left feeling defensive or resentful. Although the role of boss is superior to that of employee, this boss

TRY THIS

1. Change this evaluative statement to a descriptive one: "You really annoy me when you expect me to exercise with you. I'm just too busy."

2. Change this controlling statement to a problem-solving one: "Tonight we eat at Joe's and then go to see a movie."

3. Change this manipulative statement to a spontaneous one: "If you really loved me, you would remember my birthday and our anniversary."

4. Change this neutral statement to an empathic one: "I know your boss irritates you, but you must remember that he has very great responsibilities."

5. Change this superior statement to an equal one: "Since I earn all the money in this household, I should decide how to spend it."

6. Change this statement of certainty to a provisional comment: "The Democrats are always right, and no one is going to persuade me they are not."

tries hard not to use his position of power. The result is a more equal conversation, which leads, in turn, to better communication between the two.

COMMUNICATION SOLUTIONS IN RELATIONSHIPS

Once people have a commitment to a relationship, they can usually improve their communication within it. Better communication, including reflective listening and assertiveness, can lead to better relationships.

Reflective Listening

Chapter 3 discusses the subject of reflective listening in detail. Because this kind of listening is so important to relationships, it is worthwhile to review the main points here.

Reflective listening is listening for feelings from the other person's point of view. In this kind of listening, you put aside your own feelings and try to *hear* what the other person is really saying. If your partner says, for example, "Everyone is picking on me today," as a reflective listener, you would be sympathetic to your partner and indicate, both verbally and nonverbally, that you are ready to listen to what is bothering him or her.

The most important thing about reflective listening is that you don't try to evaluate the other person's feelings. If you respond to "Everyone is picking on me" with "You're really paranoid today," communication is likely to end. A more appropriate response might be "You sound upset. What happened?" This response sets the stage for the other person to talk about the problem. In reflective listening, the most important thing to remember is that people often just need a sounding board. Everyone feels happier when the other person in a relationship is a sympathetic listener.

I/You Messages

Sometimes it's possible to make changes in relationships by changing our ways of communicating. Rebecca Cline and Bonnie Johnson have done some valuable research that shows the importance of making careful language choices when dealing with criticism. They found that people react negatively and defensively when conversation is filled with "you" messages ("*You* didn't empty the garbage"; "*You* always foul up the checkbook"; "*You* never change the oil in the car").[17]

Cline and Johnson found that this kind of "you" talk makes the other party feel defensive. "I" messages, however ("I am afraid we will need a new car if we don't change the oil more often"), are likely to receive a much less defensive response. The reason for this is that an "I" message takes the pressure off the other person—which makes him or her more likely to focus on the feelings of the person who believes there is a problem. Here are some typical "I" messages: "When I am left alone at a party, I feel very shy and embarrassed"; "I can't concentrate when the room is such a mess"; "I feel uncomfortable when we have the only yard in the neighborhood where the grass isn't cut."

Assertiveness

Sometimes communication goes astray because we don't express ourselves clearly or we are not certain what we want. **Assertiveness** is taking the responsibility of expressing needs, thoughts, and feelings in a direct, clear manner. Let's say, for example, that you always put things away, but your roommate seldom does, so your apartment is always a mess. You have several options in this situation. You could clean up after you and your roommate with a lot of sighs and significant looks showing you are unhappy, or you could make an indirect verbal comment ("I wish our apartment were a little tidier") and hope your roommate will get the hint. These approaches, however, are not assertive. If you want to make an assertive statement that might change your roommate's behavior, you should say something on the order of "I'd like it if you would wash the dishes and put them away after you use them." You could also make a statement about how you feel. "I feel like the whole kitchen is dirty when there are dirty dishes in the sink."

Neither of these comments should make your roommate feel defensive since you are not evaluating his or her behavior.

Often it's hard to tell what another person is feeling, so it is useful to make clear statements about your emotional state:

> *I feel very anxious if you don't call me when you are going to be late.*

> *I'm not mad at you. I'm mad at my boss, and I need some time to cool down before I can talk to you.*

> *I feel that if we go to your mother's house over the holidays, I will be too rushed and I won't be able to meet my deadlines.*

Our definition of assertiveness includes the responsibility to be as clear as possible. You can fulfill this responsibility by planning what you want to say before you say it. This is particularly useful when a situation is charged with emotions. Thinking your words through in advance helps to make the situation clear in your own mind.

RESOLVING CONFLICT

From time to time, all of us face conflict in our interpersonal communication. Sometimes conflict destroys a relationship; other times, if the participants can work it out, the relationship become stronger.

When two people are in conflict and have decided that nothing will be served by avoidance or aggression, the option left open to them is **conflict resolution**—negotiation to find a solution to the conflict. Conflict arises because two individuals do not have compatible goals. Through the negotiation process, the two try to find out how they can both reach their goals. For the negotiation to be considered successful, both sides must be satisfied and feel that they have come out ahead.

Deborah Weider-Hatfield, a researcher in this area, has suggested a useful model for resolving conflict.[18] In this model, each individual looks at the conflict *intra*personally. Then the partners get together *inter*personally to work out the problem.

In the first stage, *intrapersonal evaluation*, each person analyzes the problem alone. This analysis is accomplished through a series of questions: How do I feel about this problem? How can I describe the other person's behavior? What are the facts?

It is important not to confuse facts with inferences. If you have an untidy roommate, for example, a fact might be that he doesn't pick up his clothes. An inference would be that he is trying to irritate you by not hanging them up. Throughout this intrapersonal process it is important to *describe*—not judge—the other person's behavior.

In the second stage, the parties in the conflict get together to work out an *interpersonal definition* of the problem. It is important that both parties believe there is a problem and can define what it is. Partners in conflict often do not see the problem in the same light; in fact, one person might not even believe there is a problem. Therefore, in this stage, it is important that each person listen carefully. To aid in listening, it is useful for each person to check the accuracy of what he or she has heard by paraphrasing what was said. The same is true for feelings. Because feelings are intense in a conflict, it is important for each partner both to express his or her own feelings and to make sure he or she is listening accurately by trying to paraphrase the feelings of the other. Then it is useful for each person to describe the other person's behavior. At the end of this stage, both partners should agree on the facts of the problem.

In the third stage, the partners should discuss *shared goals*. Still focusing on the problem, the individuals should ask, "What are *my* needs and desires?" and "What are *your* needs and desires?" Then they should work to see whether their needs and goals overlap. Let's look at the tidy and untidy roommates. The tidy roommate wants to have things picked up and the dishes washed. The untidy roommate hates doing housework and doesn't care if the apartment is in disorder. Thus their goals in housework are incompatible. Nonetheless, they like each other and like sharing an apartment. Each is also concerned that the other partner be happy. In this case, then, they have found some goals in common.

At the fourth stage, the partners must come up with possible *solutions* to the problem. Here it is useful to create as long a list as possible. Then each individual can eliminate solutions he or she considers unacceptable. One partner's list might look like this:

- Clean the apartment every week.
- Pay someone to clean the apartment.
- Move out.

The second partner's list might be:

- Clean the apartment once a month.
- Use paper plates and plastic cups.
- Eat only fast food.

When the roommates look at each other's lists of solutions, they both decide there are some items they can't live with. Neither can afford to hire someone to clean, and they decide that disposable dishes are not good for the environment. One also says she really doesn't want to move out, and the other admits that a steady diet of fast foods is not very appealing.

In the fifth stage, the partners move on to *weighing goals against solutions*. Since the roommates want to live together and they want each other to be happy, their task is to choose a solution or solutions that will help them to reach these goals. Looking at their lists, they discover only two items remain. ("Clean the apartment once a week" and "Clean the apartment once a month"). Some compromises are inevitable at this stage. In this particular situation, the roommates decide to do a thorough cleaning of the apartment every two weeks. Also, the tidy roommate agrees to stop nagging, and the untidy roommate agrees to pick up after herself in the common living areas. These solutions may not be entirely satisfactory to either party, but they are a compromise that both hope they can live with.

Since all resolutions are easier to make than to keep, the last stage of the process is to *evaluate* the solution after some time has passed. Does the solution work? Does it need to be changed? Should it be discussed again at a later date? As we mentioned earlier, it is not easy to change human behavior. When partners work to resolve conflict, even when they come up with good solutions, there is likely to be some backsliding. It therefore makes good sense to give partners a chance to live up to their resolutions. Letting time pass before both negotiators are held accountable helps to achieve this goal.

Although these guidelines can be useful in many situations, it must be pointed out that not all conflicts can be resolved. If partners cannot find any goals that they share, or if they cannot agree on solutions that will enable them to meet their goals, then the conflict will probably not be resolved. Also, although this model looks good on paper, it is much like the chair you see advertised in the local discount store. The sign says "A child can put it together in ten minutes," but when you get it home you find there are thirty nuts and bolts and a dozen separate pieces, and after two hours' work you have something that only vaguely resembles a chair. In the same way, this model sounds simple in theory, but it is not always easy to put into practice. Human communication is so complex, and there are so many ambiguities and subtleties in meaning, that each person in a negotiation must bring careful thought and analysis to each stage of the process. When both partners are committed to a relationship, however, there is a good chance that conflict can be worked out using this or a similar process.

RELATIONSHIPS THAT WORK

Most relationships can be improved when the partners understand how to communicate with each other. Conflict occurs in all relationships; it's how it is worked out that allows the partners to find satisfaction and happiness together.

What is a relationship that works? It is one where there is intimacy and self-disclosure. When you save up the good things that have happened to you to tell to your partner, that is a good relationship. It is a relationship where you can share the good and the bad things you feel. It is a partnership where you can solve problems and feel happy that you have solved them. Most important, a relationship is the psychological space where you and another person are closest to being your truest selves. It can happen with a marriage partner, with a best friend, or with a parent or child. For us to be happy, it is important that it happen with someone.

In this section we present ideas that may contradict information in the text and may or may not reflect the views of the authors. The important thing is that you read the material, discuss it with your classmates or friends, and make up your own mind.

One Person Can Change a Relationship

Dr. Barry L. Duncan and Dr. Joseph W. Rock, psychologists and family therapists, believe that couples must take a new approach to conflict. They contend that even though partners follow standard formulas of using "I" rather than "you" language or try to resolve conflict by defining and talking about the problem, they end up stating the problem in different words but never arrive at resolution. They also believe that problems can be solved by one member of the couple—even when the other is resistant.

Their theory is this: The relationship between two people is a system. Regardless of how strong one personality may be, that person is part of a system and is therefore influenced by his or her partner's behavior. This means that if one person changes his or her behavior, the other person will change too, and thus, the relationship is changed.

The psychologists deal with three kinds of behavior that can be changed: power disparities, jealousy, and communication problems. We will deal only with communication since that is the focus of this chapter. Below we list three problems and some of the remedies the authors suggest. Note that all of these responses are high in unpredictability.

1. Your partner is unwilling or unable to communicate as much as you would like him or her to.

   Change the strategies you have used before. Be less available for conversation. Don't make a great attempt to begin a conversation or keep one going. When conversation does start, cut it short.

   Discuss his or her silence in a positive way. "We are so close we don't always have to talk." "I feel good when you're quiet because it means everything is all right with us."

2. Your partner makes lots of complaints and you feel frustrated because you can't help him or her.

   Accept his or her complaints. Encourage complaining rather than trying to stop it. Express negative rather than positive opinions you have about the topic. Introduce complaints at every opportunity.

3. Your partner accuses you of something you didn't do.

   Don't explain or defend yourself because that will start an argument. Turn the problem on your accuser: "You're feeling insecure about my feelings for you."

Source: Barry L. Duncan and Joseph W. Rock, "Saving Relationships: The Power of the Unpredictable," *Psychology Today,* Jan.–Feb. 1993, pp. 45–50.

QUESTIONS

1. From what you know about their approach, do you think that Duncan and Rock believe that couples can sit down and work out problems in a rational way? Why or why not?

2. How does their approach differ from Gibb's approach for dealing with the categories of defensive communication, which suggests that problems can be solved by rephrasing how you talk about them?

3. The most radical approach that Duncan and Rock suggest is that if a couple is having problems, it might be possible for one person to bring about change. Why do they believe this is true? Do you think they are correct?

4. Duncan and Rock's approach seems to suggest a considerable amount of manipulation. Is manipulation an ethical issue in a relationship?

■ SUMMARY

The most important relationships in our lives go through five stages: initiating, experimenting, intensifying, integrating, and bonding. Relationships that remain superficial go through only the first or second stage.

Relationships that come apart also go through five stages: differentiating, circumscribing, stagnating, avoiding, and terminating. When a relationship is ending, the participants often make statements that summarize the relationship and comments that indicate whether the relationship will continue in any form. Many relationships end when a third person intervenes in some way.

Good relationships need commitment and dialog. Commitment is a desire by both partners to continue the relationship and to take responsibility for problems that occur in it. Dialog occurs when the parties in the relationship have ongoing conversations about the relationship itself. An important part of dialog is discussing conflict when it arises.

When people evaluate their relationships, they should look at their roles and the expectations they have of their partners. As circumstances change, it is important to renegotiate roles. When a relationship is in trouble, it's a good idea to look at costs and rewards. Costs are the problems in the relationship, and rewards are the pleasures.

Communication problems in a relationship include criticism, complaints, avoidance, aggression (including indirect aggression), and defensive behavior. Criticism is a negative evaluation of a person for something he or she has done or the way he or she is. Complaints are different from criticism in that they are not necessarily directed to a specific person. Criticism and complaints should be carefully structured, so that they don't cause problems in a relationship. Avoidance is the refusal to talk about the problems in relationships. Aggression is the intent to injure another person, either physically or verbally. Indirect aggression is showing resistance by refusing to do something or doing it in an unsatisfactory way.

Strategies for avoiding defensive communication include describing rather than evaluating, problem solving with a partner rather than trying to control him or her, being spontaneous rather than manipulative, using empathy rather than remaining neutral, aiming for equality rather than superiority, and being provisional rather than certain.

Several communication strategies can help improve a relationship. Assertiveness helps both partners because needs, thoughts, and feelings must be expressed in a direct, clear manner before they can be acted upon. Reflective listening, the kind of listening where you concentrate on the other person's feelings and avoid evaluating what he or she is says, is helpful in developing empathy. It is also useful for persons involved in a disagreement to use "I" rather than "you" messages.

Using a model of conflict resolution can help reduce conflict in a relationship. The steps involve evaluating the conflict intrapersonally, defining the nature of the conflict with your partner, discussing the goals you and your partner share, deciding on possible solutions to the problem, weighing goals against solutions, deciding on a solution that will reach the goal, and evaluating the solution after some time has passed.

NOTES

[1] Mark L. Knapp, *Interpersonal Communication and Human Relationships* (Boston: Allyn and Bacon, 1984), pp. 35–44.

[2] Mark L. Knapp, Roderick P. Hart, Gustav W. Friedrich, and Gary M. Shulman, "The Rhetoric of Goodbye: Verbal and Nonverbal Correlates of Human Leave-Taking," *Speech Monographs* 40 (1973): 182–198.

[3] For more information on how couples come apart, see Stephen P. Banks, Dayle M. Altendorf, John O. Greene, and Michael J. Cody, "An Examination of Relationship Disengagement Perceptions: Breakout Strategies and Outcomes," *Western Journal of Speech Communication* 51 (1987): 19–41, and William W. Wilmot, Donal A. Carbaugh, and Leslie A. Baxter, "Communication Strategies Used to Terminate Romantic Relationships," *Western Journal of Speech Communication* 49 (1985): 204–216.

[4] Diane Vaughan, *Uncoupling: How Relationships Come Apart* (New York: Random House, 1990).

[5] Margaret A. Farley, *Personal Commitments* (San Francisco: Harper & Row, 1986), p. 18.

[6] Ibid., p. 21.

[7] Deborah Tannen, *That's Not What I Meant!* (New York: Morrow, 1986), p. 124.

[8] "The Rat in the Spat," *Psychology Today* (Sept.–Oct. 1993): 12.

[9] Karen Tracy, Donna Van Duesen, and Susan Robinson, "'Good' and 'Bad' Criticism: A Descriptive Analysis," *Journal of Communication* 37 (1987): 46–59.

[10] Ibid., p. 48.

[11] Ibid., p. 50.

[12] Daniel Goleman, "Why Job Criticism Fails: Psychology's New Findings," *The New York Times*, July 26, 1988, p. C1.

[13] Jess K. Alberts and Gillian Driscoll, "Containment versus Escalation: The Trajectory of Couples' Conversational Complaints," *Western Journal of Speech Communication* 56 (1992): 394–412.

[14] Ibid.

[15] Jack Gibb, "Defensive Communication," *Journal of Communication* 11 (1961): 141–148.

[16] Hal Witteman, "Analyzing Interpersonal Conflict: Nature of Awareness, Type of Initiating Event, Situational Perceptions, and Management Styles," *Western Journal of Speech Communication* 56 (1992): 248–280.

[17] Rebecca J. Cline and Bonnie McD. Johnson, "The Verbal Stare: Focus on Attention in Conversation," *Communication Monographs* 43 (1976): 1–10.

[18] Deborah Wieder-Hatfield, "A Unit in Conflict Management Education Skills," *Communication Education* 30 (1981): 265–273.

CAHN, DUDLEY D., JR. *Letting Go: A Practical Theory of Relationship Disengagement and Engagement,* Albany: State University of New York Press, 1987. This book looks at research about failed relationships and focuses on how poor self-concept and communication may play a part in failure. The book is research-oriented and scholarly.

CROSBY, JOHN F. *Illusion and Disillusion: The Self in Love and Marriage,* 4th ed. Belmont, CA: Wadsworth, 1991. Crosby zeros in on difficulties in love and marriage and what can be done about those difficulties. This is a serious book with sophisticated case studies to support the author's analyses.

FISHER, BRUCE. *Rebuilding: When Your Relationship Ends,* 2d ed. San Luis Obispo, CA: Impact, 1992. This excellent and insightful book treats denial, loneliness, guilt and rejection, grief, anger, letting go, self-concept, friendships, love, trust, sexuality, responsibility, singleness, and freedom.

FITZPATRICK, MARY ANNE. *Between Husbands and Wives: Communication in Marriage.* Newbury Park, CA: Sage, 1988. The author defines five types of relationships and shows how couples communicate in each of them. The book is a scholarly study with lots of statistical data.

GOTTMAN, JOHN. *Why Marriages Succeed or Fail.* New York: Simon & Schuster, 1994. After studying more than 2,000 married couples, Gottman has discovered that intuitions about why marriages succeed or fail are wrong. The most serious threats to marriages, he says, are criticism, contempt, defensiveness, and stonewalling. Useful examples, valuable self-tests, and practical advice make this book interesting and important.

GRAY, JOHN. *Men Are from Mars, Women Are from Venus: A Practical Guide for Improving Communications and Getting What You Want in Your Relationships.* New York: HarperCollins, 1992. The idea that men and women are from different planets provides the metaphor used to illustrate the commonly occurring conflicts between men and women. In fifteen delightful chapters, Gray offers valuable insights, engaging examples, and advice that seems sound, useful, and on target.

GUMPERT, GARY, AND SANDRA L. FISH. *Talking to Strangers.* Norwood, NJ: Ablex, 1990. Focusing on therapeutic communication, this book contains a series of articles about people solving problems by using computers, talk radio, advice columns, and television evangelists. The articles about computers are especially fascinating.

VAUGHAN, DIANE. *Uncoupling: How and Why Relationships Come Apart.* New York: Random House, 1990. Through extensive research and dozens of case histories, Vaughan explains the underlying patterns beneath disintegrating relationships. She takes us through the process of uncoupling, from the initial secret awareness of discomfort and the display of discontent through the breakdown of cover-up, trying to patch things up, and going on. A thorough, well-documented treatment with numerous examples.

PART

III

COMMUNICATING IN GROUPS

KEY TERMS

brainstorming

cohesiveness

commitment

consensus

groupthink

norms

questions of fact

questions of policy

questions of value

roles

rules

small groups

Small Groups: Characteristics

CHAPTER OBJECTIVES

After reading this chapter, you should be able to:

1 Describe the situations in which group decision making is superior to individual decision making.

2 List the characteristics of a small group.

3 Tell the difference between norms, rules, and roles.

4 Distinguish between different types of groups.

5 Explain how the physical setting can help a group to function better.

6 Explain how a group becomes cohesive.

7 List and explain the steps in group problem solving.

n issue of a city newspaper announces the following coming events:

■ **WORK FOR HUMAN RIGHTS.** Attend an Amnesty International meeting. March 11, 7 P.M., at St. Paul's Church.

■ **ENVIRONMENTAL ACTION GROUP.** Another day went by, and did you think of the beauty of our planet? Or that every day that very beauty is slipping away? What will our children have to look forward to? Please take action. Come to a meeting. No strings attached. Meet our new senator; plan for Earth Week; showing of *Medicine Man* and *Trip to Wintergarden and the Rainforest!* All welcome. March 11, 9 P.M., Room 257 Memorial Hall.

■ **THE EXCHANGE,** a support group for women in business, will meet at 6 P.M., Tuesday, March 15, at the Women's Business Development Center.

A campus paper announces upcoming events:

■ **WOMEN IN COMMUNICATIONS.** Meeting tonight at 7:30 in 106 Business Administration Building. Rita Sobol will discuss newspaper editing.

■ **STUDENT ORGANIZATION FOR LEADERSHIP DEVELOPMENT.** Leaders of the future are the ones who take the time to learn today. Leaders lead. Learn to become a leader. S.O.L.D. meets in Room 405 Student Services Building at 7 P.M. tonight. We're S.O.L.D. on leadership.

If people from another planet were to land on U.S. soil and pick up a newspaper, they might think that Americans spend most of their time in meetings. They wouldn't be far from wrong. All over town and all over campus people are meeting for business, political, educational, religious, social, and personal reasons. Regardless of the purpose of these meetings, they have something in common. They all bring together **small groups**—gatherings of three to thirteen members who meet to do a job or solve a problem.

Small groups are essential in helping society function efficiently, and many of us spend several hours each week communicating in such groups. We might take part in a seminar discussion, talk with a group of coworkers about improving job conditions, or discuss with family members how to make the household run more efficiently. Many of us belong to service or professional groups. Many of these groups are involved both with completing tasks and with social life.

Whatever groups we belong to, we want them to function efficiently. But participation should also be pleasurable; we want to meet, get on with the job, and then spend some time socializing with other group members.

This chapter and the next one discuss how groups work. In this chapter, we note the characteristics of small groups and how such groups go about solving a problem.[1] In Chapter 9, we concentrate on how to effectively lead or participate in a group.

 ## WHY DISCUSS?

When a group has a job to do, its main form of communication is discussion. Group members meet to exchange information and ideas in an effort to better understand a particular issue or situation. The executive council of the Student Activities Organization discusses how many major activities it wants to sponsor for the forthcoming academic year. The tenants' committee discusses ways of improving the apartment complex; the social committee discusses security arrangements for an upcoming concert.

Not all people like discussion. Many find it time-consuming and boring. What, then, is the value of discussion?

In a democratic society, one of the first assumptions is that no one person will make the decisions for everyone. Discussion is a way for everyone to participate and be heard. It is a forum where ideas are proposed and then modified in response to group feedback.

Group decision making is often superior to individual decision making. Those who study small groups have found that people who work in groups accomplish more than people who work alone.[2] Other research has found that students learn better in classroom discussion groups. When exam time comes, they will do better and find the task more enjoyable if they join a study group.

Often a group can do a job more efficiently than an individual. The study group is a good example: rather than outlining every chapter, each member of the group can outline one chapter and share it with other members. Or take the case of the executive council of the Student Activities Organization discussing how many major activities to sponsor for the forthcoming year. This is clearly a group project; no individual can do the job as well. First, the group talks about how many activities per year the group has sponsored in the past and how popular the activities were. The group's historian provides this information. The group's treasurer offers a report on how much money the group currently has and how much the activities are likely to generate. The group's social chairperson discusses a list of possible activities. If preparation for this discussion were left to one individual, it would be an overwhelming job.

If you have worked in a group, you probably have discovered that motivation increases when everyone works together.[3] If five roommates decide to redecorate their apartment, it is much more fun if everyone pitches in and helps. Also, the five roommates are likely to come up with more ideas about how to do things than if only one person takes on the project. People are also likely to be more motivated when others are depending on them.[4] If one roommate, for example, has to strip the windowsills before the others can paint, he or she is likely to get the job done so that the others can go ahead with what they have to do.

When people work in groups, they have opportunities to ask questions when an idea or issue is not clear. In addition to learning faster, group members are able to absorb more information.[5] Not only does more information become available, but group members can help decide which information is important.

We can see how this works in a practical situation. Let's say that the state has a new recycling law that says all individuals and organizations must recycle aluminum, glass, and paper. Your university appoints ten people to a group to work out the details of how this will be done. The group is made up of hall directors, students, faculty, and the buildings and grounds staff. When the group meets, its members agree that recycling will work best if people on campus don't have to expend very much effort. They decide that the most effective way to organize recycling is to provide places on every floor of every campus building where people can put things for recycling. Because nobody knows how many collection areas this will require, the group members decide to split up. Faculty will scout the floors and best collection sites in all the classroom buildings, the hall directors will look at the dorms, and the students will check out all the remaining buildings. The staff from buildings and grounds is assigned to find a central location for the collection of all recycled materials. Because the members of the committee split up the jobs, no one is responsible for too much work. When they meet again, they will have enough information for the group to work toward the next phase.

When you see how effectively a group can solve a problem, it's no surprise that groups are so important. In one study of 200 top- and mid-level managers in eight different organizations, the researchers found that senior managers spent an average of 23 hours a week in meetings and mid-level managers 11 hours.[6] If a quarter to a half of each work week is devoted to meetings, it's important that we all learn how to work in groups.

CHARACTERISTICS OF SMALL GROUPS

All small groups have common characteristics. They reflect the culture in which they occur; they have norms—expectations that group members have of how other members will behave; they have rules—formal and structured directions for behavior.

Cultural Values

When Americans think they should solve a problem at work or in the community, their first instinct is to form a group. Even President Clinton's operational style places an emphasis on teamwork and deliberation with his tendency to form task forces and committees. Once the group begins to function, everyone is more or less equal. If someone wants to talk, he or she is given a chance. If all in the group cannot agree on a solution, then the group takes a vote and the majority will decide.

This kind of group-forming and group-operating behavior seems so natural that we don't think twice about it: it is part of our culture. We should not assume, however, that other cultures work the same way. When one of our authors asked a Polish friend why the Poles didn't organize child-care cooperatives, her friend replied, "In Poland, we never work in groups."

Most societies have some dominant kind of problem-solving mechanism, but it may differ greatly from culture to culture. In many countries men are much more likely than women to make decisions about workplace and community issues. In many of these same countries, only elder members of the group can participate in decision making.

Seventy percent of the world lives in a collectivist society—a society whose loyalties are to the family or, more broadly, to the clan, the tribe, or the caste.[7] In these groups problem solving and decision making are most likely to occur within the family or the clan. If a group were formed that included members from different clans or families, the way the participants worked to solve a problem would depend on how they perceived the solution would affect their own families or clans.

Americans who join a group in another country cannot assume that the group will function in the same way that an American group does. In a campus setting, if American students work with international students, they should also be sensitive to the different ways the group work may be perceived. In some cases it might be appropriate to explain how American groups work.

Group Norms

Norms are the expectations group members have of how other members will behave, think, and participate. These norms are informal—they are not written down. Members assume that others understand the norms and will follow them.

A daily staff meeting of the editors of a college newspaper shows how norms operate. All the editors (associate, managing, and city editors, as well as editors of the opinion, campus, and sports sections) look to the editor in chief not only to set the agenda for the meeting but to begin it, to recognize participants, and to maintain control throughout the meeting. The editor in chief assumes that all editors will attend each meeting, be on time, bring the necessary information that pertains to their areas, and generally act in a polite and responsible manner. In other words, they will follow the norms of behavior for their daily staff meeting. The editor's manner and demeanor sets the tone for all meetings.

In familiar settings, we take group norms for granted. But if we join a group where the norms are not so obvious, we might just sit back and listen until we figure out what the group norms are. For example, a new person appointed to a board of directors will probably try to get a sense of how the group operates before he participates.

CONSIDER THIS

What **roles** does gender play in group communication? Three writers on gender claim that women in mixed groups are interrupted, ignored, or circumvented. When they try to talk to male group members, they receive little serious attention. If women want to be heard, they have to work much harder than men.

Source: Nancy Hoar, "Genderlect, Powerlect, and Politeness," in Linda A. M. Perry, Lynn H. Turner, and Helen M. Sterk (Eds.), *Constructing and Reconstructing Gender: The Links Among Communication, Language, and Gender* (Albany: State University of New York Press, 1992), pp. 127–161.

QUESTIONS

1. As a group participant in groups that include men and women, what can *you* do to avoid these situations?

2. What strategies can women use to get serious attention in the group?

3. What other effects might occur in groups because of gender differences? Can these be avoided?

Norms are important because they give a group some structure. If members know how to behave, the group will function more efficiently. Also, outsiders can look at the group's norms to see whether they want to join the group. If, for example, you feel comfortable only in informal settings, you will probably not want to join a group that has numerous rituals and ceremonies.

Group norms also govern how participants communicate with each other. This may be especially true in male-female interactions. It is important that group members be treated equally and that all members are given sufficient consideration and concern by all others. Any differences in the way people are treated should be based on their needs or roles in the group and not on gender. See the "Consider This" box for a discussion of the influence of gender on group communication.

Group Rules

Unlike norms, **rules** are formal and structured directions for behavior. Rules may dictate what jobs group members should do, how meetings should be conducted, how motions should be introduced, and so on. The rules help a meeting to progress and ensure that everyone can be heard but no one person will monopolize the floor. Sometimes, when order and decorum are especially important, a group will appoint a *parliamentarian* to see that the rules are properly interpreted and followed.

Not all groups have rules. Informal groups such as a book club have norms such as meeting at different homes, providing food, and being prepared to discuss a particular book. A community group such as the Junior League, on the other hand, has rules, bylaws, voting, minutes to approve, and even penalties for not attending regularly. These distinctions between groups are likely to be based on informality and formality or perhaps on size. Formal and large groups generally have both norms and rules. Small and informal groups usually have norms but few rules.

DIFFERENT TYPES OF GROUPS

From your own experience, you can probably distinguish several different kinds of groups. For example, you are probably a member of informal social groups. When you were young, you went to school with members of a social group of friends, you met and socialized with friends at work, and you frequently saw friends from church. All these were social groups; all had norms associated with belonging, but there were few, if any, rules. These are informal groups.

Many groups are task-oriented—that is, they serve to get something specific accomplished. Task-oriented groups often have problem-solving or decision-making goals. Problem solving involves using some specific procedure—like the one we discuss later in this chapter—to resolve the difficulty (problem) under consideration. Decision making, of course, occurs within the process of problem solving whenever alternatives emerge and

What norms and rules unite this group?

choices must be made. When a group is designated a "decision-making group," its task is recommending action—making clear choices among several possibilities.

A task-oriented problem-solving group in the workplace might be designated to solving the problem that smokers present. That is, what should be done to protect nonsmokers and yet protect the rights of smokers as well? A task-oriented decision-making group might be charged with presenting a variety of possible alternatives to management, yet this group does not solve the problem. That is left to management.

Many decision-making groups operate in our society. Juries are one example. Groups can be delegated to decide who is to receive an award, or who might be a guest speaker, or what kind of activities the group might like to support. A classroom professor experienced the operation of a decision-making group when students in one class met and recommended to him that the date of an examination be changed from the day after homecoming weekend to any of three possibilities the group presented. He presented the three alternatives to the class, and a vote determined the new date.

There is another important kind of group meeting as well. The information-sharing group can be found in corporations, schools, churches, families, and service clubs and in social fraternities and sororities and among faculty in departments on campus. Whenever people meet to be informed and to inform others, to express themselves and to listen to others, to get or give assistance, to clarify or hear clarification of goals, or to establish or maintain working relationships, information sharing becomes the purpose. Such groups are necessary when people plan to do business together over a long period.

In all groups, whether focused on a task or information sharing, there is a social dimension as well. Task functions or information-sharing functions are closely interrelated with social dimensions. The degree to which members concern themselves with the task or with information sharing affects the social dimension. The degree to which members show concern for relationships within the group has a direct effect on task accomplishment or information sharing as well. In some faculty meetings, department members converse, tell jokes, and communicate informally before the formal agenda is begun. This behavior establishes an effective social climate before the information sharing takes place.

SMALL-GROUP EFFECTIVENESS

Why do some groups succeed and others fail? Why do some come up with creative solutions for problems while others fall short? Why do some groups have members who get along and other groups have members who are always fighting?

Research shows that effective small groups have certain common characteristics: they have a sense of solidarity, they are able to focus on their task, and they have a task that is appropriate for their particular group.[8]

Solidarity can come from sharing common interests (baseball trivia, exercising), from knowing each other at work, or from sharing some social time together before and after group meetings.

Focus comes from a leader or member who tries to keep the group directed toward its subject. This is the person who says, "That's an interesting point, but our problem is to. . . ."

Appropriateness occurs when a group and its task are well matched. For example, a student group cannot solve the problem of a deficit in the university budget. However, it might be able to solve a problem like screening strangers who enter dormitories or finding a better way to publicize elections for student senators.

In addition to having solidarity, focus, and task appropriateness, a truly effective group must be of a workable size, must meet in appropriate surroundings with suitable seating arrangements, and must inspire its members to feel cohesiveness and commitment.

Workable Size

A group works best when all its members can communicate and interact with one another. For a group to be effective, it should have anywhere from three to thirteen members. Research indicates that an ideal size for a group is five members.[9] If a group consists of too many members, it cannot work effectively to solve problems or do the job at hand. In such cases, it should be broken up into smaller groups—each with a job to do. The student government, for example, is usually broken down into committees: the Social Committee, the Food Advisory Committee, the Constitutional Revision Committee, and so on. The committees then study the issues and make recommendations to the larger body, the student government.

A group may be too large if all members do not have an opportunity to speak or if all members do not participate in group decisions or actions. When this occurs, it is time to break the group into still smaller units. With the student Social Committee, for example, some members could check out the availability of certain musical groups, while other members could conduct a poll to see which musicians the students would like to have on campus.

Groups can also be too small. When there is a lot of information to gather or when the task requires specialized skill or knowledge from its members, it is important to have enough members to do the job.

For example, if a department is all computerized, it may be faced with many decisions. Some people might be assigned to find the best kind of computer software—or the best available software for updating what the department already has. Then the question may be how to get everyone to use the system or to check their E-mail. Others might be assigned to establish computerized networks with other departments or programs on campus, or how to develop instructions for getting on electronic bulletin boards. If there are enough members to investigate each of these areas, no single person will have too much to do.

An Appropriate Meeting Place

The place where a group meets will often influence the general atmosphere of the meeting. A group that meets in a classroom or a conference room will probably be more formal than a group that meets in someone's room or apartment.

The meeting place can be chosen on the basis of who the group members are and what they want to accomplish. Members who know each other well might want to meet in someone's home; when members do not know each other well or if the group wants to continue to attract new participants, it would be better off meeting in a public place.

Sometimes the meeting place will be determined by what the group wants to accomplish. The parents' group seeking citywide support for a tax increase in order to add new classrooms to the high school might meet in the high school cafeteria. Travel Abroad, a group of interested citizens who enjoy sharing slides and talks about their travels, might gather in the meeting room of the local public library.

Suitable Seating Arrangements

Seating of group members should not be left to chance, with each member choosing a chair. Donald C. Stone, a professor of public service, believes that seating is important if people are going to pay attention at meetings.[10] For small groups, Stone recommends seating people where they can all see one another's faces. A circular table would serve this function, as would classroom desks or small tables placed in a circle. For larger groups, Stone recommends a U-shaped arrangement of tables. In this arrangement people should sit only on the *outside* of the U. Otherwise, they will have their backs to one another.

Stone also makes recommendations about chairs. The perfect chair, he says, is one that has a little padding on the seat. If the chairs have hard seats, people will not be comfortable in them for very long; if they're too soft, group members might be tempted to doze off.

Cohesiveness and Commitment

As a positive force, **cohesiveness** is the feeling of attraction that group members have toward one another.[11] It is the group's ability to stick together, to work together as a group, and to help one another as group members. **Commitment** is the willingness of members to work together to complete the group's task. When members are committed, the group is likely to be cohesive. There are few more powerful and satisfactory feelings than the feelings of belonging to a group and of being loyal to that group.

Although cohesiveness is often a matter of group chemistry, an effective group leader can help cohesiveness to develop when the group meets the first few times. A good leader will make certain that all members are introduced and, if appropriate, are given a chance to say something about themselves. Cohesiveness will also be helped if members have a chance to do a little socializing before and after the meeting. Finally, during the discussion, a good leader will try to draw out the quieter members. The more everyone participates, the better the chance for group unity to develop.

Groupthink

Social psychologist Irving Janis, having made a careful study of groups, found that cohesive groups can become victims of **groupthink**, a group dysfunction in which the preservation of harmony becomes more important than the critical examination of ideas.[12] Janis's point was simply that groups can bring out the worst as well as the best in people.[13] Because it can limit group effectiveness, group members need to be sensitive to its operation.

Cohesive groups often show signs of unity. For example, the campus radio station staff wears T-shirts with the station logo. Staff members show mutual support by filling in for each other on broadcasting shifts, and they help newcomers learn their jobs. Many of the group members form lasting friendships and spend free time together.

Although our society depends on groups to make decisions, and we spend more and more time in groups, not all group decisions are superior.

What are some of the advantages of working in a group?

TRY THIS

Because groupthink can bring out the worst in groups, see if you can identify the following problem areas in a policy- or decision-making group of which you are a member:

■ Check to see whether group members are overly concerned about getting along and preserving group harmony. These conditions may foster groupthink.

■ Ask whether group members think it is their responsibility to make a decision or to set a policy. Do they think they will be harmed or injured in any way by making the decision? These are further conditions that are likely to foster groupthink.

■ Check to see if group members are absolutely certain everyone agrees. Do they know for sure that everyone goes along with the idea? If they haven't actually checked, their assumptions may be wrong.

Source: R. J. Welch Cline, "Detecting Groupthink: Methods for Observing the Illusion of Unanimity," *Communication Quarterly* 38 (1990): 112–126.

That is, group decisions can be just or unjust, fair or discriminatory, sensitive or insensitive to the needs of others; they can be responsible or irresponsible, respectful of or in violation of people's rights. In a dormitory, for example, students on one floor decided unanimously to designate a lounge area as a permanent "No-Talk Study Area" where students could go at any time if they needed total quiet for study. When the ruling was put into effect, students found they had eliminated the meeting place of a number of important campus groups that could find no other convenient place to meet.

Two students on the dorm floor already knew about the groups that met in the lounge. Because of the high cohesiveness, solidarity, and loyalty of the deciding group, however, these students chose not to speak up. Their decision not to speak up is a direct result of groupthink.

The essential idea about groupthink is that it helps us understand why some groups do not exhibit the kind of critical thinking essential to ethical and responsible problem solving and decision making. And it should be clear, too, that groupthink can occur in groups of all kinds. Although our example is a dormitory group, such actions can occur in clubs, committees, boards, teams, or work units. Groupthink is sometimes hard to detect, but detection is worth the effort. When you are part of a group, you want that group to be the best. Groupthink can limit a group's best efforts.

Most groups that work efficiently use some kind of process to discuss a problem. Many procedures work equally well: what is important is that the steps help the group to focus on the problem. Many groups use a sequence of steps that is similar to the one you see in Figure 8-1. Let's look at each of these steps in some detail.

Choosing a Topic

If you are in a class, you may be required to pick a topic your group can discuss. How do you choose a topic? How do you find a subject that all group members will find interesting enough to work on?

Your first approach might be to look at your own school. Are there any problems or improvements your group might like to tackle? How's the housing? Does registration run smoothly? Does the bookstore have fair prices? Is the library open at convenient times? Any of these questions might lead to an interesting discussion.

Take a look at the community. Are there any problems there? How do students get along with the townspeople? Are students good neighbors? Do the banks cash out-of-town checks without adding a service charge? Do the local merchants realize how important students are to the economy of the town? Are there issues in the city council or county commissioners' office that might affect the school?

If your group is interested in attacking a broader social issue, the supply is almost limitless. World peace, foreign policy at the end of the cold war, abortion, and attacking the federal deficit are all issues that are hotly debated and will continue to be debated in the future. Discussing one of these topics in your group might be a good way for everyone to become informed about an important issue.

When a group cannot find a topic that all members consider interesting, it should try brainstorming. In **brainstorming** all members of the group

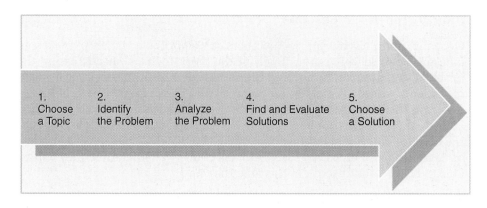

1.
Choose
a Topic

2.
Identify
the Problem

3.
Analyze
the Problem

4.
Find and Evaluate
Solutions

5.
Choose
a Solution

FIGURE 8-1
**Solving a
Problem**

**What are the
advantages and
disadvantages of
democratic
decision making
in a group?**

throw out ideas—however far out they might seem. The goal of brainstorming is for the group to be as creative as possible. No one should make judgments about the ideas during the brainstorming session. If members fear that their ideas might be condemned, they will be less willing to share some of their wilder thoughts.

Once the group runs out of ideas, it's time to stop brainstorming and take a look at the topics that were generated. Sometimes one idea is so good that everyone says, "That's it." More commonly, however, the group will have to evaluate the ideas. Each topic should be assessed in terms of whether all members are willing to work on it and whether it can be narrowed enough to permit comprehensive research. For example, taking on the problems of the country's landfills (garbage dumps) is too big a job. However, the group might be able to research and discuss the problems with the local landfill.

Identifying the Problem

Once the group has a topic, its members can work toward identifying a specific problem. At this point, much of the work focuses on narrowing the problem so that it can be covered thoroughly. For example, let's say a group of students wants to work on reducing crime. They narrow the problem to crime on their campus. They narrow it even further to rape, and they then identify the specific problem: getting the campus administration to accept the need for additional lighting on campus. Notice that through this process of narrowing and focusing, the group has come up with a topic they will be able to handle and discuss in the time they have.

What kind of procedures do groups follow in problem solving or decision making? One method is for a leader to impose a process on members and then give them negative reinforcement if they deviate. For example, one leader in a group said she operates by majority rule—if more than half of the members agree, the proposal becomes group policy. One aggressive member who did not agree to this not only met with disapproval but was asked to leave.

A second method is tradition. Groups follow rules and procedures because they are habitual. For example, in one group members always take a vote to confirm important decisions. Why? Because that is the way it has always been done.

The third and most important kind of process is equality of members. Anyone can lead the group when he or she thinks it appropriate; all members have important information, equal status, and the opportunity to influence and control decisions.

Source: Marshall Scott Poole, "Group Communication and the Structuring Process," in Robert S. Cathcart and Larry A. Samovar, *Small Group Communication: A Reader*, 6th ed. (Dubuque, IA: Brown, 1992), pp. 147–164.

QUESTIONS

1. Think of a group to which you belong. How are procedures in the group determined?

2. Is this system of selecting procedures effective for this group? Would a different system for selecting procedures work better for this group?

3. How might a system for selecting procedures be changed?

The most important thing the group can do in this stage is to identify a problem that is manageable. One of the biggest mistakes groups make is choosing a problem that is so broad that it cannot be adequately covered.

Analyzing the Problem

THE FIRST QUESTIONS

Groups can take several approaches to analyzing problems. Sometimes it is useful to know what has caused the problem; other times it's enough to acknowledge that the problem exists. For example, a group that wanted to raise student awareness about donating blood did not need to explore why the American Red Cross needs blood. The problem was that students were not donating blood. Another group became interested in establishing a pregnancy crisis center because several local newspaper articles indicated that pregnant students had nowhere on campus to turn for assistance. This group, too, acknowledged that a problem existed.

Before making a final choice of topics, a group might want to find out how extensive the problem is and how many people are affected by it. For instance, citizens in one community wanted to establish an exchange of guns for toys. However, a neighborhood survey discovered that few people owned guns. In checking with the local police, the citizens discovered that few gun-related deaths occurred in their community. The group discovered that guns affected so few people in their area that they did not pursue their plan.

The group should also ask whether anyone else is trying to solve the problem now or has tried to solve it in the past. For example, a group that wants to solve the problem of poor student preparation for college should check with local school administrators to see if someone has been, is, or will be working on this problem—as well as to learn whether or not administrators consider it a problem. It could be that the group can add to the work that other people have already done or are in the process of doing.

Once the group has gone through this initial analysis, it should decide whether to proceed or to find a new topic. If it decides to proceed, it's ready to begin defining terms.

DEFINING TERMS

The group should define any terms related to its problem that might be vague or ambiguous. For example, a classroom group decided that the campus mailroom took too long to deliver mail. Since individual members in the group defined *too long* in various ways, the group had to arrive at a precise meaning for the term. After some discussion they agreed that *too long* was anything over 24 hours. A community group that wanted to start a program to teach illiterate persons how to read and write first had to define *illiterate*. Did it apply only to people who could not read or write? What about a person who could do some reading and writing but not enough to function in ordinary society? From a practical point of view, was this person also illiterate?

SEEKING OUT INFORMATION

To understand a problem fully, a group will need to seek outside information. The kind of information will vary depending on the problem or task. To get information, individual members may each investigate a different aspect of the problem. First they might decide to interview people who have had experience with the problem. For example, if they were trying to find out why library hours had been cut, one group member could interview the

TRY THIS

Here is a list of possible discussion topics. Which words and phrases need defining?

1. Should parents who send their children to private schools receive tuition tax credits?

2. Should welfare mothers receive federal money for abortions?

3. Should the government limit the availability of guns?

4. Should the government prohibit broadcasters from showing violent programs on television?

5. Should government control violent videogames?

6. Should public money be used for artworks considered obscene or blasphemous?

director of the library and others could interview students or faculty to see if they were affected by the reduced hours.

Many subjects require research that extends beyond personal experience. A group that is discussing the problem of harmful household products being dumped in landfills would find it useful to interview an expert, such as a chemistry professor. Groups can also find background information on their subjects in the library. Chapter 11 has many suggestions on library research.

A group will work more efficiently if every member prepares for each meeting. Then when the group meets, all members will be ready for discussion and able to move on to the next task.

DECIDING ON THE WORDING OF THE FINAL QUESTION

Once the problem is analyzed, the next step is to phrase it as a question. A well-worded question should summarize the group's problem; it should be simply and clearly worded; it should focus on a single central idea. It should use neutral terminology and present a specific problem for the group to solve. Depending on the topic, it should take the form of a question of fact, a question of value, or a question of policy.

Questions of fact deal with what is true and what is false. Examples of these questions might be: How can we protect the drinking water supplies of our largest cities? In what ways can we reduce gun-related deaths in our nation? Does sexism affect our lives? What are note-taking skills?

Questions of value are questions of whether something is good or bad, desirable or undesirable: Is recycling a beneficial activity? To what extent is the violence depicted on television and in videogames harmful to people in our society? Is fraternity or sorority membership worthwhile?

Questions of policy are about actions that might be taken in the future. Such questions are often asked in institutional settings, such as schools, businesses, or organizations, and they usually include the word *should:* Should colleges increase the number of required courses? To what extent should business and industry assume the responsibility for cleaning up the environment? Should all students be required to have real-world work experience as part of their college education? Should businesses be required to hire more minority workers?

Note that many questions of policy also involve fact and value. For example, "Should students be required to take a course in AIDS education?" is a question of policy, but it also has questions of fact and value built in. The questions of fact might include: Is there enough information on AIDS to justify a course? Can AIDS awareness be taught? Can the institution handle the number of students who would take a required course? Would such a course make a difference? The questions of value might include: Is teaching AIDS awareness beneficial and important?

When a group is engaged in fact-finding, it is most likely to use questions of fact. If some students, for example, are curious about how much money is spent on college athletics, some of their fact-finding questions might be: What percentage of the student activity fee is spent on athletics? What percentage of the total college budget is spent on athletics? What percentage of salaries paid at the college goes to coaches? These and other fact-finding questions will help them to gather information about how much money is budgeted for athletics.

When a group is going to make recommendations, it will use questions of value or questions of policy. A group considering the parking problem on campus might ask: Should first-year students be permitted to bring cars on campus? Should faculty and staff be given the first choice of parking spots? Should everyone be required to pay for parking stickers? Research into these questions will help the group move to the point where it can make recommendations.

Finding and Evaluating Solutions

Most problems do not have a single easy solution. Sometimes there are a number of alternatives, and the way a group looks at these alternatives is an important factor in the group's effectiveness. Not only must a group suggest alternatives that are realistic and acceptable, but it must also look at both the negative and the positive consequences of all the alternatives.

Other times a group has difficulty finding appropriate solutions. If members cannot come up with good solutions when they work together, they may find it helpful to work separately for a while, with each member coming up with two or three solutions to present at the next meeting. Some research has shown that when people work alone, they often come up with more innovative ideas than they would in a group.[14]

Sometimes a group can think of several solutions, but some will have to be discarded because they are impractical. In a group that wanted to teach adults to read and write, for example, someone suggested that unemployed elementary school teachers should be hired to teach illiterate adults. Although everyone agreed this was a good idea, no one could find a way to get the money to pay the teachers.

To see if their solutions are practical, the group should list each one along with its advantages and disadvantages. Some of the questions a group can ask about proposed solutions include: Will the solution solve the problem? Is it practical? Is permission necessary to put the solution into effect? Who will implement the solution? How much money will it cost? How much time will it take? If a solution doesn't pass such scrutiny, the group will have to keep working until it finds one that does.

To see if decisions are practical, the group should consider the same types of questions raised regarding solutions. Solutions and decisions are similar because they are both group products or outcomes. Some questions regarding a group's decisions might be: What are their relative merits and demerits? What is the best decision the group can support? How will the group's decision be put into effect? To what extent does it satisfy the group's criteria for an effective decision? How will the effectiveness of the decision, once put into effect, be measured?

Ideally the group should work toward **consensus**—the point at which all group members agree. This must be done, of course, while balancing concerns regarding groupthink—defined previously as a group dysfunction in which the preservation of harmony becomes more important than the critical examination of ideas. If gaining consensus is impossible, group members may have to choose their solutions by putting ideas to a vote, with the majority determining the outcome. Some groups decide on a solution too quickly because they want to get the task done. This is a mistake: a group is only as good as its solution.[15]

 ## SUMMARY

A small group is made up of people who get together to solve a problem. Groups can often solve problems better than individuals because they generate more ideas and the work can be divided among the members.

Small groups have norms, rules, and roles, and they vary from one culture to another. Small groups are often more characteristic of a democracy than of other forms of government.

For a small group to be effective, it must have a common goal, a workable size (usually from three to thirteen members), an appropriate meeting place, and suitable seating arrangements. Groups that work effectively are cohesive. However, when group members start to think too much alike, there is a danger of groupthink.

Groups that meet together to solve problems should use a problem-solving sequence to structure their work. A common sequence is that the group chooses a topic, identifies the problem, analyzes the problem, finds and evaluates solutions, and chooses the best solution.

■ NOTES

[1] For a thorough overview of small-group communication, see Steven A. Beebe and John T. Masterson, *Communicating in Small Groups: Principles and Practices*, 4th ed. (New York: HarperCollins, 1994); John K. Brilhart and Gloria J. Galanes, *Effective Group Discussion*, 7th ed. (Dubuque, IA: Wm. C. Brown, 1992); Donald G. Ellis and B. Aubrey Fisher, *Small Group Decision Making: Communication and the Group Process*, 4th ed. (New York: McGraw-Hill, 1994); Charles Pavitt and Ellen Curtis, *Small Group Discussion: A Theoretical Approach*, 2d ed. (Scottsdale, AZ: Gorsuch Scarisbrick, 1994); Gerald L. Wilson and Michael S. Hanna, *Groups in Context: Leadership and Participation in Small Groups*, 3d ed. (New York: McGraw-Hill, 1993).

[2] John E. Baird, Jr., and Stanford B. Weinberg, *Communication: The Essence of Group Synergy* (Dubuque, IA: Wm. C. Brown, 1977), p. 126.

[3] Elizabeth W. Flynn and John F. LaFaso, *Group Discussion as a Learning Process* (New York: Paulist Press, 1972), pp. 102–103.

[4] Baird and Weinberg, *Communication*, p. 125.

[5] R. Victor Harnack, Thorrel B. Fest, and Barbara Schindler Jones, *Group Discussion: Theory and Technique*, 2d ed. (Englewood Cliffs, NJ: Prentice-Hall, 1977), p. 14.

[6] Daniel Goleman, "The Group and the Self: New Focus on a Cultural Rift," *The New York Times*, December 25, 1990, pp. 37, 41k.

[7] Ibid.

[8] Ibid.

[9] H. A. Thelen, "Group Dynamics in Instruction: Principle of Least Group Size," *School Review*, 57 (March 1979): 142. Also see F. F. Stephen and E. G. Mishler, "The Distribution of Participation in Small Groups: An Exponential Approximation," *American Sociological Review*, 17 (1952): 598–608, in *Small Groups: Studies in Social Interaction*, ed. A. P. Hare, E. F. Borgatta, and R. F. Bales (New York: Knopf, 1965), pp. 358–369.

[10] Bill Lawren, "Seating for Success," *Psychology Today* (September 1989): 16–20.

[11] Steven A. Beebe and John T. Masterson, *Communicating in Small Groups: Principles and Practices*, 4th ed. (New York: HarperCollins, 1994), p. 113.

[12] I. L. Janis, *Victims of Groupthink* (Boston: Houghton Mifflin, 1972), p. 9.

[13] Ibid., p. 3.

[14] Goleman, "The Group and the Self: New Focus on a Cultural Rift," pp. 37, 41.

[15] R. J. Welch Cline, "Detecting Groupthink: Methods for Observing the Illusion of Unanimity," *Communication Quarterly*, 38 (1990): 112–126.

■ FURTHER READINGS

BEEBE, STEVEN A., AND JOHN T. MASTERSON. *Communicating in Small Groups: Principles and Practices*, 4th ed. New York: HarperCollins, 1994.   This well-written, well-documented, illustrated textbook covers the essentials of small-group processes and problem solving. The text includes chapters on theory, group formation, relating in groups, group climate, leadership, and problem solving.

BRILHART, JOHN K., AND GLORIA J. GALANES. *Effective Group Discussion*, 7th ed. Dubuque, IA: Brown, 1992. An excellent, comprehensive textbook on small groups and group discussion. The text contains a balance between empirically grounded theories of the dynamics of small-group communication and specific practical procedures and techniques for improving the functioning of groups. Written for the beginning student.

COREY, MARIANNE SCHNEIDER, AND GERALD COREY. *Groups: Process and Practice*, 4th ed. Pacific Grove, CA: Brooks/Cole, 1992. Marianne is a licensed marriage and family therapist; Gerald is a licensed psychologist. In this 439-page book, the authors use examples, guidelines, basic issues, and key concepts to explain the "how to" and "why" of group process and practice. Unique are the individual chapters on groups for children, adolescents, adults, and the elderly. A strong research base is provided.

ELLIS, DONALD G., AND B. AUBREY FISHER. *Small Group Decision Making: Communication and the Group Process*. New York: McGraw-Hill, 1994. The value of this book is its overriding emphasis and focus on communication as *the* organizing element in groups. The authors establish a framework; describe the communication process; and then discuss structural elements, communication, behavioral standards, decision making, leadership, conflict, and improving effectiveness. A solid research-based book.

JANIS, IRVING LESTER. *Groupthink: Psychological Studies of Policy Decisions and Fiascoes*. Boston: Houghton Mifflin, 1983. Although Janis focuses on foreign relations, his thesis concerns the psychological effects that groups have on individual and group thinking. Numerous case studies are provided. This is an insightful volume full of discussion applications.

JOHNSON, DAVID W., AND FRANK P. JOHNSON. *Joining Together: Group Theory and Group Skills*, 4th ed. Englewood Cliffs, NJ: Prentice-Hall, 1993. This paperback provides the theory and experiences necessary to develop an understanding of group processes and effective group skills. The authors stress an experiential approach to learning by including brief, clear theoretical explanations followed by exercises—more than eighty that supplement and illustrate the ideas discussed.

PAVITT, CHARLES, AND ELLEN CURTIS. *Small Group Discussion: A Theoretical Approach*, 2d ed. Scottsdale, AZ: Gorsuch Scarisbrick, 1994. The authors' goal is to have students develop their own natural theories about group discussion. The greater students' understanding of theory, the more options they will have when they choose how to act in groups. Thus, the authors cover topics central to an understanding of decision-making discussions in small groups, but they purposely downplay the importance of group discussion skills training.

ROTHWELL, J. DAN. *In Mixed Company: Small Group Communication*. Fort Worth: Harcourt Brace Jovanovich, 1992. Rothwell uses extensive research and a unifying theme of communication competence in this innovative, user-friendly textbook. He treats themes such as power, communication competence, gender and ethnicity, conflict, and decision making.

TUBBS, STEWART L. *A Systems Approach to Small Group Interaction*, 4th ed. New York: McGraw-Hill, 1992. Tubbs emphasizes traditional problem-solving methods as well as interpersonal relations and personal growth. As the pioneer of the systems approach in groups textbooks, this book is widely known and respected for its combination of theory and research blended effectively with skill development through cases and readings.

WILSON, GERALD L., AND MICHAEL S. HANNA. *Groups in Context*, 3d ed. New York: McGraw-Hill, 1993. The authors provide a comprehensive and up-to-date introduction to group discussion. They effectively combine theory, research, and practical guidelines; however, the unique perspective of this volume is the application of group discussion to a wide variety of career, community, and social contexts. A useful textbook.

Roles and Responsibilities: Leading, Managing, and Participating in Conflict

CHAPTER OBJECTIVES

After reading this chapter you should be able to:

1 Define the ways in which a leader can influence followers.

2 Tell what is meant by an interactionist approach to leadership.

3 Describe the four basic responsibilities of all group members.

4 Distinguish between democratic, authoritarian, and laissez-faire leaders.

5 List the procedures that should be established at the beginning of a group meeting.

6 Explain how a leader can help a group to progress.

7 Distinguish between task, maintenance, and negative roles, and give examples of each.

8 Explain how conflict can have some value for a group.

9 Explain the ways in which conflict can be managed in a group.

ost Americans spend a good deal of time in meetings. A faculty member at your school might go to four or five meetings a week. The end of the work day does not mean the meetings are over. If you are on the board of such community groups as the YMCA, the literacy council, or the public library, you can count on filling after-work hours with even more meetings.

Yet if you were to ask people what they dislike most about their jobs or community activities, they would probably mention the number and quality of the meetings. William N. Yeomans compiled a list of what people dislike about meetings[1] that probably reflects some of your own feelings:

- People don't know why the meeting was called.

- No one is clear about what is to be accomplished.

- There is no agenda or timetable.

- Meetings run too long.

- Meetings are boring.

- People tell "war stories."

- There are too many items to be covered.

- No one wants to talk about the real problems.

- Some participants are not interested, should not be there.

- There are too many distractions, interruptions.

- The leader has already decided on a course of action. The meeting is only a rubber stamp.

- People attack one another.

The problems Yeomans lists are common to all groups. The extent to which a group suffers from any or all of these problems depends on how much control is kept over its meetings. Some of this control is exerted by group leaders. They are responsible for keeping the meeting on track, for sticking to the agenda, and for not permitting certain people to monopolize the group.

The leader, however, is not the only one at fault when a group functions poorly. Many group participants sit back and observe an ineffective and boring meeting without doing anything to make the meeting move faster or more efficiently. A group can function only as well as the combination of its leaders and its participants. What, then, are the responsibilities of the people who make up a group?

Before answering this question, let's begin our discussion by looking at responsibilities in general. After a brief overview of responsibilities, we will look specifically at leaders—how they come to lead and what their styles of leadership are. Then we will move on to participants and the roles they play in groups.

TRY THIS

Think about and respond to the following questions regarding group leadership. Are there any correct answers to these questions? On what issues do answers to these questions depend?

1. How far should leaders push uncooperative or unproductive group members?

2. What obligations do leaders have to either fill in for or cover for unproductive group members?

3. What role should group leaders play in motivating or empowering group members? Is motivation or empowerment a leader's responsibility?

4. To what extent are leaders responsible to or responsible for group members? For group success or failure?

5. What are some of the ethical issues leaders must face in performing leadership functions? Do group members face these same issues?

When it comes to responsibilities, all group members need to be accountable. Often, we believe that only leaders are accountable; this relieves participants of responsibility. But there are some basic responsibilities all group members must fulfill if groups are to be successful. Even the leader's success depends on members fulfilling these responsibilities because no leader is likely to be successful alone.

What are some of these responsibilities? First, all group members need to be adequately prepared for discussion. This means that they have gathered the necessary information, done the required reading, or performed the important thinking before the meeting. Second, they need to think carefully during the discussion process. This means they must show concern for the discussion process by being objective and listening carefully. Third, they must be willing to share their ideas and reflections with others. To have ideas and not share them is like not having the ideas at all; they are useful only when they are offered to the group for consideration and discussion. And fourth, those members who do not support the group's recommendations must be willing to say so while the group is deliberating, rather than waiting until after decisions are made.

Some readers may think that one advantage of a group is that the responsibilities outlined above can be distributed among group members. What we are saying is that *each* member should fulfill *all* these responsibilities. If just this minimum list of responsibilities is assumed by each group member, there will be far more assurance of a successful group discussion.

WHAT IS A LEADER?

243

LEADING,
MANAGING, AND
PARTICIPATING
IN CONFLICT

If we were asked to make a list of all the leaders in our lives, most of us could probably come up with at least a hundred. Some of the people on our list hold recognized leadership positions: the president of the United States, a state senator, the principal of our elementary school. Others do not have formal leadership positions but are leaders because a group acknowledges them as such: the student who organizes a study group to prepare for an examination, the employee who puts together a car pool, the friend who gets people together to purchase tickets for a group to attend a rock concert. The characteristic that all these leaders have in common is that they exert some kind of influence. A **leader**, then, is a person who influences the behavior of one or more people.

Why is one person more influential than another? Why are some people leaders and others followers? Where do leaders get their power to influence others? What kind of power do they have?

How Leaders Influence Followers

Some leaders influence their followers through the sheer force of their personalities. Others wield influence because they are in a position of power in an organization and the people they lead are their subordinates. Most often, however, leadership is a combination of factors. Researchers have identified five sources of influence for leaders: reward power, coercive power, legitimate power, expert power, and referent power.[2]

Who is in charge in this group? How do you know?

REWARD POWER

A leader can have influence if he or she can reward the followers; this is known as **reward power**. In an organization, reward can take such forms as promotions or pay raises. If the leader is liked and admired, he or she can reward followers by praising them, giving them approval, recognizing them, or giving them attention. On the campus newspaper staff, for example, the editor rewards her subordinates by giving them good stories to cover and praising the stories they write.

COERCIVE POWER

Coercive power is the power to punish. In an organization the leader could punish followers by demoting them or refusing to raise their pay or, more drastically, by firing them. Leaders can also exercise coercive power by criticizing their followers or refusing to pay attention to them. For example, a manager may not assign new projects to employees who have not "paid their dues." Employees who have not sat on the benches or walked into the trenches don't get the new projects.

LEGITIMATE POWER

In a formal organization, a leader is influential because he or she is "the boss." The people who report to the leader must comply because of the organizational hierarchy and its rules. This constitutes **legitimate power**. In the military, for example, the lower ranks must always defer to the higher ranks; ability and personality are not factors.

EXPERT POWER

Expert power denotes the influence and power an expert has because he or she knows more than anyone else. For example, Shin and Nikisha have formed a group of international students to study the problem of having no common meeting place on campus. Although the group has six other members, Shin and Nikisha spearhead the group because they have done the most research on the problem.

REFERENT POWER

Leaders with **referent power** enjoy influence because of personality. Members look up to them, want their approval, and try to emulate them. For example, a student who writes a humor column for the campus newspaper is greatly admired. Because of this widespread admiration, many students defer to her judgments on a variety of subjects.

Figure 9-1 shows when these five sources of influence come from organizations or from personality and where they overlap.

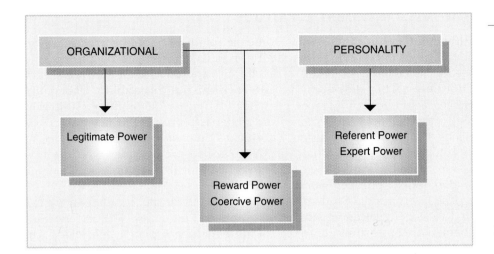

Figure 9-1
**Sources of
Influence**

How People Become Leaders

What makes a person a leader? Why do some people always take on leadership roles, regardless of the situation they are in? Why do people rise to leadership positions in organizations? Robert A. Baron and Paul B. Paulus, writers on organizational theory, believe leaders arise because of their personality traits and the situations in which they find themselves. These two factors work together in what they call an interactionist approach to leadership.[3] Let's look at these elements in more detail.

PERSONALITY

We have all heard the term *born leader*, and we all know individuals who fit this description. Most people like and admire these people. They take charge of situations, they are the people who others turn to, and they are the ones who come up with the most creative solutions. They can cut through the discussion to identify the essence of the problem, and they show the ways in which the group can make a decision. All these traits are internal—they are found in the personality of the leader.

SITUATION

In many situations people emerge as leaders because they have the competence and the skill to solve the problem. The person who emerges as leader is the one who is best able to meet a specific group's needs. These characteristics are external in that they depend on the situation and on the kind of skill or expertise needed to solve the problem. For example, if a group of students is assigned to make a videotape and only one student knows how to run a video camera, he or she will be the leader—at least until everyone else has learned.

THE INTERACTIONIST APPROACH

Although there are times when someone might become a leader solely on the basis of outstanding personality or skills, most often people become leaders when their personalities or skills are appropriate for a *particular* circumstance. This describes the **interactionist approach** to leadership. Since various circumstances demand different personalities or different skills, the person who becomes the leader is the one who best meets the needs of a particular situation. This means that leadership is not limited to a small group of individuals; anyone can become a leader who meets a group's needs at a given time.[4] Let's look at an ideal situation to see how the interactionist approach works.

The International Students Association meets for the first time in the fall and decides to set an agenda of programs and activities. The club decides that its three priorities are to recruit more members, plan a sightseeing trip to Washington, D.C., and present a panel on world peace. The executive committee gets together and figures out which people in the organization will be best to work on each project. They all agree that Ranjan would be their best recruiter. Although he is not very organized, everyone likes him, and he is usually good at persuasion. Ranjan, then, is chosen to lead this particular activity because of his personality. The committee appoints Ming to head the group that will plan the trip to Washington, D.C., because she has been to Washington several times and knows the city well. Ming, then, is chosen because of her knowledge and skills. Luis is chosen to organize the panel on world peace and contact speakers. In previous work with the association, Luis has always done an outstanding job when he handled such activities. He is goal-oriented, and he presents himself in a professional way. He is therefore the right choice for a job that requires both personality and competence. Although leaders do not always emerge in such a clear-cut way in real life, this example shows how the interactionist theory of leadership works to confer leadership on various people.

Gender can play a role in group discussion, too. It often has an effect on the personalities of the members, the situation, and even the interactionist approach. Read the "Consider This" from Mary Monedas to get one perspective on the role gender plays. As you read, think about the influence gender would have in a mixed-sex group if the men felt just as Mary Monedas has described.

■ LEADERSHIP STYLES

The manner in which a leader exerts control over a group is called **leadership style**. Styles can range from the leader who tells the participants exactly what to do to the leader who depends on participants to point the way. No one leadership style is the best in all situations: how a leader acts should depend on the job to be done. We can see how this works in three different leadership styles: authoritarian, democratic, and laissez-faire.

CONSIDER THIS

Leadership style is the amount of control a leader exerts over a group. Mary Monedas, a researcher on gender, claims that in our society there are certain traits associated with gender. She writes:

Men have a socialized tendency to dominate, control, and subordinate women to maintain their power. When situations do not proceed in traditional ways, they fall back on these tendencies to appear confident. They are accustomed to being in control, and when women claim authority or any aspect of power, men may lose their energy, initiative, and joy because of this loss of power and control.

Source: Mary Monedas, "Men Communicating with Women: Self-Esteem and Power," in Linda A. M. Perry, Lynn H. Turner, and Helen M. Sterk (Eds.), *Constructing and Reconstructing Gender: The Links Among Communication, Language, and Gender* (Albany: State University of New York Press, 1992), pp. 197–208.

QUESTIONS

1. If women control groups that include men, are men likely to react in the way Monedas describes?

2. If men act in the way Monedas describes, is it possible to restore their energy and initiative? How?

3. In mixed groups, might there be ways to resolve gender problems before they occur? How?

The Authoritarian Leader

The **authoritarian leader** holds the greatest control over a group. He or she takes charge by deciding what should be talked about and who should talk. This leader approves some ideas and discards others. Most of the discussion in the group is directed to the leader for approval.

Although this style of leadership does not sound very desirable, there are situations where it can work quite well. Authoritarian leaders often gain their position because they are the only group member with expertise. Sometimes a group starts out with an authoritarian leader but later operates more democratically. For example, members of a committee are meeting for the first time in the academic year, and only one person has served on the committee before. In the beginning this member may have to be more authoritarian, but group members will start to play greater roles as they gain experience.

CONSIDER THIS

"Do women perform as well as men in small task groups?" This is a question raised by J. Dan Rothwell in his book *In Mixed Company: Small Group Communication*. How well women perform depends on the type of task involved and the gender balance in the group. In general, men excel when the tasks involve mathematical expertise or physical strength, and women excel at verbal tasks. Thus, women would be expected to excel in most group discussions.

But women's ability to perform is also affected by the gender composition of the group. That is, if a woman is alone in an otherwise male group, her performance will be adversely affected. The opportunities for her to speak, to show she is competent, to indicate she has a contribution to make are low in such situations. The larger the group, too, the lower these odds are.

Women benefit when group composition is diverse. When women are fairly represented in groups, better group participation and more representative group participation will likely occur.

Source: J. Dan Rothwell, *In Mixed Company: Small Group Communication*, (Fort Worth: Harcourt Brace Jovanovich, 1992), pp. 83–84.

QUESTIONS

1. Do you agree with these findings? Is gender balance in groups likely to have the effects stated above?

2. In what ways can balanced-gender groups be promoted or encouraged? Who would be in the best position to promote or encourage this?

3. How would you go about getting gender balance in groups to which you belong? Do you believe the advantages would outweigh any disadvantages to these groups?

An authoritarian leader is often best when a group must do a job very quickly. For example, a group is meeting to write a grant proposal that is due in two days. One person takes charge of the project and appoints other members to do various tasks. This is the most efficient way to get the job done in the available time.

Authoritarian leaders will be ineffective if group members are equal in experience, knowledge, or status. Such members are likely to resent an authoritarian leader and will not cooperate.

The Democratic Leader

A **democratic leader** is one who lets all points of view be heard. Rather than decide things personally, he or she will throw out ideas and let the group react to them. Ideally, such a leader keeps the discussion on track but makes a real attempt to let all members be heard. The group is never told what to do, though the leader may suggest a direction to take. Leadership in a democratic group is often functional: it may vary with the task and may even move from one individual to another when the group finds doing so would be appropriate. All members have a chance to contribute, and information can move among them as well as back and forth to the leader.

Democratic groups work best when members are equal in status and experience and when there is sufficient time to solve the problem. Due to its open nature, a democratic group provides more opportunity for originality and creativity than does an authoritarian group. Since members share in the decision making, there is also greater motivation. Because members identify with the group, they are more interested in helping the group achieve its goal.

The Laissez-faire Leader

The **laissez-faire leader** does very little actual leading. He or she might call the group together, but that's about it. Such a leader neither suggests any direction nor imposes any order on the group. In some groups there is a reluctance to name one person as leader. Support groups, such as groups for people with cancer or for people who were abused as children, might feel uncomfortable with an acknowledged leader since the members attend for the purpose of helping one another. As members of the group they want to be able to respond to a particular member's problem rather than be tied

What kind of leader do you think this group has: authoritarian, democratic, or laissez-faire? Why did you reach this conclusion?

TRY THIS

1. What do you think is the most effective style of leadership? Why?
2. What specific behaviors would you like to see leaders demonstrate in support of their leadership style?
3. Is one style of leadership more appropriate than others? Which one? Why?
4. Are there leadership behaviors you consider inappropriate? Which ones? Why?
5. If you were in a situation in which a leader was using a leadership style you considered inappropriate or ineffective, what could *you* do, as a member of the group, to try to change the situation?

to a schedule or topic. However, these groups could fall into a pattern where the discussion is so unstructured that they don't provide very much help to anyone.

LEADING THE GROUP

The role of a group leader is to help the group get the job done. To do this the leader must have a certain sense of detachment. He or she needs to look at the group from a different perspective than other members—the perspective of "Is the group functioning as well as it should?" "Is the group making progress?" "What can I do to make the group work better?" Leaders can help groups work better when they establish procedures, help the group move, raise questions, focus on answers, delegate responsibility, and encourage social interaction.

Establishing Procedures

Every formal small-group meeting should be conducted according to a plan that organizes the group's work. This plan, called the group's *procedures,* specifies how the group should operate. Most informal groups, such as book clubs, do not follow a plan.

If the group is meeting for the first time, the person who has convened the group should ask it to elect a leader. If the members do not know one another, it is a good idea for all participants to introduce themselves before a leader is chosen. If appropriate, the convener might also ask members to tell why they joined the group and what they would like the group to accomplish.

Many groups function more efficiently if someone volunteers or is elected to act as secretary. This person keeps a record of what goes on at every meeting. This record can take the shape of formal minutes that are read at the next meeting or a simple list of topics the group has discussed that members can refer to when necessary. At all meetings, if group members make motions to pass resolutions, each resolution should be recorded exactly as the member worded it, along with the tally of votes for and against it.

After the members have been introduced and someone agrees to take notes, the leader can briefly state what the group's work will be for that meeting. Once the work has been outlined, the discussion is ready to begin.

Many groups structure their time with an **agenda**—a list of all the items that will be discussed during the meeting. In Chapter 8 we discussed the problem-solving sequence. This is an excellent sequence for a group with a single problem to solve. Many groups, however, have a variety of matters to handle during a meeting. These groups are more likely to use an agenda that begins with the reading and approval of the minutes from the last meeting and proceeds to reports of officers, boards, and standing committees; reports of special (ad hoc) committees; special orders; unfinished business; and new business. Figure 9-2 shows a typical agenda.

Throughout the meeting, the leader should give everyone a chance to participate. If the leader includes everyone in the first meeting, it is a clear sign that all members' opinions are welcome.

The purpose of the agenda is to keep the meeting on track so that all topics can be covered in the time available. Also, an announced agenda allows group members to anticipate and prepare for the subjects to be discussed.

FIGURE 9-2
Agenda

Wood County Area Arts Council
Meeting Agenda
February 1, 1995
A. Approval of January 4, 1995, minutes
B. Treasurer's report
C. Social Chair's report
   1. Valentine's Day update
   2. April social activity plans
D. Special Projects Chair's report
   1. Verdant Gardens Art Project
   2. Council Museum Tour
E. Arts report
F. Committee reports
   1. Program Committee
   2. Fund-raising Committee
G. Correspondence
H. Executive Director's report
I. Unfinished business
   1. Public awareness program
   2. Support for a council brochure
J. New business

Group members need to be aware of hidden agendas, if possible, because they can interfere with the group's process. **Hidden agendas** are unannounced goals, subjects, or issues that are important to individual members or subgroups but are not on the group's public or stated agenda. For example, in a classroom group one member is more interested in social life than in the topic the group is supposed to be discussing. This person often asks questions about dorm life, football games, or other weekend activities. Finally, the group leader politely asks this person to stick to the assigned topic.

So the group leader does not embarrass any one member, he says something to the effect that "It might be better if we all tried to stick with the group's assigned topic for now," or "We have a limited amount of time. If we could all keep our comments directed to our topic for today, we might be able to complete our task." Most hidden agendas lose their force when recognized. Often they can be recognized and controlled subtly, without causing group members embarrassment or loss of face. It is important not to publicly chastise or condemn group members on whose participation the group must then depend.

Helping the Group to Progress

Groups cannot move ahead when members spend too much time dealing with trivia or with only a single aspect of a problem. An effective small-group leader will move the group toward the next topic when a sufficient amount of information has been presented, when information is being repeated, or when the discussion becomes too trivial. The leader might say, "I think we are beginning to repeat ourselves. Let's move along to the next issue."

Helping the group move along requires some assertiveness on the part of the leader. Leaders must be willing to interject themselves and enforce the group's agenda. This requires some discretion and diplomacy because group members do not like to be bossed. A leader might say, for example, "Excuse me for interrupting you, Sabrina, but I wonder if we might hear what some of the others are thinking."

Summarizing is one good way to help the group progress. It alerts the group to where it has been, what it has accomplished, where it is now, and where it is going. A final summary and a statement of goals for the next meeting is also a good way to close each group meeting. "Today we had a disagreement over whether we should lease our equipment to outsiders or permit only our own students to use it. At our next meeting, I think we should work to resolve this issue."

Raising Questions

One of the ways a leader can be most helpful is to raise pertinent questions. Sometimes, during discussion, it is easy for a group to lose sight of its original goal. A group of students, for example, might be discussing the issue of date rape and get diverted to the subject of unfriendly law enforcement officials. If the group leader says, "Is this directly related to the problem of date rape?" the group will realize that it is not and will get back on the subject.

Sometimes a group will try to discuss a subject but will lack sufficient information. A group discussing faculty and student parking might realize that it doesn't know how many parking places are assigned to each group. The leader may ask someone to find this information. If it is not known, he or she may ask members to count the spaces in the various lots.

Information that the group receives must be evaluated. Some information may be insignificant, irrelevant, or invalid. Appropriate questions for the leader to ask include: How recent is the information? Who is the source? Might the source be biased? Facts and opinions should be scrutinized carefully for possible errors or misinterpretation.

Focusing on Answers

To accomplish its task, a group needs answers. If the function of the group is to solve a problem, members need to keep their attention on possible solutions. An effective group leader will focus members' attention on the need for answers and will support members who work toward answers.

Focusing on answers involves evaluating alternatives by considering their advantages and disadvantages. A useful leadership role is played by members who ask such questions as: What consequences are likely to occur? What are the costs going to be? What barriers have to be overcome? How serious are the barriers?

Sometimes solutions call for a plan of action. If your group decides that the only solution to its problem is to demonstrate against the administration, members would be faced with making plans for that demonstration. How are you going to publicize your grievances, get recruits, and carry out the protest? Effective leadership helps a group plan carefully for the action it has decided to take.

Delegating Responsibility

Many people do not want to become leaders because they think that leadership involves too much time and trouble. These people often see a leader as the one who does all the work. This should not be true in any group. A good leader should be able to delegate responsibility to the group's members. If a group is going to do research, for example, the leader could assign some members to go to the library, some to interview experts, and others to coordinate and present the information to the group.

Some leaders do not delegate because they believe they are the only ones who can do the job right. If you are one of these people, you should consider taking a risk and letting some of the other people do some of the work. You might be surprised how well they do it. Also, sharing the work makes participants feel more involved and committed.

Are all group
members partici-
pating in solving
the problem?
How can you tell?

Encouraging Social Interaction

Social interaction occurs in a group when people feel recognized and
accepted, unthreatened, and valued by other members. The more friendliness, mutual trust, respect, and warmth exhibited, the more likely the members are to find pleasure in the group and to work hard to accomplish the
group's goals. The use of first names and the use of such words as *we, us,*
and *our* will help group members feel a sense of belonging. The group
leader can also strengthen social interaction by encouraging shy members
to speak, by complimenting worthwhile contributions, and by praising the
overall accomplishments of the group. Group leaders should also plan to
leave a little time before and after a meeting so members can socialize.

PARTICIPATING IN GROUP DISCUSSION

Roles in Discussion

Groups, like individuals, can be defined as mature or immature. Often an
immature group is a new one. It is overly dependent on its leader and, in
the beginning, is often passive and unorganized. As the group matures, it is
able to function independently of its leader, and its members become
actively involved and capable of organizing their discussions.[5]

Although most groups have a specified leader, the leader does not have
total responsibility for giving the discussion a direction or for moving the

group along. In most groups, an individual member may temporarily take over the leadership from time to time. For example, a member who temporarily leads a group may have more information or experience in a certain area than the usual leader.

Individual group members continue to play the same roles in groups as they do in any other communication. A person who likes to take charge is likely to want the role of group leader. A person who is shy is going to be as hesitant in a group as in any other kind of communication. In addition to the roles we play in life, however, some roles are specific to small-group communication. Kenneth Benne and Paul Sheats, in a classic study, have pointed out that group members play task and/or maintenance roles.[6]

TASK ROLES

Task roles are those that help get the job done. Persons who play these roles help the group come up with new ideas, aid in collecting and organizing information, and analyze the information that exists. Task roles are not limited to any one individual; they may be interchanged among the members as the group goes about its job. Following are some of the common task roles.

INITIATORS-EXPEDITERS. Members who act as *initiators-expediters*—by suggesting new ideas, goals, solutions, and approaches—are often the most creative and energetic of the group. When the group gets bogged down, they are likely to make such statements as "What if we tried . . ." or "I wonder if . . . would solve our problem."

How early does group behavior begin in your culture? Might this differ from group to group?

Initiators-expediters often can suggest a new direction or can prevent the group from losing sight of its objectives. They are not afraid to jump in and give assistance when the group is in trouble. Often too, they are the ones who hold the light so others can see the path.

INFORMATION GIVERS AND SEEKERS. Individual members may both seek information and give it. Since lots of information will lead to better discussion, many members will play these roles. *Information givers* are often the best-informed members of the group. They might have had more experience with the subject or even be experts on it.

The more complex the subject, the greater the group's need for *information seekers.* These are people who are willing to go out and research the subject. They might agree to interview experts, or they might go to the library to do research. If the group has very little information on a subject, it might be necessary for several members to play the role of information seeker.

The roles of information giving and seeking are the most important in any group. The information the group gets provides the foundation for the entire discussion. The more group members who play these roles, the better the quality of group discussion.

CRITICS-ANALYZERS. *Critics-analyzers* are those who look at the good and bad points in the information the group has gathered. These people see the points that need more elaboration, and they discover information that has been left out.

The critic-analyzer is able to look at the total picture and see how everything fits together. People who play this role usually have an excellent sense of organization. Often they can help keep the group on track: "We have mentioned this point twice. Maybe we need to discuss it in more depth." "Maybe we should go back and look at this information again. Something seems to be missing."

MAINTENANCE ROLES

People who play **maintenance roles** focus on the emotional tone of the meeting. Since no one wants to spend his or her entire time being logical, gathering information, and doing the job, it is important that some emotional needs be met. People who play maintenance roles meet these needs by encouraging, harmonizing, regulating, and observing.

ENCOURAGERS. *Encouragers* praise and commend contributions and group achievements: "You really did a good job of gathering this information. Now we can dig in and work."

The best encouragers are active listeners. They help in rephrasing points to achieve greater clarity. They do not make negative judgments about other members or their opinions. Encouragers make people feel good about themselves and their contributions.

CONSIDER THIS

"In ideal group situations all group members trust each other." Do you consider this a correct statement? What factors in a group situation might lead to distrust between group members? Read the following excerpt, and then answer the questions below:

Inherent in a culturally diverse community are problems of racial, ethnic, and gender prejudice. There are many members of the community who have grown up with negative beliefs about other races and ethnic backgrounds as well as the role and place of women. This is not a perception peculiar only to white Anglos; it is common across races and ethnic groups. This diversity in experience can lead to differences in ideas about who can be trusted.

Source: Richard E. Porter and Larry A. Samovar, "Communication in the Multicultural Group," in Robert S. Cathcart and Larry A. Samovar, *Small Group Communication: A Reader*, 6th ed. (Dubuque, IA: Brown, 1992), pp. 390, 382–392.

QUESTIONS

1. Have you ever felt that someone from another ethnic background is not trustworthy?

2. Do you think other group members may feel this way?

3. Can you see how distrust can prove difficult for a group to handle or how lack of trust can prevent or inhibit group progress?

4. What can be done to dissipate these feelings of distrust among people of different cultural backgrounds?

HARMONIZERS-COMPROMISERS. Those who help to resolve conflict in the group, who settle arguments and disagreements through mediation, are the *harmonizers-compromisers*. People who play this role are skillful at discovering solutions acceptable to everyone. Harmonizers-compromisers are especially effective when they remind group members that group goals are more important than individual needs: "I know you would like the library to be open on Sunday morning, but we have to find the times that are best for everybody."

REGULATORS. As their name implies, *regulators* help regulate group discussion by gently reminding members of the agenda or of the point they were discussing when they digressed: "We seem to be wandering a little. Now, we were discussing . . ."

Good regulators also find ways to give everyone a chance to speak: "Vilma, you haven't said anything. Do you have any feelings on this subject?" Sometimes the regulator has to stop someone who has been talking too much: "Roberto, you have made several interesting points. Let's see what some of the others think of them." A regulator who is too authoritarian, however, might find that others resent him or her. In this role, it is important to word statements or questions tactfully.

OBSERVERS. *Observers* aid in the group's cohesiveness. They are sensitive to the needs of each member: "I think we have ignored the point that John just made. Maybe we should take some time to discuss it."

■ CONFLICT IN GROUPS

When individuals meet in a group to solve a problem, there's no guarantee of agreement. **Conflict**—expressed struggle between at least two individuals who perceive incompatible goals or interference from others in achieving their goals—might arise at any stage of discussion: in defining the problem, in deciding how to go about solving it, or in choosing the solution.

Group conflict generally occurs for one of several reasons. The first, and perhaps the easiest to solve, is conflict about procedure. How often should the group meet? What form should the minutes take?

To keep such conflict from occurring, the group should discuss and resolve issues of procedure at its first meeting. If it does so, it is not likely to face further conflict in this area.

The second source of conflict is the desire of individual members for power. Research has found that in business and corporate settings a group often becomes a focal point for power struggles.[7] However, power struggles are not so common in classroom groups. If one person wants power, the problem is often solved by making him or her chair. If this doesn't solve the problem and members continue their power struggle, the group will probably not work very efficiently.

The third source of conflict, and one of the greatest in classroom groups, is that some members often work harder than others. When a lot of work must be done and some people do very little, the harder workers feel anger and hostility—especially if the group is working for a grade. Like power struggles, this kind of conflict is difficult to resolve. Since few students are willing to tell the instructor about such inequality, their only hope is to confront the group members who are not working and use peer pressure to persuade them to change. If this approach doesn't work, it might console them to know that most instructors have a good idea of who does their work and who doesn't.

Although these three kinds of conflicts can interfere with group work, not all conflict is harmful. The fourth kind of conflict, conflict about substantive issues, can be rewarding. Let's look at this area more closely.

CONSIDER THIS

What first comes to your mind when conflict is mentioned? When asked their first reaction to the word *conflict*, people from different nations responded with the following words: *fight, anger, pain, war, impasse, destruction, fear, mistake, avoid, lose, control, hate, loss, bad,* and *wrongdoing.* Often, the benefits of conflict are not seen because of just such a negative haze. But here is what one author of a book on conflict says about the values of conflict:

Many conflicts can serve as opportunities for mutual growth if we develop and utilize positive, constructive conflict resolution skills. Indeed, conflict can serve as one of the engines of personal development and social evolution, generating opportunities to learn from and adapt to the diversities and differences that are natural and healthy characteristics of our society. Conflict can bring out into the open alternative ways of thinking and behaving. It can challenge us to manage our lives in ways that utilize our differences for mutual growth and benefit.

Source: Dudley Weeks, *The Eight Essential Steps to Conflict Resolution: Preserving Relationships at Work, at Home, and in the Community* (Los Angeles: Tarcher, 1992), pp. 4, 7.

QUESTIONS

1. Do you think this author is being too optimistic about conflict?

2. Have you ever experienced any of the benefits of conflict outlined in the paragraph above? Others not mentioned there?

3. Can you think of *any* situations in which conflict might lead to your own growth and benefit? What are these situations?

The Value of Substantive Conflict

Substantive conflict occurs when people have different reactions to an idea. It is likely to occur when any important and controversial idea is being discussed. As in all exchanges of ideas, people's opinions and perceptions are influenced by their culture, upbringing, education, and experience. These perceptions cause them to react differently to ideas and can create conflict in a group. For example, a classroom group is assigned the question of whether a physician should be able to help a suffering patient commit suicide. Even though group members may not have read anything on this subject, when they hear the discussion question, they are still likely to have opinions based on their perceptions. Ricardo, 18 years old and a devout Catholic, is shocked by the possibility. He thinks, "What's there to discuss? Everyone should be against this idea." However, Maria, another group member, who is 40 years old and has returned to school, has another reaction. She thinks, "I wish someone had helped my mother to die. She went through terrible suffering in the last weeks of her life."

Although two group members start out strongly disagreeing, they will not necessarily continue to do so. When the group members begin their research, they read current cases and report their findings to the group. One group member has followed the recent events in the life of Dr. Jack Kevorkian and provides a case-by-case historical base for group analysis. Another member brings in a *Time* magazine article about a devout Catholic family who let their mother commit suicide. Still another student discovers the case of a doctor who told his patient how many barbiturates she would need to kill herself. The doctor had been treating this patient for many years and knew that her disease would not respond to treatment.

As the group discovers this information, Maria and Ricardo find that because they have more information, their opinions are beginning to shift. Maria realizes that a physician-aided suicide may take different forms, some less preferable than others. Ricardo is also adjusting his point of view. Maria has told the group about her mother's suffering, and Ricardo, finding himself very moved by her account, begins to question his previous position.

However this group resolves its question, the conflicts of substance between Maria and Ricardo have had a good effect on the group—especially since both have been willing to hear new information and listen to different points of view. By the time the group completes the project, its members will have a better understanding of the ideas and can make a better decision. Also, because group members have worked together to learn, and the learning has been rewarding, the group has become more cohesive. Although conflict in a group may be disruptive, it can work in the group's favor. Substantive conflict can help group members to see other points of view and motivate them to seek additional information.

MANAGING GROUP CONFLICT

There are times when conflict can slow a group down or even bring it to a screeching halt. When conflict arises, the group leader has to step in and try to help group members resolve it. The approach the leader takes should depend on the seriousness of the conflict. Robert Blake and Jane Mouton, who have written about ways to resolve conflict, suggest five ways of managing it.[8]

Avoidance

Sometimes groups argue over points that are so minor that they are not worth the time. If the leader sees this happening, she should suggest that the issue doesn't seem very important and that the group should move to another topic. For example, when one group disagreed about the time its banquet should begin, the leader pointed out that there was little difference between 6:30 P.M. and 7 P.M. and that it would be more productive to choose the earlier time and move on.

Accommodation

Accommodation occurs when people on one side of an issue give in to the other side. If a leader sees accommodation as a possibility, she should attempt to find out how strongly people feel about the sides they have taken. If the issue is not really important to one side, the leader might suggest that they give in. For example, when a group was planning a children's day, members argued over whether they should spend money for a clown or for pony rides. The side that favored pony rides decided that children would also enjoy a clown, so they were willing to give in.

Competition

Competition can cause considerable harm to a group. It occurs when one side cares more about winning than about other members' feelings. When a leader sees competition rising, he should try to deflect it before members get entrenched in their positions. Sometimes individual members feel competitive with one another, and they use the group sessions to work out their feelings. If this is happening, the leader might point out to each member privately that the conflict is keeping the group from working together.

Collaboration

In collaboration, people who are in conflict try to work together to meet the other person's needs as well as their own. Collaborators do not attack one another; instead they try to understand opposing points of view and work hard to stay away from anything that might harm the relationship. For example, a faculty committee was asked to choose one curriculum proposal to send to the state for funding. Since they received two—one for a women's studies minor and the other for a leadership minor—they had to make a choice. Both proposals were well thought out and clearly written, but members of the committee were divided as to which proposal they favored. After many hours of discussion, they decided to choose the women's studies proposal, but they saw many points in the leadership proposal that could make the women's studies proposal even stronger. By combining the two proposals, they had a true collaboration.

Compromise

In compromise, each side has to give up something to get what it wants. This involves a kind of bargaining in which each side makes an offer of what it will sacrifice. Compromise will work only when each side believes that what it gets is fair and that it has gained at least a partial victory. For example, a fraternity was planning its annual banquet and dance. One side favored holding it at the Elks hall and making it a formal party, whereas the other side wanted to hold it at a rustic lodge and make it a casual party. The group finally compromised: the party would be held at the Elks, but it would be informal.

EVALUATING GROUP PERFORMANCE

Since you are learning how groups work, toward the end of each meeting your group should evaluate its performance. The first and most important question your group should ask is whether it made progress toward finishing its job or solving its problem. Your instructor may have evaluation forms to help you answer this question. Another way of evaluating group work is for each member to take one minute to write down what the group has accomplished during its session and then compare notes with other members.

If the group has not made progress during its session, it is useful to answer the following questions: Did members stick to the topic? Did everyone come prepared with the material the group needed? Was everyone able to participate and contribute? Did the atmosphere encourage members to try to understand other members' points of view? Was time used efficiently? Was the leader skillful in helping members to participate and voice their opinions? If the group answers "no" to any of these questions, it will have an idea of where it needs to make improvements.

The group should also consider whether the process of group work has been rewarding. Do members feel good about what they accomplished? Were they satisfied with the roles they played? Would they like to work with this group again?

Successful work in groups can be rewarding and even exhilarating. Group work gives you a chance to play an active role in your own learning. Therefore, when you have an opportunity to work in a group, make your best effort. Even work in a classroom setting prepares you for the workplace and for participation in the life of your community.

SUMMARY

A leader is a person who influences the behavior of one or more people. Leaders gain influence through five kinds of power: reward, coercive, legitimate, expert, and referent.

One theory of leadership is that people become leaders because of their personality and the situations in which they find themselves. These two factors work together in an interactionist approach.

Leaders tend to fall into three categories: authoritarian, democratic, and laissez-faire. An authoritarian leader takes charge of a group—a style that is most successful when the group has little information or experience. A democratic leader gives everyone a chance to participate in decision making. This style of leadership works best when members are equal in status, education, and experience and when there is sufficient time to solve the problem. The laissez-faire leader does little leading. This kind of leadership works best in self-help groups.

A group leader has six responsibilities: to establish procedures, to keep the group moving, to raise questions, to focus on answers, to delegate responsibility, and to encourage social interaction.

Participants in group discussion play a variety of roles. Members in task roles focus on getting the job done; members in maintenance roles are concerned with the emotional tone of the group.

Substantive conflict can be disruptive, but it can also help group members come to better decisions. One important task of a leader is to manage conflict in a group. He or she should determine how serious the conflict is and take one of the following approaches: avoidance, accommodation, competition, collaboration, or compromise.

NOTES

[1] William N. Yeomans, *1000 Things You Never Learned in Business School* (New York: McGraw-Hill, 1985), pp. 108–109.

[2] Hugh J. Arnold and Daniel C. Feldman, *Organizational Behavior* (New York: McGraw-Hill, 1986), pp. 120–121.

[3] Robert A. Baron and Paul B. Paulus, *Understanding Human Relations*, 2d ed. (Boston: Allyn & Bacon, 1991), pp. 214–245.

[4] Ibid., p. 245.

[5] P. Hersey and K. H. Blanchard, *Management of Organizational Behavior: Utilizing Human Resources*, 4th ed. (Englewood Cliffs, NJ: Prentice-Hall, 1982), pp. 152–155.

[6] Kenneth D. Benne and Paul Sheats, "Functional Roles of Group Members," *Journal of Social Issues*, 4 (1948): 41–49.

[7] Goleman, "The Group and the Self: New Focus on a Cultural Rift," *The New York Times*, December 25, 1990, pp. 37, 41.

[8] Robert R. Blake and Jane S. Mouton, *The Managerial Grid* (Houston: Gulf Publishing, 1964). Also see Robert R. Blake and Jane S. Mouton, *The New Managerial Grid* (Houston: Gulf Publishing, 1978), p. 11.

FURTHER READING

BELASCO, JAMES A., AND RALPH C. STAYER. *Flight of the Buffalo: Soaring to Excellence, Learning to Let Employees Lead*. New York: Warner Books, 1993

Not only do the authors explain the new leadership role for executives, but they guide readers with nuts-and-bolts prescriptions on how to get people to be responsible for their own performance. An excellent, readable, motivational book by two business professionals.

BETHEL, SHEILA MURRAY. *Making a Difference: Twelve Qualities that Make You a Leader.* New York: Berkley Books, 1990.   In this well-written book, Murray discusses such characteristics as mission, big thinking, high ethics, change mastery, sensitivity, risk taking, decision making, wise use of power, effective communication, team building, courage, and commitment. Examples upon examples make this a readable book.

FISHER, ROGER, ELIZABETH KOPELMAN, AND ANDREA KUPFER SCHNEIDER. *Beyond Machiavelli: Tools for Coping with Conflict.* Cambridge, MA: Harvard University, 1994.   The authors offer a step-by-step system for dealing with the conflicts that are part of our changing world. Their conflict-management tactics are applicable to persuading employers, community officials, and business associates alike. Here are 151 pages of practical, readable, interesting information.

HELGESEN, SALLY. *The Female Advantage: Women's Ways of Leadership.* New York: Doubleday Currency, 1990.   From studying four successful female leaders, Helgesen explores how female leaders make decisions, schedule their days, gather and disperse information, structure their companies, hire, and fire. This is a book that celebrates the strengths of women and the differences between male and female leadership styles. Male leaders tend to emphasize the value of vision. Women leaders, on the other hand, strive for the development of a voice. Helgesen explains these differences and many more.

HOCKER, JOYCE L., AND WILLIAM W. WILMOT. *Interpersonal Conflict,* 3d ed. Dubuque, IA: Brown, 1991.   In this 303-page book, the authors systematically examine those components that contribute to the conflict process, with an emphasis on communication behavior. This is a well-written, thoroughly documented (close to 500 sources) textbook for the serious student.

KOHN, ALFIE. *Punished by Rewards: The Trouble with Gold Stars, Incentive Plans, A's, Praise, and Other Bribes.* Boston: Houghton Mifflin, 1993.   In this follow-up book to his *No Contest: The Case against Competition* (Houghton Mifflin, 1986) Kohn cites hundreds of studies to prove people actually do inferior work when they are enticed with money, grades, or other incentives. A great book for leaders because Kohn discusses precisely what it takes to motivate others in two chapters on the roots of motivation. Many examples, solid research, a comfortable writing style, and excellent insights make this a valuable book.

LULOFS, ROXANE SALYER. *Conflict: From Theory to Action.* Scottsdale, AZ: Gorsuch Scarisbrick, 1994.   This text is based on the assumption that effective behavior in conflict situations requires participants to analyze the situation and choose behavior appropriate to it, without sacrificing their own values and beliefs. Although this book covers all the essentials in an effective, thorough, and well-researched manner, it adds to what others have done. Each chapter provides brief narratives and longer case studies—personal descriptions of conflict situations—that help readers apply the theory discussed. A solid volume for the serious student.

MOORE, ROBERT, AND DOUGLAS GILLETTE. *King, Warrior, Magician, Lover: Rediscovering the Archetypes of the Mature Masculine*. New York: Harper San Francisco, 1990. The value of Moore and Gillette's work is not just in their view of masculinity—one *not* rooted in control and domination; the value is more in the foundation they lay for a mature, authentic, and revitalized masculinity rooted in creativity and the empowerment of the self and others. For males this is an effective guide to transforming their personalities in positive, specific directions.

WEEKS, DUDLEY. *The Eight Essential Steps to Conflict Resolution: Preserving Relationships at Work, at Home, and in the Community*. Los Angeles: Tarcher, 1992. Weeks offers readers what he labels "the conflict partnership process" to help resolve personal and professional differences. His process, based on principles of human behavior and communication, is designed to remove fear and eliminate ineffective approaches. His examples are drawn from business, family, and community situations. An easy-to-read book, although it lists no sources for additional information.

PART
IV

COMMUNICATING
IN PUBLIC

KEY TERMS

audience
    analysis

central idea

demographic
    analysis

general purpose

informative
    speech

personal
    inventory

persuasive
    speech

specific purpose

Getting Started

CHAPTER OBJECTIVES

After reading this chapter, you should be able to:

1 Choose a topic for a speech.

2 Assess whether the topic is appropriate for you, the audience, and the speech occasion.

3 Narrow the topic to make it manageable.

4 State a general purpose for your speech.

5 State a specific purpose for your speech.

6 State a central idea for your speech.

7 Distinguish between an informative and a persuasive speech.

8 Make some inferences about your audience's knowledge, attitudes, and interests.

Hyung Suk is the director of the Korean Cultural Center. The center gets a lot of its funding through United Way. This year the board of directors would like to add programs for children, but to do this the center will need more money from United Way. The board asks Hyung Suk to put together a presentation to show how the additional money would be used.

Cheryl is a high school music teacher. After several years of experience she is convinced that band competitions are bad for the school program. She believes that when the band is involved in competition, the students play the same pieces again and again, which limits the new material they could learn. She convinces the principal of her point of view, but he tells her she must present her case to the school board. Cheryl spends several days gathering and organizing the information she will present to the board.

Bill's best friend is getting married on Saturday. The custom among his friends is to toast the bride and groom with short speeches about each of them. Bill has been asked to speak about the groom. Since the occasion is a wedding reception, he knows his remarks should be short, light, and humorous.

Francisco is president of the Environmental Club on campus. A community activist interested in local environmental concerns has been invited to speak to the club, and Francisco is going to introduce him. Francisco begins his research by collecting details about the speaker's career and successes.

Sharon is president of the local branch of the electrical workers' union. For several months the executive committee has been negotiating with an employer about a cost-of-living pay raise. The committee now realizes that management is not going to come through and that the union will have to ask members for a vote to strike. Sharon will speak to her local branch to explain why a strike vote is necessary.

Kelly edits the opinion section of the campus newspaper. Over the past few months the newspaper has been getting fewer and fewer letters from students. Kelly knows that students in her classes have opinions about things going on around campus, but often they don't think of writing them down and submitting them to the newspaper. She asks instructors in her classes if she can speak to her classes about contributing to the newspaper. They agree, and she organizes a short presentation.

All these people are in a position where they are going to give a speech. Their speeches are not going to be given in large auditoriums before vast audiences; they are part of the routine of school and work. People give speeches like this every day. They make presentations (to committees or boards of directors), hold workshops (for community members or professionals), or conduct seminars (for people who want to learn something). Whatever the purpose, all these forms of speaking have a speaker and an audience.

Public speaking involves the same elements as other forms of communication: sender-receivers, a message, a channel, and feedback. The speaker is the main sender-receiver, although audience members will also respond as sender-receivers by providing nonverbal feedback or asking questions. The message in public speaking is the most structured of all communication. The speaker works on the message beforehand, carefully planning what he or she will say. Usually the channel is the voice and gestures, but some speakers enhance the channel by using graphics such as computer-generated visuals, posters, or slides. Feedback to a speech usually comes from the entire audience rather than from one or a few individuals. Typical feedback would be applause or laughter.

Public speaking has some of the characteristics of transactional communication, although its transactional nature differs from that of interpersonal and small-group communication. When an audience is small and the speaker can see everyone, continuous and simultaneous communication between the speaker and the audience can exist. However, when an audience is very large, it's difficult to say that all the communication between the speaker and the audience is continuous and simultaneous. Let's say, for example, that several instructors on campus require their classes to go to hear a speech. The auditorium, which holds 500 people, is packed. One group of students sits in the back, in the shadows. This group has no intention of listening to the speaker. Because the auditorium is large, the speaker isn't aware of them and is unable to say something that will engage their attention. In this situation there is probably little communication between the speaker and these members of the audience.

The transactional elements of past, present, and future usually apply to public speaking. Some people go to hear a speaker because they have past experience in the subject and want to learn more. How they react to the speech and the speaker may depend on how the speaker and the topic tie into their past experience or whether it is of value to them in the future. For example, in a speech class, students will look forward to hearing some student speakers because, in the past, they have been interesting.

The transactional element of roles is also present in public speaking. Steve Allen, who because of his career as a comedian and an actor has often been asked to give speeches, offers an interesting perspective on the role of the speaker:

> I learned very early in my experience as a speaker—as distinguished from an entertainer—that if there were five hundred individuals present, they were perceiving not one Steve Allen at the lectern, but five hundred separate me's.
>
> To give just a few illustrations:
>
> A young woman, to whose father I might bear a physical resemblance, might perceive me primarily as a male, to some degree physically attractive.
>
> An elderly conservative Republican gentleman in the front row might perceive me primarily as a notorious Democrat or liberal.
>
> A tailor in the audience might perceive me as someone attired unfashionably.

A fan of my television comedy program might perceive me as too stuffy and serious on this particular occasion.

A poorly educated person might perceive me as someone who uses too many big words.

One of my sons might perceive me as just "Dad."

My wife might perceive me as having put on a bit too much weight recently.[1]

SELECTING A TOPIC

Most of the people in the examples at the beginning of the chapter did not have to select a topic for a speech—the topic grew out of the work they were doing. On other occasions people are asked to speak on their area of expertise, but the specific topic is left up to them. Dr. Randolph Shine, a prominent local psychiatrist, is asked to give a speech for the Alliance for the Mentally Ill, and he chooses the subject of how families can provide the necessary support for the mentally ill. Sherill Goldman, an active volunteer for local organizations, is asked to speak to the Literary Society, and she decides to talk about the rewards of and need for volunteer work.

Since you are in a speech communication course, you will have to make several speeches during the course of the term, and the choice of topic will probably be left up to you. Choosing the topic is one of the most difficult parts of making a speech, so let's take a look at how to go about it.

The most important consideration in choosing a topic is to find a subject that interests you. If the subject is one that you like, you are going to be more motivated to research it and your presentation will be more lively. How do you find a subject that is interesting and that will also lead to an effective speech? Let's look at some areas that you should investigate.

Making a Personal Inventory

The first place to look for a topic is within yourself. You can begin by making a **personal inventory**, which involves appraising your own resources. What are you interested in? Would your interest make a good speech? Sometimes a hobby will lead to a good speech. A hobby can make you an expert about any number of subjects—rap musicians, computer games, or Elvis memorabilia.

Another area you might examine is how you spend your free time. If you listen to music or play an instrument, you might have the basis for a speech. Are you interested in nutrition, or do you like to cook? Maybe you can tell your audience something about food that they would find interesting.

Have you done anything unusual? One student gave a speech on how to

How might this professional baker adapt a speech on making bread to a group of amateur cooks?

teach a cat to do tricks—something most cats are reluctant to do. Have you been to any unusual places, or have you done something unusual—such as foraging for food in the woods?

Sometimes people have unique skills. Do you have the ability to make old cars run? Are you familiar with laser technology and how it works? Are you particularly good at entertaining children? Do you have any innovative ways of studying you can share with others?

Often the books, magazines, and newspapers you read will offer possibilities for speech topics. Hundreds of thousands of articles are published in magazines and newspapers every year. Most of these articles are about what people are currently interested in and could lead to ideas for speech topics. To get some idea of the range of topics covered, take a look at the *Readers' Guide to Periodical Literature*. Here you will find hundreds of different subjects from which to choose.

What newspapers and magazines do you read? What sections do you turn to first? Are there issues in these sections that might result in good speeches? For example, if you always read the sports section, you know that scores and accounts of games are unlikely to provide material for speeches. Well-written sports pages, however, also include stories on important issues in sports. Typical examples: Are the public pressures on athletes too great? What percentage of college athletes graduate? How should we define *amateur*? Should the Olympics be held only in Greece to keep politics out of sports?

Newspapers and magazines are also the best source of information for what is going on in your city or state, the nation, and the world. Even though you might not ordinarily pay attention to this kind of news, take an hour or so some day to leaf through a big-city newspaper or a news magazine such as *Time* or *Newsweek*. What subjects catch your attention? What's going on in the community or in the nation that might affect you and the people you know? For example, what is the local zoning board up to? Do you know that this is the board that decides how many people can live in a single dwelling? This is certainly an issue that affects students, who often need to save money by living with four or five others.

What is the state legislature up to? If you are attending a college or university supported by state money, this is an important question, since your state legislature will decide how much money your college will get and even how much tuition you will be paying. The federal government also makes many decisions that affect us all (nuclear power plants and health care reform) and many that affect college students in particular (drinking age and student loans). What about on the world stage? What effect has the end of the Cold War had? How do you view America's position toward Bosnia? Somalia? Russia? Haiti?

Your college library probably subscribes to hundreds of magazines. Take a look at some you are not familiar with. Magazines such as *Scientific American*, *Psychology Today*, and *Consumer Reports* cover dozens of subjects that could make good speech topics.

Sometimes the books you read can inspire speech topics. Generally, nonfiction books (which deal with facts and true stories) offer better speech topics than do works of fiction. Every year in this country, thousands of nonfiction books are published on subjects ranging from dieting to nuclear physics. If you were to look at the card catalog entries on a computer screen in the library, you would probably find dozens of book titles that would suggest good ideas for speech topics.

Whenever you seek a speech topic, remember that you will do best with material you know something about. While you are making a personal inventory, your emphasis should be on discovering interests and skills that you have and would like to share with others. Figure 10-1 diagrams the various sources where speech topics might be sought.

Brainstorming

In Chapter 8, we discussed brainstorming in groups. You can brainstorm all by yourself, too. As we noted earlier, *brainstorming* is a technique of free association. You take a subject—cars, for example—and think of everything that might possibly be related to this subject. The goal of brainstorming is quantity—to come up with as many ideas as possible.[2]

When you are ready to brainstorm, it is a good idea to sit in a comfortable chair and relax with a paper and pencil by your side. Once you are comfortable, think about something you are interested in (maybe from your personal inventory) and write down everything that comes into your mind. Don't try to edit any of your ideas—in fact, don't even think about them. Work quickly and make your list as long as possible. After you have finished with one topic, try other areas that seem promising. Some possibilities might include your major, your reading interests, school-related subjects, and so forth.

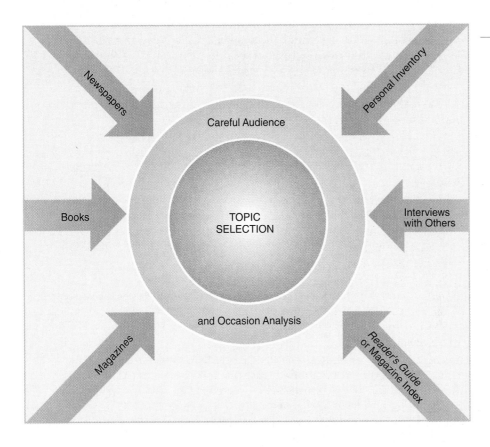

FIGURE 10-1
Finding a Topic

Let's say, for example, that we were going to brainstorm on the subject "food." Our list might look something like this:

Diet	*Poisoning*
Entertainment	*Nutrition*
Health	*Preparation*
Recipes	*Science*

After you have come up with a brainstorming list on a subject, go back and look at it with a more critical eye. Eliminate any topic from your list if it doesn't look as though it will work, or if it is an aspect of the subject that does not really interest you. In our list of food topics, for example, we might decide that we don't know much about recipes, preparation, or food poisoning, so we eliminate them from the list. Also, we might group the topics of diet, health, and nutrition because they are closely related. Entertainment does not seem to relate enough to our immediate audience, so we eliminate it too. Now we are left with science.

Since science is a broad concept, we brainstorm a little more to see what could come under this heading:

TRY THIS

Take the following test regarding your choice of a subject for a forthcoming speech:

Yes	No	
[ ]	[ ]	Can you predict that this subject will motivate you to *want to* research, organize, and present a speech to your audience?
[ ]	[ ]	Is the subject within your experience?
[ ]	[ ]	Do you have access to the additional material you will need?
[ ]	[ ]	Does the subject lend itself to interesting, attention-holding material?
[ ]	[ ]	Can you make the subject significant and relevant to your listeners?
[ ]	[ ]	Will you be able to adapt the subject to your listeners' needs, interests, and experiences?
[ ]	[ ]	Can you still give the speech despite the limitations imposed on you by the occasion or by the assignment?
[ ]	[ ]	Can you limit your subject and still treat it adequately in the time you have?
[ ]	[ ]	Will you be able to provide your listeners with some new ideas or information?
[ ]	[ ]	Will your subject pose some intellectual challenge for you and for your listeners?

Now, go back and give yourself 10 points for each "yes" you recorded. At 100 points, you know you have a winning subject on your hands. At 80 or 90 points, you can predict that it will be a winner (but there are no guarantees). At 70 points, you might consider selecting another subject. At 60 or 50 points (or less), make another selection; the one you just considered would be troublesome for you or your listeners.

- Food storage and handling
- Foods that help you live longer
- Preparing foods for schoolchildren
- The use of pesticides and their effects

These four aspects of science are individual topics and could not be covered in a single speech about food science. We need to narrow it even more to create a manageable speech topic. We might simply eliminate food storage, the use of pesticides and their effects, and handling and preparing foods for schoolchildren because we don't have as much interest in them.

Sometimes when you brainstorm, you find that your list does not yield anything you want to talk about. In this case, brainstorm again about another subject. It might take two or three brainstorming sessions before you find a topic you really like that is sufficiently narrow to be discussed effectively in a brief speech. Once you find a topic, you need to test whether it will work in a speech.

 TESTING THE TOPIC

When choosing among possible topics, you should consider three questions: (1) Is the topic appropriate for your audience? (2) Is it appropriate for you? (3) Is it appropriate for the speech occasion?

Appropriate for the Audience?

To determine whether a topic is appropriate for an audience, you have to ask whether you can speak about it on a level the audience can understand. Does the subject require specialized or technical knowledge? Can you talk about this subject in a language everyone will understand? Can you make this topic interesting for your audience? Does the audience have enough background to understand the subject? Answers to these questions will help you decide whether the topic will be appropriate.

Appropriate for You?

A topic is appropriate for you if it meets this test: Can you get involved in it, and is it interesting enough to motivate you to do the necessary research? A student studying air traffic control would probably have a high interest in air disasters—especially those caused by mistakes on the part of traffic controllers. A student studying restaurant administration would probably find it interesting to research the causes of food poisoning. Someone with a collection of African coins would be motivated to learn even more about the subject.

To give a good speech you are also going to have to speak with confidence and expertise. Do you know about the subject? Can you learn enough about it to give a speech? There is nothing worse than getting up before an audience and realizing that you don't know what you are talking about!

Appropriate for the Occasion?

The first consideration here is whether you are giving the right kind of speech for the occasion. An after-dinner speech, for example, should have a light touch and not be too long, since it will occur when members of the audience have just eaten and are not feeling at their most alert. On the other hand, if you are giving a speech at a seminar, this will be an opportunity to speak on a more complex topic. In a classroom setting, you will

CONSIDER THIS

♀♂ Here is some advice found in a college public speaking textbook published in the mid-1960s.

Generally, women are more interested than men in subjects related to the feminine gender, such as women's clothing, cosmetics, house-work, the rearing of children, the local ladies' aid society, home decoration, etc. On the other hand, men show strong masculine interests in rough competitive sports like football. More than women, men tend to enjoy technical and scientific subjects, particularly those related to mechanics, electronics, and engineering. Since more men than women serve as chief breadwinners for their families, they are more apt to be interested in matters pertaining to occupations and professions—but remember the possible exceptions.

Source: Win Kelley, *The Art of Public Address* (Dubuque, IA: Brown, 1965), p. 25.

QUESTIONS

1. What problems will you encounter if you stereotype listeners according to their gender?

2. Is any of the advice from this 1965 textbook relevant today? Why or why not?

3. Are there topics today that are more appropriate for one gender than for the other? What are those topics?

4. In what ways can speakers make topics relevant to both sexes?

probably be given only a limited time to speak, so you have to decide whether you can cover your topic adequately in the time you have.

If you are speaking at a special occasion, you should tie some aspect of the speech into the occasion itself. If the speech is for some kind of ritual occasion such as a graduation or bar mitzvah, certain conventions are expected of the speaker. At a graduation, for example, a speaker typically has some words about the future for graduates. At a bar mitzvah, a Jewish ceremony initiating a boy into religious adulthood, it would be appropriate to praise the young man and his parents.

Another consideration is whether you can fit the speech into the time limits of the occasion. Usually a speaker is given some idea of how long to speak. In a speech class, this is always true. You must consider whether you can cover your topic or whether you need to narrow it down so you can cover it adequately within the time allowed.

For many of us, making a final decision about a topic is difficult—especially when we are faced with several good options. When you are deciding on a topic for your speech class, however, it is important that you choose a single topic well ahead of the date when the speech is due. If you don't do this, you will waste a lot of time doing unfocused and unusable research on several topics. If you have several topics that seem equally appropriate and you just can't make up your mind, put all the topics in a hat and draw one out. Now that you have one topic, stick with it.

■ NARROWING THE TOPIC

A common mistake made by beginning speakers is trying to cover a topic that is too broad. If you wanted to talk about a social issue, such as crime, racial equality, or educational reform, you would discover so much relevant material that you would not even be able to read it all, let alone cover it in a single speech. If you tried to cover the entire topic, your treatment would have to be so superficial that your speech would not be very meaningful. Let's say you wanted to speak on the subject of education. You could probably divide education into 100 or more different subsections. Do you want to talk about elementary schools or high schools? Special education? Bilingual education? If you choose elementary education, there are still many possibilities. Do you want to talk about how children learn? About curriculum? About educational games? About interactive learning?

Narrowing a topic is the process of finding the specific aspect of a subject that will best meet the time restraints and other demands of the speaking situation. Let's see how three different students narrowed their subjects for speeches.

Baljit, a student from India, has been taking a health class and becomes interested in the issue of health in third-world countries. She is particularly interested in infant mortality since two of her cousins back home had babies who became seriously ill.

She decides to see what she can find on the topic and goes to the library to use a computer database to see what is available. After Baljit types "infant mortality" and "third world," the computer comes up with hundreds of entries. Baljit realizes that the topic is much too large and that she will have to narrow it. As she looks at the titles of some of the articles, she realizes that several are about infant formula. Since she knows several young women in her country who use infant formula rather than breast-feed their babies, she decides to pursue this subject.

When she types "infant formula" and "third world" into the computer, she still finds the subject is too broad—there are more than forty articles on the subject. Since she wants to stay with the topic of infant formula and cannot narrow it down any more on the computer, she decides to look at some of the articles to see if she can tighten her focus even more.

After looking at several articles, Baljit finds that the following issues are addressed:

- Infant formula is safe for babies only if it is mixed with the correct amount of pure water.

- The manufacturers of infant formula consider the third world to be a lucrative market for their product.

- Manufacturers of infant formula are using advertising that manipulates third-world mothers into thinking that formula is better for their babies.

- Infant formula is safer than breast milk if the mother has AIDS.

- Poor women often dilute infant formula to make it last longer.

All these subjects sound interesting to Baljit, but she realizes that she can't cover them comprehensively enough in a 5-minute speech. She decides not to deal with the manufacturers of infant formula and their advertising campaigns and to concentrate instead on health issues. Once she has narrowed down the subject to how infant formula affects health, she finds seven articles that are relevant and uses the material from them as the basis for her speech.

Jeff knows that he wants to talk about some aspect of baseball. He uses brainstorming to narrow down his topic. He writes "Baseball" at the top of the page and lists everything he can think of under this heading. His final list looks like this:

Baseball

History	*Injuries*
College	*Collector's cards*
Professional	*Trivia*
Salaries	*Televising of games*
Expansion teams	*New wild-card rules*
Organization and administration of the sport	*Role of commissioner*
Free agency	

Although this list might not cover every aspect of baseball, it covers Jeff's main interests. He now studies this list and looks for something he can talk about. Since he is a collector and is always looking for new baseball cards, he decides that "Collector's cards" is the aspect that interests him the most. His speech title will be "The Challenge of Collecting Baseball Cards." He has narrowed his subject so he can present information that will be useful and interesting to his audience.

Sherri, a mother of two preschool children, has returned to school to get her degree. She has had many problems in arranging for baby-sitters, and she knows she wants to give her speech on some aspect of child care for preschool children. She goes to the library and finds several articles about child care. Some focus on psychological problems; others discuss families where both parents work; yet others deal with professional standards in child-care institutions. Sherri finds these articles interesting but decides that she wants to focus on practical information that will help others who face her problem. Finally she asks herself, "What would be the ideal child care arrangement for my family?" Her answer to the question becomes the topic of her persuasive speech: "Colleges Should Provide Child Care for Student Parents."

By starting with a subject they found interesting, Baljit, Jeff, and Sherri were able to work with it and narrow it in a way that would make it manageable for a speech. Now they are ready to start thinking about the purpose for which they will be giving the speech.

▌ SELECTING A PURPOSE

Whenever you give a speech you should have a good idea of your purpose or reason for speaking. Having this purpose in mind beforehand is very much like planning a trip: if you know where you're going, you are able to plan the route ahead of time. In the same way, having a purpose for your speech will help you to look for materials, organize and outline your speech, and adapt your speech to the needs and interests of your audience.

There are three stages in working out the purpose for your speech: (1) selecting the general purpose, (2) selecting the specific purpose, and (3) stating the central idea.

The General Purpose

When you are asked to state a **general purpose** for your speech, you should tell whether you intend to inform or to persuade. **Informative speeches** generally concentrate on explaining—telling how something works, what something means, or how to do something. A speaker who gives an informative speech usually tries to give his or her audience information without taking sides. For example, if a speaker is giving an informative speech about using animals for research, he will not state whether he is for or against it; he will let members of the audience make up their minds. When the subject is controversial, the informative speaker will present all sides of the issue. In an informative speech about running for fitness, for example, you could give the advantages (physical fitness and feeling good) and the possible disadvantages (shin splints and other injuries).

In a **persuasive speech** the speaker takes a particular position and tries to get the audience to accept and support that position. For example, a speaker tries to persuade her audience that it should oppose welfare reform. Someone else tries to persuade the audience to support making volleyball a varsity sport or to sign a petition against chemical dump sites in the community. In a persuasive speech, the speaker concentrates on looking for the best information available to support his or her point of view.

Often the same subject could lead to either an informative *or* a persuasive speech—depending on your wording of the topic and your approach. Say your subject is the ethics of abortion. If you choose as your topic "The Ethical Issues of Abortion" and cover the ethics on both sides of the issue, the wording of your topic and your approach are appropriate for an informative speech. But if your topic is "Abortion: The Wrong Choice," you clearly have a persuasive speech, because you have made up your mind and are in favor of one particular side of the issue. Here are some other subjects that are phrased first as informative (*I*) and then as persuasive (*P*) topics:

I: Latino Interests and Concerns

P: Latinos Must Form Their Own Political Party

I: Environmental Conservation Means Energy Efficiency

P: Energy Efficiency Requires People to Change Their Habits

I: Stress Reduction Programs Can Be Successful

P: People Need to Learn How to Control Stress in Their Lives

Sometimes it's difficult to fit a speech firmly into an informative or a persuasive slot. In a persuasive speech, informative material often plays an important role. If you are speaking in favor of political candidates, it is natural to use information about their background and voting record. In an informative speech, even when you try to present both sides, one side might seem more persuasive than the other to some audience members.

The Specific Purpose

After you have decided whether the general purpose of your speech is to inform or to persuade, you must then decide on a **specific purpose**. The statement of your specific purpose will help you focus on precisely what you want to accomplish—that is, it will help you define exactly what you are going to inform or to persuade your audience about. In deciding your specific purpose, you should follow four guidelines.

1. *State your purpose clearly and completely.* Examples of a specific purpose statement would be:

    To inform my audience about the value of daydreams

    To explain to audience members how to stay physically fit

To persuade audience members not to buy products from advertisers who use sexist advertisements and commercials

To persuade audience members to become better organized and plan their time better

2. *State your purpose in terms of the effect you want to have on your audience.* What information do you want to give to your audience, or what do you want them to think or do when the speech is over? In an informative speech the main effect you seek is to have your audience remember the information. For example:

To inform my audience about the ways volunteers can contribute their time to worthwhile organizations

To inform my audience about how they can improve their study habits

In a persuasive speech, however, the effect you might want is for audience members to take direct action:

To persuade my audience to donate blood to the Red Cross

To persuade my audience that a low-fat diet will reduce their risk of heart attacks and other health problems

3. *Limit your purpose statement to one idea.* Keeping your purpose statement limited to one idea will help you to narrow your topic and keep it specific. Notice that each of the above examples has only one idea. If the first example had been "To inform my audience about the value of daydreams and how to use them to escape, relax, and rethink," the speaker would have had two topics to cover rather than one and the speech would lack focus.

4. *Use specific language in your purpose statement.* The more precise your language, the clearer the ideas will be in your mind. For example, "To persuade my audience to fight crime" is too vague a topic. By *crime*, do you mean drugs, date rape, kidnapping, murder, or something else? You could rephrase your purpose like this:

To persuade my audience that everyone can help control shoplifting

or

To inform my audience about the ways that shoplifting occurs

Once you have determined your statement of purpose, you should subject it to some tests. Does it meet the assignment? You might discover, for example, that your opinions on a subject are so strong that you are unable to talk about it without favoring one side over the other. This means your subject is better for a persuasive speech than for an informative one. If you have been assigned an informative speech, then you should keep this subject for a later time.

Another important test is to ask whether you can accomplish your purpose within the time limits of the speech. If your speech purpose is too broad to fit in the allotted time, you will have to either narrow the topic fur-

TRY THIS

Here is a list of speech topics and purposes. Which word should go in the blank, *inform* or *persuade*?

1. To _____ the audience that they should be smart about nutrition.
2. To _____ the audience of the real risk of AIDS.
3. To _____ the audience how to avoid business rip-offs.
4. To _____ the audience of ways to help the homeless.
5. To _____ the audience to put their strengths to work for them.
6. To _____ the audience to take advantage of the national student exchange.
7. To _____ the audience of the common causes of cancer.
8. To _____ the audience how crime can affect them.
9. To _____ the audience to avoid unnecessary auto repair.
10. To _____ the audience to make a good night's sleep a priority.

Answers: 1. p 2. I 3. I 4. I 5. p 6. p 7. I 8. I 9. p 10. p

ther or find a new topic. One speaker discovered, for example, that her purpose, "To inform my audience about physical fitness," was too broad; too many issues were involved. She rephrased her purpose: "To inform audience members how low-impact aerobics can improve their health."

The Central Idea

Whereas the specific purpose expresses what we want to accomplish when we give the speech, the **central idea** statement (also called the *thesis statement*) establishes the main thrust of the speech. Everything in the speech relates to the central idea. In an informative speech, the central idea contains the information you want the audience to remember, in a persuasive speech, it tells audience members what you want them to do.

The difference between a specific purpose and a central idea statement is illustrated in the following examples. Notice that the central idea explains the *why* or the *how* of the specific purpose.

Specific Purpose: To persuade my audience to protect themselves against car theft.

Central Idea: Car thefts occur because people buy cars attractive to car thieves, leave the cars in areas where theft is likely to occur, and are careless in locking their cars or securing valuables.

Specific Purpose: To inform my audience about how to make sure their drinking water is safe.

Central Idea: People can do three things to ensure their drinking water is safe: (1) have it tested; (2) reduce exposure to bacteria, lead, and disinfection products; and (3) purchase an activated-carbon filter.

Specific Purpose: To persuade my audience that it pays to write effective complaint letters.

Central Idea: Effective complaint letters should include all the relevant material, be neat, be written to the person in charge, establish rapport, state the problem succinctly, explain the action you would like taken, and end on a positive note.

The central idea should be stated in a full sentence, contain one idea, and use precise language. Sometimes it is not possible to come up with a central idea statement until you have finished organizing and outlining the speech. When you start working on your speech, you should have a tentative central purpose in mind; when you have finished organizing and outlining the speech, you can refine it.

Ivan decided on a speech topic and a specific purpose right away. His parents had just finished building a new house, and many of the materials that were used in the construction had been recycled. Ivan decided to give a speech with the specific purpose "To inform my audience how recycled materials can be used in building houses." Ivan knew his central idea would contain information about the kinds of recycled materials that could be used, but the specific concepts did not emerge until he had a rough outline:

I. *The United States builds a million houses each year, and many of the materials traditionally used are in short supply.*

II. *Waste paper products can be used to replace wood that is not visible.*

III. *Shredded tires, plastic, melted scrap steel, and iron can be used throughout the house.*

Once Ivan had completed his outline, he knew his central idea would be "The United States can save many of its scarce resources by building houses from recycled materials."

TRY THIS

To what extent should speakers pay attention to the values implied in their topic choices? Are the following topics ever appropriate? What are the ethical implications of these topics?

- How to get out of paying a speeding ticket

- How to shoplift without being detected

- How to get into an athletic event without paying

- How to cheat on a college examination

- How to get out of paying income taxes

ANALYZING THE AUDIENCE

Margaret Hernandez is the director of an organization called Citizens for a Better Environment. The organization has decided that its priority for the year is to conduct a campaign to get people to avoid buying products with excessive packaging or with packaging that is difficult to recycle. Since much of the campaign will consist of educating the public, Ms. Hernandez has scheduled several speeches throughout the community. She will speak to all kinds of audiences: on Monday to sixth graders in a middle school, on Wednesday to senior citizens, on Thursday to a college class, and on Friday to landfill managers in a statewide meeting.

In her speeches Ms. Hernandez always talks about packaging. However, she does not make the same speech to every audience. Instead, she adapts her material to make it appropriate for each particular group. Before she makes the speech to sixth graders, she finds out from their teacher that they have started a unit on recycling in their social studies class, and so they have some knowledge of the need to recycle. Ms. Hernandez decides to talk about two product packages that sixth graders are likely to know about: peanut butter and catsup. In this speech she discusses how difficult it is to recycle plastic and points out that they can help the recycling effort by urging their parents to buy these products in glass containers.

When Ms. Hernandez goes to speak to senior citizens, she assumes that many of them eat frozen dinners that can be heated in the oven or microwave. She brings in one brand of dinner that has three layers of packaging and uses this as a starting point to talk about the problems of packaging. She takes a similar approach with the college students. This time, however, she uses a package of microwave popcorn, a popular item in the dormitory. She asks students to imagine how large the trash pile would be if, in one week's time, half the students in the dorm made microwave popcorn in throwaway containers. Before she leaves, she gives the students a handout on how to make popcorn in containers that can be reused.

When Ms. Hernandez prepares to talk to the landfill managers, she knows that her speech should take a different direction. Since they run the landfills throughout the state, they are well aware of the problems of too much trash and garbage. Ms. Hernandez decides that her focus with this group will be on public education. Because there are only two branches of Citizens for a Better Environment, she tells the managers how to set up similar organizations in their own communities. She also recommends some activities they can engage in to educate the public.

The Role of the Speaker

In all of the above examples, Ms. Hernandez was playing the role of the speaker. Whenever you play this role, the audience has certain expectations of you. When an audience comes to hear you, it expects that you will be knowledgeable about your topic and that you will present what you know in an interesting way. Ms. Hernandez is a competent speaker not only because she knows her subject but also because she knows her audiences.

What Ms. Hernandez has done is to use audience analysis to adapt her subject matter to the specific characteristics of each group. **Audience analysis** is the process of finding out what the members of the audience already know about the subject, what they might be interested in, what their attitudes and beliefs are, and what kinds of people make up the audience. In your role as speaker you should consider audience analysis as one of the most important parts of your preparation.

Audience Knowledge

One important aspect of audience analysis is to take into account how much the audience is likely to know about a subject. In a practical sense, we can make only an educated guess about our audience's knowledge. We can assume that if we are talking to a lay audience and we pick a topic related to a specialized field of knowledge (CD-ROM, electronic book technology, laser surgery, health care, behavioral psychology), we will have to explain and define a lot of basic terminology before we can go into the subject in any depth. For example, when Sam spoke to his class about dietary fat, he had to explain such terms as *saturated*, *polyunsaturated*, and *hydrogenated* before he could talk about anything else.

On some subjects we can assume that audiences have a base of general knowledge. If we are speaking on vitamins, we can assume most people know that vitamins are good for us and even that vitamin C is particularly good for preventing and treating colds. But a general knowledge about other vitamins should not be taken for granted.

Speakers should realize that although people have general information about many subjects, they usually don't know the specifics. Most people know, for example, that the Constitution guarantees us the right to free speech. Yet if you were to ask them what *free speech* means, they would probably be a little fuzzy on a definition or on what is encompassed by the term. Would they know, for example, that the courts regard ringing a bell or burning a flag as a form of free speech?

To give another example, when speaking to a college audience about her recent trip to mainland China, Ming assumed that most of her listeners would know approximately where China is located and that most of them would know that China is ruled by a Communist government. She figured, however, that most of them would not know much about such important Chinese ideas as communal farming or the Cultural Revolution, and so she took some time to explain them. Once she had given this background information, her speech and slides about what she had seen and done made much more sense.

In a college speech class, you can get some idea of how much your audience knows about your subject by asking your friends and classmates what they know. If you have been asked to speak before a group you belong to, you can ask a couple of members what they know about the subject. If they don't know very much, you can assume that your audience won't either and that you will have to start by giving basic information. When you are speaking to community or professional groups, often the program chairperson who is responsible for finding speakers will be able to give you some information about audience members' level of knowledge and also about what is likely to interest them.

Audience Interest

Some subjects seem to be inherently interesting. Books on the best-seller list usually are about diet, exercise, and money. If you look at the topics covered by popular magazines, you will discover that self-help or self-improvement is the category of articles that appears most often. However, most of us do not want to be limited to speaking about physical fitness, diet, and self-help. Instead, we have to find a way to make other subjects appealing to our listeners.

One way to interest an audience in a topic is to point out that it has importance and relevance to them. Jan, an English major and a tutor in the Writing Center, wants to give a speech on the importance of writing skills. She knows that most students would like to improve their grades, but she also knows that most of them do not want to listen to a lecture on English composition. She decides to call her speech "Five Tips for Better Grades on Papers" and concentrates on giving specific and practical advice.

Another way to attract an audience's interest is to get listeners involved in the subject. Christian wants to persuade his audience that a cheap way to travel and see America is to get involved in American Youth Hostels. He begins his speech with some specific stories about staying in various hostels across the country. He goes on to tell how many students take advantage of hostels, where they are located, and what staying in hostels involves—the commitment to helping out by cooking meals and cleaning up. Even though his audience might not have had an interest in the subject to begin with, his examples are so compelling that he creates an interest.

Since you will be speaking on a subject that interests you, it might be useful to spend some time thinking about why you find this area so intriguing. What things about it caught your attention in the first place? If you can recreate your own enthusiasm for a subject, you will have a better chance of exciting your audience's interest too.

Audience Attitudes and Beliefs

When planning your speech, you also need to consider your audience's attitudes and beliefs about your subject. Often you will be speaking before an audience that shares your beliefs—as when you speak before your club or your church group. The Sierra Club (a conservation group) will appreciate a speech on the environmental position of the federal government. The Marketing Club will be interested in hearing from a local sales representative who has surpassed all previous sales records. Fellow employees will be interested in listening to a speech by an expert on profit sharing. College students will favor a proposal requiring instructors to put copies of their examinations on file at the library. These subjects tie into the attitudes and beliefs of the audience members.

But sometimes your audience may not have any particular attitudes or beliefs about your subject. They may not have enough information to make up their minds, or they may not care enough to have an opinion. The latter will be especially difficult to deal with. If you want to appeal to an indifferent audience, you will have to try especially hard to make your listeners feel that the speech has relevance and importance to them. Alexis, for example, wanted to speak to his class about the importance of voting in the student government election. He knew that most of his listeners believed that voting was a good idea but that when election day came, few of them would actually vote. To motivate them, he began his speech by pointing out that student government controls three areas of high interest to students: concerts, athletics, and food service.

Sometimes your own beliefs run contrary to those of your audience, and your speech may be met with hostility. If you think your audience may be opposed to your ideas on a subject, you have to plan your speech carefully. Robin, for example, knew that her classmates would be opposed to the idea of expanding the number of class periods during the day because it meant both earlier and later class periods. Yet, by researching her topic carefully and presenting reasons for the expansion (to make more courses available to students), she was able to show that an expansion was necessary. Her audience might not have been happy about the expansion, but they had a better understanding of the reasons for it. In his speech, Kamil set out to persuade members of his speech class that the college should increase the amount of support it gives to student government. He expected his audience to be resistant to the idea because of the number of letters by con-

CONSIDER THIS

The issue of free speech versus "hate speech" is particularly important at universities because they are supposed to be symbols of open thought and discussion. As you read the following examples, try to answer these questions: To what extent can colleges guarantee free speech and, at the same time, satisfy the demands of all students to be protected from verbal assault? Should college speech codes forbid language that demeans individuals on the basis of race, national origin, religion, sex, sexual orientation, disability, or age?

1. At the University of Wisconsin, one student was put on probation and made to take a course in ethics or East Asian history for stealing a roommate's bank card. He was accused of discrimination because his roommate was Japanese.
2. Dr. Leonard Jeffries, head of the African American Studies Department at City College, New York, was dismissed from his post as chairman because of a speech he made. He said that Jews and the Mafia conspired to make Hollywood movies that portrayed blacks offensively, and he blamed rich Jews for the slave trade.
3. At the University of Pennsylvania some dorm residents shouted insults at a group of black sorority women making noise outside late at night. The women said the words shouted included "the N-word" and "black water buffaloes." The student who admitted shouting "water buffalo," not "black water buffalo," was accused of racial harassment and threatened with expulsion.

cerned students printed in the college newspaper. However, he was able to show that interest in student government was increasing, that student government had a positive effect on campus concerns that directly related to students, and that more money could be used in advantageous and responsible ways. Not all of his classmates were persuaded, but after the speech was over, several told Kamil they thought his ideas were worth considering.

People's attitudes and beliefs affect how speeches are received. Sometimes, despite our "free" society and despite the protection of free speech, our ideas are not considered acceptable. Notice, for example, in the "Consider This" on free speech that just because free speech *should* exist does not mean that it *does* exist.

Since people's attitudes and beliefs will affect how your speech is

4. A columnist for the University of Pennsylvania student newspaper attacked affirmative action and called Martin Luther King, Jr., an adulterer and a plagiarist. The columnist was accused of racial harassment. The entire 14,000-copy run of the newspaper in which the column appeared was confiscated by angry black students, but the university took no action against them.

5. When Michigan State University was looking for a new president, they located one of their leading candidates in Dale Lick, 55, president of Florida State University. As a candidate, Lick had excellent credentials. As it turned out, he withdrew his name because of the outrage that resulted from a comment he had made four years previously while president of the University of Maine. The comment, "A black athlete can actually outjump a white athlete on the average, so they're better at the game [of basketball]," prompted a trustee to say, ". . . There is no way we can have this man as a candidate."*

*Source: *The New York Times*, May 30, 1993, sec. 4, p. 3.

QUESTIONS

1. Should universities regulate free speech?

2. Should codes specify what is punishable very precisely, drawing distinctions between that which is harassing, intimidating, or threatening on the one hand and that which is offensive on the other? What is your position?

received, it is absolutely essential that they be considered when your speech is in the planning stage. Important clues to people's attitudes and beliefs can be discovered through audience demographics.

Audience Demographics

Even if you have no specific information about your audience's knowledge, interest, and attitude toward your subject, certain factual information about the audience members can tell you a great deal. **Demographic analysis** reveals data about the characteristics of a group of people, including such things as age, sex, education, occupation, race/nationality/ethnic origin, geographic location, and group affiliation.

What generalizations would you make about this audience from looking at the individual members? How would the make-up of this audience influence the material you would put in your speech?

When we work with demographic information, we generalize about the *entire audience*; our generalizations might not be true of individual members. For example, on the basis of demographic data we have gathered, we might generalize that the age of our speech class audience is between 18 and 27—even though one member is in his fifties. In the same way, we can make generalizations about the class's educational level or about its racial composition. And on the basis of such generalizations, we can make some predictions about what might interest the people in this audience and what they might be knowledgeable about.

One caution about generalizing. There is a great deal of change going on in the world today, with concurrent changing demographics. This makes the need for analyzing audiences even more important, but it means, too, that we have to be sensitive and responsive to the differences we discover. To analyze without sensitivity and responsiveness has the same effect as not analyzing at all. What good is it, for example, to discover that audience members are extremely well informed on a topic, very gender sensitive, or made up of a majority of people of different ethnic groups if there is no willingness to change one's approach because of this new information? Let's consider each of the demographic characteristics in turn.

AGE

As a speaker you need to have a sense of the age range of your audience because interests differ with age. College-age people are usually interested in school, future jobs, music, and interpersonal relationships. Young parents are often interested in subjects that might affect their children, such as school bus safety and school board policy. Middle-aged people tend to be focused on their jobs, and older adults tend to be interested in issues related to leisure activities and health. However, not all subjects are age-related. Computers, elections, and world and national news, for example, have interest for most age groups because they affect everyone.

Sometimes the same subject can be of interest to various age groups if it is adapted to each group's particular concerns. Take the subject of nutrition. If you were speaking to an elementary school audience, you would probably not go into detail about vitamins and minerals because you would have problems keeping the attention of the children. Instead, you might use puppets (one that eats junk food and another that eats good food) or put your speech into a story with characters the children could identify with. If you talked about nutrition to pregnant women, you could adapt your speech to the needs of the fetus, assuming that every mother-to-be has a high interest in having a healthy baby. When you speak to older adults, you could talk about their particular nutritional needs, such as the importance of calcium to avoid bone deterioration.

It is sometimes difficult to generalize with respect to age. Look, for example, at "college-age" people. The average age of college students is no longer about 20. It is now around 26, and it is likely to go higher with an increasing nontraditional population. Students, and others, need to be sensitive in their classrooms and in the workplace to age differences and need to avoid stereotyping in their speeches.

GENDER

The gender of audience members can also be important. In a speech that's open to the public, you will probably have both men and women in your audience. If you have either an all-male or all-female audience, it will probably be because you are talking to a club or organization whose members are all of one sex. The topic of your speech will then be influenced more by the organization itself than by the sex of its members. For example, the American Association of University Women has long been interested in education. If you were speaking to this group, its interest in education would be more important than the fact that the group is all female.

Speakers must be sensitive and responsive to the gender issue. If you deliver a speech to a mixed audience but do not acknowledge the presence, and appeal to the needs of both genders, not only will you miss the mark—your speech may even seem sexist and inappropriate. For example, many volunteer organizations once included mostly homemakers. A speech to one of these organizations now needs to address working women's less flexible, more demanding schedules, which limit their time for volunteer commitments.

EDUCATION

The audience's level of education is important to a speaker because it gives some idea of the group's knowledge and experience. We can assume that the more education people have, the more specialized their knowledge. Lawyers, doctors, and Ph.D.'s all have specialized knowledge; however, they might have little information about subjects other than their own. Your main consideration when you prepare a speech is whether your audience has the same knowledge you have or whether you will have to start with the basics. For example, if you are a biology major, don't assume that your speech class will know what the terms *homeostasis* and *morphology* mean. Although people might have a general idea of what these words mean, they might not know their precise scientific definitions.

OCCUPATION

The occupation of audience members may influence how you approach some topics. Sometimes occupation indicates an area of specialized knowledge: paramedics and nurses know about the human body; lawyers know about legal rights; social workers know about social problems. Occupation can also indicate interest in a subject. Most professional groups would probably be interested in a speech about ethics in their profession. Factory workers might be interested in the workings of a union or how to form one. If you are speaking to an occupational group, try to adapt your speech to that audience's job interests.

RACE/NATIONALITY/ETHNIC ORIGIN

Politicians have whole audiences made up of a single racial or ethnic group. To identify with these groups, they eat knishes with Jews, burritos with Mexicans, and soul food with African Americans. When they speak to one of these groups, they try to identify with their goals and aspirations.

If you are speaking to a group with members from diverse backgrounds, you should be particularly careful in your use of language. If your audience includes foreign students, they may have problems understanding slang and colloquial expressions. If you are in a class with people from different ethnic groups, some of your classmates might not understand experiences that are typical of your own group. For example, not everyone has gone to summer camp, and not everyone has eaten kim chi.

It used to be that awareness of cultural diversity usually occurred as a result of foreign travel. Today, however, there is a continuous flow of immigration to the United States. Ethnic populations are increasing, and these new racial and ethnic populations tend to hold on to their own customs.[3] This creates increasing challenges for speakers.

One thing speakers cannot do is reduce all cultures, or even one culture, to a single type. In their book *Our Voices*, Alberto Gonzalez, Marsha Houston, and Victoria Chen make it clear that "there is not 'one' style of any particular ethnic group any more than there is 'one' style of Anglo-American

How do speakers make certain their speech will be appropriate for their audience? Cristina Stuart tells how one group of speakers had little sense of their audience:

I remember a group of bank managers who asked me to advise them on the presentations they were giving to school graduates. Naturally they hoped to encourage these young men and women to open bank accounts, but somehow they weren't having the success they had hoped for. It was hardly surprising. These middle-aged men didn't realize the need to understand their audience. It was no good talking about security, savings, and pensions to a group of people who were longing to spend, spend, spend. Once the bank managers made their talk relevant to sixteen-year-olds, their presentations were successful.

Source: From Cristina Stuart, *How to Be an Effective Speaker* (Chicago: NTC Publishing Group, 1993), p. 11.

QUESTIONS

1. How could these bank managers have improved their knowledge of high school graduates?

2. What might the bank managers have said in the speech to identify with their audience?

3. What appeals could the bank managers have made that would be of direct interest to their audience?

communication."[4] What this means, more than anything else, is that speakers need to be sensitive and responsive to diverse audiences. The more information and knowledge they have about their listeners, the better they will be able to specifically adapt their speeches to the needs of those audience members.

GEOGRAPHIC LOCATION

Your audience's geographic location may affect the content and approach of your speech. If the federal government is giving money to improve airport runways, find out if some of this money is coming to the local airport. If the nation has been hit with a crime wave (or a heat wave), has this been a problem in your local area? If you have a chance to speak in a town or city other than your own, the audience will be pleased if you know something about its area. Ralph Nader, the consumer advocate, always does some geographical research before he speaks. When he spoke on the environment to upstate New Yorkers, he mentioned specific environmental problems in their own area.

GROUP AFFILIATION

Knowing the clubs, organizations, or associations that audience members belong to can be useful because people usually identify with the goals and interests of their organizations. If you speak to a group, you should be aware of what it stands for and adapt your speech accordingly.

If you speak to the local historical society, its members will expect you to speak on a subject that has some historic angle. The campus journalism society will be interested in a speech dealing with the theory (e.g., freedom of the press) or practice (e.g., using video display terminals) of journalism. Some groups have particular issues or themes for the year, and they look for speakers who can tie their speeches into these themes.

ANALYZING THE OCCASION

When planning your speech, as well as doing audience analysis, you need to consider the occasion. Factors to take into account when analyzing the occasion include the length of the speech, the time of day, and the location of the speech.

Length of the Speech

Always stick to the time limit set for the speech. If you are giving a speech in class, you will probably be told the amount of time you can speak. If you are asked to give a speech to a group or organization, you should ask how long you will be expected to speak. When the audience has an expectation of the length of your speech, it will get restless if you go on too long or be disappointed if you run short. If your speech topic is too complicated to be covered in the allotted time, you should narrow your topic or find another subject to speak on.

More than one speaker hasn't known when to stop. Mortimer J. Adler has written about the time he was giving lectures on philosophy to college students. Student interest in the subject was great, but not great enough to sit through each of Adler's two-hour lectures. When Adler returned the next year to deliver another series of lectures, the students hid alarm clocks in the lecture hall. After an hour, all of the alarms went off. At the second lecture, a student pulled the main switch after an hour and blacked out the lecture hall. Adler got the message; he cut his remaining lectures to a listenable length.[5]

Time of Day

The time of day should also be a consideration when choosing your topic. In a classroom setting, students seem to be less alert in the early morning and late afternoon. If you are in a class that meets at one of these times, you have to pay special attention to the appeal of your presentation. An interesting topic or a topic handled in an interesting manner can get the attention of even a sluggish audience. Probably most public speeches occur at night. Since people are usually somewhat tired, the speaker has to take special care to find material that will hold the audience's attention.

Physical Setting of the Speech

The place where the speech will be given might also be a consideration. If you are not familiar with the room, you might want to take a look at it before you speak. Is the lectern where you want it? Are the chairs arranged the way you want them? Is there a public address system? Do you know how to turn it on? It is easier to make changes before the audience arrives.

A speaker we witnessed gave a speech in a large gymnasium. Arriving moments before the speech was to be delivered, he discovered the public address system had not been set up. Also, the lectern was placed in the middle of the gym instead of closer to the audience as he preferred. The final insult was that the public address system, once working, could only be heard by the center portion of the large audience. People seated at either end of the gym could not hear. The disaster could not be rectified in time to save the speech

Comfort should also be considered in a location. Many a politician has given a speech from the courtyard steps where there is no place for the audience to sit. If you are in a location where the audience cannot be comfortable, be prepared to give a short speech and get to the point before you lose your audience.

 ## SUMMARY

Whenever you are scheduled to make a speech, it is important to find a topic that interests you. Two techniques will help you discover topics: making a personal inventory, which means taking a careful look at what interests you, and brainstorming, which is a method of generating ideas through free association.

Once you have an idea for a topic, you should test whether the topic is

TRY THIS

Here is a brief survey you can use to gather information about your audience. Although this survey is designed primarily for classroom use, you can easily adapt it to a broader audience by changing some questions and adding others. Have students circle the correct response or add a response in the blank labeled "Other."

1. I am:
   A. Female
   B. Male
2. My approximate age is:
   A. 18–22
   B. 23–29
   C. 30–39
   D. Over 40
3. My primary ethnic background is:
   A. Anglo
   B. African-American
   C. Hispanic
   D. Native American
   E. Asian
   F. Other _____
4. My marital status is:
   A. Single
   B. Married
   C. Divorced
   D. Other _____
5. I live:
   A. In my parents' home
   B. In my own apartment or house
   C. In a dormitory
   D. In a fraternity or sorority
6. I am involved in: (Circle all that apply.)
   A. Athletics
   B. Student government

appropriate for the audience, whether it is appropriate for you, and whether it is appropriate for the occasion.

Whatever you plan to speak on, you should narrow the topic so that it can be adequately covered within the time set for your speech. Narrowing the topic means taking some specific aspect of the subject and speaking about that.

   C. A fraternity or sorority
   D. Intramural activities
   E. An honor society
   F. Other _____
7. I currently:
   A. Go to school full time
   B. Go to school full time and work part time
   C. Go to school part time and work part time
   D. Go to school part time and work full time
   E. Other _____
8. To what extent are you liberal or conservative in your religious orientation? (Circle the number that most closely reflects your attitude.)

   Liberal 5 4 3 2 1 Conservative

9. To what extent are you liberal or conservative in your political orientation? (Circle the number that most closely reflects your attitude.)

   Liberal 5 4 3 2 1 Conservative

10. How involved or committed are you on this issue?

   _____
   (Write the topic of your speech here.)
   Highly Involved 5 4 3 2 1 Not Involved

11. How informed are you on this issue?

   _____
   (Write the topic of your speech here.)
   Highly Informed 5 4 3 2 1 Poorly Informed

12. How interested are you in this issue?

   _____
   (Write the topic of your speech here.)
   Highly Interested 5 4 3 2 1 Not Interested

Every speech should have a general purpose, a specific purpose, and a central idea. The general purpose relates to whether the speech is informative or persuasive. The specific purpose focuses on what you want to inform or persuade your audience about. The central idea captures the main idea of the speech—the idea you want your audience to retain after the speech.

Audience analysis is the process of finding out what the audience knows about the subject, what it might be interested in, what its attitudes and beliefs are, and what kinds of people are likely to be present. Useful demographic information about an audience includes age, gender, education, occupation, race/nationality/ethnic origin, geographic location, and group affiliation.

In analyzing the speech occasion, the speaker should consider the length of the speech, the time of day, and the physical setting where it will take place.

NOTES

[1] Steve Allen, *How to Make a Speech* (New York: McGraw-Hill, 1986), p. 40.

[2] Alex Osborn, *Applied Imagination: Principles and Procedures of Creative Thinking* (New York: Scribner's, 1979).

[3] Alberto Gonzalez, Marsha Houston, and Victoria Chen, *Our Voices: Essays in Culture, Ethnicity, and Communication (An Intercultural Anthology)*, Los Angeles: Roxbury, 1994, p. xv.

[4] Ibid.

[5] Mortimer J. Adler, *How to Speak, How to Listen* (New York: Macmillan, 1983), pp. 71–72.

FURTHER READING

AILES, ROGER. *You Are the Message.* New York: Doubleday, 1988. Although this is a practical book full of advice and suggestions about great communication, the insights and anecdotes about the Kennedys, Reagan, Bush, and other big names in politics make it interesting. A valuable resource for anyone who has to go out and speak.

ALLEN STEVE. *How to Make a Speech.* New York: McGraw-Hill, 1988. This engaging, entertaining how-to book is simple and specific. Allen brings to bear his many years of radio and television work as both comedian and actor as well as his forty years at the lectern. Allen's focus of this work tends to be presentational skills.

DETZ, JOAN. *How to Write and Give a Speech.* New York: St. Martin's Press, 1992. Detz is a corporate speechwriter who gives practical advice on focusing the topic, assessing the audience, organizing material, simplifying and sharpening language, making humor work, handling tough question-and-answer sessions, delivering speeches with style, and getting good media coverage. A fast-paced, confidence-building book.

HENNESSY, BERNARD. *Public Opinion,* 5th ed. Monterey, CA: Brooks/Cole, 1985. The author includes several sections on conducting polls and administering questionnaires. A useful source for those interested in techniques for gaining information about their audience.

HUMES, JAMES C. *The Sir Winston Method: The Five Secrets of Speaking the Language of Leadership.* New York: Morrow, 1991. With 21 chapters divided into brief quick-read sections, this is a fast and enjoyable book. Humes is a communication consultant who presents seminars to business leaders, lectures on communication, writes speeches for presidents (from Eisenhower to Bush), and teaches speech at the University of Pennsylvania. Although brief, the book is highly recommended because of its practical, useful advice.

MAKAY, JOHN J. *Public Speaking: Theory Into Practice.* Fort Worth: Harcourt Brace Jovanovich, 1992. This textbook is thorough and complete. It focuses on research, public speaking ethics, and the history of public address. It includes excerpts from actual speeches and interviews with nationally known public speakers. It is a solid book designed for the serious student of public speaking.

PEOPLES, DAVID A. *Presentations Plus,* 2d ed. New York: Wiley, 1992. The author is an internationally celebrated speaker, presenter, and sales trainer for major corporations. This how-to book is full of illustrations, checklists, strategies, guidelines, and principles. It is interesting, entertaining, and very readable. It covers all the basics you need to present, persuade, and win.

SPRAGUE, JO, AND DOUGLAS STUART. *The Speaker's Handbook,* 3d ed. Fort Worth: Harcourt Brace Jovanovich, 1992. This is both a reference guide for the individual speaker and a textbook. It is a thorough compendium of principles, examples, and exercises that covers the issues speakers commonly confront in preparing and delivering their material. Although close to 400 pages, the book is concise and tight. It is an excellent resource.

KEY TERMS

abstracts

catalog

comparison

contrast

database

definition

example

periodicals

polls

statistics

study

supporting
    material

testimony

vertical file

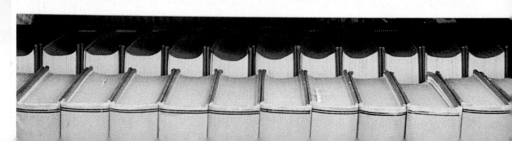

11

Finding Speech Material

CHAPTER OBJECTIVES

After reading this chapter, you should be able to:

1 Include some of your own experiences as part of your speech.

2 Gather speech information by interviewing.

3 Research your speech in the library.

4 Use the various reference tools in the library.

5 Recognize the various kinds of supporting materials.

6 Use the supporting materials that are most appropriate for your topic and your audience.

Staci was desperate. She had to give a speech, and she hadn't found a topic yet. As she sat with her friends in the student union, she said, "Come on, help me find a topic for my speech." Elena mentioned the results of a survey presented in her business class. When asked to rank factors that contributed to success in the classroom, 72 percent of the Japanese workers surveyed listed hard work first while only 27 percent of the Americans surveyed agreed. "What about talking about hard work? That would hold attention," Elena suggested. Staci said, "That's a good idea. Students are always talking about ways to get out of work."

Staci didn't have much time to prepare a speech, but she knew she should start in the library. She checked out the computerized card catalog under "Work" and found many book titles—too many. Once she located the books in the stacks, she realized she didn't have time to read them. She found a newspaper article by using the computerized index to *The New York Times,* and she found two magazine articles by using the *Reader's Guide to Periodical Literature.*

Later that night when she put together her speech, she found she didn't have much material at all. When she was organized enough to rehearse it, she found it was only three minutes long—and that was when she paused a lot. However, it was too late to do anything about it. When she gave the speech the next day, Staci's audience listened closely at first but soon lost interest. It was clear that she had not prepared well; she could say little more than that hard work matters. That was the same speech their parents had given most of them many times before. Listeners asked no questions. The speech was barely mediocre, and Staci felt embarrassed about the whole experience.

In another speech class, Eric was planning to give a speech on the same subject. Eric, however, had read an anthology in which many of the essays argued that individual opportunity is a myth—and he had disagreed with that premise so much that he had written a term paper titled "Life's Chances Are Determined by Hard Work." Eric thought this might be a good speech topic as well, so he went to the library early to see what he could find.

He found several books and a number of articles, and he learned some historical background from the writings of Jean de Crèvecoeur and Alexis de Tocqueville. He put together many note cards of information. Because he had such excellent background resources, Eric organized his speech around the history of the idea that hard work was a central idea to early American immigrants and why and how the work ethic had slowly come under attack. He ended the speech by concentrating on many factors thought to contribute to the devaluing of hard work in contemporary society: parents and teachers are so concerned about the child's self-esteem that they no longer reprimand laziness or poor workmanship; Americans tend to believe that success comes through innate ability and not through hard work; and many people seem to think that luck plays a large role in success—such as being in the right place at the right time.

The audience listened to Eric's speech with obvious interest. It was clear that he had done some research and knew quite a lot about his topic. After the speech was over, several people asked him questions, and at the end of the class someone even asked how long he had been working on the speech. By doing his research and carefully planning his speech, Eric had come across as a *credible*—that is, believable—speaker.

No doubt you would like to have the same reaction from your class that Eric had. You would like to be thought of as credible, as knowing your subject. The key to having this happen lies in the research you do for your speech. The more diligent you are about finding relevant material and adapting it to your audience, the more successful you will be when you give your speech.

RESEARCHING YOUR TOPIC: WHERE TO LOOK

Once you have decided on the topic and specific purpose of your speech, it is time to begin looking for useful information. The three most common sources you can draw on for relevant material are your own personal experience and observation, interviews, and the library. Let's look at each of these.

Personal Experience and Observation

If you have chosen a topic in which you have a strong interest, the first thing you should ask yourself is whether you have had any direct experience with the subject. Your own experience can provide interesting and valuable material. For example, when Dan spoke to his speech class on the subject "Preventing Fires in Your Home," he drew heavily on his experiences as a volunteer firefighter. Not only did he describe the tragedy of a family being burned out of their home, but he also gave some facts and figures on the causes of home fires that he had learned during his training period.

When Kelly spoke of the danger of drunk drivers, she too gave facts and figures: how many innocent victims are killed each year by drunks on the road. Then she stunned her classmates by telling them that her own sister was one of those victims. Because Kelly spoke out of personal experience, her example became much more vivid and real than if she had used only statistics from a book or an article.

Sometimes we do not put enough value on personal experience; we think that if it happened to us, it can't be important. However, relating our own experiences to the subject of our speech can often provide the most interesting material of all.

Interviewing

Interviews can be an excellent source of speech material. Because you can talk directly to decision makers, interviews are one of the best ways of gathering material on campus-related topics such as why three people are put in dorm rooms intended for two or what energy-saving devices are used on campus. Interviews are also a good way of getting up-to-date information from experts. For example, if a war breaks out in the Middle East, you can interview the person on campus who is most knowledgeable in this area. Another advantage of interviewing is that if the subject is complicated, you can ask questions about points you don't understand.

Using the Library

The library can be a rich source of material. Any library—whether large or small—has millions of pieces of information. Fortunately for users, all libraries organize their information in essentially the same way, and so once you learn how to use one library, you can use this skill in *any* library. The goal of this section is to help you make the most of your campus (or public) library to find information that will be useful in preparing speeches.

THE LIBRARY CATALOG

The library **catalog** contains information about all the material in the library and identifies where it can be found. In every college or university, the catalog is either printed on small cards housed in a many-drawered cabinet or stored on a central computer to which you can gain access through a terminal. Although most libraries now use computers, we include a brief section on "The Card Catalog" for those that do not. Both systems use call numbers. Although call numbers organize library materials by subject, to the library user their main use is to help locate the book. All call numbers that begin with "PN," for example, will be located in the same general area.

Since card and computer catalogs are somewhat different, we would like to discuss each one here.

THE CARD CATALOG. Entries are organized in three ways: by author, by title, and by subject. If you want a particular book and you know who wrote it, you can look it up by author. If you know only the title, you can look it up by title. If you don't know any authors or titles but are interested in a particular subject, you can look in the subject catalog. Figure 11-1 shows cards for the same book classified by author, title, and subject. Note that in the upper left corner of each card the call number is given.

The catalog entries not only tell you where to find the material but also give you some general information about it so you can decide whether it will be useful. Always check the date of the materials. In some subjects, the date when the material was published is not very important. However, in other subjects you will want to have the most timely information.

THE COMPUTER CATALOG. In many ways the computer catalog duplicates the card catalog: it has call numbers and entries arranged by author, subject, and title. The main difference in the computer catalog is that it almost

```
        Rovin, Jeff.
ref.
P       The encyclopedia of monsters/ Jeff Rovin.—New
        York:
96          Facts on File, c1989. ix, 390 p. : ill.; 28 cm.
.M6         Includes index.
R68         ISBN 0-8160-1824-3
1989

            1. Monsters in mass media—
        Dictionaries. 2. Popular culture—
        Dictionaries. I. Title
```

```
        The encyclopedia of monsters
ref.
P       Rovin, Jeff.
96
.M6     The encyclopedia of monsters/ Jeff Rovin.—New
        York:
R68         Facts on File, c1989. ix, 390 p. : ill. ; 28 cm.
1989        ISBN 0-8160-1824-3

            1. Monsters in mass media—
        Dictionaries. 2. Popular culture—
        Dictionaries.
```

```
        MONSTERS IN MASS MEDIA—DICTIONARIES
ref.    1989
P       Rovin, Jeff.
96
.M6     The encyclopedia of monsters/ Jeff Rovin.—New
        York :
R68         Facts on File, c1989. ix, 390 p. : ill. ; 28 cm.
1989        ISBN 0-8160-1824-3

            1. Monsters in mass media—
        Dictionaries. 2. Popular culture—
        Dictionaries.
```

FIGURE 11-1
Card Catalog: The Same Book Classified by Author, Title, and Subject

always gives you more information. Let's look at this in greater detail.

When you sit in front of a computer screen, remember that entries start with the general and, with each new screen, move to the more specific. As you can see in Figure 11-2, if you type in "biological rhythms," the computer responds with all the material in that category. If you want to look at a single entry, such as the book by Shirley Moore, you type in "12," and the screen for her book comes up. Note that at the bottom of the entry, the screen not only gives the call number but also tells exactly where the book is located in the library. In addition, the computer will tell you whether the book is available. As you can see on the third card in Figure 11-2, one copy of a particular book about Freud is available for circulation. Other information on the status of the book could tell you that the book is lost, that it is checked out (and when it will be back), or that it's in the reserve room.

Perhaps the greatest advantage of a computer catalog is that it's very easy to browse when you are using it. If you have several subjects in mind, you can easily check the computer to see what is available. You can also browse through the library's shelves without ever leaving your chair since most systems have a "shelf" command, which will show you all the items with a particular call number—items that would be shelved in the same section of the library.

If your library has its collection on computer, take some time to check the instruction manual to see how to use it best. Usually it's easy to search for books by author, title, subject, and key words, but the computer can do much more than that. The more you know about the computer, the more sophisticated and efficient your search will be.

Biological rhythms (82 citations)
[1]   Advances in climatic physiology. [1st ed.]. [1972].
[2]   An analysis of biorhythms and their effect on athletic injuries.
       / Klug, Gary A. 1973.
[3]   Analysis of periodicity of arrhythmias in patients with acute
       myocardial infarctions. / Nail, Lillian M. 1974.
[4]   Analysis of selected physiological variables and selected
       biological rhythms in the performance of track and field
       competitors. / Hall, Larry T. 1976.
[5]   Aspects of human efficiency: diurnal rhythm and loss of sleep.
       1972.
[6]   Avian breeding cycles. / Murton, R.K. 1977.
[7]   Bio rhythms [slide]. c1981.
[8]   Bioclocks [slide]. 1976.
[9]   Biological and biochemical oscillators. 1973.
[10]   Biological clocks. / Brady, John. 1979.
[11]   Biological clocks. / Cloudsley-Thompson, J. L. c1980.
[12]   Biological clocks and patterns. / Moore, Shirley. [1967].
[13]   Biological clocks and shift work scheduling. / United States.
       Congress. House. Committee on Science and Technology.
       Subcommittee on Investigations and Oversight. 1983.
— Lib All
>>>   1
>>>
To see more citations, press [NEXT] or [PREV].

Biological rhythms
Moore, Shirley
      Biological clocks and patterns. New York, Criterion Books, [1967].
      133 p. illus. 22 cm.
      Bibliography: p. 117–127.
      1. Biological rhythms. 2. Biological control systems.
Call#: QH527.M65
      East Pattee Second Floor
— Lib All
>>>   12   12 of 82
>>>

The scientific credibility of Freud's theories and therapy. / Fisher,
      Seymour. c1977.
BF173.F85F55
-Central Pattee Level 2
      Blue-
Now in Reserve Reading
      Room
      1 Available
— Lib All
>>>   st
>>>

FIGURE 11-2
**Screens from the
Computer Catalog**

LOOKING FOR ARTICLES

Periodicals—the inclusive name for magazines, journals, and newspapers—have the latest available information on a subject and are often used as source material for speeches. If you want to know, for example, what the American president said to the Russian president yesterday, the newspaper

CONSIDER THIS

♀♂ Here is the way Joyce Plath, an architectural designer, says she goes about designing a building—as told to Foss and Foss in *Women Speak*. As you read the description, see if you can see the parallels between designing a building and finding speech material.

When designing a building, Joyce first attends to the site, "noting views, neighborhood, sun angles, topography, flat areas for play or gardens, areas that should not be viewed (neighbors' houses, junk cars), and acoustics." She finds difficult sites particularly interesting. She then interviews her clients to determine "lifestyle, hobby and home-office needs, other people who may live there (parents, extended guests, future children), and, of course, budget." Making her houses fit the physical needs of the owner is a major priority for her. She also likes her houses to "capture sunlight and views and to have outside space protected from wind"; her structures also must be visually pleasing to proportion and style.

Source: Karen A. Foss and Sonja K. Foss, *Women Speak: The Eloquence of Women's Lives* (Prospect Heights, IL: Waveland, 1991), p. 34.

QUESTIONS

1. Are the parallels between designing a building and finding speech material clear?

2. Do you think there would be differences between the way women and men design buildings? Find speech material? What would these differences be?

3. Following the similarities between designing a building and finding speech material, what would be the exact procedures you would follow in finding speech material that would parallel the procedures Joyce Plath used in designing her building?

is your best source, for it will have the latest information. Magazine articles typically cover such subjects as the latest trends in a variety of popular subjects; academic journals cover the latest research.

The card or computer catalog will tell you which periodicals are held in the library, including those on microfilm. The catalog, however, does not list the articles in these periodicals. To find them, you must either check the periodical indexes in book form or use a computer designed for searching periodicals. Let's look at the indexes first.

Since hundreds of thousands of magazines and journal articles are published every month, you will need an index to find the particular articles you need. Your library is likely to have several such indexes, and, like the catalog, they classify material by author, title, and subject. When you are searching for articles in periodical indexes, you should identify the general category and then look for an index that is likely to cover that subject. For example, if you want to research preschools, the *Education Index* is likely to have more academic articles on that subject. If you are looking for articles about preschools in mass-circulated magazines, *The Reader's Guide to Periodical Literature* would be a good place to start.

Some other common indexes found in libraries are *Social Science Index; Applied Science and Technology Index; Index to Periodical Articles by and about Blacks; Books in English: Authors, Subjects, Titles; Business Periodicals Index; Monthly Catalog of United States Government Publications;* and *Consumer Index.*

Many periodicals sections of libraries have computers designed to search for articles in periodicals and journals. These computers have access to a **database**—a collection of information that can be read on a computer screen. Databases commonly found in periodical rooms are ERIC, an index to periodicals in education, and InfoTrac, an index of general interest and academic periodicals.

To use these computers, you type in the key words of the subject you wish to search. The computer will respond with all the relevant articles. Some databases also have **abstracts**—summaries of the articles. Abstracts will tell you enough about an article for you to decide whether it is worthwhile to locate the entire thing.

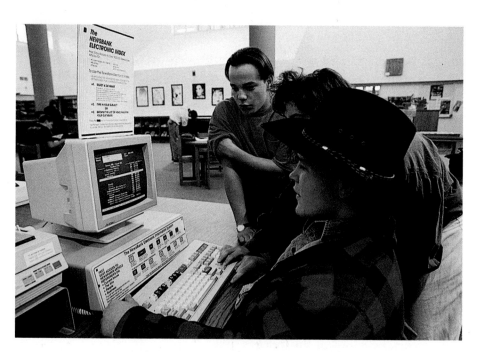

What kinds of topics are best searched for with News Bank?

Libraries can decide which indexes they want on Info Trac. What indexes are available at your library and what time periods do they cover?

Your search will be more successful if your entry is specific. The computer finds what you are looking for by matching the words you type with the same words in its database. For example, let's say you want to make a speech about how to protect your house from fire. If you type in only "fire," you could get hundreds of entries. However, if you type in "house fires," the computer will list only those titles that have both "house" and "fire" in them.

Whether you use indexes or a computer to search for articles, the actual periodical might not be available in your campus library. Thus, when you are researching, make a longer list of possible sources than you will actually use because you might be able to locate only a fraction of them.

Since libraries are always short of space, many of them have material (especially periodicals) on microfilm or microfiche. Microfilm and microfiche differ only in the method by which pages are put on the film. *Microfilm* presents data on a roll, with one page following another. In *microfiche*, a large number of pages are put on the same piece of film, which looks like a small note card. The machines needed to read each one are different. Don't let the machines intimidate you. Someone in the library will show you how to use them.

NEWSPAPERS. Most libraries have the local newspaper, papers from around the state, and a few of the important big-city newspapers. The big-city papers deal comprehensively with international and national issues, while the local papers cover information of importance to the particular area. Practically every college has *The New York Times*. This paper is particularly useful for research, since it publishes an index of many of the articles it carries. *The New York Times* is also one of the few newspapers to carry partial or full texts of such documents as Supreme Court decisions, legislation, and speeches (especially presidential ones).

If you don't see the newspaper you want on the newspaper rack, check the card catalog. Some libraries store newspapers and magazines on microfilm to save space.

FINDING REFERENCE WORKS

Every library has a reference section which contains materials that do not circulate. The reference works found in this section are factual materials that cover every subject you can think of. If you don't know very much about a subject, the reference section is a good place to begin.

ENCYCLOPEDIAS. Encyclopedias are an important part of any library's reference collection, and most libraries have several different sets. Encyclopedias contain short articles written by experts, and they are a very good way to get basic information on a subject you don't know much about. They work best as a starting point. Once you have the basic knowledge, you can do further research in other sources. Most encyclopedias are arranged in alphabetical order by subject. Some of the best-known are *The American Academic Encyclopedia, The Encylopaedia Britannica, World Book Encyclopedia, Collier's Encyclopedia,* and *The Encyclopedia Americana.*

ALMANACS. Almanacs are compilations of factual material. Although they do not contain in-depth material on which to base a speech, they are useful for checking out facts. If you want to know who won the Super Bowl in 1990 or how many people were on Death Row in 1993 or how much the federal government spends on welfare, you'll find it in an almanac. Some of the most popular almanacs are *The World Almanac, Information USA, Reader's Digest Almanac, Guinness Book of Records,* and *Information Please.*

BIOGRAPHICAL SOURCES. Biographical information can be useful in many contexts and is particularly useful if you are going to introduce or speak about someone with an established reputation. Several biographical sources are available, of which the *Who's Who* series is the best known. There are the broad, general editions—*Who's Who in the World, Who's Who in America*—and there are the more specific ones: *Who's Who in Finance and Industry . . . of American Women . . . in American Politics . . . in Government,* and *. . . in Science*—to name just a few. The entries, listed alphabetically by last name, typically list birth date, names of spouse and children, school attended, and accomplishments. Other biographical sources include *Current Biography, Dictionary of National* [English] *Biography, Dictionary of American Biography, New York Times Biographical Service,* and *The Biography Index.*

Figure 11-3 shows entries for Michael Crichton, the novelist, from two biographical sources.

(a) From *Who's Who in America*:

CRICHTON, JOHN MICHAEL (MICHAEL CRICHTON), author, film director; b. Chgo., Oct. 23, 1942; s. John Henderson and Zula (Miller) C. A.B. summa cum laude, Harvard U., 1964, M.D., 1969. Postdoctoral fellow Salk Inst., La Jolla, Calif., 1969–70; vis. writer MIT, Cambridge, 1988. Writer, dir. film Westworld, 1973, Coma, 1977, The Great Train Robbery, 1978, Looker, 1981, Runaway, 1984; dir. film Physical Evidence, 1989; co-writer film, Jurassic Park, 1993, Rising Sun, 1993; author: The Andromeda Strain, 1969, Five Patients, 1970, The Terminal Man, 1972, The Great Train Robbery, 1975, Eaters of the Dead, 1976, Jasper Johns, 1977, Congo, 1980, Electronic Life, 1983, Sphere, 1987, Travels, 1988, Jurassic Park, 1990, Rising Sun, 1992, Disclosure, 1994. Recipient Edgar award Mystery Writers Am., 1968, 80; named med. writer of year Assn. Am. Med. Writers, 1970. Mem. Authors Guild, Writers Guild Am. West, Dirs. Guild Am., PEN Am. Ctr., Acad. Motion Picture Arts and Scis., Harvard Bd. Overseers, Phi Beta Kappa, Aesculaepian Club (Boston). Office: Page Jenkins Fin Svcs Inc 433 N Camden Dr Ste 500 Beverly Hills CA 90210

(b) From *Contemporary Authors*:

CRICHTON, (John) Michael 1942–
(Jeffery Hudson, John Lange; Michael Douglas, a joint pseudonym)
PERSONAL: Surname is pronounced Cry-ton; born October 23, 1942, in Chicago, Ill.; son of John Henderson (a corporation president) and Zula (Miller) Crichton; married Joan Radam, January 1, 1965 (divorced, 1970); married Kathy St. Johns, 1978 (divorced, 1980). *Education:* Harvard University, A.B. (summa cum laude), 1964, M.D., 1969. *Address:* 1750 14th St., Suite C, Santa Monica, Calif. 90404. *Agent:* Lynn Nesbit, International Creative Management, 40 West 57th St., New York, N.Y. 10025.

CAREER: Salk Institute for Biological Studies, La Jolla, Calif., post-doctoral fellow, 1969–70; full-time writer of books and films; director of films and television movies, including a Movie of the Week, "Pursuit" (based on his novel *Binary*), American Broadcasting Co., 1972, "Westworld," Metro-Goldwyn-Mayer, 1973, "Coma," United Artists, 1978, "The Great Train Robbery," United Artists, 1979, and "Looker," Warner Bros., 1981. *Member:* Mystery Writers Guild of America West, Authors Guild, Authors League of America, Director's Guild of America, P.E.N., Aesculaepian Society, Phi Beta Kappa. *Awards, honors:* Edgar Award of the Mystery Writers of America, 1968, for *A Case of Need,* and 1979, for film "The Great Train Robbery"; Association of American Medical Writers writer of the year award, 1970, for *Five Patients: The Hospital Explained.*

WRITINGS—Novels, except as indicated; published by Knopf, except as indicated: *The Andromeda Strain* (Book-of-the-Month Club and Literary Guild selection), 1969; *Five Patients: The Hospital Explained* (nonfiction: Doubleday Book Club selection), 1970; (with brother Douglas Crichton, under joint pseudonym Michael Douglas) *Dealing: Or, the Berkeley-to-Boston Forty-Brick Lost-Bag Blues,* 1971; *The Terminal Man* (Book-of-the-Month Club selection), 1972; *Westworld* (also see below), Bantam, 1974; *The Great Train Robbery* (also see below; Book-of-the-Month Club and Reader's Digest selection), 1975; *Eaters of the Dead: The Manuscript of Ibn Fadlan Relating His Experiences with the Northmen in A.D. 922,* 1976; *Jasper Johns* (nonfiction), Abrams, 1977; *Congo,* 1980; *Electronic Life: How to Think about Computers* (nonfiction), 1983.

Screenplays: "Westworld," Metro-Goldwyn-Mayer, 1973; "Coma" (based on the novel by Robin Cook), United Artists, 1977; "The Great Train Robbery" (based on his novel of the same title), United Artists, 1978; "Looker," Warner Bros., 1981. Also author of "Runaway," 1984.

Under pseudonym John Lange, except as indicated; all novels; published by New American Library, except as indicated: *Odds On,* 1966; *Scratch One,* 1967; (under pseudonym Jeffery Hudson) *A Case of Need,* 1968; *Easy Go,* 1968, published as *The Last Tomb,* Bantam, 1974; *Zero Cool,* 1969; *The Venom Business,* 1969; *Drug of Choice,* 1970; *Grave Descend,* 1970; *Binary,* Knopf; 1971.

SIDELIGHTS: From his pseudonymous potboilers to his best-selling novels, from his popular films to his critically-acclaimed nonfiction studies, Michael Crichton has found success in virtually every field into which he has ventured. Best known for his suspense-filled novels *The Andromeda Strain* and *The Terminal Man* and as the writer-director of such like-minded movies as "Looker" and "Coma," Crichton has an "approach to writing [that] is consistent from work to work," according to Robert L. Sims in his *Dictionary of Literary Biography* article about the writer. "He fully exploits the techniques available to the omniscient author, controlling every facet of his plots, which are constructed as suspensefully as [an Alfred] Hitchcock film."

In fact, the famed film director was a major influence on the young Crichton. "I'd always wanted to direct movies," he tells Ned Smith of *American Way.* "My first hero was Alfred Hitchcock—I knew who [he] was long before I knew who Charles Dickens was. . . . I guess one of the reasons I identify with him now is that it seems to me we get a lot of the same criticism." Some of that criticism focuses on the fact that Crichton's heroes, like Hitchcock's, "are one-dimensional figures whose psychological makeups are determined by the particular drama in which they are involved," as Sims explains. "By and large, [Crichton's] characters tend to be exceptional people (scientists, psychiatrists, doctors, etc.) possessing specialized skills, who find themselves in extraordinary situations. [The author] often uses flashbacks to develop his characters. Although his plots are more memorable than his characters, the success of his fiction depends on human fallibility."

Figure 11-3
Biographical Sources

GOVERNMENT DOCUMENTS. Documents pertaining to city, state, and federal government are an important part of the collection in most libraries. Many of these documents describe how government is run. If you are doing a speech on any aspect of government policy, it would be useful to scan this information. Typical city (or county) information will cover such subjects as budget allocations, social service agencies, maps, and surveys. Many state governments publish yearly almanacs, which contain information such as the number of people in the state, the longest river, per capita income, and so on. Most states also publish information about state law and state tax structure. Often libraries also carry tourist and promotional information about the state. Since state and local governments differ in how they publish and organize information, ask the reference librarian for help if you want to use this material.

The United States government is the biggest publisher in America. To find out what it is publishing, check the *Monthly Catalog of United States Government Publications*. This is an index to articles about various federal departments. Here are some of the departments covered:

Agricultural Cooperative Service
Census Bureau
Centers for Disease Control
Civil Rights Commission
Congress
Education Department
Environmental Protection Agency
Fish and Wildlife Service
Justice Department
National Center for Health Statistics
National Portrait Gallery
State Department
Supreme Court

Since federal government publications are so extensive, few libraries carry all the articles listed in the *Monthly Catalog*. If your library does not have the material, you have two choices: you can write for the material (the catalog tells how to do this) or you can ask your librarian for the location of the nearest federal depository library. A federal depository library is a regular library, but it is also one in which the federal government has chosen to put all of the documents it publishes. There are 1350 federal depository libraries in the United States, so there is probably one not very far from where you live. (Your own library might be one.)

THE VERTICAL FILE. If you need more information on a subject, or if you need a subject for a speech, see if your library has a vertical file. (Some local libraries may call it a pamphlet file.) Most libraries receive hundreds of publications from consumer groups, business, industry, and the consumer divisions of state and federal government. To make these available, libraries file them alphabetically by subject matter in filing cabinets called the **vertical file**. If you opened a drawer of your library's vertical file, you might find the following subjects:

Commercial treaties
Communication
Compost
Computers
Conservation of natural resources
Consumer education
Consumer price index
Container gardening
Contraceptives

TRY THIS

Where do you find good material to use as a speaker? The answer, of course, is anywhere and everywhere. Once you become sensitive to seeing and hearing good examples, illustrations, aphorisms, and anecdotes in everyday life, you will be amazed at how much information you will discover.

Try this right now. On a notepad, jot down a list of all the possible topics or topic areas that have the potential for development into a speech. Come up with one idea for each of the following subject headings:

■ An example from your own history

■ A story about family or friends

■ An idea from a book or article

■ A news story

■ A story from television or radio

■ An example used by another speaker

■ An interview with an expert

How successful were you? If you always carry a notepad and jot down incidents when you see or hear them, you will be amazed at how quickly the ideas accumulate. Some of the very best ideas for speeches are simple, everyday things to which people can easily relate.

MISCELLANEOUS MATERIAL.   In addition to the reference material already discussed, every library has a miscellaneous collection of material of interest to its patrons. For example, many libraries have telephone books from around the country, annual reports from corporations, historical and genealogical information that is used for researching a family tree, and books about local history.

USING INTERLIBRARY LOAN

When your own library doesn't have a book or an article you need, it can usually obtain it from some other library. Since each library has a specific procedure for requesting books through interlibrary loan, check with one of the librarians. You will have to plan ahead if you want to use this service. A photocopy of a magazine article will take about ten days; a book might take longer.

USING THE LIBRARY STAFF

Whatever the size of a library, its librarians are its single greatest resource. All their education and experience has been devoted to finding and organizing information, and because of this training they are able to help you find anything you want to know. Although you should be able to do most of your library work on your own, you should not be afraid to ask for help when you need it.

TAKING NOTES

Since library research is time-consuming, there is no sense in having to do it twice. Careful note taking will help you use your time efficiently. Make sure to copy source information completely and accurately. This will help you if you should need to find the material again. Also, if you are asked about any of the sources you have used, you can tell someone where to find them.

Whether it is for footnotes, endnotes, or bibliographies, make certain you copy the author's full name correctly. In addition, for a book, copy the title of the book, place of publication, name of publisher, publication date, and page numbers you have used; for an article, copy the author(s), the title of the article, title of periodical, volume number, date, and page numbers. Figure 11-4 shows sample note cards.

SUPPORTING MATERIAL: WHAT TO LOOK FOR

Once you have learned where to look for information, your next project is to find supporting material for your speech. **Supporting material** is information that backs up your main point and provides the main content of the

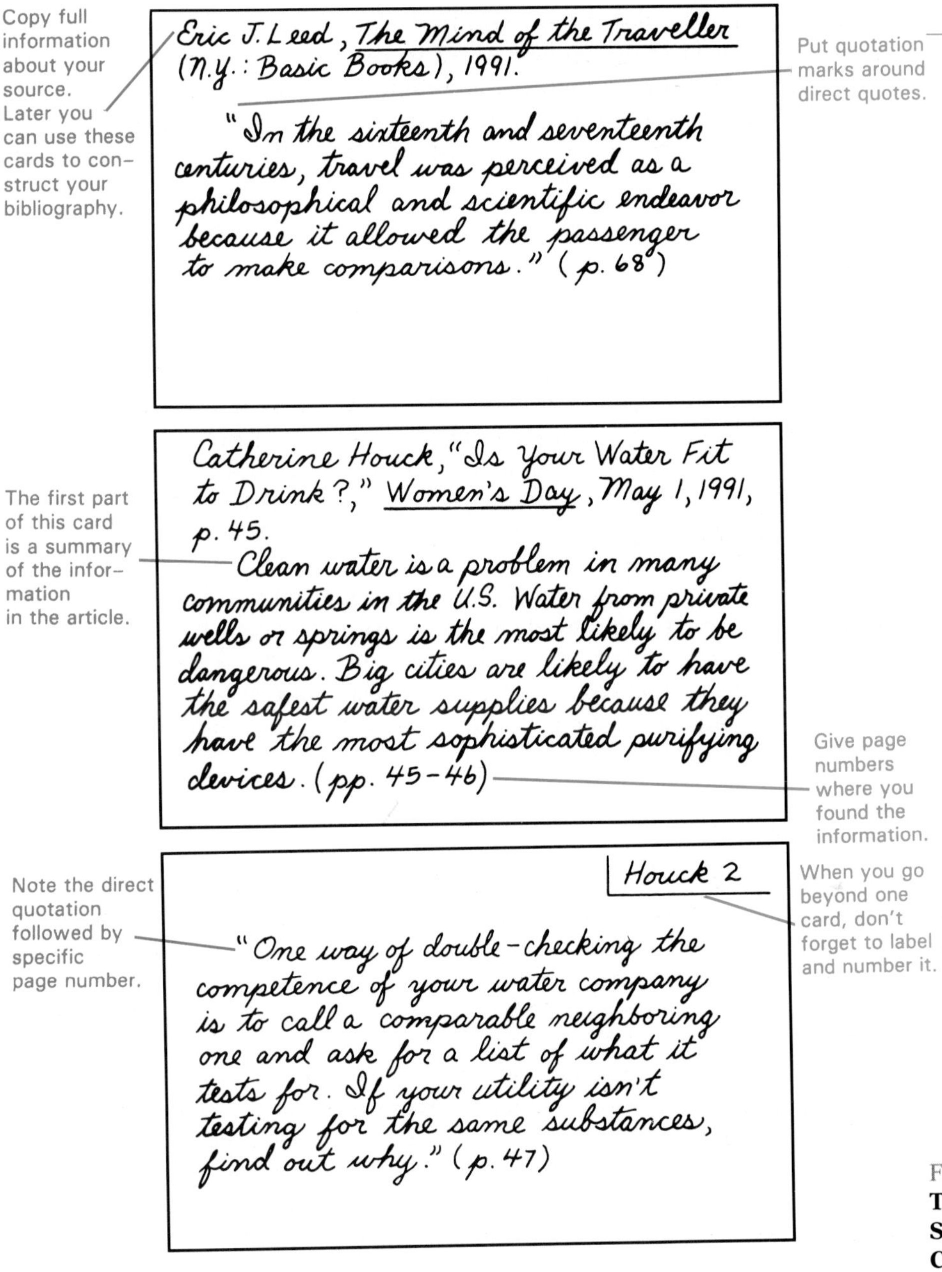

Copy full information about your source. Later you can use these cards to construct your bibliography.

Put quotation marks around direct quotes.

> Eric J. Leed, *The Mind of the Traveller* (N.Y.: Basic Books), 1991.
>
> "In the sixteenth and seventeenth centuries, travel was perceived as a philosophical and scientific endeavor because it allowed the passenger to make comparisons." (p. 68)

The first part of this card is a summary of the information in the article.

> Catherine Houck, "Is Your Water Fit to Drink?," *Women's Day*, May 1, 1991, p. 45.
> — Clean water is a problem in many communities in the U.S. Water from private wells or springs is the most likely to be dangerous. Big cities are likely to have the safest water supplies because they have the most sophisticated purifying devices. (pp. 45–46)

Give page numbers where you found the information.

Note the direct quotation followed by specific page number.

> Houck 2
>
> "One way of double-checking the competence of your water company is to call a comparable neighboring one and ask for a list of what it tests for. If your utility isn't testing for the same substances, find out why." (p. 47)

When you go beyond one card, don't forget to label and number it.

FIGURE 11-4
Taking Notes: Sample Note Cards

speech. To find effective material you need to return to the specific purpose of your speech. Let's say you are interested in art and you want to speak on how to visit a museum, and your specific purpose statement is "to inform the audience about how they can enjoy their visit to an art museum." Now you have to find supporting material that will help you achieve your goal of informing the audience about museums.

Before you begin to look for such material, you should think about what might work in your speech and make some notes about what to look for. Your notes might look something like this:

How many museums are located in this area?	Look for names and locations.
What kinds of collections exist?	Identify the different types of collections, e.g., modern, historical.
What guidebooks are available at each museum?	Collect some sample guidebooks.

By thinking out the speech beforehand, you save yourself time because you won't need to read everything about museums. You will have a good idea of what you are looking for and can pass over information that does not serve your purpose. Sometimes you might find some interesting material you hadn't thought about. If it fits into your speech, use it.

Every speech you put together should have supporting material for the main content of your speech. Some of the material you will find through library research; other material can come from your personal experience or from interviews.

In the sections that follow, we are going to discuss some types of supporting material. Each time you prepare a speech, you should decide which types will work best for your particular speech.

Comparison

Comparisons point out the similarities between two or more things. For example, Sidney, who spoke about the use of peer evaluation in one of his classes, used this comparison:

> *Think of peer evaluation as a reflection of real life. Like real life, it includes people who take it seriously and those who do not; opportunities to assist friends and hurt enemies; and even a wide range of possible, and often contradictory, viewpoints—none of them necessarily accurate, but all of them contributing to an understanding of what is being evaluated.*

You can often use comparisons to help your audience imagine something that is outside its experience. For example, Gretchen wanted her audience to understand that the human body, even in its scrubbed and sanitized condition, is *not* clean—from a microbial standpoint:

> *Our bodies are like a microbial version of Jurassic Park. Microbes thrive, for example, on the desert of the forearm, in the cool woods of the scalp, and in the tropical forest of the armpit. Life on humans, however, is most abundant in the tropics. Trillions of bacteria, viruses, protozoa, and fungi thrive in the warm, hairy, humid terrain of the armpits and groin.*

Sometimes a comparison can show us a new way of looking at something. We have often heard the United States referred to as a "melting pot" of different races and nationalities. Wanting to use the same concept but not the same cliché, the Rev. Jesse Jackson found a new comparison:

> *America is not like a blanket—one piece of unbroken cloth, the same color, the same texture, the same size. It is more like a quilt—many patches, many pieces, many colors and many sizes, all woven and held together by a common thread.*[1]

Contrast

Contrasts point out the differences between two or more things. A contrast might tell how baseball is different from softball or how an all-terrain bike is different from a standard ten-speed. One student who was speaking on the subject of keeping a diary made this contrast:

> *Men's and women's diaries are very different from each other. In most cases, men's diaries concentrate on their public life, women's on their private life. Men seldom write of wives and children; women have numerous entries about their families. Most important, women write of their feelings, and men write of their deeds.*

It can be effective to contrast the familiar with the unfamiliar. This student, just back from an exchange program in Poland, informs her class of the difference between an American (familiar) and a Polish (unfamiliar) university education:

> *Unlike American students, high school students in Poland have no guarantee of admission to a college or university. After leaving high school, the Polish student takes a stringent examination which involves weeks and weeks of study. Even though the students study hard, only a small percentage will be admitted.*
>
> *Once the students are admitted to the university, they spend 30 to 35 hours in class each week whereas American students seldom spend more than 18 hours. In Poland textbooks are not common. If a student is studying biology, for example, the teacher will prepare a list of acceptable books which are available in the library. The student then submits a request for the book in the library and has to wait two or three days for it.*

Definition

A **definition** is a brief explanation of what a word or phrase means. Use definition whenever you suspect that some people in your audience might not know what you are talking about. After you define something, it also might be appropriate to give an example. This student gives a definition followed by an example in her speech:

CONSIDER THIS

⚥ In the following passage Julia T. Wood talks about the way communication is used to shape reality.

Society is a human creation that we constantly remake through communication in private and public settings. Your voice will join those of others to shape the meaning of gender and the concrete realities of being men and women in the coming years. You will also influence attitudes toward diversity either by reinscribing the view that differences are divisive or by affirming them a source of individual and collective enrichment, regeneration, and growth. What gender and culture will mean in the future is up to you. In your private relationships, public interactions, professional engagements, and civic activities, you will create and communicate new visions of who we can be and how we will live.

Source: Julia T. Wood, *Gendered Lives: Communication, Gender, and Culture* (Belmont, CA: Wadsworth, 1994), pp. 309–310.

QUESTIONS

1. Have you ever thought of *your* voice shaping the meaning of gender and others' concrete realities? What responsibilities does this imply for *you* as a speaker?
2. Do you think Wood is exaggerating when she says, "What gender and culture will mean in the future is up to you?" Why or why not? What decisions will you make in finding material that will reflect what *you* think gender and culture mean?
3. As you find material to support your speech, what specific things can you do to "communicate new visions of who we can be and how we will live"?

Fatigue is decreased ability of an organism to perform because of prolonged exertion. Have you ever studied and studied for a tough examination only to go into the examination completely tired out and exhausted? Fatigue may seem physical to you, but often it's a sign of mental distress—especially if you are particularly fearful about the exam.

Examples

An **example** is a short illustration that clarifies a point. Commonly used in speeches, examples can come from personal experience, from research, or from imagination.

Often you will choose a topic for a speech because you have some personal involvement in it. Ask yourself whether you can provide any examples from your own experience. Nothing beats "I know what I'm talking about because I've been there," as you can see in this speech against drinking and driving:

> *Three years ago, I was a senior in high school. One night my best friend Jeff called and asked if I wanted to go out to the lake and have a few beers. Since I had planned to see my grandmother, who was in the hospital, I told him I couldn't go but to give me a rain check.*
>
> *There was no next time. That night Jeff and three of my other friends were killed in an accident. According to the police report, they hit a tree while going 75 miles an hour. All of them had alcohol in their blood.*

Not all personal examples will be so dramatic. Another student uses a commonplace experience to make her point in a speech about how college students are affected by inflation:

> *Last year, when I bought a current CD at the college bookstore, it cost $12.99. This year, in doing the research for this speech, I checked back at the bookstore. The same CD is now priced at $13.99. That's how inflation affects us.*

RESEARCH.   Often if you have not had personal experience with a topic, you can use the examples you find in your research. When you do this, however, be sure to cite your source. A common way of doing this is to say, "In the latest issue of *Newsweek* . . ." or "according to a January 1995 issue of *Popular Science*. . . ." A student who was giving a speech on why the hair dye industry should be regulated used this example that she found during her research:

> *A current issue of the magazine* In Health *tells about a woman who was dyeing her hair. As soon as she applied the dye, her vision blurred, her face swelled, and she began to feel dizzy. Suddenly, she couldn't breathe and passed out. Fortunately her son was in the house and called the paramedics. It turned out that she had had an allergic reaction.*

HYPOTHETICAL EXAMPLES.   Sometimes speakers use hypothetical examples—examples that are made up—to illustrate a point. A speaker should always tell the audience if an example is hypothetical. When this student spoke about the need to use infant seats, he involved his audience in his example. The words "imagine yourself" cue the audience that the example is hypothetical:

> *Imagine yourself in this situation. You are taking your 2-year-old son out for an ice cream cone. You don't bother to strap him in his seat because*

the ice cream shop is less than a mile away. As you are traveling about 25 miles an hour, a car pulls out in front of you. As you slam on your brakes, your son is still moving at 25 mph—right into the windshield.

Statistics

Statistics—which are facts in numerical form—have many uses in a speech. Being factual material, they are a convincing form of evidence. Quite often, a speaker who uses statistics is seen as someone who has done his or her homework.

Sometimes statistics can support your speech in a way no other information can. Juan, for example, wanted to speak about religion and the college student. He ran across a survey in the newspaper *The Chronicle of Higher Education*, which reported that 83 percent of first-year college students attend a religious service. The poll also found that 32 percent were Roman Catholic and that the largest Protestant affiliation was the Baptists with 18 percent. Twenty-nine percent identified themselves as born-again Christians.[2] With these data Juan could show that there was considerable interest in religion—at least among first-year students.

Statistics are easy to find. Many books contain nothing but statistics, such as the *Statistical Abstract of the United States*. Many state governments also publish books about statistics within their jurisdictions. Often you don't have to make a special search for statistics; the sources you use for your speech will have figures you can use.

RULES FOR USING STATISTICS

USE THE BEST POSSIBLE SOURCES. If you see the headline "World's Food Supply Failing to Keep Pace," it will be much more believable if it comes from *The New York Times* than from one of the tabloid newspapers by the checkout stand in your local supermarket. Pick your statistics from well-respected sources.

MAKE SURE THE INFORMATION IS UP TO DATE. Figures on military spending in 1973 are useless—unless you want to compare them with figures for the current year. If you do this, you must account for inflation.

USE STATISTICS THAT SHOW TRENDS. We can often tell what is happening to an institution or even a country if we have information from one year to another. There is even a Trends Research Institute, based in Rhinebeck, New York, with its own *Trends Journal* designed to follow major trends in every area of life. Ardath, a student in a speech communication class, wanted to show that the "fitness boom" never really became a deep, widespread, and effective phenomenon:

> *The data are conflicting and subject to interpretation. Obesity is up, but heart disease death is down. High-fat cheese is increasingly popular, but*

so is low-fat milk. Smoking has declined, but the decline might be slowing. High-profile, influential Americans have become more physically active, but most other Americans have not. It seems clear that even in the sweaty heat of its fitness craze, America did not become a nation of health nuts. Translated into numbers, perhaps one-third of Americans get enough physical activity to confer some health benefits, and about 70 percent of America managed to miss the big fitness fad.

USE CONCRETE IMAGES. When your numbers are large and may be hard to comprehend, using concrete images is helpful. Notice, for example, that in the preceding example Ardath avoided most numbers, preferring more concrete images. He rounded off the percentages he quoted to make them easier for listeners to understand. In a speech on smoking, Garret cited statistics from an October, 1993, issue of *USA Today* saying that typical smokers smoke 25 cigarettes a day, 500,000 in a lifetime. He said, "Each day you smoke, you shorten your life expectancy by two hours and fifty-five minutes. You lose nearly a day of the future for every eight days you smoke." He used another, more concrete image to drive this point home:

> *If we built a monument to everyone who died from smoking just last year, it would be seven times as long as the Vietnam Memorial wall.[3]*

Testimony

When you cite **testimony**, you use another person's statements or actions to give authority to what you are saying. Experts are the best sources of testimony. Suppose you are planning to speak about NCAA violations and you get some of the information from the athletic director of your school. When you use this information in your speech, tell your audience where it came from. Because the information is from an expert, your speech will have more authority and be more convincing than if you presented only your own opinions.

Testimony can also be used to show that people who are prominent and admired believe and support your ideas. For example, if you are going to persuade your audience to take up swimming for fitness, it might be useful to mention some famous athletes who swim to stay fit. If you want people to sign your petition to build a new city park, mention other citizens who are also supporting this park.

Testimony can be made up of direct quotations. You can quote what public figures or celebrities are saying, or you can quote historic figures by using books of quotations found in the reference section of the library.

Try to use quotations that are short and to the point. If they are too lengthy, your speech could end up sounding like everyone but yourself. If you have quotations that are long and wordy, put them into your own words. Whether you quote or paraphrase, you should give credit to your source.

Polls

Polls are surveys of people's attitudes, beliefs, and behavior. Quite often polls are conducted on controversial subjects. If you want to know how the American public feels about abortion, health care reform, or environmental issues, you will probably be able to find a poll.

National polls also can provide useful information as to what particular segments of the population think or know about an issue. There are numerous polling organizations. Often, however, a single poll may yield far more information than what is necessary for a speech. Since all that information would be overwhelming for listeners, you must decide how much or how little to use. Try to select responses to share that will appeal precisely to your classmates' ages and socioeconomic circumstances.

When your statistics come from a survey, you should look to see how many and what kinds of people were questioned. For example, if you discovered survey results saying that 30 percent of the American public eats with chopsticks, you might find the statistics fairly startling and you might be tempted to use it—until you note that the survey included only 100 people and that many of them were Chinese immigrants.

Studies

As the term implies, a **study** is an in-depth investigation of a subject. The subject might be anything—from how white rats run mazes to how newspapers present political news. Studies are found in popular magazines, newspapers, and academic journals. If you are interested in finding what research has been done in a particular field, check the indexes for such periodicals. For example, Table 11-1, based on a table from *Statistical Abstract of the United States*, offers comparative information about salary offers to candidates for bachelor's degrees from 1980 to 1991.

TRY THIS

To support your speech topic, try to find at least one piece of each kind of supporting material: comparison, contrast, definition, examples, statistics, testimony, polls, and studies.

Which pieces of supporting material do you predict will hold audience attention the best? Why?

TABLE 11-1
SALARY OFFERS TO CANDIDATES FOR BACHELOR'S DEGREES, 1980 TO 1991

Field of Study	Salary Offer	
	1980	1991
Accounting	$15,516	$26,642
Business	14,616	24,019
Marketing	13,740	23,713
Engineering		
Civil	18,648	29,658
Chemical	21,612	37,492
Computer	(NA)	32,280
Electrical	20,280	33,190
Mechanical	20,436	33,999
Nuclear	20,016	32,175
Petroleum	23,844	38,882
Engineering technology	19,020	30,098
Chemistry	17,508	26,836
Mathematics	17,700	27,370
Physics	(NA)	29,227
Humanities	12,888	23,567
Social sciences	12,864	21,375
Computer science	18,696	30,696

SOURCE: Adapted from *Statistical Abstract of the United States*, 112th ed. (Washington, DC: Department of Commerce, Bureau of the Census, 1992), p. 172.

ADAPTING SUPPORTING MATERIAL TO YOUR AUDIENCE

Because each kind of supporting material may work better with some audiences than with others, you should keep your audience constantly in mind as you build your speech.[4]

Consider, for example, a speech about videocassette recorders (VCRs). If you were going to speak to a group of potential customers, you would give some technical information from a magazine such as *Consumer Reports* about various VCR brands: what the various options are—such as the number of shows that can be recorded—whether four heads are better than two, and so on. If you were speaking to parents, you might want to talk about some of the best videos for children. In this case you might want to quote some experts on the subject. For an audience of schoolteachers, a discussion of how videos can be used in the classroom would be appropriate, and your supporting material could include statistics on how videos enhance learning.

You also need to consider the attitudes of the audience toward your topic. If your audience is suspicious of you or your message, you will probably do best with facts and figures and with quotations and testimony from people your audience respects. Citing *evidence* in the form of statistics and facts will give you a better chance of persuading them to accept your point of view.

Finally, you should consider what kind of supporting material will hold your audience's attention. If you are speaking to a young and potentially restless audience, examples and narratives will probably hold their attention best.

Since audience members often come from a variety of backgrounds, no one form of supporting material will work uniformly well. If you have an adult audience with different levels of knowledge and different attitudes, you should use a variety of supporting material. In the following extract, the speaker begins with a statistic and then goes on to give an example:

> *A California study of 3,000 divorced couples found that one year after the divorce, the woman's income had dropped 73 percent while the man's had increased 43 percent.*
>
> *Karen Jackson is one of these women. Last year she was living with her three children in a comfortable middle-class neighborhood. Now she is living in a slum and needs food stamps to feed her children.*

Presenting a variety of supporting material is like offering a variety of fruit in a fruit bowl. Some people will like the grapes and others will like the peaches, but everyone will be pleased to find something that appeals to them.

■ SUMMARY

When you are putting together material for your speech, you should consider drawing on three areas: your own experience, interviews with others, and research in the library. Depending on the topic, one of these sources might provide better information than others.

Library material is organized into three categories: books, periodicals, and reference works. Book titles, authors, and subjects are all listed in the library catalog. Magazine and journal articles can be located through periodical indexes. Reference material includes encyclopedias, almanacs, biographical yearbooks, government documents, and vertical files.

Supporting material forms the main content of every speech. Supporting material includes the following: comparisons, which are similarities between two or more things; contrasts, which point out differences; definitions, which give the meaning of words or phrases; examples, which illustrate points; statistics, which are facts in numerical form; testimony, in which the statements or actions of others are used to give authority to the speech; polls, which indicate what a selected group of people think, feel, or know about a subject; and studies, which are in-depth investigations.

When choosing supporting material for a speech, you should consider which kinds will be appropriate for the audience. To make this choice, consider the audience's level of knowledge about and attitude toward your topic, and ask which material will best hold the audience's attention.

 NOTES

[1] Jesse Jackson, Excerpts from text of Jesse Jackson's remarks prepared for the Democratic Convention, *The New York Times*, July 18, 1984, p. 12A.

[2] "This Year's College Freshmen: Attitudes and Characteristics," *The Chronicle of Higher Education*, January 30, 1991, pp. A30–A31. As cited in Alexander W. Astin, "The American Freshman: National Norms for Fall 1990" (American Council on Education and University of California at Los Angeles).

[3] Michael Gartner, "The Smoke Police Are Hot on the Case," *USA Today*, August 18, 1993, p. 11A.

[4] See Jo Aprague and Douglas Stuart, *The Speaker's Handbook* (San Diego, CA: Harcourt Brace Jovanovich, 1984) for an excellent sourcebook for material on the principles of speech communication.

FURTHER READING

BARZUN, JACQUES, AND HENRY F. GRAFF. *The Modern Researcher*, 5th ed. New York: Harcourt Brace Jovanovich, 1992. This is an outstanding book full of useful ideas for serious researchers. The section on research includes chapters entitled "Finding the Facts," "Verification," and "Handling Ideas." For those looking for suggestions to help improve their writing, the section entitled "Writing" also is very good.

FITZHENRY, ROBERT I., ED. *The Harper Book of Quotations*, 3d ed. New York: HarperPerennial, 1993. An excellent reference source for anyone's personal library, this book includes over 6500 quotations on a wide variety of ideas, subjects, people, and places.

GRONBECK, BRUCE E., RAYMIE E. McKERROW, DOUGLAS EHNINGER, AND ALAN H. MONROE. *Principles and Types of Speech Communication*, 12th ed. Glenview, IL: Scott, Foresman, 1994. This is the speech communication textbook that has been around the longest. It is included here for its excellent chapter "Developing Ideas: Finding and Using Supporting Materials." The book is thorough, complete, and well written. An excellent resource.

PARTNOW, ELAINE. *The Best of Quotable Women: From Eve to the Present*. New York: Facts on File, 1991. In most of the standard books of quotations, men dominate. This book is made up of quotations by women.

RUBIN, REBECCA, ALAN M. RUBIN, AND LINDA J. PIELE. *Communication Research*, 3d ed. Belmont, CA: Wadsworth, 1993. The usefulness of this volume is in its emphasis on information sources. It covers how to search the communication literature, write and organize research papers, design the research project, search on-line computer databases, and discover other relevant material. A terrific guide for beginning researchers.

STACKS, DON W., AND JOHN E. HOCKING. *Essentials of Communication Research*. New York: HarperCollins, 1992. This book, written for communication students, is designed as an introduction to the study of communication research. Throughout the book the authors use communication-related examples for explanation and illustration. It is mentioned here because of its excellent 30-plus-page chapter "Getting Started: Library Research."

TODD, ALDEN. *Finding Facts Fast: How to Find Out What You Want and Need to Know*, 2d ed. Berkeley, CA: Ten Speed Press, 1979. Alden designed this as a useful, concise tool for accessing information quickly. It is a readable book guaranteed to save time and energy.

TUCKER, RAYMOND K., RICHARD L. WEAVER II, AND CYNTHIA BERRYMAN-FINK. *Research in Speech Communication*. Englewood Cliffs, NJ: Prentice-Hall, 1981. Chapter 3, "Documentary or Library Research," discusses types of library research, procedures in library research, suggestions for library researchers, and its values and limitations of library research. It is a practical approach designed for all researchers and writers.

WILSON, JOHN F., AND CARROL C. ARNOLD. *Public Speaking as a Liberal Art*, 6th ed. Boston: Allyn and Bacon, 1990. The authors approach public speaking as an art and discuss some general problems—rhetorical invention, style, delivery, and the like. Chapters 4 to 6, on invention, are cogent and especially relevant here.

Organizing and Outlining the Speech

CHAPTER OBJECTIVES

After reading this chapter, you should be able to:

1 Organize and outline your speech.

2 Identify the six patterns of organization for a speech and choose the best one for your purpose.

3 Explain the function of an introduction and be able to write one.

4 Explain the function of a conclusion and be able to write one.

5 Explain the function of transitions and be able to write them.

6 Use both full-sentence and key-word formats to outline a speech.

7 Write a bibliography for your speech.

Julie learned how to organize her ideas in a high-school English course. Mrs. Goudy, her English teacher, told her class that a good outline gets you started right, keeps you under way, and gets you to your destination. Mrs. Goudy stressed two fundamentals: (1) keep it simple, and (2) make sure that whatever organizational pattern you choose is instantly intelligible to your readers.

Julie decided to put Mrs. Goudy's ideas to work as she began to put together her first major speech project for the semester. She selected a topic she knew would be important and relevant for her listeners: anxiety. Her roommate, Mai, always seemed to be anxious. Also, she knew that investigating the topic might help her reduce the anxiety she often experienced around exam time. This interest alone was enough to spark her own curiosity.

Julie remembered that her father had a couple of books on the subject, and she had seen a recent article on anxiety, so she knew she could get plenty of information. The first thing she did, however, was brainstorm about the subject. She came up with the following possible angles:

- The body's response to anxiety
- Causes of anxiety
- Methods of reducing anxiety
- Recognizing anxiety signals
- Time management and anxiety

Julie decided to focus on methods of reducing anxiety. She thought that would hold her listeners' attention since many students had already expressed anxiety about the speeches they would be giving. She began her research with the idea of informing her classmates about how to reduce anxiety.

Julie got to the library early, and using "anxiety" as her key term, she consulted a variety of indexes that led her to recent articles in *Science*, the *American Journal of Psychiatry*, and *Psychology Today*—all excellent sources. In addition, by using the computerized card catalog, she located five recent books. She had sources and she had time, so she began taking notes. She collected different kinds of material: a definition of anxiety, a contrast between anxiety and stress, several examples or practical applications of the methods of anxiety reduction, and some useful statistics. As she collected her information, she kept asking, "Will this hold my listeners' attention?"

Julie collected far more information than she would need for her 5-minute informative speech, but the excess gave her many choices as she began to form her presentation. She decided to begin with all the signs of anxiety; her listeners would clearly and quickly identify with them, and she would capture the audience's attention. Then she would define the word, and as a transition into the body of her speech, she would tell how many college students suffer from symptoms of anxiety (78%)—this, to get them to focus on her methods.

CONSIDER THIS

A speech is not a chicken fillet. It needs bones. Without some sort of skeleton, it will just lie on the plate. If you want your material to get up and walk, organize it. Give it some structure.

A good speech outline should start you out in the right direction, keep you underway successfully, and get you where you planned to be.

Source: C. Barry McCarty, *Well Said and Worth Saying* (Nashville, TN: Broadman, 1991), p. 45.

Julie decided that each main head in the body of her speech would be one method for dealing with anxiety. Her single bold point would be that there are specific, simple methods for dealing with it. She had notes on at least six different methods, but she had excellent examples for only three. Given her time limit (5 minutes), she decided she would use the three points for which she had the best examples. Coincidentally, these were the three points easiest to explain as well: positive self-talk, relaxation training, and physical activity.

For her conclusion, Julie summarized her ideas, then alerted listeners to books and articles on the topic. She saved one of her best comments for the end. Julie's college had a psychological counseling center with specialists who dealt with students experiencing high levels of anxiety. Not only did Julie come prepared with this information; she had created a flyer that indicated the location, and hours of the counseling center and the names of the available psychologists. Since hers was not a persuasive speech, she did not try to persuade students to seek help; she simply told them where to find more information, material, and help.

Julie wrote out a complete outline that she was required to turn in to her instructor. She condensed the outline to just key words, and she put these on several 3 × 5 cards. She began practicing her speech using the cards. Because she had been so thorough in her research, because she was so familiar with her material, and because she chose an important and relevant topic, she could speak on it conversationally and comfortably.

When the time came to deliver her speech, her delivery was smooth. Julie felt strong and in control. The structure of her speech was easy for her to remember and instantly intelligible for her listeners. After the speech, several classmates told her she had done a terrific job. One student asked her a question she had not answered in her speech: "Is use of the college counseling center free of charge?" "Not only is it free," Julie replied, "but they never release the names of students who go for help."

Relate Points to Your Specific Purpose and Central Idea

The points you make in your speech should relate directly to your specific purpose and central idea. In this speech, "The Challenge to Excel," notice that all the main points do this.

Specific Purpose: To inform my classmates about the four things required to excel.

Central Idea: No matter what people's abilities are, there are four things they can do to excel.

Main Ideas:
   I. Learn self-discipline.
  II. Build a knowledge base.
 III. Develop special skills.
 IV. Bounce back from defeat.

Distinguish between Main and Minor Points

When organizing your speech, you should distinguish between main points and minor points. If you do this, the speech will flow more naturally and will seem logical to your listeners. The **main points** are all the broad, general ideas and information that support your central idea; the **minor points** are the specific ideas and information that support the main points. Say that the purpose of your speech is to persuade your audience to learn to incorporate computer-generated graphics into their research papers. The central idea of your speech is that they can illustrate their ideas better and more efficiently by using a computer. Your main point would have this broad, general idea: "Computers help you draw faster, revise drawings more easily, and produce a better-looking, better-illustrated paper." Your minor points will explain the main point in more specific terms: (1) most people do not draw very well; (2) a computer enables you to draw like a professional, even if you don't have drawing skills; (3) revising and changing drawings is easy and efficient. All these minor points help to explain the ways in which the computer is more effective and efficient for illustrating ideas.

If you have difficulty distinguishing between major and minor points, write each of the points you want to make on a separate index card. Then spread all the cards out in front of you and organize them by main points, with minor points coming under them. If one arrangement doesn't work, try another. This is the advantage of having each point on a separate card.

Phrase All Points in Full Sentences

If you write all your points in full sentences, it will help you think out your ideas more fully. Once your ideas are set out in this detailed way, you will

TRY THIS

For each of the following sets of sentences, identify the main point with an *M* and the minor or supporting point(s) with an *S*.

____1. There are thousands of different kinds of dolls.
____2. *Nesting dolls* is the term for dolls that fit inside each other.
____3. Baby dolls resemble infants.

____1. Don't wear anything that glitters.
____2. Don't wear all-black or all-white clothing.
____3. If you are appearing on television, be careful what you wear.

____1. The amount of agricultural land under cultivation does not support the population.
____2. Famine can occur for many reasons.
____3. Population exceeds the food sources.
____4. Unusual weather, such as drought, occurs.

In each of the next sets there are *two* main points. Find them and match them with the correct minor points.

____1. Certain signs indicate that your pet is too fat.
____2. Cut back food by one-third.
____3. It tires easily after a little exercise.
____4. Put your pet on a diet.
____5. Use low-calorie fillers such as rice or cottage cheese.
____6. It looks fat (or everyone calls it "Butterball").

____1. Some studies indicate that people who drink coffee in large amounts are more prone to heart disease.
____2. Caffeine can cause birth defects such as cleft palate and bone abnormalities.
____3. Decaffeinated coffee is a good alternative to coffee with caffeine.
____4. If you want to break the caffeine habit, cut down by a cup or two a day.
____5. People who drink large quantities of coffee may be endangering their health.
____6. You can break the coffee-caffeine habit.

Answers: The main points are:
- There are thousands of different kinds of dolls.
- If you are appearing on television, be careful what you wear.
- Famine can occur for many reasons.
- Certain signs indicate that your pet is too fat.
- Put your pet on a diet.
- People who drink large quantities of coffee may be endangering their health.
- You can break the coffee-caffeine habit.

be able to discover problems in the organization that might need more work.

Give All Points a Parallel Structure

Parallel structure means that each of your points will begin with the same grammatical form. For example, on a speech about ways to lose weight, this speaker started each suggestion with a verb:

- Exercise at least three times a week.
- Eat low-fat, high-energy snacks such as fruit.
- Count your daily fat intake.

▎ PATTERNS OF ORGANIZATION

Once you have researched your speech, have decided on a specific purpose, and have listed the main points, you are ready to choose an organizational pattern. This organizational pattern will mainly affect the **body**—the main part of the speech. (Introductions and conclusions are discussed later in the chapter.)

The body of the speech is made up of your main points. Most classroom speeches should not have more than four or five main points, and many of them will have no more than two or three. Your choice of how many main points to use will depend on your topic. If you want to cover a topic in depth, you will use fewer main points. If you want to give a broad, general view, you might want to use four or five main points.

There are many ways to arrange the main points in your speech. Your choice will depend on what best suits your material. In this section we will discuss six possible arrangements: time order, spatial order, cause and effect, problem-solution, motivated sequence, and topical order.

Time Order

Time order, or chronological order, is used to show development over time. This pattern works particularly well when you want to use a historical approach. For example, in a speech about the development of beer, the speaker arranged her main points in chronological order:

Specific Purpose: To inform my audience about the development of beer.

    Central Idea: Beer had a long history before it came to America.

      Main Points: I. Brewing originated in Babylon, where barley grew wild as early as 6000 B.C.

II. In 2800 B.C. it was used as a mortuary offering, played a part in religious worship, and was used in medicine.

III. The Greeks learned brewing from the Egyptians, and the Romans learned about beer from the Greeks.

IV. American brewing began in 1584 when the British brewed beer from corn (maize) during their first attempt to colonize Virginia.

Time order is often used to explain a process. The process could be anything from how to wrap a gift to how to apply for a student loan. This student used time order for describing the process of making beer:

Specific Purpose: To inform my audience of how beer is made.

Central Idea: Making beer involves three stages: mashing, boiling, and fermentation.

Main Points:
I. Mashing occurs in three stages, each raising the temperature of the finely mashed malt to a new level.
II. The wort (what is left after mashing) is boiled in a copper tank or kettle.
III. Fermentation begins when the yeast is "pitched" into the wort.

Spatial Order

When you use **spatial order**, you refer to a physical or geographical layout to help your audience see how the parts make up the whole. To help your audience visualize your subject, you explain it by going from left to right or from top to bottom, or in any direction that best suits your subject.

For example, a student decided that spatial order is the best way to explain the layout of the campus to parents and potential freshmen who are taking a campus tour. He organized his campus tour speech from the outside of campus to the inside as a series of concentric circles:

Specific Purpose: To inform my audience about the layout of the campus.

Central Idea: The campus is laid out logically as a series of concentric circles.

Main Points:
I. Parking and athletic complexes occupy the outermost circle.
II. The dormitories, fraternities, and sororities occupy the next concentric circle.
III. Next to the center circle are the library, the student union, and the classroom buildings.

IV. The center circle of campus is occupied by the administrative offices.

Spatial order works particularly well when the speech focuses on a chart or diagram. When using the visual aid, the speaker naturally moves from top to bottom or from left to right. For example, when a student decided to speak on the topic "Who Makes Decisions on Campus," she used a spatial order and worked from top to bottom on a flowchart showing who the administrators were and what they were responsible for:

Specific Purpose: To inform my audience about who makes decisions on campus.

Central Idea: Campus business is divided into two branches: the administrative branch and the academic branch.

Main Points: I. The president is the chief administrative officer of the college and the main spokesperson for the college in the community.
II. The academic vice president is responsible for everything that concerns classes, such as curriculum and faculty.
III. The administrative vice president is responsible for all nonclass activity, such as law enforcement, revenues, and payroll.

Cause-and-Effect Order

A speaker who uses **cause-and-effect order** divides a speech into two major parts: cause (why something is happening) and effect (what impact it is having). Here is how a speaker used a cause-and-effect arrangement to talk about "Why Smart People Fail":

Specific Purpose: To inform my audience why smart people sometimes fail.

Central Idea: Smart people sometimes do things that lead to failure.

Main Points: I. Smart people are defined as those with very high IQs.
II. Causes for their failures include arrogance, isolation, recklessness, and overreaching.
III. Failures (effects) include loss of high-paying, high-profile jobs; public humiliation; loss of opportunity; and even loss of fortunes.

You do not always have to start with the cause and end with the effect. In this speech, "Why Smart People Fail," main points II and III could have been reversed: the speaker could have first used examples of some of the

**How might this
speaker use
comparison and
contrast to make
her point?**

possible effects of high IQ and then could have continued with the causes. If you are using a cause-and-effect order, begin with the aspect most likely to capture the audience's attention.

Problem-Solution Order

Like speakers who use a cause-and-effect arrangement, a speaker who uses a **problem-solution order** also divides a speech into two sections. In this case, one part deals with the problem and the other deals with the solution. For example, look at this outline for a speech titled "Protect Yourself from Shopping-Mall Crime":

Specific Purpose: To inform my audience how to protect themselves from shopping-mall crime.

Central Idea: You can protect yourself from shopping-mall crime by parking close to elevators, having purchases delivered, accompanying small children at all times, and carrying as little cash as possible.

Main Points: I. Shopping malls attract muggers, car thieves, child molesters, drug peddlers, and pickpockets.
  II. Shoppers can take several precautions to protect themselves from shopping-mall crime.

Here is another example from a speech titled "Americans Need to Know about the Third World":

Specific Purpose: To persuade my audience that American schools need to teach students more about the Third World.

Central Idea: Americans must know about the Third World because what happens in these countries affects all of our lives.

Main Points: I. Most Americans have negative impressions of the Third World from the mass media.

II. Most Americans are ignorant of the impact that the Third World has on American trade.

III. Most Americans do not know how the Third World influences political decision making among the superpowers.

IV. American teachers and curriculum planners must add material about the Third World to the school curriculum.

V. Textbook publishers should add Third World material.

Motivated Sequence

The **motivated sequence**, developed by Professor Alan H. Monroe in the 1930s,[1] is also a problem-solving pattern of arrangement. The sequence is designed to persuade listeners to accept a point of view and then motivate them to take action. The full pattern has five steps:

1. *Attention:*   The speaker calls attention to the topic or situation.
2. *Need:*   The speaker develops the need for a change and explains related audience needs. This is the problem-development portion of the speech.
3. *Satisfaction:*   The speaker presents his or her solution and shows how it meets (satisfies) the needs mentioned.
4. *Visualization:*   The speaker shows what will result when the solution is put into effect.
5. *Action:*   The speaker indicates what kind of action is necessary to bring about the desired change.

Any persuasive problem-solving speech can be adapted to the motivated sequence. Notice how this speaker uses the pattern in "To Cheat or Not to Cheat: That Is the Question":

Specific Purpose: To persuade my listeners that they should take a strong stand to eliminate academic dishonesty.

Central Idea: Unless you are willing to take a strong stand to eliminate academic dishonesty, cheating is likely to continue and will hurt us all.

Main Points: I. [*Attention*] The decision to cheat or not can be difficult to make—especially when you are under a lot of pressure.

II. [*Need*] Often students face the temptation to be academically dishonest daily, whether it be cheating, helping others to cheat, or plagiarism.

III. [*Satisfaction*] Students need to focus on the value of honesty, the importance of integrity in academic matters, and the privilege of a college education.

IV. [*Visualization*] Academic honesty is important to educational growth: aim for learning, grades that represent solid effort, feelings of self-worth and integrity, and a clear conscience about never having helped others to cheat.

V. [*Action*] Think about academic honesty. If you have ever cheated, don't do it again. If you haven't, don't start. If you get caught, the price you may pay is too great.

Topical Order

When your speech does not fit into any of the patterns described so far, you will probably use a topical pattern of organization. You can use a **topical order** whenever your subject can be grouped logically into subtopics. Here are some examples: four ways to save money for college, three systems for selecting a major, inexpensive ways to travel abroad, or five foods that help you live longer.

In the next sample, a student uses a topical order in a speech titled "Native Americans." Topical order is the only choice for this speech, which treats Native American culture, beliefs, respect for the planet, and contributions. Time order would work if the student were to consider the history of Native Americans. A spatial order would work to compare and contrast various Native American tribes from different geographical locations, to describe where the tribes now are located, or perhaps to show how a living site is laid out spatially. A problem-solution order might work if the student wanted to look at the problems faced by Native Americans and suggest various solutions to these problems. For example, the motivated sequence could be used to examine feelings about adoption among Native Americans.

Specific Purpose: To inform my audience about the importance of family in Native American culture.

Central Idea: To protect their values, continue their traditions, and maintain their families, Native American tribes are trying to keep children from being adopted by outsiders.

Main Points:

I. Native American tribes have values that are different from mainstream American society.

II. Native Americans believe their traditions will die out if their children are adopted by outsiders.

III. Native Americans want to maintain their families, for values and traditions must be taught to children while they are young.

TRY THIS

Which organizational pattern might you use for each of the follow-ing speech topics?

1. Health care for AIDS victims
2. Four ways to overcome snoring
3. How to find your way around the library
4. Immigration: more diversity for the United States
5. The history of the university

Answers:

1. Problem-solution order or motivated sequence 2. Topical order 3. Spatial order 4. Cause-and-effect order. 5. Time order.

In a persuasive speech on what can be done to conserve natural resources, a student speaking on the topic "Conservation: What You Can Do" used a topical order to show what can be done:

Specific Purpose: To persuade my audience that everyone can contribute to conserving natural resources.

Central Idea: Conservation means practicing the Four R's of reduce, reuse, repair, and recycle.

Main Points:
   I. Reduce consumption and waste.
  II. Reuse what can be reused.
 III. Repair what can be fixed.
  IV. Recycle what can be recycled.

THE SPEECH INTRODUCTION

The **introduction** is the opening statement of your speech. It gives the audience members their first impression of you, it introduces them to the topic, and it motivates them to listen. The introduction is very important: if you don't hook audience members in the beginning, you might never get their attention.

It is possible to outline an introduction. The outline would be especially valuable to beginning speakers who want to make certain everything impor-tant is included.

There are no hard and fast rules for introductions. If you have a wonderful idea for one, use it. If you need some guidance in preparing it, many introductions have some or all of the following elements:

- Get attention
- Announce your topic
- Preview your central idea and main points
- Establish your credibility

We think it is useful to write out the complete text of your introduction because it gives you added confidence when you begin your speech. However, your instructor might want you to do it differently, so be sure to follow your instructor's directions.

Stating Your Purpose, Central Idea, and Main Points

In most situations, a speaker will use the introduction to tell what he or she is going to talk about. When a speaker does this, the audience can turn its attention to the topic and begin to concentrate. Although you do not have to mention the topic in your very first words, you shouldn't wait too long. By the time you reach the end of your introduction, your audience should know what you intend to accomplish and the central idea of your speech. By including this information in your introduction, you are providing a signpost about the direction you will be taking. For example:

> *The physical abuse of children is a serious problem in this country, and today I want to talk about how bad the problem is and some of the things we can do about it.*

In your introduction, you might also want to preview your main points. Not only does this give members of the audience a sense of your direction, but it also helps them to follow your speech more easily. The student speaking on the physical abuse of children previewed her main points this way:

> *Since this problem covers such a broad area, I would like to limit my talk to three areas: parental abuse of children, social agencies that deal with abuse, and what the ordinary citizen can do when he or she suspects a child is being abused.*

Getting Attention

In addition to telling your audience what you are going to talk about, your introduction should arouse attention and interest. Gaining attention is not just a matter of getting audience members to listen to your first words—they would probably do that anyway. It is rather a matter of creating interest in your subject. You want your audience members to think, "This really sounds like an interesting subject" or "I am going to enjoy listening to this speech."

Certain techniques are proven to be attention getters. Let's look at them and at the functions they serve. Note that sometimes a speaker might use more than one of these techniques.

USE SOME HUMOR

Research shows that speeches with some humor produce a more favorable reaction to the speaker.[2] Often a speaker will use humor in his or her introduction. This is how a speaker began her speech for Senior Recognition Day:

> *Greetings to you, seniors, who invited me to address you today and who soon will be able to decide whether that was a mistake. Greetings to you, colleagues, and to you, freshmen, and most special greetings to anyone who came even though you were not required to.[3]*

USE AN EXAMPLE

Short examples often work quite well in introductions. They can be personal examples, or they could have happened to someone else. A student used this example to spark interest in her speech:

> *Gilbert is 42 years old. He has three children, ages 17, 10, and 4. Gilbert never read to his two oldest children or helped them with their school-work. If they asked for help with reading, Gilbert's reply was, "Ask your mother." Last week everything changed. Gilbert read* The Cat in the Hat *to his 4-year-old. It was the first time Gilbert had ever read to one of his children. In fact, it was the first time Gilbert had read anything aloud at all.*
>
> *Gilbert had been illiterate. For the past four months he has been learning to read through a program in the literacy council. I am Gilbert's teacher.*

REFER TO THE OCCASION

If you are asked to speak for a special occasion or if a special occasion falls on the day you are speaking, make a reference to it, as in the following:

> *I am very honored to have been asked to give a speech for Founders' Day. This occasion has a special meaning for me because, one hundred years ago, when this college began, my great-grandmother was in its first class.*

SHOW THE IMPORTANCE OF THE SUBJECT

Showing the audience that the subject is important to their own lives is a good way of getting and keeping attention. Not only does this student let his listeners know how important the subject is to them, but he also keeps their attention by building suspense:

I would like to speak on a topic that affects, according to a recent Roper poll, close to 74 percent of Americans. Sometimes it nags at us day in and day out. Often it makes us feel inadequate because we can't measure up— we can't accomplish what we hope to, or we can't do as well on things as we would like to. This is something that takes a toll on us physically, mentally, and emotionally. What is this thing that makes us feel we have lost control over our day-to-day routine? It is the daily grind.

USE STARTLING INFORMATION

Using information that startles or surprises your audience is a good device for gaining attention. Gail, citing a number of current sources, tells us about foods that fight cancer, using examples the audience can easily relate to:

A review of 170 research studies from 17 nations revealed that people who ate the most fruits and vegetables had about half the cancer rates of those who ate the least fruits and vegetables.

Tomato products contain lycopene. That's what makes tomatoes red. It is also found in watermelons and apricots, and it fights off pancreatic cancer.

Spinach, broccoli, kale, and dark green lettuces lower the risks of many different kinds of cancers. The darker the vegetable the better.

A good way to avoid cancers linked to the colon, stomach, lung, and liver is to eat garlic, onions, and scallions.

Are statistics easier to understand if you put them in a bar graph?

An all-around cancer package contains oranges, grapefruit, lemons, and limes, and these need to be eaten as often as possible.

For those concerned about breast cancer, cabbage, cauliflower, brussels sprouts, broccoli, kale, mustard greens, and turnips will help.

Studies show we need to strive for five or more servings of fresh fruits and vegetables daily.

USE QUESTIONS

Questions get audience members involved right away because they will mentally answer the questions as you ask them. Sometimes questions can be used to build suspense. Here's how one student began her speech about buying a secondhand car:

> *How do you shop for a secondhand car? Do you look for a particular model, or do you go in to see what's available? Is there any kind of research you can do before you go to the car lot? Is there any way of knowing what a particular car is worth? Are secondhand cars ever under warranty by the dealer? These are some of the questions many of us ask when we go to buy a secondhand car. Today, I am going to try to give you some answers.*

USE PERSONAL EXAMPLES

Don't be afraid to refer to your own life when you can tie examples from it into your subject. Personal examples make a speech stronger because they are a way of showing that you know what you're talking about. This speaker used an example from his own experience to begin a speech about dropping out of school:

> *Seven years ago I was a teenage dropout. I went away to college because my parents wanted me to. I moved into a dorm, made lots of friends, and began to have a wonderful time—a time that was so wonderful that I only occasionally went to class or studied for an exam. The college, realizing that first-year students take time to adjust, put me on probation for the first year. In the second year, however, I had to settle down.*
>
> *I tried to study, but I didn't have any idea of what I was studying for. I didn't have a major and I had no idea of what I wanted to do with my life. Finally I asked myself, "What am I doing here?" I could come up with no answer. So after finishing the first semester of my sophomore year, I dropped out. It was the second-best decision I ever made. The first-best was to come back to school—at the grand old age of 27.*

Sometimes examples from your life help tell your audience why you are qualified to speak on your subject. If the audience thinks you have some experience or expertise, you will have more credibility as a speaker:

Today I am here to persuade you never to take up smoking. You might think it is a case of the pot calling the kettle black. In the past you may have seen me smoke at every possible opportunity. All I can say is that if I had one wish, I would like to be a nonsmoker. Why do I want to give it up? Let me tell you what you might not know. Every morning I cough for half an hour when I get out of bed. I have thrown away countless clothes because I have burned tiny holes in them with cigarette sparks. The windows of my house and car are covered with a greasy yellow film from smoke. Worst of all, my favorite cat won't sit in my lap because she hates smoke.

Why haven't I given it up? Because it is a powerful addiction that is very hard to break. But today, here, with all of you as my witnesses, I want you to know that I have just passed my first week without any cigarettes.

USE A QUOTATION

Sometimes you can find a quotation that will get your speech off to a good start. A well-chosen quotation can also give credibility to your speech. When a journalism student spoke to her class about what goes into television reporting, she quoted Bill Whittaker, a correspondent for CBS:

> *I think most people think it's glamorous and exciting and fast-paced and fun. And it is. But what they fail to realize is how demanding it is, how much it requires of you. CBS can call you at any hour of the day or night and ask you to get out of your bed, catch a plane and fly to Nowhere, U.S.A., and stand in the mud and rain and talk about a flood.*[4]

Additional Tips for Introductions

When writing an introduction to a speech, remember these points as well:

1. Although you might want to build curiosity about your speech topic, don't draw out the suspense for too long. The audience will get annoyed if it has to wait to find out what you're going to talk about.

2. Keep your introduction short. The body of your speech contains the main content, and you shouldn't wait too long to get there.

3. In planning your speech, be sure to adapt the topic to the occasion and to the audience. Before you start to speak, ask yourself whether there is anything in the situation that you did not anticipate and need to adapt to. For example, did someone introduce you in a particularly flattering way? Do you want to acknowledge this? Did your audience brave bad weather to come and hear you talk? Do you want to thank them?

Here is a speaker who, for a short time, violates all of the "rules" of a good introduction. Do you think this introduction is effective?

The energy in that room was so low, I almost hesitated to do my normal opening, which almost always works. I deliberately start a presentation the wrong way. I mean, the worst possible way. I lay a stack of pages (supposedly the text of my speech) on the lectern and start reading. Eyes glued to the page. Flat monotone voice. No gestures. In other words, just like my two predecessors on that podium.

I decided to go with it anyway. After I was introduced, I stepped up to the lectern and proceeded to do everything I could to sabotage my own likability and drive the energy of the audience into the ground. It worked beautifully. In a second, the boredom in that room was so thick you could cut it with a chainsaw.

I glanced up a couple of times as I droned on—not to make eye contact with my listeners, but just to make sure that they were still tuned out. It was perfect. I saw people yawning, gazing blankly, reading newspapers, checking watches.

Then, about a minute into my speech, I raised my voice, picked up my "notes," tossed them behind me, and stepped out from behind the lectern. A ripple of surprise and a murmur of suspense *went through the audience. I could see it in their faces: "What is this guy up to?" No question, I now had their undivided attention.*

"How many of you completely tuned out while I was talking from that lectern?" Lots of sighs of relief, but no hands. "Oh, come on! Be honest! I just got through boring you to tears! Admit it! How many of you tuned me out completely in the first five seconds *of my so-called 'speech'?" Grins now, expressions of relief, and a massive* show of hands.

From that point on we were off and running.

Source: Bert Decker (with James Denney), *You've Got to Be Believed to Be Heard* (New York: St. Martin's Press), 1992, p. 67.

QUESTIONS

1. From his introduction, what do you think the speaker was going to talk about?

2. Notice that he says his so-called introduction only lasted about five seconds. Could he have gone on much longer without losing his audience?

3. How does he indicate that he was taking a risk with this introduction? Is it a risk you would be willing to take?

THE SPEECH CONCLUSION

A good **conclusion** should tie a speech together and give the audience the feeling that the speech is complete. It should not introduce any new ideas.

If you have not had very much experience in public speaking, it is especially important that you plan your conclusion carefully. No feeling is worse than knowing that you have said all you have to say but do not know how to stop. If you plan your conclusion, this won't happen to you.

In preparing a conclusion, it may be helpful to follow a model. Just as in following a model for the introduction, this can help ensure that all essential parts are included. This is, perhaps, more important for beginning speakers than for those with more experience. As we said when introducing a model for introduction preparation, speakers who follow models without deviation may find themselves giving lackluster, mechanical speeches.

A conclusion should:

- Signal the end of your speech. (You could say "The last thing I would like to say . . ." or "Finally, . . ." Please note that the words "In conclusion I would just like to say that . . ." are overused. Try to find an original signal.)

- Summarize your main points.

- Make a memorable final statement.

This model is designed to show beginning students what they are supposed to work toward as they prepare their conclusions. Try not to let this model stifle your creativity or imagination.

As with introductions, certain kinds of conclusions are used time and time again. When you are working on your conclusion, consider one of these. Note that even though the conclusions are of different types, speakers should try to give them an inspirational quality. They should make the audience feel that the speech was terrific and that they would like to hear this speaker again.

Summarize Your Main Ideas

If you want your audience to remember your main points, it helps to go back and summarize them in the conclusion of your speech. The student whose topic was "Five Tips for Improving Term Papers" concluded her speech this way:

> Let me briefly summarize what you should do whenever you write a term paper. Use interviews as well as books, show enthusiasm about the subject, paraphrase quotations, don't pad your paper, have your paper printed on a quality printer, and proofread your paper before you hand it in. If you follow these hints you are certain to do better in the next paper you write.

Use a Quotation

If you can find a quotation that fits your subject, the conclusion is a good place to use it. A quotation gives added authority to everything you have said, and it can often help sum up your main ideas. In his speech to persuade the audience not to make political choices on the basis of television commercials, this student used a closing quotation to reinforce his point:

> An executive in the television industry once wrote, "Television programming is designed to be understood by and to appeal to the average 12-year-old." Since none of us are 12-year-old voters, I would suggest that we fight back. There is only one way to do that. Turn off the television set.

Inspire Your Audience to Action

When you give a speech, especially a persuasive one, your goal is often to inspire an audience to some course of action. If this has been the goal of your speech, you can use your conclusion to tell audience members precisely what they should do. In the following example, a student has been trying to persuade members of her audience to join campus organizations. Notice how she motivates them to take this action:

> We often hear that college is not part of "real life." Real life, however, is made up of clubs and organizations—all of which function to make decisions about our community, our lives, and even the course of democracy. This campus has 159 different clubs and organizations. If you are not a member of one of them, I encourage you to join today. If you join one of them, you become part of campus life. If you start working with an organization, you are preparing yourself for life in the "real world." On the table by the door there are lists of all of these organizations along with their telephone numbers. Please pick up a list on your way out. I'm sure you will find that at least one organization has something for you.

Additional Tips for Conclusions

1. Work on your conclusion until you feel you can deliver it without notes. If you feel confident about your conclusion, you will feel more confident about your speech.
2. If you tell your audience you are going to conclude, do it! Don't set up the expectation that you are finished and then go on talking for several more minutes.
3. Don't let the words *thank you* or "Are there any questions?" take the place of a conclusion.
4. Give your conclusion and leave the speaking area if appropriate. If you don't do this, you will ruin the impact of your conclusion and perhaps even your entire speech. (Leaving the speaking area may not be appropriate if there is a question period following the speech.)

■ SPEECH TRANSITIONS

The final element to work into your speech is **transitions**—comments that lead from one point to another to tell your audience where you have been and where you are going. Transitions are a means of smoothing the flow from one point to another. For example, if you are going to show how alcohol and tobacco combine to become more powerful than either acting alone, you might say:

We all know, then, that cigarette smoking is hazardous to our health and we all know that alcohol abuse can kill, but do you know what can happen when the two are combined? Let me show you how these two substances act synergistically—each one making the other more powerful and dangerous than either would be alone.

Now you are set to speak about their combined effect.

Tips for Transitions

In writing transitions, you should pay attention to these points:

1. Use a transition to introduce main heads and to indicate their order: "First . . . Second . . . Third . . ."; "The first matter we shall discuss . . ."; "In the first place . . ."; "The first step . . ."; "Let us first consider . . ."; and the like.
2. Write out your transitions and include them in your speech outline. A transition that is written out and rehearsed is more likely to be used.
3. If in doubt about whether to use a transition, *use it*. Since a speech is a one-time event, listeners cannot go back. Do everything you can to make the job of listening easier and more accurate.

■ PREPARING AN OUTLINE

An **outline** is a way of organizing material so you can see all the parts and how they relate to the whole. Outlining your speech will help you organize your thoughts and discover where your presentation might present problems in structure.

The Outline Format

Your speech will be organized into an introduction, a body, and a conclusion (with transitions connecting them). Since the introduction and the conclusion deal with so few points, they are usually not outlined, although some people prefer to outline them. As previously noted, outlining can help you see whether all essential parts are included. This is especially important for beginning speakers. We use Roman numerals to designate the main points of the body of the speech, as demonstrated in the previous example about speech organization.

MAIN AND SUPPORTING POINTS

The outline sets forth the major portion of the speech—the body—and shows the content's organization into main and supporting (minor) points. Remember that the broad, general statements are the main points; the minor points contain the more specific information that elaborates on and supports the main points.

STANDARD SYMBOLS AND INDENTATION

All outlines use the same system of symbols. The main points are numbered with Roman numerals (I, II, III) and capital letters (A, B, C). Minor, more specific, points are numbered with Arabic numerals (1, 2, 3) and lowercase letters (a, b, c). The most important material is always closest to the left-hand margin; as material gets less important, it moves to the right. Note, then, that the outline format moves information from the general to the more specific through the use of numbers, letters, and indentation.

I. University
   A. College of Arts and Sciences
      1. English
      2. History
      3. Mathematics
      4. Psychology
      5. Science
   B. College of Business Administration
      1. Accounting
      2. Economics
      3. Finance
      4. General Business
   C. College of Education
      1. Early Childhood Education
      2. Elementary Education
      3. Secondary Education
      4. Special Education

Another thing you should note about the outline format is that there should always be at least two points of the same level. That is, you can't have just an A and no B; you can't have just a 1 and no 2. The only exception to this is that in a one-point speech, you would have only one main point.

Full-Sentence and Key-Word Outlines

There are two major types of outlines: full-sentence and key-word. A **full-sentence outline** is a complete map of what the speech will look like. All the ideas are stated in full sentences. In a full-sentence outline it is easy to spot problem areas and weaknesses in the structure, support, and flow of ideas. This type of outline is useful as you plan and develop your speech.

Key-word outlines give only the important words and phrases; their main function is to remind the speaker of his or her ideas when delivering the speech. Sometimes speakers will add statistics or quotations to key-word outlines when such information is too long or too complicated to memorize. Some speakers prepare a full-sentence outline on the left and a key-word outline on the right, as in the following example. The key-word outline enables the speaker to avoid having to look at his or her notes all the time.

Produce should be carefully washed before you eat it.	Wash produce
Breads without preservatives should be refrigerated.	Refrigerate bread
Meat should not be eaten raw.	No raw meat

The main points (whether presented in full sentences or by key words) are sometimes put on cards—one to a card. We will discuss the reasons for this in Chapter 13.

 ## THE BIBLIOGRAPHY

At the end of your outline you should have a **bibliography** of all the material you have used in preparing your speech. This bibliography should include everything you have read (books, newspapers, magazines) and all the people you have interviewed. Figure 12-1 shows how items should be listed in a bibliography. At the end of this chapter, following the sample outline, you will find a sample bibliography.

Following the style used by the Modern Language Association (MLA), bibliography entries would look like this:

A BOOK
   McCullough, David. *Truman.* New York: Simon & Schuster, 1992.

A MAGAZINE
   Myers, D. G. "Pursuing Happiness: Where to Look, Where Not to Look." *Psychology Today* July/Aug. 1993: 32–35+.

AN INTERVIEW
   Hoff, S. Personal interview with Steven Hoff, President, Campus Committee on Student Personnel (CCSP), Nov. 1994.

Following the style used by the American Psychological Association (APA), bibliography entries would look like this:

   McCullough, D. (1992) *Truman.* New York: Simon & Schuster.

FIGURE 12-1
Sample Bibliographical Entries

To help you do your own outline, here is a sample speech titled "Controlling Stage Fright" by Annie Metzger of Bowling Green State University, done in outline form. The topical outline works well for this particular speech because all the main points are illustrations of the central idea. The speech outline appears on the left, our commentary on the right. (Please note that the page numbers in the speech are for the outline and should not be part of the speech itself.)

Title

Controlling Stage Fright

By stating your specific purpose and central idea, you will be able to stay on track while you are doing your outline.

Specific Purpose

To inform classmates about ways for controlling stage fright.

Central Idea

Academic, mental, and physical preparation is required for controlling stage fright.

Whenever you add a new main point, ask yourself whether it ties in directly with your purpose and central idea.

Introduction

Did any of you ever see that episode of *The Brady Bunch* where Marsha had to give a speech and her mom told her to picture the audience in their underwear? Well, Mrs. Brady was actually advising a very good public speaking tool. The idea is that picturing others undressed makes them less threatening to the speaker, according to Antoni A. Louw, writing on stage fright in a recent issue of *Training and Development*. This, along with many other tricks, can be used to diminish speech anxiety. Stage fright, as it is also known, can be controlled using academic, mental, and physical preparation.

The opening example about *The Brady Bunch* relates closely to student interests; thus, it will grasp attention well. The question, too, adds to its attention value.

Notice the use of the source here in the introduction. It proves at the outset that Metzger has done her homework.

Transition

In the August 1991 issue of *Sales and Marketing Management*, Edward Walsh defines stage fright as "unjustified and potentially destructive self-awareness" (p. 54). It is this destructive self-awareness that causes adrenaline to course through the body. Nathalie Donnet, in an article on nervousness in *Training and Development*, explains that that is what causes mouths to dry

Although a bit long, this transition has some obvious benefits. First, it provides Metzger an opportunity to provide two more excellent sources. Also, it allows her to talk briefly about the signs of

out, muscles to twitch, voices to quiver, hands to shake, knees to get weak, and stomachs to churn. (p. 21) Although symptoms of anxiety are always present in everyone before presentations, they can be controlled by using academic, mental, and physical preparation. Let's look at academic preparation first.

Body

I. By academic preparation I mean things like making the speech as interesting as possible and practicing the speech over and over again so that you become familiar with it.

   A. There are many aspects that go into an interesting speech.

      1. In his 1991 article "How to Think On Your Feet," Stephan Rafe points out that a dynamic opening is important. (p. 61)

      2. Roger Ailes, in his 1988 book *You Are the Message*, recommends that speakers focus their energy *into* their speech to help keep audience attention. (p. 166)

   B. Practice the speech as much as possible.

      1. Perform the entire speech (including visual aids, introduction, and conclusion) at least three times.

         a. First, use a mirror.

         b. Second, have a good friend listen to it.

         c. Third, use a tape recorder.

      2. In 1991, Walsh, in "Tips to Better Talks," says this is the time to clarify sections of the speech that are unclear. (p. 56)

Transition

Academic preparation is one part of mental preparation; the other part of mental preparation is visualization. Visualization also can help speakers counter stage fright.

---

anxiety. Finally, it gives her a chance to remind her listeners of the main points of the speech and what she plans to talk about first.

Metzger develops the first main point under Roman numeral I. Note that this point is stated in a full sentence.
Subpoints are all stated as full sentences. Metzger even stated items below this level in full sentences. Notice her continuing use of good sources. In this subpoint, too, Metzger uses a strong source to support her point.

Notice how tightly Metzger's points are tied together. Each subpoint relates precisely to the point that it is subordinate to in the outline. Metzger's use of sources continues to enhance her credibility.

Notice that this transition serves two purposes. Not only does Metzger remind listeners of the point just covered, she forecasts the points to come as well.

II. Positive thinking, pausing to organize thoughts, and "embracing" the audience are techniques used by the professionals to counter speech anxiety.

    A. Being positive means both thinking and talking.

        1. Ailes says to think thoughts such as "This is an opportunity to improve on a skill I'll need one day" (p. 166).

        2. Burns, in his 1991 article "Combating Speech Anxiety," suggests positive talk such as "I'm going to do a great job! I can do this"(p. 30).

    B. Ailes says speakers should pause a second longer than they think they should before starting a speech. (p. 166)

        1. The pause allows speakers to organize what comes next.

        2. The pause helps coalesce the audience—to get them to focus on the same thing. (Ailes, p. 166)

    C. Antoni Louw, a practiced public speaker, "embraces the whole audience" as part of his mental preparation.

        1. He pauses when he steps to the lectern.

        2. He focuses on the back of the room first.

        3. Then, within the space between the lectern and the back of the room, he "embraces the audience" (p. 22).

Transition

All this mental stuff is fine, but when speakers' stomachs start to tie up in knots, all the mental preparation used to control stage fright may not seem to help much. That is when physical preparation comes in handy.

The second main point is stated in a full sentence, as are all the subheads.

Once again, notice how tightly points are tied together. Also, notice Metzger's use of sources—they are all excellent and well placed.

Notice how Metzger now has constructed parallel points. All points at the same level in the outline are similarly structured.

In this transition, Metzger, does three things: (1) She makes a general reference to her last two points. (2) She focuses on the next point. (3) By saying "preparation used to control stage fright," she keeps audience attention on the central thesis.

III. To minimize butterflies, nervous twitch-
es, and shakes, speakers can use warm-
up, breathing, and progressive relaxation techniques.

    A. Nathalie Donnet, director of the
Studio for Effective Expression, lists
three warm-up exercises:

        1. Roll the neck.

        2. Shrug the shoulders.

        3. Yawn and stretch.

    B. Burns says it is important to breathe
from the diaphragm before and dur-
ing speeches. (p. 30) Ron Hoff, in his
book *"I Can See You Naked,"* says to
do it for two minutes. (p. 54)

    C. Donnet explains progressive relax-
ation.

        1. Tighten all muscles of the body
one by one.

        2. Release the tension all at once to
achieve the "rag-doll effect."

        3. Repeat this again and again until
speech time. (p. 21)

Notice how Metzger's third main head includes all three of the subpoints (A,B,C) that follow.

Notice how she uses her sources.

Throughout her speech Metzger does an excellent job of using her sources. They are well integrated into her material.

Conclusion

Academic preparation involves knowing a
speech very well and being as animated as
possible when presenting it. Mental preparation is thinking positively about every aspect
of a presentation. Physical preparation, such
as warm-ups, proper breathing, and progressive relaxation, can help nervous speakers,
too. All these help in controlling stage fright.
You can control stage fright before it controls you. Having butterflies is normal; what
I've tried to do is help you get them to fly in
formation.

In Metzger's conclusion, she first summarized the three points she covered in the speech. She reminded listeners of her central thesis: help in controlling stage fright. Her final comment about the butterflies is an old quote, but used fairly creatively, and appropriately here.

Bibliography

AILES, ROGER, *You Are the Message,* New
York: Doubleday Currency, 1988.

AILES, ROGER, WITH JON KRAUSHAR.
"Public Speaking Survival Strategies,"
Working Woman, November 1990, pp.
118–121.

BURNS, ROBERT EDWARD. "Combating
Speech Anxiety," *Public Relations Journal,*
March 1991, pp. 28, 30.

This bibliography lists (in MLA style) all the sources the speaker used in preparing the speech. If she (or anyone else) wants to check her infor-mation, the bibliography tells where to look.

DONNET, NATHALIE. "Making Nervousness Work for You," *Training and Development*, April 1989, pp. 21–23.

HOFF, RON. *"I Can See You Naked,"* Kansas City: Andrews and McMeel, 1992.

LOUW, ANTONI A. "Stage Fright, Break Your Barriers," *Training and Development* (February 1992): p. 19.

RAFE, STEPHAN C. "How to Think On Your Feet," *Small Business Report*, May 1991, pp. 58–61.

WALSH, EDWARD F. "Tips to Better Talks," *Sales and Marketing Management*, August 1991, pp. 54–56.

SUMMARY

The principles of organization include selecting information that relates to the specific purpose and central idea; distinguishing among the introduction, body, and conclusion of the speech; distinguishing between main and minor points; and phrasing all points in full sentences with parallel structure.

Six patterns of organization work well for organizing speeches; time order, using a chronological sequence; spatial order, moving from left to right, top to bottom, or in any direction that will make the subject clear; cause-and-effect order, showing why something is happening and what impact it is having; problem-solution, explaining a problem and giving a solution; motivated sequence, following the steps of attention, need, satisfaction, visualization, and action; and topical order, arranging the speech into subtopics.

The purpose of the introduction is to set the tone for the speech, introduce the topic, and get the audience's attention. Some attention-getting devices are using humor, giving personal examples, referring to the occasion, showing the importance of the subject, telling startling information, asking questions, and using quotations.

The speech conclusion should signal the audience that the speech is over and should tie all the ideas together. In their conclusions, speakers often summarize main ideas, use quotations, and inspire the audience to take further action.

Speech transitions help an audience follow where a speaker is going. They introduce main heads and may be written into the speech outline.

An outline is a way of organizing material to highlight all the parts and how they relate to the whole. In most cases, the body of the speech is what is outlined—the introduction and conclusion are handled separately.

The outline shows the organization into main and minor points through the use of standard symbols and indentation. Many speakers like to construct two outlines: a full-sentence outline for organizing the speech and a key-word outline to summarize the main ideas and to function as notes during delivery of the speech.

Your outline should be followed by a bibliography—a list of all of the material from other sources that you have used in your speech. All the items should be stated in a standard bibliographical form.

◼ NOTES

[1] Bruce E. Gronbeck, Raymie E. McKerrow, Douglas Ehninger, and Alan H. Monroe, *Principles and Types of Speech Communication,* 12th ed. (New York: HarperCollins, 1994), pp. 193–223.

[2] Charles R. Gruner, "Advice to the Beginning Speaker on Using Humor—What the Research Tells Us," *Communication Education,* 34 (April 1985): 142.

[3] Rebecca C. Jann, "What They Should Have Told Me When I Was a Senior," *Vital Speeches of the Day,* November 1, 1983, p. 51.

[4] Shirley Biagi, *Newstalk II* (Belmont, CA: Wadsworth, 1987), p. 165.

◼ FURTHER READING

BOYD, STEPHEN D., AND MARY ANN RENZ. *Organization and Outlining: A Workbook for Students in Basic Speech Courses.* Indianapolis: Bobbs-Merrill, 1985. This workbook can be used by individuals without direction. It helps develop proficiency by systematically providing principles, frequent examples, sample exercises, and possible answers. It begins by discussing points of focus of speeches and ends with the complete outline.

BRICKMAN, GAYLE F., AND LYNNE E. FULLER. *Organizing for Impact: A Practical Guide for the Public Speaker.* Dubuque, IA: Kendell/Hunt, 1986. The authors provide a systematic approach for putting together a presentation: analyze your audience; brainstorm for a topic; develop the topic to a suitable length; derive pertinent, clear main points; then use their "branching sheet" to make certain that all main components are in place. A practical, useful book full of specific suggestions and guidelines.

COOK, JEFF SCOTT. *The Elements of Speechwriting and Public Speaking*. New York: Collier (Macmillan), 1989. Cook has written a readable 242-page paperback that includes the essentials. Chapter 4, "Speech Construction," the longest (35 pages), contains specific information on the introduction, the body, and the conclusion, with numerous supporting examples.

LUCAS, STEPHEN E. *The Art of Public Speaking*, 5th ed. New York: McGraw-Hill, 1995. In this best-selling textbook, Lucas offers a thorough, clear, and lively examination of public speaking. One special strength is his heavy reliance on narratives, extracts from speeches, speech outlines, and sample speeches. Although all parts of the text are strong, the book is listed here because of its three outstanding chapters on organizing and outlining: "Organizing the Body of the Speech," "Beginning and Ending the Speech," and "Outlining the Speech." A well-written, well-researched book.

NOONAN, PEGGY. *What I Saw at the Revolution*. New York: Random House, 1990. Noonan writes about what it was like to be a speechwriter for a U.S. president. She wrote speeches for both Ronald Reagan and George Bush. Chapter 5 is particularly interesting since it describes all the writing and revisions of a speech before it is actually delivered.

ROSS, RAYMOND S. *Speech Communication: The Speechmaking Process*, 9th ed. Englewood Cliffs, NJ: Prentice-Hall, 1992. From the number of editions this book has gone through, it should be clear this is tried and tested material. Chapter 5, "Organizing the Speech," offers readers a thorough examination of the topic, as does Chapter 6, "Outlining the Speech." Clear writing, specific examples, with a focus on easy comprehension have always guided Ross's works.

SAMOVAR, LARRY A., AND JACK MILLS. *Oral Communication: Message and Response*, 8th ed. Dubuque, IA: Brown, 1992. In this classic book on public speaking, the authors consider organization in Chapter 10. Other chapters include "The Core Statement," "Formulating Main Points and Subpoints," "Patterns of Relationship," "Strategies of Arrangement," "Outlining the Message," and "Beginning and Ending the Speech." Excellent writing with specific examples.

KEY TERMS

articulation

*computer-
  generated
  graphics*

diagram

enunciation

*extemporaneous
  speaking*

flip chart

graphs

*impromptu
  speaking*

inflection

monotone

*organizational
  chart*

pace

poster

pronunciation

tables

visual aids

Delivering the Speech

CHAPTER OBJECTIVES

After reading this chapter, you should be able to:

1 Show attentiveness to your audience.

2 Achieve a conversational quality in your speech.

3 Distinguish among the four types of delivery.

4 Use body movement, eye contact, and gestures to enhance your speech.

5 Identify the elements that affect how you sound, and adjust them to improve your delivery.

6 Use visual aids to increase your audience's attention and understanding.

7 Employ several techniques to control your nervousness.

8 Outline the steps to follow in practicing your speech.

inny DeVries had been out of college for two years. She had majored in social work and was now working for the Department of Social Services. Most of her work involved finding foster homes for problem children and helping the children adjust to their new families. Ginny loved her work, and when the Social Work Club at her alma mater asked her to speak she was excited by the opportunity. She decided to speak on the subject "Foster Care for Problem Kids," and she hoped to inspire some of the future social work graduates to choose the area of foster care for their own careers.

In preparing her speech, Ginny gathered facts and figures about foster care in the state. She prepared two charts: one a list of characteristics that make up a good foster home, the other a graph showing the percentage of children who stay out of trouble once they have been in a foster home. In addition to her factual and statistical material, she had a large number of examples and anecdotes based on her own experience. She organized all this material into a full-sentence outline—choosing items she thought would be particularly interesting to her audience.

Ginny had not done any public speaking since her speech class in college, but she remembered that it had been very helpful to practice her speech beforehand. Once it was organized, she gave the speech in her living room—pretending it was filled with an audience. On the first run-through she discovered it was 20 minutes long, whereas she had been asked to speak for only 15 minutes. She worked to cut it back and also added a couple of transitions to make the speech run more smoothly. When she had finished her editing and revising, she tried giving the speech again—this time in front of a mirror. She found her speech was the right length and the transitions worked well, but she wasn't using enough gestures. She made notes on the margins of her note cards to move around a little more and use more gestures. This she would practice in her next run-through. Feeling satisfied with her progress, she went to bed.

The next morning she woke up with a new idea for the introduction. She made a few notes and then went off to work. During her lunch hour, she shut her office door and ran through the speech again. As she was giving it, she made an effort to add gestures and to move around. This time the speech went so smoothly that she felt confident and went back to her work.

That evening, on her way to give the speech, she was feeling a little nervous, but she told herself that she was in good shape: the speech was well prepared and she knew she could deliver it well.

When she arrived in the room where she was to give the speech, she was still feeling a little apprehensive, so she took the remaining time to look over her note cards again.

When she stood up to speak, she started with a humorous anecdote, thus winning the complete attention of the audience. Ginny felt that she was off to a strong start and that this was going to be a good speech. As she spoke, she remembered to look around the room—particularly toward the back row and corners. She also looked at individual audience members. When she was two-thirds through the speech, she noticed some restlessness, so

To what extent can public speaking be an instrument for changing ourselves? Do you believe women need this tool more, or differently, than men? Read this example, and then answer the questions that follow it:

Susan Faludi, in an article called "Speak for Yourself," published in The New York Times Magazine, *felt that public speaking connected her to a political movement because it was a way to reform public life. What she did not realize, however, was how public speaking transformed her life. It was public speaking that helped her both prove and change herself. These results challenged and motivated her. Now, despite any nervousness, these results caused her to be even more determined than ever to speak in public.*

Source: Susan Faludi, "Speak for Yourself," *The New York Times Magazine,* January 26, 1992, p. 29.

QUESTIONS

1. What do you think Faludi meant when she said "prove" and "change" herself? What kind of proof? What kind of changes?

2. Do you think public speaking can prove or change you? Explain.

3. Does Faludi's conclusion make sense? If you prove and change yourself through public speaking, will you want to do more of it?

she added an anecdote. Immediately she had the audience's attention again.

When the speech was over, the chairperson asked if there were any questions. With barely a pause, several hands went up. Ginny answered dozens of questions—all of them dealing with different aspects of her work. The questions went on for so long that the chairperson had to call a halt— campus security had come to lock up the room. As the audience left the room, the chairperson told Ginny that this was the best speech the Social Work Club had heard all year. She added, "We'll be sure to invite you back next year." As Ginny drove home, she felt very good about herself. She thought, "I would like to do this again. It was a lot of work, but it really paid off."

A good speech can bring even more satisfaction to the speaker than it does to the audience. There is nothing quite like the experience of communicating your ideas, having them understood, and having an entire audience respond to you in a positive way. Yet speaking to an audience does not come naturally; it is a skill you have to learn. By now you have begun to master the skill of finding material and putting your speech together; now it is time to shift focus to delivering your speech.

Attentiveness

You might wonder how a speaker could be inattentive to his or her own speech. Yet it's quite possible to be present and functioning as a body while not being there in spirit. When Shakela's friend complimented her on the speech she had given in speech class, Shakela replied, "You know, it's almost like I wasn't there at all. I don't remember looking at anyone and I barely remember what I said."

Not being attentive to your own speech is really a matter of internal noise: you are so overcome with the mechanics and anxiety of giving a speech that you forget this is basically a human encounter between a speaker and listeners.

Attentiveness means focusing on the moment. It means saying to yourself that you have come to tell your listeners something important and that you are going to do your very best to communicate with them. It is also a matter of being aware of and responding to your listeners' needs. To ensure that you will be attentive to your audience, you can do several things:

1. *Pick a topic that is important to you.* If you are speaking on something of great interest and importance to you, it is likely that you will communicate your interest and enthusiasm to your audience. Also, if you can get involved in your subject, you are likely to feel less anxiety about giving your speech.
2. *Do all the work necessary to prepare the best speech possible.* If you work on your speech—organize and practice it—you will be much more confident about it and will feel less anxious when the time comes to give it. Then you will be able to concentrate on delivering your speech.
3. *Individualize your audience members.* Try to think of your audience as individual human beings rather than as a mass of people. As you give the speech, think: "I am going to talk to Kristen, who sits in the second row. Gabriel always looks like he is going to sleep. I am going to give a speech that will wake him up."
4. *Focus on the audience rather than on yourself.* As you speak, look for audience feedback and try to respond to it. The more you focus on the audience members and their needs, the less likely you are to feel anxiety.

Ginny followed these four guidelines when she gave her speech. She select-ed a topic, "Foster Care for Problem Kids," that was important to her; she did the work necessary to prepare the best speech she could; she looked at individual audience members; and she focused on the audience rather than on herself. At one point, noting some restlessness in her audience, she even added an unplanned anecdote to her speech.

Conversational Quality

Some of our models for public speaking come from orators who address huge audiences. Their voices rise and fall dramatically, their gestures are large and expansive, their voices big and booming. Although this might be an effective speaking technique for some occasions, such as political rallies and religious revivals, it is usually most effective to use a conversational quality in public speaking.

When you use a conversational quality you talk to your audience in much the same way you talk when you are having a conversation with another person.[1] The value of a conversational tone in public speaking is that it gives the impression that the speaker is talking *with* the audience rather than *at* it. Notice how this speaker uses conversational language and the word *you* to involve his audience:

> *Have you ever felt embarrassed—I mean really embarrassed—where you never wanted to show your face in public again? Has your face ever turned red when lots of people were watching you? I would guess that you have had this experience once or twice in your life—I know I have. But—have you ever wondered what happens to us physically and psychologically when we are embarrassed?*

How do you achieve a conversational tone in speaking? The most useful way, right from the planning stage, is to imagine giving your speech to one person or to a small group of people. Have a mental picture of this person or persons, and try to talk directly to them in a normal, conversational man-ner. This will help you to achieve the right tone.

However, a conversational tone doesn't mean being casual. A speech occasion is more formal than most conversations. Even though you're aim-ing for a conversational tone, you shouldn't allow long pauses or use such conversational fillers as "O.K." or "you know." You should also avoid some of the slang and "in" jokes or expressions you would use in casual conver-sation. Here are a few additional hints on how to achieve a conversational quality:

- When you give your speech, imagine you are giving it to someone you know.

- Use contractions such as *don't, can't, isn't,* and *weren't.* They create a more informal tone.

CONSIDER THIS

In 1919 Eugene Lang was the nine-year-old son of an immigrant family who scraped for a living. To save the nickel street-car fare, he walked two miles back and forth to Public School 121 in Harlem. From those humble beginnings, Lang went on to found the Refac[sic] Technology Development Corporation and to become a wealthy international industrialist.

In 1981 Lang's old school, P.S. 121, invited him to give the commencement address to the sixth grade class. Lang began his speech by urging the students to work hard and stay in school so that they, too, could achieve success. About midway through the address, Lang realized that his paralyzingly dull speech was meaningless to the poor black and Hispanic children who made up his audience. Suddenly, he broke from his prepared text and told the astonished youngsters something that did change their lives. Lang decided he would do more than merely urge them to finish school and go to college. He promised to put up the money to provide a college education for every student who applied himself and earned high enough grades to be admitted to college. For Lang and his sixth-grade listeners, it was the most exciting speech he could give or they could hear.

In 1985 Time *magazine told the story of Lang's spontaneous commencement address and reported that not one of the fifty-two students still in the New York area had abandoned school. In 1987 the*

- Use words everyone will understand.
- Use an outline rather than writing out your speech word for word.

TYPES OF DELIVERY

Think about a particularly good speech you have heard. Do you remember how it was delivered? From notes? From a manuscript? From memory? Was the speaker making a few brief, off-the-cuff remarks?

There are essentially four methods of delivery: making impromptu remarks, speaking from a manuscript, memorizing the speech, and delivering extemporaneously.

speech was the subject of a piece on CBS's "Sixty Minutes."

Though not all of us can afford to give away a college education to our audiences, we can supply another ingredient that made Lang's message come alive: commitment. Lang knew that it meant nothing to tell those kids to stay in school unless he really cared about their staying in school. And for him caring meant doing what he could to help them achieve the goal he urged them to pursue. In the "Sixty Minutes" interview Lang said that the most valuable thing he gave those kids was not tuition but attention. To give a great speech you must care about your topic and care about getting your listeners to embrace it and act upon it.

Source: C. Barry McCarty, *Well Said and Worth Saying* (Nashville, TN: Broadman, 1991), pp. 17–18.

QUESTIONS

1. How can you make a commitment in your own speeches?

2. Notice the importance of audience analysis in public speaking. Could Lang have changed his speech in another way, without promising a college education to each student, and still have been successful?

Impromptu Speaking

Impromptu speaking is the giving of a speech on the spur of the moment. Usually there is little or no time for preparation. Sometimes your instructor might ask you to give an impromptu speech in class. Other times you might be asked to give a toast or offer a prayer at a gathering, or you may make a few remarks at a meeting.

If you are asked to give an impromptu speech, the most important thing is not to panic. Your main goal is to think of a topic and organize it quickly in your head before you start to speak.

In finding a topic, look around you and consider the occasion. Is there anything you can refer to? Decorations? A friend? A photo that recalls a time together? Formal occasions usually honor someone or something, and the person or thing being honored can provide a focus for your speech: "I am delighted to be at this yearly meeting of documentary filmmakers.

Documentary filmmaking is one of the noblest professions. . . ." Other times you might want to refer to the place or the people: "I am happy to be here in Akron again. The last time I was here . . ." or "I am very touched by the warm reception you have all given me. . . ."

In impromptu speaking it's essential to keep your remarks brief. No one expects you to speak for more than a minute or two. The audience knows that you are in a tight spot, and it doesn't expect a long and well-polished speech.

Speaking from a Manuscript

Speaking from a manuscript involves writing out the entire speech and reading it to the audience. When you read a speech you can get a clear idea of how long it is, so manuscript speaking is a good method when exact timing is necessary. Because a manuscript also offers preplanned wording, political leaders often favor this method when they speak on sensitive issues and want control over what they say. When Louisa, for example, decided to run for president of the student government, she prepared a 5-minute speech in manuscript form for her appearance on the campus television station with the other candidates. Louisa knew that having a manuscript would help her stay within her time limit and would also help her say exactly what she wanted to say. However, she knew that she had to be very familiar with the manuscript so she could break away from it to establish eye contact too.

When using a manuscript, speakers find that it is difficult to sound spontaneous; if listeners think they are being read to, they are more likely to lose interest. Experienced speakers who use manuscripts are often so skilled at delivery that the audience is not aware the speech is being read. Beginning speakers, however, have difficulty making a manuscript speech sound spontaneous and natural.

Feedback is another problem in speaking from a manuscript. If the audience becomes bored and inattentive, it is difficult to respond and modify the speech; the speaker is bound to the manuscript. A manuscript also confines a speaker to the lectern—because that's where the manuscript is.

Speaking from Memory

Speaking from memory involves writing out the entire speech and then committing it to memory word for word. It has the same advantages for speakers as the manuscript method: exact wording can be planned, phrases and sentences can be crafted, and potential problems in language can be eliminated. Also, a memorized speech can be adapted to a set, inflexible time limit. Francisco, who was running against Louisa in the student election, decided to memorize his speech. He decided this was a good idea because he wanted exact wording but he also wanted the freedom to move around. Feedback was not a problem to Francisco because he was speaking to a television audience via the campus's closed-circuit television station. In other situations, however, responding to feedback can be a problem because it is difficult for the speaker to get away from what he or she has memorized. A speaker who gets off track or is distracted may forget parts of the speech or lose the place.

A memorized speech can create considerable pressure. Not only does the speaker have to spend hours memorizing the speech, but he or she is also likely to worry about forgetting it. In addition, making a memorized speech sound natural and spontaneous requires considerable acting talent.

Extemporaneous Speaking

When using the **extemporaneous speaking** method, a speaker delivers a speech from notes. The speaker might commit the main ideas of the speech to memory—possibly also the introduction and conclusion—but will rely on notes to remember most of the speech.

The extemporaneous method has several advantages. It permits flexibility so that a speaker can adjust to the feedback of listeners. For example, if a speaker sees that several audience members do not understand something, he or she can stop and explain. If the audience looks bored, the speaker can try moving around or using a visual aid earlier than planned. The extemporaneous method is the one method of delivery that comes closest to good conversation because a speaker can be natural and responsive to the audience.

One disadvantage of the extemporaneous method is that the speaker may stumble over or grope for words. However, much of this problem can be overcome by rehearsing the speech beforehand. Sometimes speakers want to use exact words or phrases. Although in extemporaneous speaking the speech as a whole is not memorized, there is nothing wrong with memorizing a particularly important sentence—or having it written down and reading it from a note card.

For the beginning speaker, the extemporaneous method is the best type of delivery. In addition to eliminating heavy burdens for the speaker (writing out or memorizing the speech), it enables a natural and spontaneous style of speaking. It also makes the listeners a central element in the speech, for the speaker is able to respond to them at all times.

HOW YOU LOOK

Appearance

As you rise from your chair and walk to the lectern to give your speech, the audience's first impression of you will come from how you look. Audience members will notice how you are dressed, whether you walk to the lectern with confidence, and whether you look interested in giving this speech.

On days when you are going to make a speech it is a good idea to look your best. Not only does looking good give the audience a positive impression of you, but it also gives you a psychological boost.

Try to stay away from clothing that might distract from your speech. For example, avoid T-shirts with writing on them. The message itself may be distracting, and audience members will divert their attention by trying to read or to guess what your T-shirt says if some of it is hidden by the lectern. Also, avoid accessories you might be tempted to play with. Scarves or jewelry worn around the neck can be troublesome in this regard.

When you are giving a speech in public, wear what the audience would expect you to wear. If it's a formal occasion, wear dress-up clothing; if it's informal, wear what you think everyone else will wear. If you don't know this, ask the person who has invited you to speak.

Body Movement

Movement usually causes a response. Blinking turn signals on a car attract more attention than tail lights; most of us prefer motion pictures to still photos; the most interesting commercials show the products working. By the same token, a speaker who uses some movement is likely to attract more attention than a speaker who stands absolutely still.[2] Of course, this does not mean that all movement is good. To be effective, your movement should be carefully coordinated with your speech. For example, if you want to stress your most important point, you might indicate this nonverbally by moving closer to your audience. If you want to create intimacy between you and your audience as you are telling a personal story, you could sit on the edge of the desk for a brief period.

Avoid movement that might be distracting. Probably you have seen a speaker (or teacher) who paces back and forth in front of the room. This movement is not motivated by anything other than habit or nervousness: as a result, it's ineffective.

Speakers cannot move around very much if they depend too heavily on their notes. If you must constantly return to the lectern to consult your notes, you will not be able to move very far. The better you know your speech, the more you will be able to experiment with movement.

When you are planning how to deliver your speech, you should consider whether to include deliberate body movements. If you leave these movements to chance, you might not move at all or might move in a way that distracts your listeners. For example, when Navita planned her speech about battered women, she decided to stay behind the lectern when she talked about policy but to move in front of the lectern when she talked about individual women. So that she wouldn't forget, she wrote reminders about moving on her note cards.

Eye Contact

In our culture, it is considered extremely important to look into the eyes of the person we are talking to. If we don't, we are at risk of being considered dishonest or of having something to hide. However, this is not true from culture to culture. There are sharp differences between cultures, although many people are not aware of them. Eye behavior varies according to the environment in which we learned it. We respond to social norms.

In some cultures, for example, there are rules governing whom you should and should not look at. One report says that in Kenya, men and their mothers-in-law must turn their backs to each other—they have no eye contact at all.[3]

Our point here is simply to underscore the existence of cultural differences. Often, Americans think everyone behaves the same as they do. In situations where cultural diversity exists, difficulties in social interaction and communication may arise if we are not sensitive or responsive to these differences. Eye contact, of course, is just one aspect of cultural diversity. Careful audience analysis may uncover differences in other areas of nonverbal communication, language, rules of social situations, social relationships, and even motivation.[4]

Public speakers talk to a broad range of audience members. Speakers in our culture are expected to scan the audience and to look directly into the eyes of individual audience members.[5] Not only is this expected, but it is a standard of excellence by which effectiveness often is gauged. Be careful about judging speakers from other cultures by standards which they have not learned and to which they do not personally subscribe.

Facial Expressions

Facial expressions are the most difficult movements to change. Since we seldom have a chance to see our own faces while we are communicating, it is difficult to know what we are expressing. Generally, however, this is an area of movement that you don't have to worry about *unless you get some negative reaction.* For example, if someone remarks that you looked bored to death while you were giving a speech, this is an area you should work on for your next speech.

Gestures

When we speak, most of our gestures are made up of hand and arm movements. We usually use gestures to express or emphasize ideas or emotions. Most of us are too stiff when we speak and could benefit by using more gestures. The best way to add more gestures to your speech is to practice in front of a mirror. Always aim for gestures that look spontaneous and that feel natural to you.

Posture

Posture is a matter of how we walk and stand. It can give the audience all sorts of messages. If you drag your feet or slouch, you could be communicating that you are lazy, sick, tired, or depressed—none of which you would want to communicate when giving a speech.

Also remember that the way you sit in your seat, rise and walk to the lectern, and return to your seat after the speech can leave as much of an impression as the posture you use during your speech.

When giving a speech, we usually don't have a good idea of our eye contact, facial expressions, or general body movement. Because we don't have a very good sense of how we look to others, a speech class is a great opportunity to get some feedback. Try to listen to critical remarks from your instructor and classmates without feeling defensive. If you can learn from your mistakes, you will improve every time you give a speech.

■ HOW YOU SOUND

When members of a speech class have a chance to see themselves on videotape, most of them react more negatively to how they sound than to how they look. Few people really like their own voice.

Our voice reveals things about us that might be far more important than the words we speak.[6] How loud, how fast, how clear and distinct the message—all are part of the information we send about ourselves.

The voice is also a powerful instrument of communication. Because it is so flexible, you can vary it to get the effect you want. You can speak in a loud voice and then drop to a mere whisper. You can go through basic information quickly and then slow down to make a new and important point. You can even use your voice to bring about a change of character. Notice how many different voices your favorite actress or comedian uses.

We have some idea of how we look to other people because we can see ourselves in a mirror. However, very few of us have any idea of how we sound, and once we find out, most of us would like to make some changes. When members of a speech communication class were asked to identify the things they most disliked about their voices, the most common complaints were poor articulation, speaking too fast, not sounding confident, and not having enough expression.

Volume

Many students who thought they did not sound confident enough attributed this fault to not speaking loudly enough. As one student wrote, "I sound as soft as a mouse." Her comment reflects the perception in our society that a weak and hard-to-hear voice implies the speaker has little confidence. You don't want people to think that about you. In a public speaking situation, you have to speak loudly enough so that people in the back row can hear you. Because your voice-producing mechanism is so close to your ears, you probably think you are speaking louder than you really are. This means that you probably need to speak in a louder voice than you feel comfortable with.

Always check out the back row to see if people can hear you there. Generally you can tell if they are straining to hear you, and often they will give you some nonverbal sign (e.g., leaning forward) that you need to speak louder. If the place in which you are speaking is unusually large, you could even ask if people in the back can hear. If people have to strain to hear you, they probably will not make the effort unless you have something extraordinary to say.

Using a Microphone

If you are speaking in a large auditorium or in a room with poor acoustics, there might be a microphone at the lectern. The rules for using microphones are simple: make sure it is turned on, don't blow into it to see if it's working (it could ruin it), adjust it to your height, and stand 8 to 12 inches away from it while you speak.

Pace

Like volume, pace is easy to vary. **Pace** refers to how fast or how slowly you speak. If you speak too fast, you may be difficult to understand. If you speak

TRY THIS

Below is a list of paired words that sound somewhat alike. Read them so that they can be distinguished.

accept	except
access	excess
adapt	adopt
amplitude	aptitude
are	our
Arthur	author
ascent	accent
axe	ask
comprise	compromise
consecrate	confiscate
consolation	consultation
disillusion	dissolution
immorality	immortality
line	lion
martial	marital
Mongol	mongrel
pictures	pitchers
statue	statute
vocation	vacation
wandered	wondered

Source: John P. Moncur and Harrison M. Karr, *Developing Your Speaking Voice*, 2d ed. (New York: HarperCollins, 1972).

too slowly, you risk losing the attention of your audience. If audience attention seems to be drifting away, try picking up your pace. Usually you don't know that you have been going too fast until someone tells you so after your speech is over. If you are told this, guard against the mistake in the future: in your next speech, write reminders on your note cards to slow down.

Ideally a speaker varies his or her pace. Speaking fast and then slowing down helps keep the attention of the audience. Also, don't forget the benefits of pausing. Making a pause before or after a dramatic moment is a highly effective technique. The next time you are watching a comedian on television, notice how he or she uses pauses.

Pitch and Inflection

As we noted in Chapter 5, *pitch* is the range of tones used in speaking. **Inflection** is a related concept. It refers to the change in pitch used to emphasize certain words and phrases. The person who never varies his or her speaking voice is said to speak in a **monotone.**

Sometimes a person's voice might not seem very interesting because of lack of inflection. If you listen to professional newscasters or sportcasters, you will discover that they use a lot of inflection. By emphasizing certain words and phrases, they help direct listeners' attention to what is important. Emphasis can also bring about subtle changes in meaning. Try reading the following sentence emphasizing a different word each time you read it. You should be able to read it in at least eight different ways.

You mean I have to be there at seven tomorrow?

The best way to get inflection in your voice is to stress certain words deliberately—even to the point of exaggeration. Try taping something in your normal voice and then in your "exaggerated" voice. You might be surprised to find that the exaggerated voice is more interesting.

Enunciation

Enunciation is made up of articulation and pronunciation. **Articulation** is the ability to pronounce the letters in a word correctly; **pronunciation** is the ability to pronounce the whole word. Not only does good enunciation enable people to understand us, but it is also the mark of an educated person. Most of our articulation problems go back to the people from whom we learned our language. If our parents, teachers, or peers pronounced words incorrectly, we probably will too.

Three common causes of articulation problems are sound substitution, omission of sounds, and slurring. Sound substitution is very common. Many people say "dere," "dem," and "dose" for "there," "them," and "those." In this case a *d* is substituted for the more difficult *th* sound. The substitution of a *d* for a *t* in the middle of a word is widespread in American English. If you need any proof, try pronouncing these words as you usually do: "water," "butter," "thirty," "bottle." Unless you have very good articulation, you probably said "wader," "budder," "thirdy," and "boddle."

Some people believe they have a speech defect that makes them unable to produce certain sounds. This can be easily checked. For example, if you always say "dere" for "there," make a special effort to make the *th* sound. If you are able to make it, you have a bad habit, not a speech defect.

We also commonly omit sounds. For example, we sometimes say "libary" for "library." And we frequently omit sounds that occur at the ends of words, saying "goin" for "going" and "doin" for "doing."

Slurring is caused by running words together. We use such phrases as "Yawanna go?" and "I'll meecha there." Slurring, as with other articulation problems, is usually a matter of bad speech habits, and it can be overcome with some effort and practice.

Once you are aware of a particular articulation habit, you can try to change it. Changing a habit is not easy, since the habit has probably been a part of your behavior for many years. Sometimes it helps to drill, using lists of words that give you trouble. It also helps to have a friend remind you

TRY THIS

You can practice correct articulation by saying each of the following tongue twisters three times, rapidly. If you have trouble with one or more of them, try working on exercises on the sound that gave you the problem.

1. She sells seashells on the seashore.
2. Rubber baby buggy bumpers.
3. The little lowland lubber was a lively lad, lucky, liberal, and likable.
4. The theme is there for them.
5. Betty battled bottles for thirty days.
6. Fanny Finch fried five floundering fish for Frances Fawlie's father.
7. While we waited for the whistle on the wharf, we whittled vigorously on the white weatherboards.
8. Meaninglessly meandering Melina managed to master Monday's memory work.
9. We apprehensively battled with the bragging apprentices, but they broke away from our blows and beat a poor retreat.
10. Grass grew green on the graves in Grace Gray's grandfather's graveyard.

Source: Adapted from Glenn R. Capp, G. Richard Capp, and Carol C. Capp, *Basic Oral Communication* (Englewood Cliffs, NJ: Prentice-Hall, 1990), p. 247.

when you mispronounce a word. Once you become accustomed to looking for the problem, you will catch yourself more often. If you have several articulation problems, do not try to solve them all at once. Work on one sound at a time; when you can handle that sound, then attempt another one.

Pronunciation is a matter of saying words correctly. Probably you have a bigger reading vocabulary than speaking vocabulary but don't know how to pronounce many of the words you read. If you are in doubt about how to pronounce a word, check it in the dictionary.

USING VISUAL AIDS

Visual aids are devices such as charts, graphs, and slides that help illustrate the key points in a speech. Visual aids serve three functions: they help hold

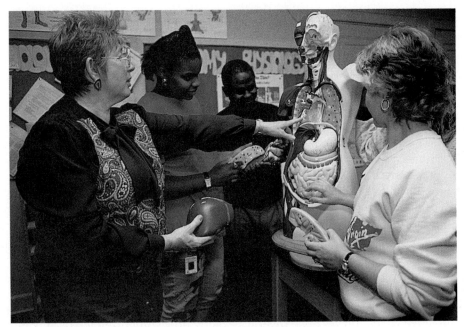

Why would spatial order work well for this presentation?

the attention of the listeners, they provide information in the visual channel, and they help the audience remember what you've said. A study has shown that if members of an audience are given only verbal information, after three days they will remember a mere 10 percent of what they were told; if they are shown material without verbal communication, they will remember 35 percent. However, if both verbal and visual information are provided, they will remember 65 percent after three days. Just because you have a visual aid, however, does not mean that your audience will automatically give you its attention. A poorly designed or inappropriate visual aid will not keep an audience's attention.

Types of Visual Aids

Your visual material should help make your topic lively and interesting to the audience. There are numerous types of visual aids to choose from. In making your choice, ask yourself which kind of visual material would best illustrate your topic and appeal to your listeners.

THE CHALKBOARD

Since a chalkboard exists in every classroom, it is the most accessible visual aid. It works particularly well if you write key words or phrases while you are talking. You can also use it to draw very simple diagrams.

When you use the chalkboard, it's important that you write quickly to avoid having your back to the audience any longer than necessary. Once you have the word or diagram on the board, turn around, stand next to it, and as you explain, point to it with your hand. Make sure that your writing is large and dark enough for the entire audience to read.

THE ACTUAL OBJECT

Sometimes it is useful to use the thing you are talking about as a visual aid. An audience likes to see what you are talking about—especially if the object is not familiar to them. One student brought a violin and viola to class to demonstrate the differences in the sounds and the looks of the two instruments. Another, explaining how to make minor adjustments on one's car, brought a carburetor. Still another borrowed a skeleton from the biology department to illustrate a speech on osteoporosis, a bone disease.

MODELS

A model is a replica of an actual object that is used when the object itself is too large to be displayed (e.g., a building), too small to be seen (e.g., a cell), or inaccessible to the eye (e.g., the human heart). A model can be a very effective visual aid because it shows exactly how something looks. It is better than a picture because it is three-dimensional. For example, a student who was discussing airplanes used in warfare brought in models of planes he had constructed.

POSTERS, DIAGRAMS, AND CHARTS

A **poster** consists of lettering or pictures, or both. The purpose of a poster is to enhance the speaker's subject. For example, when speaking about the style of electric cars, a student used a poster showing pictures of one make to show how the batteries had been incorporated into the overall design of the car. A poster may also be used to emphasize the key words or thoughts in a speech. A student who spoke on how to save money on clothes used a poster to list the following points:

1. Decide on a basic color.
2. Buy basics at one store.
3. Buy accessories at sales.

Not only did the poster provide the audience with a way to remember the points, but it also gave, in visual form, the general outline of the speech.

A **diagram** may range from a simple organizational chart to a complex rendering of a three-dimensional object. Diagrams are particularly valuable in showing how something works. For example, in a speech about storing toxic wastes, a student used the diagram in Figure 13-1 to show how waste can be stored in a salt cavern. Including a drawing of the Empire State Building was particularly useful because it gave the viewer an idea of the depth of the mine.

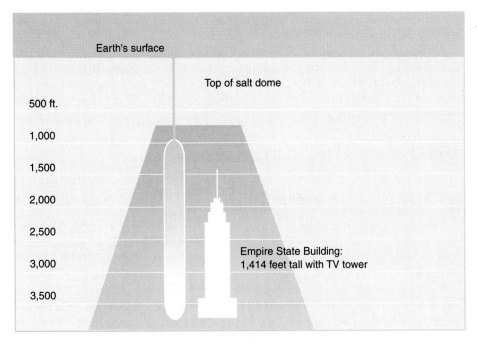

FIGURE 13-1
**One Cavern's
Size**

An **organizational chart** shows the relationships among the elements of an organization, such as the departments of a company, the branches of federal or state government, or the committees of the student government. For example, note how a speaker used the organizational chart in Figure 13-2 to show how the academic side of a university is organized and how a

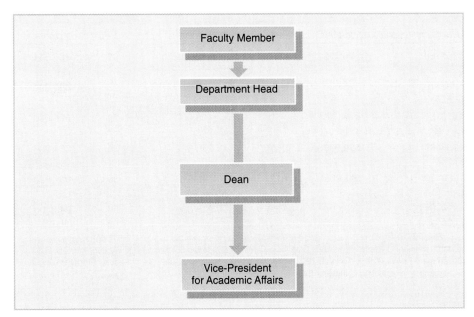

FIGURE 13-2
**Organizational
Chart**

student wishing to express dissatisfaction should approach people in a specific order beginning with a faculty member.

A **flip chart** is a series of pictures, words, diagrams, and so forth. It's called a flip chart because it is made up of several pages that you "flip" through. A flip chart is best used when you have a complicated subject which needs several illustrations or when you want to emphasize several points in your speech.

TABLES AND GRAPHS

These visual aids are easy to prepare and can be used to condense a lot of information into a useful, understandable form. Perhaps most important, anyone can make them because no special skills are required.

Tables are columns of figures arranged in an order that enables the viewer to easily pick out the information needed. For example, when a student spoke about the need for more female professors, he used Table 13-1 as his visual aid.

Graphs are statistical material presented in a visual form that helps viewers see similarities, differences, relationships, or trends. There are three commonly used graphs: bar, pie, and line. If you want to see a variety of graphs available, look in any issue of *USA Today*. We show a bar graph in Figure 13-3 and a pie graph in Figure 13-4.

A line graph is particularly useful in showing trends over a period of time

TABLE 13-1

NUMBER AND PERCENTAGE OF FACULTY MEMBERS BY GENDER, 1959–1991

Year (No. of Institutions)	Male Faculty		Female Faculty		Total
	Number	%	Number	%	Number
1959–60 (2,008)	296,773	78	83,781	22	380,554
1969–70 (2,525)	346,000	77	104,000	23	450,000
1979–80 (3,152)	479,000	71	196,000	29	675,000
1988–89 (3,565)	559,000	70	246,922	30	804,000
1989–90 (3,535)	577,298	70	246,922	30	824,220
1990–91 (3,559)	592,000	70	248,000	30	840,000

SOURCE: National Center for Education Statistics, *Digest of Education Statistics 1993,* Washington, DC; U.S. Government Printing Office (October 1993): 173. Table 167, "Historical Summary of Faculty, Students, Degrees, and Finances in Institutions of Higher Education, 1969–70 to 1990–91."

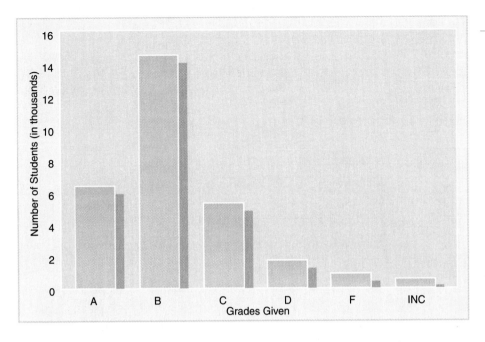

FIGURE 13-3
**Bar Graph:
Grading of
Students in One
University**

or in making comparisons. For example, a student who was trying to persuade his audience that the university should provide additional parking used the line graph in Figure 13-5 to show how the number of commuting students had increased.

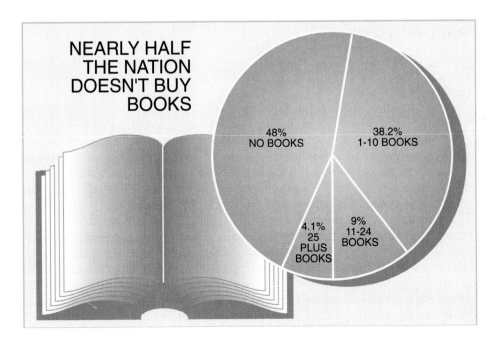

FIGURE 13-4
Pie Graph

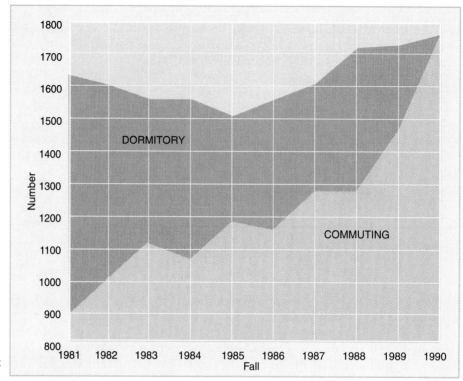

FIGURE 13-5
**Line Graph
Comparing
Resident and
Commuter Student
Populations**

PROJECTED MATERIAL

Videos, slides, and other projected material are useful visual aids. When
you are using projected material, remember that it should enhance, not
replace, your speech.

   If you decide to use a video, you have two choices: you can use one made
by other people or you can make your own. If you are making a long speech,
a preprogrammed video can be a very good visual reinforcement of what
you are saying. A student who gave a speech on how applicants are propa-
gandized by college admission tapes followed her speech with the college's
own admissions video. The students were amazed at the difference between
their perception of the college and the tape's portrayal of it.

   If you have access to your own video camera, you can make your own
tape and customize it to match your subject and your audience. One student made a videotape illustrating four basic karate moves for his speech.
Because video is so easy to work with, he was able to stop the tape, talk
about the move, then go on to the next one. Another student, speaking
about parking on campus, made a short video of students trying to find a
place in a full parking lot. Her video was an effective way of persuading her
audience of the need for additional student parking areas.

   You may have slides you could use in a speech, or you may have access to a set of slides that have been commercially produced. Since you are giving a speech rather than a slide show, however, you should limit the number of slides you use. One student who had traveled to China decided to limit her slides to those of the Great Wall. She figured this single site would be of greatest interest to her audience.

Overhead projectors are a very easy way of showing visual material. With an overhead, a page from a book can be projected and enlarged on a movie screen—which is much less complicated than copying from the book onto a chart. With an overhead projector you can also draw your information on an ordinary-sized piece of paper and then transfer it to a transparency for projection.

HANDOUTS

When material is complex or when there is a lot of it, audience members may need a handout. For example, a student who spoke about the calories in fast food gave audience members a handout showing caloric values of specific foods. Other times a handout is useful to reinforce the points you are making in your speech. A student who spoke about ten ways to recycle made a handout of her main points and distributed it at the end of her speech.

If you use handouts, choose the best time to pass them out. If you distribute your handouts too early, the audience will read them and ignore you. Also, most people dislike having a handout read to them. If your handout repeats the points you are making, give it out when your speech is over.

YOU AS A VISUAL AID

Often you can be the best visual aid—especially if you want to show your audience how to do something. For example, if you're telling audience members how to improve their golf swing, bring your clubs and demonstrate.

Computer-Generated Graphics and Multimedia

If you do not draw or letter well but have access to a computer, consider computer graphics. Many of the computer spreadsheets make it easy to convert figures to graphs. Check to see if one of your computer labs has a software program that will do this. Several software programs offer a variety of drawings and typefaces. For optimum clarity, make sure that your printer produces clean copy.

Numerous options are becoming available to speakers today. You may have seen some of the potential when you watched football games and noticed the visuals used to introduce the game. Many such innovations have come about as a result of the computer and are referred to as **computer-generated graphics.** The ordinary computer user may not yet have the capacity to produce visuals like you see on television—which often cost thousands of dollars to produce—but well-thought-out visuals, projected on a screen or on a computer, can give your presentation a professional and sophisticated look.

A computer with a graphics program can generate visual materials. Computers are best for processing numerical data and then converting that data into bar, line, and pie graphs. Having computer-generated graphs enlarged is a relatively simple, inexpensive process. Photocopiers can enlarge images, sometimes to 200 percent of the original size. The end product is worth the time, effort, and money. You can emphasize portions of your material by highlighting or coloring in areas. Even darkening the lines of a line graph or adding press-on letters for headings on a large copy can enhance visual presentation and effect.

To add even more emphasis to a presentation, you can mix in other media as well. The word *multimedia* refers to various media (text, graphics, animation, and audio) used to deliver information. Often these products are also interactive—users can choose from a variety of information options. For example, Lyndrey used computer graphics to illustrate parts of the human body for his speech on proper exercise techniques, and he gave his presentation a more professional look by converting computer-generated images into transparencies showing muscles during exercise. He projected these images during his speech. Computer-generated images can show machines, buildings, almost anything.

As we write this, techniques combining CDs with television and computers and computer-generated graphics with video cameras are bringing sophisticated capabilities to the nonprofessional as well as the professional. Many of these resources are already being used in high-quality workplace speeches and sales presentations. Check to see if you have access to such technology.

Although we give some advice about using visual aids in the section that follows, there is a major caution that needs to be made regarding using these supporting materials. Remember, computer-generated graphics and media are props that should support and enhance your main ideas, not take their place. It is sometimes easy to forget that you are the main actor, speaker, and focus of the speech and that visuals must be chosen to fit *your* purpose, *your* physical setting, and *your* audience's needs.

Rules for Using Visual Aids

You want a visual aid that will really work for you. The wrong one could detract from your speech and make it much less effective.

When you are considering a visual aid, keep the following rules in mind:

1. *Use the visual aid to supplement, not replace, the speech.* The visual aid should not become the whole show. It should be a useful addition to support the speech.
2. *Choose visual aids for points that need more explanation.* Look over your speech and decide which details could be better explained by a visual

387
DELIVERING THE
SPEECH

Could the speaker position himself better in showing this visual aid?

aid. Is there a particular statistic you want to stress? Will something be more easily understood if your audience could see it? Will it help your speech to show your main points visually?

3. *Show the visual aid only when you are ready for it.* Put the visual in an inconspicuous place; then, when you are ready to use it, take it out. When you are finished with it, put it away. You don't want it to compete with you for attention.

4. *Make sure everyone can read the visual aid.* When making a chart, use a dark marker with a thick tip so you can draw bold lines that will show up. If you have any doubts, check your visual aid beforehand. Set it up in the front of the room and stand in the farthest corner to see if you can read it. If you can't read it easily, fix it so you can.

5. *Before your speech, check the room to see if your visual aid can be easily displayed.* If you are using projection equipment, find the electrical outlets and see if the room has blackout curtains. If you are hanging a chart, decide how to hang it. Are you going to need tape or thumbtacks?

6. *Practice with your visual aid before the speech.* If you are using some sort of chart, stand next to it and point to it with your right or left hand rather than standing in front of it with your back to the audience. Practice using any kind of equipment until you can operate it quickly and easily. If you are using something complicated, such as projection equipment, consider having a classmate run it for you. If you do this, practice with him or her. When practicing with your visual aid, check to see how much time it takes. If it is going to take too much time, decide how you will cut back.

7. *Talk to the audience, not to the visual aid.* You may need to look at your

CONSIDER THIS

These days it is becoming increasingly important to develop skills that will serve us well in a competitive and "downsized" job market. When many others possess credentials or experiences similar to our own, we must search for qualities which will set us apart from the field and contribute to ongoing personal and professional success. One quality we should cultivate is an often neglected aspect of self-improvement which I refer to as "communication image."

Source: Ruth Olscamp, "The Way We Speak Influences What Others Think about Us," *At BG* 23 (Spring 1993): 8.

QUESTIONS

1. What is "communication image"? (It represents everything that we are and everything others perceive us to be when we communicate our ideas to them.)

2. How can *you* best develop and perfect your communication image? What areas need the most work?

3. Do you agree with Olscamp that one's communication image will "set you apart from the field and contribute to ongoing personal and professional success"—or do you think she is overstating the case? Explain your answer.

4. What are the best ways you have to develop a positive communication image?

5. Do you think there is a difference between men and women in how hard they must work, or in what ways they must work to cultivate a "communication image"? Why or why not?

visual aids occasionally, but remember to maintain eye contact with the audience.

8. *Maintain control of the speech situation.* Since visual aids can distract audience attention away from you, keep them simple.

CONTROLLING NERVOUSNESS

In studies of what makes people anxious, public speaking always ranks right up there at the top. Public speaking makes people nervous, no matter how famous or how experienced they are. Winston Churchill, who became one of the most famous statesmen and orators of the twentieth century, fainted dead away the first time he gave a speech.[7] Willard Scott, a television weather announcer, says, "Each day, as soon as I get out of bed, when I know that I've got to go on the air, I have a panic attack in the form of anticipation."[8]

Speaker anxiety has been well documented. While most people have a normal heart rate of 70 beats a minute, as a person anticipates giving a speech, the rate may increase from 95 to 140. Once he or she begins speaking, it can jump from 110 to 190. As the person proceeds with the speech, however, the heart rate begins to drop.[9]

No matter how nervous a speaker might be, there is some comfort. Studies have shown that *most audience members do not realize that a speaker is nervous.* Even observers who are trained to look for anxiety cues usually do not see them in a speaker.[10] This means that if your palms sweat, your knees shake, or your mouth is dry, you are probably the only one who knows it.

A good deal of research has been done on the subject of anxiety. Researchers have found that about 10 percent of college students have an intense fear of public speaking and will even go as far as to drop a public speaking course they need in order to graduate. The other 90 percent have fears they can overcome; they are nervous but it doesn't impair their ability to make a speech.[11] Although people who are phobic often need professional help to conquer their speaking phobia, people who have normal anxiety can usually find at least one strategy that helps them deal with their nervousness by themselves.

Unfortunately, there is no single sure-fire formula that reduces every person's anxiety before a speech. However, some strategies work for many people and are thus worth trying to see if they will work for you:

1. Dress in comfortable clothes—but clothes that show you have made some kind of special effort for this speech. Psychologically, it is important to feel confident and in control.
2. Practice some positive self-talk. Whenever a negative idea appears ("I'll never get through this speech"), replace it with a positive one ("I'm feeling nervous, but that won't stop me from doing a good job.") Give yourself no negative messages. Don't say, "I know I'm going to blow it" or "I'm so nervous I'm never going to get through this speech." Saying such things, whether out loud or to yourself, feeds your fears and makes them worse than they already are.
3. Be well prepared. Do not wait until the last moment to put your speech together. And don't just go over the speech in your mind. Stand up. Say the speech aloud, using only notes as many times as you need to remember your main points.
4. Concentrate on your message. When you believe you have something important to share with your listeners, it is easier to get excited about what you plan to tell them. Along with concentrating on your message, focus on your audience. Think about really communicating with them

CONSIDER THIS

Mark Twain once told of a Missouri farmer who ran five times for the state legislature without winning. It wasn't because he didn't practice his speeches. He practiced his campaign talks every day while milking. He referred to himself as "your humble aspirant." He referred to his audiences as "my enlightened constituents." He talked of "obtaining a mandate" for his "legislative mission."

Then one evening his cow balked at his speeches and kicked him in the teeth.

With his front teeth knocked out, the farmer could speak only words of one syllable. The result was he won his next election and kept getting reelected.

The farmer found out the hard way the language of leadership.

Source: James C. Humes, *The Sir Winston Method: The Five Secrets of Speaking the Language of Leadership* (New York: Morrow, 1991), pp. 58–59.

QUESTIONS

1. What is the moral of this story?

2. What implications does this story have for all speakers?

3. Is there a formal style of language and an informal style of language that students must choose between when they decide how to frame their ideas with words?

---

about your important message. The point is to take your focus from yourself and aim it at the message and toward your listeners.

5. Picture yourself doing well. Use positive mental imagery. If you can imagine yourself walking to the front of the room, speaking to a responsive audience, hearing your words flow without hesitation, and receiving a positive response from listeners, you have a visual image of success. Run replays of this visual image of success often.

6. If your anxiety is high, ask your instructor if you can speak first or second so you don't have to sit there and worry more. Sometimes anxiety increases if you have to sit and wait to speak.

7. Take several deep breaths on the way to the front of the room. An increased respiratory rate because of nervousness can cause you to feel short of breath. Also, it can inhibit good vocal production. Taking several deep breaths can break this cycle and have a calming effect.

8. Remember that your audience is made up of people just like you. They want you to do well; they are supportive. Nervous, uncomfortable

speakers make listeners ill at ease and embarrassed; that is why planning and thorough preparation are so important.

9. Move around if possible. Moving releases nervous energy and restores a feeling of calm. Don't pace, and don't make extraneous, nonpurposeful movements, but try to gesture and move when you use transitions and personal examples.

10. Pick out friendly faces and make eye contact with these people. An encouraging, supportive expression on a listener's face can do wonders to promote confidence and reassure speakers they are on the right track.

11. Give yourself a reward after your speech, and congratulate yourself for having succeeded. Even though your speech might not have been perfect, remind yourself that you were able to do it.

PRACTICING YOUR SPEECH

Practice will help you give a better speech. You may hesitate to practice systematically—probably because you feel silly talking to an empty room. Yet if you go into a store to buy a new piece of clothing, you probably spend a lot of time in the dressing room looking at it from several angles. By practicing, you are doing the same thing with a speech. You are trying it on to see if it fits; if it doesn't, you will have time to make the necessary alterations.

How can you practice delivery so you will feel comfortable with the content and language of your speech and yet not get so locked in that your words sound memorized or mechanical? Here is a plan that seems to work well for most speakers.

Preparing Your Speech

Before you give your speech in a practice session, you should do the following:

1. Prepare the content thoroughly. Your speech will be no better than the effort you've put into it. Do you have a clear statement of purpose? Do the materials you have collected support this statement of purpose? Have you done enough research to provide support for each of your main points?

2. Organize your content into a full-sentence outline. Have you made the proper distinction between main idea and supporting points? Does your outline flow clearly and logically? Are you quite clear about what you are going to say in your introduction and conclusion? Is your conclusion worded in such a way that you can end the speech and sit down without feeling awkward?

3. From your full-sentence outline, prepare a key-word or short-phrase outline that you can use while you rehearse and also while you give your speech. Put your key-word outline on a series of 3 × 5 cards. Can you follow the speech from this outline? Have you written out phrases or quotations that you want to quote precisely? Can you read the cards easily?

Trying Out Your Speech

During the tryout session, emphasis should be on the content of the speech and whether it is working the way you imagined it in your head. (There is often a big difference between the way we imagine something will sound and the way it really sounds.) In this session you want to actually say the words—stopping to clear up imprecise language, maybe adding a transition, trying out the conclusion. In this practice session, it will take you a while to get through the speech because you will be making corrections as you go along.

Practicing Actual Delivery

The next stage is to actually deliver the speech. As you practice your delivery, try to imagine an audience.

1. Stand against one wall and look over your "audience." Remember to establish eye contact with people in all parts of the room.
2. Check your starting time. In this practice session you want to find out how long your speech is.
3. Deliver the speech all the way through without stopping. As you speak, remember to look at your "audience."
4. When the speech is over, check your ending time.
5. Now analyze your performance: Did any parts of the speech give you difficulty? Did the speech seem clearly organized? Check your outline. In giving the speech, did you leave anything out? Was your outline clear and easy to follow? How about time? Do you need to add or delete any material to make the speech the proper length?
6. Make the necessary changes and practice the speech again.

You should practice delivering the speech until you feel comfortable with it. As you practice, try to use wording that sounds natural to you. Every time you speak, your wording should be a little bit different—otherwise your speech will sound mechanical. Also, as you practice, you should become less and less dependent on your notes. Try to consult them as little as possible.

If you think you will need a lot of practice to feel comfortable with your speech, it is better not to rehearse it all at one time. Put the speech away for a few hours or even overnight. The next time you approach it, you may be surprised to find fresh ideas or ways of solving problems that hadn't occurred to you before.

TRY THIS

Many speakers think their work is done after they say the final words of their conclusion. However, some of the most valuable work begins after the speech is over. This is the time to ask whether you reached your goal and to discover what effect you had on your listeners.

Here are some questions that you need to ask yourself after you give a speech:

1. Did I follow the plan for my speech? Did I stick to my outline and cover the material I wanted to cover? Did I keep my central idea in mind?
2. Was my speech completed in the time allotted for it? If it was too long, did I go too slowly or did I have too much material? If it was too short, did I talk too fast or did I have too little material?
3. Did I pay attention to my audience? Do I have a sense of how they responded to my speech? If audience members started losing interest, did I do anything to try to reengage them?
4. Did I make eye contact with the audience? Was I conscious of using appropriate gestures to make certain points?
5. Did I have a well-defined conclusion? Did I communicate to my audience that the speech was finished?
6. The next time I speak, what things should I change?

Your answers to these questions should help you improve every time you get up to speak. Remember, the goal of your speech communication class is to help make you an effective communicator. Part of this involves having the right information to help you improve, but part of this, too, involves *you* putting this information to work for *you*.

 SUMMARY

Good delivery in a speech involves attentiveness—focusing and paying attention to giving the speech. It also involves achieving a conversational quality in your speech.

The four ways of delivering a speech are speaking impromptu, with very little preparation; speaking from a manuscript; speaking from memory; and speaking extemporaneously, from notes. For the beginner, extemporaneous speaking is the best type of delivery because it permits the speaker to depend on notes and still sound spontaneous.

All speakers should be aware of how they look and what they can do to look better. Speakers should concentrate on what they wear and on their body movement, eye contact, gestures, and posture so that they appear at their very best.

How the speaker sounds is also an important consideration in public speaking. Speakers should pay special attention to volume, pace, pitch and inflection, and enunciation. If they find they have a problem with one of these areas, they should work to improve it.

All speakers should consider using visual aids in their speeches. Visuals help to hold attention and to clarify information. Common visual aids include the actual object, models, chalkboards, posters, diagrams, charts, tables, graphs, computer graphs, videos, and handouts. When using visual aids, make sure that they can be easily read and that they enhance the speech rather than take it over.

Practically everyone is nervous about giving a speech. Most people, however, can overcome their nervousness. Some ways of handling speech anxiety are to acknowledge that the anxiety exists, practice positive self-talk, anticipate difficult situations that could arise, practice the speech beforehand, focus on the audience while speaking, and reward yourself once it's over.

The final step in getting ready to deliver a speech is to practice it. Your practice should include rehearsing delivery of the speech, imagining an actual audience, checking the speech for clarity and organization, and checking its length.

NOTES

[1] See Alan Garner, *Conversationally Speaking* (New York: McGraw-Hill, 1981). Also see Les Donaldson, *Conversational Magic: Key to Poise, Popularity and Success* (West Nyack, NJ: Parker, 1981), and Robert E. Nofsinger, *Everyday Conversation* (Newbury Park, CA: Sage Publications, 1991).

[2] Timothy G. Hegstrom, "Message Impact: What Percentage Is Nonverbal?" *Western Journal of Speech Communication* 43 (Spring 1979): 134–142.

[3] Mark L. Knapp and Judith A. Hall, *Nonverbal Communication in Human Interaction*, 3d ed. (Fort Worth, TX: Holt, Rinehart and Winston, 1992, p. 310.

[4] Michael Argyle, "Intercultural Communication," in Larry A. Samovar and Richard E. Porter (Eds.), *Intercultural Communication: A Reader*, 6th ed. (Belmont, CA: Wadsworth, 1991), p. 43.

[5] Ibid.

[6] See Jeffrey C. Hahner, Martin A. Sokoloff, Sandra Salisch, and Geoffrey D. Needler, *Speaking Clearly: Improving Voice and Diction*, 2d ed. (New York: Random House, 1986).

[7] "Teaching the 'Sir Winston' Method," *The New York Times*, March 11, 1990, p. F7.

[8] Associated Press, "Weatherman Tells Phobics of His Panics," October 14, 1984.

[9] Michael T. Motley, "Taking the Terror Out of Talk," *Psychology Today* (January 1988): 47.

[10] Ibid.

[11] William T. Page, "Helping the Nervous Presenter: Research and Prescriptions," *Journal of Business Communication* 22 (2): 10.

 ## FURTHER READING

CRANNELL, KENNETH C. *Voice and Articulation*, 2d ed. Belmont, CA: Wadsworth, 1990. Crannell has written a book designed to help readers speak clearly and skillfully. It is fairly evenly divided between learning and doing. Many interesting and varied exercises are included. Crannell does not advocate standardized speech; rather, he encourages readers to retain unique cultural aspects of their speech while making their speech and voices more flexible and effective.

DECKER, BERT. *You've Got to Be Believed to Be Heard.* New York: St. Martin's Press, 1992. Decker trains over 10,000 executives and professionals each year. This book is full of examples and how-to exercises designed to establish a foundation to help readers speak and listen. The central goal of this book is to help speakers win the emotional trust of others. Enjoyable reading.

DETZ, JOAN. *How to Write and Give a Speech.* New York: St. Martin's Press, 1992. Detz has designed this how-to book as a practical guide for executives, public relations people, managers, fund-raisers, politicians, educators, and anyone who has to make every word count. It includes a never-fail formula for a successful speech, ways to increase chances of getting a laugh, important things to leave out of your speech, places to research your speech, tips for organizing, ways to get publicity, and survival tactics. Much practical advice here.

HOFF, RON. *I Can See You Naked.* Kansas City: Andrews and McMeel, 1992. In the ancient folklore of presentation instruction, it was held that visualizing your audience naked helped reduce nervousness. Of all the books on public speaking, this is perhaps the most fun to read. Asking the question "What *is* a presentation?," Hoff covers the first 90 seconds, nervousness, being boring, understanding the audience, dealing with questions, learning from others, and things that will make your next presentation even better.

HAHNER, JEFFREY C., MARTIN A. SOKOLOFF, SANDRA L. SALISCH, AND GEOFFREY D. NEEDLER. *Speaking Clearly: Improving Voice and Diction*, 4th ed. New York: McGraw-Hill, 1993. This is a drill book for increasing effectiveness in voice and diction. The authors treat dealing with nervousness; the speech process; the sounds of American English; diction, including consonants, vowels, and diphthongs; voice production; and vocal expressiveness. This is an excellent, well-constructed textbook, and the chapter on dealing with nervousness is very helpful. Also accompanied by a set of audio cassettes for drill and practice.

McCARTY, C. BARRY. *Well Said and Worth Saying.* Nashville, TN: Broadman Press, 1991. McCarty takes readers step by step through the process of putting together and delivering a speech. This 152-page book has five chapters:

"Preparing the Speech and the Speaker," "Organizing Your Ideas," "Supporting Your Ideas," "Style: Clothing Your Thoughts with Words," and "Speaking the Speech: Delivery." Brief, but straightforward advice.

ST. JOHN, PATRICIA. *Beyond Words: Unlocking the Secrets to Communicating.* Walpole, NH: Stillpoint Publishing, 1994. This is a sensitive, touching, meaningful book about what is required to unlock the secrets to strengthening community, cooperating within families, communicating within organizations, and empowering social institutions. St. John, partially responding to her own poor eyesight (approaching blindness by the time she was eight), has gone into the different worlds of dolphins and autistic children to learn how to break through the barriers of nonverbal communication. She inspires readers to discover their own capacities for communicating with others.

SCHLOFF, LAURIE, AND MARCIA YUDKIN. *Smart Speaking: Sixty-Second Strategies for More Than 100 Speaking Problems and Fears.* New York: Plume (Penguin), 1992. The authors address common problems in chapters such as "I Don't Like the Way I Sound," "Conversational Blocks," "Nerves," "My Presentation Is Next Week—Help!" "Tough Situations," "Awkward Moments," and "We're Not Communicating." Practical advice in nutshell form.

STUART, CRISTINA. *How to Be an Effective Speaker.* Chicago: NTC, 1993. In this 238-page paperback, the author, managing director of Speakeasy Training Ltd., covers all the essentials of public speaking, including listening, preparation, writing a talk, delivery, body language, coping with nerves, finding your voice, practicing and rehearsing, relaxation exercises, understanding audience, questions and answers, using visual aids, humor, and hints on reading. She also gives advice on persuading, convincing, and selling. Practical and useful material.

KEY TERMS

anecdote

comparison

composition

definition

etymology

example

explaining

function

informative
speech

rhetorical
questions

The Informative Speech

CHAPTER OBJECTIVES

After reading this chapter, you should be able to:

1 Get the attention of listeners.

2 Increase listener understanding.

3 Aid listener retention.

4 Use specific strategies in informative speeches.

Aeron is studying hotel and restaurant management. He works in a motel close to the university to help pay for his education. When he is assigned to give an informative speech, he decides to explain how hotels and motels cut corners to keep their prices down. In preparation for the speech, he interviews local motel managers, uses a current textbook required for one of his classes, and finds several related books on hotel management in the library.

Sylvia is a journalism major, and she was one of the students assigned to cover the visit of a politician to campus during the last election. In her informative speech titled "There's No Business Like News Business," she talks about how the news media gains from political campaigns. Like Aeron, she supplements one of her current textbooks, *Formation of Campaign Agendas* by Holli Semetko, with books and articles from the library. She visits the offices of the local newspaper, and she arranges an interview with the political editor.

Before Kevin decided to go back to school, he was involved in a marriage that ended in divorce. He now felt far enough away from it that he could look at and talk about it objectively. With so many marriages now ending in divorce, it was a topic he knew would interest the class. His speech, "Until Death Do Us Part," was based partly on his own experience, but Kevin also talked to a divorce lawyer; consulted the *World Almanac and Book of Facts* and the National Center for Health Statistics for current information and statistics; read Catherine Kohler Riessman's book *Divorce Talk*; and used articles from *Man and Woman*, *New Woman*, *Business Week*, *U.S. News & World Report*, and *The New York Times Magazine* to fill in additional details.

Selah spent last summer involved in a co-op—which is a real-world work opportunity for students still in school. Now, she is working part time for the co-op office. Her job is to give speeches around campus informing students about the co-op program. According to the records of the co-op office, only 40 percent of students are aware of the co-op office and its services. Selah has put together a speech based on her own experience and the material provided by the director of the university's co-op office. She has a three-fold job: to give examples of the real-world work experience students can gain, to indicate what employers of co-op students are looking for, and to provide a step-by-step process for getting involved. At the end of each speech she provides a handout that covers all the essential material.

Aeron, Sylvia, Kevin, and Selah all have something in common: they are gathering information. Like a majority of people in the United States, much of what they do is concerned with producing, processing, and distributing information.

The need for high-quality information demands skill in our ability to produce and deliver it. Although some of this information is delivered in written form, much of it is oral: the teacher before the class, the radio or television reporter broadcasting to an audience, the professional sharing ideas with colleagues, the employer explaining policies to employees—all of them need oral skills to convey information.

The **informative speech**—one that defines, clarifies, instructs, and explains—is a common phenomenon in our society. If we are going to prosper in the information society, the ability to give an informative speech is a necessary skill.

GOALS OF AN INFORMATIVE SPEAKER

With so much information available, it is surprising that listeners don't buckle under from information overload. When listeners are so swamped with information, we face a serious problem as speakers. We have to ask ourselves, "How can I, as an informative speaker, make *my* information stand out?"

Getting Attention

The first goal of a speaker is to get the attention of audience members. In most public speaking situations there are many distractions: people come in late, the air conditioner fan turns on and off, a fly buzzes around the room, the microphone gives off feedback.

Once you have attention, there is no assurance that you will keep it. Attention spans are short. You have probably noticed that as you listen to a speech or lecture, your attention wanders—even when you are interested in the message. Since this pattern of wandering attention is characteristic of most listeners, as a speaker you have to work to get attention back again.

The best way to get and keep attention is to create a strong desire to listen to your material. Ask yourself whether your material is *relevant*. Does it apply to the people in your audience? If it doesn't, how can it be adapted to them?

If the audience perceives the information as *new*, it is more likely to pay attention. New doesn't necessarily mean a subject no one has ever heard about—it might be a matter of a new perspective or a new angle. Certain topics are going to provoke a "ho-hum" reaction from the audience. You don't want your audience to think "Not another speech about jogging . . . or dieting and nutrition . . . or getting organized." When one student chose to speak on physical fitness, he wanted to give a new perspective to an old topic. He ran across an article that said too much running might be dangerous and decided to base his speech on some of the dangers of exercise. He used material from the article to plan an introduction which would get the attention of the audience. He began:

> *David Nieman, an administrator in public health, knew that it was important to exercise. His own form of exercise was distance running. However, he noticed that soon after he ran in a marathon, he would catch a cold or get the flu. He began to question other runners and found that they had the same problem. Finally, in a survey of 2300 runners who had run the Los Angeles Marathon, he found a surprising result: the more these*

runners trained, the more likely they were to get sick. After looking at these results Nieman began to question whether strenuous exercise was good for your health.[1]

Although audience members knew this speaker was going to speak on physical fitness, most of them did not expect such a speech to begin by questioning the value of exercise.

Increasing Understanding

Since the goal of an informative speech is to give the audience new or in-depth information on a subject, it is particularly important that a speaker put together a speech that audience members will understand. Several things will help understanding: language choice, organization, and illustrations and examples.

LANGUAGE CHOICE

In our highly technological world, many of us speak a specialized language that is understood only by people in the same field. Because we are so accustomed to this language, we often don't realize that other people don't know what we are talking about. If you are giving a speech that uses technical or specialized vocabulary, you must take the time to define your terms, or consider whether you can avoid technical terms altogether.

Why would an informal, conversational tone work best with this audience?

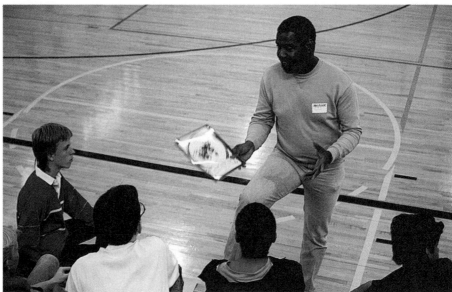

ORGANIZATION

Organization not only helps you put your speech together but also helps listeners understand what you are talking about. A good organizational pattern will show how ideas relate to one another and will help listeners move from one idea to another. You probably know that as a listener your attention will wander if the speaker is rambling or you have trouble finding the main points of the speech.

ILLUSTRATIONS AND EXAMPLES

Probably the greatest key to understanding is an ample supply of illustrations and examples. If you are going to explain a principle that might be unfamiliar to your audience, use an example to show what it is or how it works. For example, a student who was explaining three basic body types held up pictures to illustrate each type. When he held up a picture of a thin, lightly muscled person, the meaning of the term *ectomorph* was immediately clear.

Helping Retention

An important goal of informative speaking is to have your listeners remember what you said once the speech is over. Listeners are more likely to remember speeches in which they feel some kind of emotional involvement. This involvement might range from sympathy when they hear about an adult who can't read to high personal interest in a speech about how to get a better job. For the speaker, then, the goal is to involve listeners by speaking about subjects which they can identify with or which have an impact on their lives.

When you want people to remember certain points, it is useful to give these points special emphasis. Sometimes this can be done with verbal cues: "This is my most important point" or "If you remember only one thing I said today, remember this." Sometimes you can use a cue after a point: "Now let me show you how important what I just said can be to you." A point can be emphasized, too, by repeating it, by changing your rate of speech, or by pausing just before you say it.[2]

 ## STRATEGIES FOR INFORMATIVE SPEECHES

There are different types of strategies for presenting material in informative speeches. Each type requires a special skill. Sometimes all of these types can be found in a single speech; usually at least two will be used.

CONSIDER THIS

Although we have not talked about ethics in relation to informative speaking, speakers need to be concerned about ethics whenever they are involved in communication. Keep the question "What is ethical behavior?" in mind as you read the following excerpt:

A colleague approaching retirement has had a long and distinguished career teaching communication. She returned to her office visibly upset after a class one day. When questioned, she said she had just had a student announce in the introduction to his speech that his purpose was to teach the class how to make a lethal poison using ingredients people either already had in their homes or could easily buy. "Moreover," she said, "to stress the significance of the topic, he assured us that this substance would kill any living animal, certainly even the heaviest human being."

Upon hearing this, her colleagues' reactions were, "That's scary" or "That's frightening. What did you do?" Her answer told us that our friend really was upset for two reasons. She said, "I sat there thinking of the rash of teenage suicides, even copycat suicides, we've been hearing about lately, and all the other meanness in the world. I wrestled with my conscience for about a minute and a half, and then, for the first time since I started teaching, I interrupted a speaker, told him I didn't think we needed to hear this information, and asked him to be seated."

Source: George L. Grice and John F. Skinner, *Mastering Public Speaking* (Englewood Cliffs, NJ: Prentice-Hall, 1993), p. 29.

QUESTIONS

1. To what extent do you agree with this teacher's actions?

2. What else could this teacher have done?

3. What should this teacher do now to help this speaker understand her concerns?

4. Is there any way to make this speech?

5. Whose interest is greatest, the right of the student to make the speech or the right of the audience to not hear harmful information?

Defining

A **definition**—an explanation of the meaning of a word or phrase—can often make a critical difference in whether your audience understands your speech. Sometimes it's sufficient to give a dictionary definition; other times a speaker must expand by using his or her own words. For example, in defining public relations this speaker says:

> *As I see it, public relations is defined in terms of public opinion and behavior.*[3]

Kristjan, another speaker, took the traditional definition of the media and contrasted it with an updated version of what the media will come to mean for all of us in the year 2000. Notice that Kristjan doesn't just provide a bare-bones definition. He offers three brief examples to show listeners exactly what his definition ("interactive, individualized, seeking one's own level") means for them:

> *The word* media *once implied "one-way" and "lowest common denominator." That isn't true any longer. We live in a digital world. And in the digital world the word* media *suggests interactive, individualized, seeking one's own level. When you wake up in the morning in the year 2000, you will have a section (not the whole paper) called* The Daily Me, *devoted to people, places, and ideas that interest you. When you turn on the car radio, it will automatically play "important" news. When you want to look at a movie, the system will recommend an excellent one, just as your sister-in-law would have.*

This speaker defined what he meant by "media environment" by contrasting what people wanted in different decades:

> *In the '50s, we liked Ike, suburbia, and lots of kids. Back then, TV was really special—since only 10 percent of people had television. In the '60s, we simultaneously broke all society's rules and TV's sound barrier . . . television penetration hit 90 percent! In the '70s, we sang Me, Me, Me, and in the '80s we negotiated for more, more, more. But the grab it, snatch it, and "take it all" extremism of the '80s has given way to the time-crunching '90s.*
>
> *Consumers today are stuck between a clock and a hard place . . . and the '90s are governed by demand for convenience and speed in virtually everything that touches our lives. Faster food, faster news, faster mail, fax, fax, fax.*[4]

Definition can also go beyond explaining words or phrases. Four useful ways to define concepts in a speech are by etymology, example, comparison, and function.

ETYMOLOGY

Etymology, the study of the origin and development of words, can be used as a basis for definition. For example, when discussing romantic love and the intense feelings that occur, one speaker pointed out that the word *ecstasy*, which is a common label for emotions during the time of romantic love, is derived from a Greek word meaning "deranged"—a state beyond all reason and self-control.[5] She went on to show that the word *deranged* accurately describes the state of mind that exists early in romantic relationships. The *Oxford English Dictionary* provides the best source for word etymologies.

EXAMPLE

An **example** is something that is used to illustrate a point. When using an example, a speaker often either points to an actual thing or points out something verbally. This speaker defines a *feminist* by giving a series of examples of what a feminist believes in:

> *What is a feminist? Someone male or female who believes the world cannot work well as long as there are separate and unequal distinctions based on sex; someone who believes that issues like poverty disproportionately affecting women and children today are as significant as the issues of wealth and weapons which at this point in our history disproportionately involve men. Feminists are women and men who are tired of caricatured distinctions between the sexes which reinforce prototypes of macho strong men and passive female dependency. Feminists know that these stereotypes keep us from fulfilling our own potential and from recognizing others. And feminists know that until we utilize the creative capacity of half the human race which has been excluded from decision making, the world can never be whole.*[6]

This listener is getting three kinds of information. What are they? Because he is getting different kinds of information is he more likely to remember it? Why or why not?

TRY THIS

For each of the following ideas, decide which kinds of definitions would work in a speech: etymology, function, example, or comparison.

*an incomparable
experience
awesome dreams
ethical
free speech*

*independence
great instructor
recession
unbeatable bargain
well done*

COMPARISON

Comparisons point out the similarities between two or more things. LaPriel was talking about the information highway. At one point in his speech he compared this information frontier to the old one:

> *This frontier, like the real ones that precede it in history, offers up the same fundamental questions and challenges. Will large information "ranchers"—like media and cable companies—control vast tracts of intellectual property and vast numbers of channels on which to deliver it? Or will the electronic frontier be broken up into little plots, each owned by a "farmer"—that is, owned by each of us?*

The speaker's entire speech is based on defining change as desirable. He establishes the desirability of change at the outset through comparison, then develops his speech from there.

FUNCTION

With certain topics it's useful to define by **function**—showing how a thing performs or how it can be used. Speakers may stress an object's usefulness, advantages, benefits, convenience, or service. Ashtin was talking about virtual reality. First, she gave a dictionary-type definition so the audience would clearly understand what she was talking about. But notice how she stressed virtual reality's usefulness as she continued:

> *Virtual reality is a computer simulation usually experienced through headgear, goggles, and sensory gloves that lets the user feel he or she is*

present in another place. It lets you feel like you're actually at the mall, in the middle of Tom Clancy's latest thriller, or visiting your sister and her family half a world away.

Describing

Many times your audience will be able to visualize what you are talking about if you describe it be creating a picture for them. This speaker, for example, created a vivid picture in his speech about garbage:

> *In just a few years, the most widely viewed artwork in the world may not be the Mona Lisa, or the Statue of Liberty. . . . No, it just might be a land-fill in Kearny, New Jersey.*
>
> *The state recently closed the landfill, and now it's considering one artist's idea to beautify this one-hundred-foot high mountain of buried garbage. The artist wants to turn the dump into an enormous celestial cal-endar and call it "Sky Mound." . . . It will have steel posts, earthen mounds, a plume of burning methane, and radiating gravel paths aligned with the seasonal movements of the sun, the moon, and the stars.[7]*

SIZE OR QUANTITY

Notice how Marshall helped his listeners visualize the size of our national debt:

> *Most people have difficulty comprehending just how much a billion or a trillion dollars is. If you began counting dollar bills at the rate of one a second, it would take you 11.57 days to count to $1 million. At that same rate—one dollar bill a second—it would take you 31.69 years to count to $1 billion. And at that same dollar-a-second rate, it would take you 31,688.09 years to count to $1 trillion. And the current national debt is more than three-and-a-half times that much.[8]*

SHAPE

In a speech on insect control in gardening, one student used the following description of a cabbage worm:

> *It looks like a brilliant yellow-green caterpillar that begins at a length of an inch or so with about the circumference of your little finger. It has anten-nae coming from its head with numerous short pudgy feet. As it chomps away at garden cabbage throughout the summer, it extends its length from two to three inches, and it grows in circumference to about the size of the large part of your thumb.*

WEIGHT

Since people have a hard time visualizing large numbers, speakers need to relate them to something from the listeners' own experience. One speaker was trying to impress her listeners with how much a million was. She said that a class in Des Moines, Iowa, collected 1 million bottle caps. How much did they weigh? According to the speaker, these caps weighed 2½ tons: "They were put into 200 bags and the bags were so heavy it required a moving van to take them away."

COLOR

Color is an obvious component of description and serves quickly to call up mental pictures. In this speech the speaker makes a vivid use of color when discussing race:

> *In truth God made no black or white people but a flower garden of beautiful persons of colors ranging from cream to oven-burnt brown. No person is white; were he truly white and void of melanin or pigmentation, the ultraviolet radiations from the sun would burn him up. No one is black either; were one black, he would be a perfect receptor of the sun's radiations—and his body temperature would rise rapidly to over 106 degrees, into a fever so severe that he too would burn up.*[9]

COMPOSITION

Composition, a description of the makeup of a thing, can be a useful part of description. Sometimes an analysis of composition can help an audience understand an abstract concept. To describe a *global village*—a term that has been used a lot but seldom explained—a speaker used demographic figures for the world's population to create a representative global village of 1000 people:

What members of the audience cannot see the visual aid? What could the speaker do to improve the situation?

According to the World Development Forum, if you lived in a representative global village of 1000,

- *564 citizens would be Asian*
- *210 Europeans*
- *86 Africans*
- *80 South Americans*
- *60 North Americans*

Of the 1000, religions would be represented this way:

- *300 Christians*
- *175 Moslems*
- *128 Hindus*
- *55 Buddhists*
- *47 Animists*
- *85 smaller religious groups*
- *210 without religion or atheists*

Of this group:

- *60 would control half the total income*
- *500 would be hungry*
- *600 would live in shantytowns*
- *700 would be illiterate*[10]

FIT

You can often describe something by the way parts belong together or the relationship among parts. A mental picture emerges when listeners can fit all the parts into a proper relationship.

Say you are speaking about the campus newspaper and you want to explain how all the parts fit together. You talk about the responsibilities of the editor, then of the jobs of the features, news, and sports editors and what their relationship is to the editor. Next you talk about the roles of the business manager and advertising department and the relationship these people have to the editor. If you discuss how all these people fit into the overall structure, your audience will have a good idea of how the newspaper works.

Explaining

Almost everything that we know how to do was explained to us at one time or another. We were not born knowing how to do such things as cook or play volleyball—someone told us how to do them. Many of the questions we ask are requests for explanations. What does this concept mean? How does this work? How do I get there? **Explaining**, then, is the process of making something clear.

The most common form of explaining is when you teach someone to do something. Usually this is a matter of breaking the process down into steps. For example, in this speech on how to make a toasted cheese sandwich with an iron, the speaker used the following steps:

TRY THIS

A cliché is a phrase, metaphor, or expression that has been worn
out by overuse. Often, as we convey information to others, we fall
into using clichés because we are familiar with them, because we
don't try to think of other alternatives, or simply because it is the
best way we can think of to convey an idea.

Kilpatrick, in his book *The Writer's Art* describes clichés as "poor,
tired, but comfortable and familiar cubbyholes to which we retreat
when imagination fails us. . . . They fall like casual dandruff on the
fabric of our prose."*

In the spaces provided, show how you would rephrase/avoid the
clichés offered by McCarty:†

Last but not least _____

Bright as the sun _____

Clean as a whistle _____

Cool as a cucumber _____

Dark as night _____

Dead as a doornail _____

Easy come, easy go _____

Free as a bird _____

Fresh as a daisy _____

Good as gold _____

Hard as a rock _____

Light as a feather _____

Old as the hills _____

Pretty as a picture _____

Quiet as a mouse _____

Red as a rose _____

Shake like a leaf _____

Sharp as a razor _____

Ugly as sin _____

White as a sheet _____

---

* James J. Kilpatrick, *The Writer's Art* (Kansas City: Andrews, McNeel and Barker,
1984), p. 5.
† C. Barry McCarty, *Well Said and Worth Saying* (Nashville, TN: Broadman, 1991),
pp. 118–119.

1. Gather what you need: bread, cheese, margarine, aluminum foil, and an iron.
2. Heat the iron to medium-high.
3. Make a sandwich from the cheese and bread. Butter both sides of the bread on the outside.
4. Wrap the sandwich in aluminum foil.
5. Place the iron on each side for about 20 seconds. (Check to see if you need more time.)

Using Numbers

Few people can visualize large quantities, such as millions or billions. Therefore it's useful if these figures are put into some kind of perspective. For example, your audience would probably be impressed to learn that *Jurassic Park* (the movie) cost $60 million to make and made more than $200 million. However, if you relate this figure to the price of movie tickets, you will begin to speak in terms of the audience's pocketbook and the example will thus have more impact.

How does a model help to make this speech more meaningful?

When you work with numbers, here are some simple rules to follow:

- If numbers are unusual or surprising, explain why. Usually the best way to do this is to quote an expert.
- Round off large numbers.
- If you have a lot of numbers, try to convert them to percentages.
- Look for opportunities to replace numbers with words. For example, it's easier to understand "Over half the people said . . ." or "A majority believed. . . ."
- Try to relate numbers to something familiar. For example, say "The number of people killed in the earthquake was equal to the entire student body of this college."
- If possible, try to compare numbers. For example, "Forty-five percent of the seniors but only three percent of the first-year students believed. . . ."
- Look for trends, especially from one year to another: "In 1981, the average TV viewer watched network programming. By 1994, however, the average viewers were just as likely to watch cable or videos."
- Use graphs and other visual aids to make numbers more concrete.

Connecting the Known with the Unknown

When listeners are unfamiliar with a subject, a speaker can help them understand it by connecting the new idea to something they already know. For example, when a British student wanted to explain the game of cricket to her American classmates, she started by listing the ways that cricket was similar to baseball. Another student, explaining how people always seem to be looking for new ways to communicate (the known), described the Teledesic proposal (the unknown). This is the proposal by Teledesic Corporation, owned by Craig McCaw and William Gates, to develop a global communications network made up of 840 satellites that would transport information ranging from ordinary telephone calls to high-resolution computerized medical images and two-way video conferences to and from any spot on the planet.

Repeating and Reinforcing Ideas

Repetition in a speech is important because it helps listeners remember key points. However, if it is overdone, speakers run the risk of boring listeners. Let's look at a format that will enable you to spread out the repetition and reinforcement in a speech.

In your introduction, *tell your listeners what you plan to tell them.* In the introduction to her speech "Creating a More Effective Voice," Michelle listed her main points: "Today I want to talk about the three main steps for changing your voice. These steps are analysis, discipline, and production."

In the body of your speech, *tell your listeners your full message* (explain your points). In Bishetta's speech, she explained each of her steps:

CONSIDER THIS

When speakers want a style and approach that will make people sit up and listen, they need to be specific. They need to show their audience exactly what they are talking about by using specific, accurate, and evocative details. Abstract generalities will not work. They need to talk about concrete things in the real world. Read the following examples, and then try your hand at description:

For example, which is more interesting: He passed between two trees, *or* He passed between a tall pine and a large oak? *The second sentence creates more of a picture in the mind. The specific is always more interesting. Specific words are also more accurate.*

Are you more moved to learn that many children are victims of sexual abuse, *or that* one of every four girls in the United States will be sexually molested before she turns eighteen?

Does the word produce *make your mouth water? What about a* Red Delicious apple *or a* tree-ripened orange?

Are you more frightened at the thought of an assailant with a formidable weapon *or* a large, dirty man who came at you with a heavy lead pipe?

Which statement alarms you: "There's a lot of pollution in major cities" *or* "People who live in New York, Detroit, and Los Angeles breathe unsafe air an average of thirty-five days per year"?

Don't say a long time ago, in the near future, *or* a lot of flowers. *Say* in October of 1066, two weeks from tomorrow, *or* 500 yellow roses.

Source: Barry McCarty, *Well Said and Worth Saying* (Nashville, TN: Broadman, 1991), pp. 106–107.

QUESTIONS

1. How might you rephrase "The person went down the road" to make people more likely to sit up and listen?

2. Since the word *very* is weak to start with, what words could be used to replace *not very hot,* a *very hot day, very angry,* and *very*

The first step in dealing with difficult bosses is to understand them. To find out what makes them tick will allow you to speak their language.

The second step is to reveal loyalty. Most bosses will give you the freedom to solve problems in your own way as long as they are convinced of your loyalty.

The third step in dealing with difficult bosses is to establish strong communication channels. With good rapport, problems can be discussed openly and directly, facts and discoveries can be given, and information that might prove valuable can be shared.

In your conclusion, *tell your listeners what you told them.* This is the place to summarize your main ideas. Bishetta concluded her speech by saying:

Now you can see how you can go about dealing with difficult bosses. You need to understand them, show loyalty, and establish strong communication channels.

Arousing Interest in Your Topic

So many things compete for each listener's attention that even though we might get attention at first, it is not always possible to keep it. You probably have had the experience of half-listening to a speaker while you wondered what was for lunch, mentally prepared a grocery list, and so on. What can you, as a speaker, do to compete with all these distractions?

AROUSE CURIOSITY

One way to make sure that you will be listened to is to create a desire to learn about your subject by stimulating your listeners' curiosity. For example, one speaker began her speech with "Have you ever wondered why you get so tired?" Another began his speech with "Do you know how to stop procrastinating?" Another started, "The real name of Captain Kangaroo is Bob Keeshan. The name of the river that flows over the Holland Tunnel is the Hudson. Five states border on the Pacific Ocean. Did you ever wonder why we are so fascinated by trivia?"

PRESENT ANECDOTES

An **anecdote** is a short, interesting story based on your own or someone else's experience. Although some speakers use them in their introductions, they are particularly useful in the body of your speech because they can get back audience attention if it is wandering.

Here is how a speaker used an effective anecdote from her own life to hold her audience members' interest:

During my freshman year [of college], I received a call that my mother had been seriously injured in a traffic accident. My father was unemployed at the time, and I was off at college. So who do you think was elected to take on the housework? Raise your hand if you think it was my father.
 No???
 Does anybody think it was <u>*me*</u>*?*
 I am truly amazed at your guessing ability.
 Or is there something in our Hispanic cultures that says the women do the housework?

Of course there is.

So I drove home from Boulder every weekend; shopped, cleaned, cooked, froze meals for the next week, did the laundry, you know the list. And the truth is, it did not occur to me until some time later that my father could have done some of that. I had a problem, but I was part of the problem.[11]

This next speaker built an anecdote from a newspaper article to startle his audience into paying attention:

A recent story from the pages of The New York Times *broke, for many people, their stereotypes of race and crime.*

Just this past August in the middle of a silent country night outside Davenport, Iowa, 17-year-old Michelle Jensen was shot to death, and her body was left along a dusty, rural road, near a cornfield—a cold-blooded, brutal murder.

Why was she murdered? Three teenage gang members wanted the keys to her Ford Escort. How did these gang members get caught? Three other members of the same gang, even after vowing to die for each other, pled guilty to lesser charges and testified against them.

But do you know what shocked the people of Davenport even more? These weren't kids from the big-city ghettos. These weren't the black and Hispanic youngsters normally referred to when speaking of gang violence. No, these were six white fellows from just down the block.[12]

BUILD ANTICIPATION

One way to build anticipation is to preview your points in the introduction. Gwendolyn, for example, said that she was going to talk about what makes Olympic champions. Then she said:

The qualities I want to talk about not only make Olympic champions, they are invaluable, too, in school, in the home, or on the job. First, champions anticipate. *They have a dream of themselves as a champion. They aim high, because often they don't just meet their goals but surpass them. They plan for trouble by anticipating possible setbacks and preparing for them. Second, champions* motivate. *They are driven not just to be the best but to do their best as well. They never quit because they know the satisfaction of completing a difficult task against the odds. Third, champions* activate. *They make their own luck because they know luck strikes those best prepared to capitalize on it. They bounce back, and their failures inspire them to try harder.*

The audience is then more likely to listen for each of her points: (1) anticipate, (2) motivate, (3) activate. Notice the way Gwendolyn kept them parallel. Framed in the same way, they were easier for listeners to remember.

BUILD SUSPENSE

Building suspense is one of the best ways of keeping attention. Esteban decided to speak on drunk driving, and he began his speech with a personal experience:

> *There was no way I could anticipate what would happen. My girlfriend, Angelica, and I were coming home from dinner out and a movie. We were on State Street, one of the main streets of my hometown, when suddenly we were sideswiped by a car. Not knowing what was going on, and thinking it was inadvertent, we continued driving. Suddenly, the car sideswiped us again. Knowing we were about seven blocks from the police station, we drove there fast. But the car that had been following us disappeared. We waited almost twenty minutes, and thinking it safe, we decided to continue toward Angelica's house. Suddenly, out of nowhere, it was behind us again. We made it to Angelica's and ran inside. The car squealed past, but forgetting the curve leading into the court where Angelica lived, the outlaw car missed the turn, ran one wheel in the gutter and another up a driveway, and broke the front axle. The police were called; all three teenage boys had been drinking.*

Esteban then went on to talk about the penalties in the state for driving while drunk, such as fines, a police record, possible license suspension, prison, and more.

Getting Listeners Involved

GET THE AUDIENCE TO PARTICIPATE

In a speech on aerobic exercises, the speaker had listeners try several of them. In a speech on self-defense, a speaker had the class practice a few simple moves. In a speech on note taking, the speaker had listeners take notes and, as they did so, taught them some shortcuts and simplified procedures.

As every magician knows, choosing someone from the audience to participate in an act is a good technique for keeping attention. Speakers can do this too. In a speech on first aid, the speaker called for a volunteer from the audience so she could point to pressure points. For a speech titled "Appearance Sells," one student asked three classmates to come to class dressed in a certain way: one was to dress casually, another in dressy clothes, and the third in businesswear.

ASK RHETORICAL QUESTIONS

Some speakers use **rhetorical questions**—questions audience members answer mentally rather than out loud. Note how one speaker asked and answered most of his own questions but left the critical one for audience members to think about:

Question 1: Which gets more status in our society?
            a. learning
            b. sports
Answer: *Sports*

Question 2: Which gets more hours of attention?
            a. reading
            b. TV
Answer: *TV*

Question 3: What causes more excitement?
            a. a new idea
            b. a new car
Answer: *A new car*

Question 4: What gets more promotion in our society?
            a. studying
            b. shopping
Answer: *Shopping*

Question 5: Essay question—Why do you think there's an education problem in our society?[13]

SOLICIT QUESTIONS FROM THE AUDIENCE

Another device is to solicit questions from the audience following the speech. A question-and-answer session encourages listeners to get involved. You might even tell your listeners at the beginning that you will take questions when you finish, which may encourage them to pay attention in preparation for asking questions.

There are, however, some useful guidelines if you plan to solicit questions from your audience. First, make sure you listen to the full question before answering it. Sometimes speakers will cut off a questioner or will focus on irrelevant details instead of the main thrust of the question. Second, if a question is confusing, ask the questioner to rephrase it. If you are still confused, rephrase it yourself before answering it. For example, say "Let me make sure I have heard you right; what you are asking is. . . . Am I right?" Finally, in responding to questions, try to keep your answers brief and to the point. This is no time for another speech. As a final check, it's also a good idea to ask, "Does that answer your question?"

Our society needs high-quality information, and one way of producing and delivering it is through the informative speech—a speech that defines, clarifies, instructs, or explains.

When giving a speech, one of the speaker's goals should be to attract and maintain attention by using information that is relevant and interesting to the audience. The speaker should work to increase understanding by making careful language choices, having the speech organized, and using illustrations and examples. Finally, the speaker should use emphasis and repetition to help the audience retain the information.

There are numerous strategies for presenting information. Some of those we discussed included defining, describing, explaining, using numbers, connecting the known with the unknown, repeating and reinforcing ideas, and arousing interest in your topic. Sometimes speakers need to use more than one strategy to clarify or explain an idea.

The speaker can get the audience involved in the speech by inviting volunteers to participate in the speech, by asking rhetorical questions, and by soliciting questions from the audience.

SAMPLE INFORMATIVE SPEECH

Here is an informative speech by Teresa Buehler of Bowling Green State University. Teresa uses a topical pattern of organization. A commentary of the speech is given at the right, a full transcription of the speech at the left. (The numbers in the outline refer to Teresa's notes listed at the end of her outline.)

Title

Your Rights for Freedom

Specific Purpose

To inform my audience about our rights for freedom and the effects of censorship.

Central Idea

Censorship poses crucial questions about our freedoms: where do we draw the line, and how do we go about censoring freedoms?

In an incident years ago, "a German visitor to the White House saw there a newspaper full of abuse of President [Thomas] Jefferson, and asked why the President did not have the fellow who wrote it hanged. 'What? Hang the guardian | The speaker begins with a historical example. The strength of the example lies in its validity and in the use of strong words

of the public morals?' asked Jefferson. 'Put that paper into your pocket, my good friend,' he told the visitor, 'and carry it with you to Europe, and when you hear anyone doubt the reality of American freedom, show them that paper, and tell them where you found it.'"[1]

The First Amendment of our U.S. Constitution gives us numerous freedoms, including freedom of the press, freedom of speech, and others. Today's society, however, has changed considerably from the society that existed when our country's founders decided the limits of these rights. Today, we are faced with two crucial questions: where do we draw the line for these freedoms, and how do we go about censoring such freedoms?

Censorship has been in existence throughout history. Rulers, church leaders, and citizens have restricted certain ideas from becoming popularly known or available. Those forms of communication most often banned were books, poetry, and sermons believed to be in conflict with the principles of a ruling church or government.[2]

In the fifth century B.C. in Greece, many philosophers, poets, and writers were banned because "their message strayed from the culture's accepted political and religious beliefs." [3] The Chinese, in 213 B.C., were ordered by their ruler, Shih Huang Ti, to burn all books that described China under previous rulers.[4]

During the Middle Ages, the Church burned the writers and their books at the stake.[5] In the sixteenth and seventeenth centuries, Henry VIII and Elizabeth I "sought out and destroyed" books that were threatening to the government or the Church."[6]

In 1791, however, Americans passed the First Amendment to the U.S. Constitution, which granted citizens the freedom of speech and press.[7] But do you know what? The Sedition Act soon followed in 1798, "stating that it was a crime to 'write, utter, or publish false, scandalous, and malicious writings or writings against the federal government, its officials and legislators, or its laws.'"[8]

---

like *hanged* and *public morals.*

Here, Teresa uses a transition between the introduction and the first main point. Toward the end of the transition, Teresa covers the two points of her central idea. This provides direction and focus for the speech.

This is Teresa's first main point: looking at censorship as it has existed in the past.

Here, Teresa included five examples to support her main point about censorship's existence throughout history.

Teresa saved the most important example of the first main point for the end. Her listeners may have been familiar with the First Amendment, but many probably did not know the Sedition Act.

These forms of censorship have not been dropped altogether. Many countries overseas as well as closer to home and at home still burn books and use other forms of censorship for inappropriate materials.

Censorship in today's society takes various forms. Each freedom guaranteed to citizens of the United States by the Constitution has its own unique form of restriction.

Freedom of expression and speech is the most controversial of the freedoms given to us by the First Amendment. I will look at obscenity, pornography, music, TV and radio, books, and artwork.

Obscenity is any use of vulgar language which stimulates "impure thoughts."[9] Material is considered by a review board. Books found to be obscene are banned, preventing any sales of those books.

Pornography is thought to be "a practice of sex discrimination which sexualizes the subordination of women and which eroticizes violence against women."[10] Before movies are released, they are reviewed for their moral suitability. Licenses must be obtained and ratings are given.

Music censorship takes various forms.[11] All forms of music have been censored.[12] Rock and roll albums must have warning labels placed on them saying "Explicit lyrics—parental advisory" if the words of the song are considered inappropriate for younger listeners.[13] If a label is not placed on a recording that is explicit, then the lyrics must be printed on the cover so parents can read the words.

Famous groups that have been censored include the Beatles, the Rolling Stones[14], and George Michael's "I Want Your Sex."[15]

TV and radio have restrictions placed on them as well. The Federal Communications Commission regulates the shows broadcast by stations.

Books in libraries may be restricted. Books inappropriate for younger children are restricted to adult usage. Some books are even banned from libraries altogether; Madonna's book was banned from a number of libraries.

Artwork also is censored—especially by the

In this transition, Teresa connects the former main head with the main head to follow.

Teresa's first main point was the past; this main point has to do with the present.
Teresa forecasts each of the points she wants to cover under this subpoint.

In this case Teresa offers a definition first.

Once again, Teresa begins this point with a definition.

Here, Teresa used a visual aid to show what she was talking about. She brought an album with the label on it, and she brought one with lyrics on it for comparison.

government. Government-supported artists can lose their funding. Certain works by artists may be for restricted audiences only. In some cases, works can be banned from observation altogether.

Freedom of the press also has lost some of its power in recent years. For example, for "national security" reasons, laws have been passed which forbid the release of military and security secrets.[16] The Sedition Act imposes fines and imprisonment on anyone who openly criticizes the government.[17] UNESCO, the United Nations Educational, Scientific, and Cultural Organization, censors the release of international information.[18] Publishers, editors, and reporters, too, avoid topics that would reflect badly on advertisers, and they may avoid stories that do not meet social expectations.[19]

Sometimes it is easy to forget the numerous forms of censorship we utilize in our society. Lines are being drawn, and censorship is taking place![20] We've looked at the past and the present. What does the future look like?

Censorship is likely to continue into the future. Edward Iwata, in his article "A Scary Future" in the journal *Editor & Publisher*, states, "Journalists and scholars at a recent First Amendment conference . . . predict . . . military censorship, government secrecy, and corporate control over newsrooms."[21] Iwata cites Tom Wicker, a reporter for *The New York Times*, as seeing "a need to crack down on fiery words and actions that could set off violence."[22]

The Thomas Jefferson Center for the Protection of Free Expression commissioned a study on American attitudes toward free speech and free press. It found 90 percent of those surveyed thought government should not be able to tell citizens what to say, but on a separate question 58 percent said government should be allowed to censor.[23]

I've looked at censorship past, present, and future. I have looked at the line and how people go about censoring our freedoms. Our freedom is important. Who governs our public morals, and where is the line drawn? Where should it be drawn, and who should draw it? Thomas Jefferson would probably have an answer to these questions. Do you?

This is Teresa's second subpoint. It is parallel to her point about freedom of speech and expression. Teresa uses three examples to support this subpoint.

In this transition, Teresa summarizes what she just said. Then she provides an internal summary.

In her conclusion, Teresa begins with the source and then cites a useful statistic.

She summarizes her three main points. Notice how she stops short of persuading her listeners?

Notes

1. C. L. Taylor, *Censorship* (New York: C. L. Taylor, 1986), p. 66.

2. Peter Galliner, "Dashed Hopes for the Press," *World Press Review* 40 (2) February 1993: 10.

3. Taylor, p. 19.

4. Taylor, p. 20.

5. Taylor, p. 20.

6. Taylor, p. 20.

7. Taylor, p. 24.

8. Taylor, p. 24.

9. Melvin Berger, *Censorship* (New York: Melvin Berger, 1982), p. 16.

10. Catherine Itzin, *Pornography: Women, Violence, and Civil Liberties* (New York: Oxford University Press, 1992).

11. Jay E. Daily, *The Anatomy of Censorship* (New York: Dekker, 1973), p. 108.

12. Daily, p. 108.

13. Judy Monroe, *Censorship* (New York: Macmillan, 1990), p. 21.

14. Monroe, p. 17.

15. Monroe, p. 18.

16. Berger, p. 30.

17. Berger, p. 31.

18. Berger, p. 39.

19. Carrie Goerne, "Study Blasts Advertisers, Fearful Media for Suppressing News," *Marketing News* (April 27, 1993): 8.

20. Robert U. Brown, "Self-Censorship Trickier than Government," *Editor & Publisher*, May 18, 1991, p. 20.

21. Edward Iwata, "A Scary Future: Journalists and Scholars Worried about First Amendment Threats," *Editor & Publisher*, June 22, 1991, p. 20.

22. Iwata, p. 20.

23. Jean Otto, "Freedom to Speak and Write," *Vital Speeches of the Day*, Jan. 1, 1992, p. 191.

◼ NOTES

[1] Peter Jaret, "The Cold Truth about Hard Workouts," *In Health*, March/April 1991, p. 38.

[2] Ray Ehrensberger, "An Experimental Study of the Relative Effects of Certain Forms of Emphasis in Public Speaking," *Speech Monographs* 12 (1945): 94–111.

[3] Harold Burson, "Beyond 'PR,'" *Vital Speeches of the Day*, December 15, 1990, p. 156.

[4] Richard Kostyra, "Communications in the Future," *Vital Speeches of the Day*, October 15, 1990, pp. 21–22.

[5] Mark L. Knapp and Anita L. Vangelisti, *Interpersonal Communication and Human Relationships*, 2d ed. (Boston: Allyn and Bacon, 1992), p. 214.

[6] Sarah Harder, "Equity by 2000," *Vital Speeches of the Day*, December 1, 1986, p. 111.

[7] Douglas E. Olesen, "The Art of Waste Minimization," *Vital Speeches of the Day,* August 15, 1990, pp. 666–668.

[8] Marilyn Vos Savant, "Ask Marilyn," *Parade Magazine* February 14, 1993.

[9] Benjamin H. Alexander, "Why Be Ugly When You Can Be Beautiful," *Vital Speeches of the Day,* January 15, 1987, p. 203.

[10] James A. Joseph, "The Genesis of Community," *Vital Speeches of the Day,* October 1, 1990, p. 749.

[11] Janice Payan, "Opportunities for Hispanic Women," *Vital Speeches of the Day,* September 1, 1990, p. 699.

[12] Don Terry, "Killed by Her Friends in an All-White Gang," *The New York Times,* May 18, 1994, p. 1.

[13] James A. Kelly, "Establishing High Standards for the Teaching Profession," *Vital Speeches of the Day,* April 1, 1991, pp. 379–380.

■ FURTHER READING

ANDERSON, JOHN R. *Cognitive Psychology and Its Implications,* 2d ed. San Francisco: Freeman, 1985. This outstanding textbook provides a comprehensive examination of the process involved in knowing, learning, and thinking. For serious students interested in the theoretical underpinnings of effective informative communication.

FRANK, MILO O. *How to Get Your Point Across in 30 Seconds or Less.* New York: Simon & Schuster, 1986. Whether speakers have a five-minute or a five-hour time limit, the essence of their talk should occur in just 30 seconds according to Frank. The value of this book is that it forces you to focus your thinking, your writing, and your speaking. In only 120 pages, Frank gets right to the heart of the matter: each chapter ends with a section called "In 30 seconds—or less." Powerful, punchy, possible!

GRICE, GEORGE L., AND JOHN F. SKINNER. *Mastering Public Speaking.* Englewood Cliffs, NJ: Prentice-Hall, 1993. Grice and Skinner's chapter "Using Visual Aids" may be useful to speakers who intend to inform. Their chapter "Speaking to Inform" is unique in that they include separate sections on speeches about people, objects, places, events, processes, concepts, conditions, and issues. Good examples in this unique approach.

LOGUE, CAL M., DWIGHT L. FRESHLEY, CHARLES R. GRUNER, AND RICHARD C. HUSEMAN. *Briefly Speaking: A Guide to Public Speaking in College and Career,* 4th ed. Boston: Allyn and Bacon, 1992. The authors include a number of chapters that are valuable to speakers intending to inform: "Creating a Speech," "Speaking Confidently," "Using Visual Aids," and "Speaking to Inform" (which includes "How We Learn"). They discuss informative speeches designed to define a problem, to analyze a problem, to report, to explain a process, to describe a product or service, and to explain a concept. Four sample informative speeches are included.

NELSON, PAUL, AND JUDY PEARSON. *Confidence in Public Speaking,* 5th ed. Madison, WI: Brown & Benchmark, 1993. In a chapter of almost 30 pages, the authors cover purposes of informative speeches, rhetorical principles of informative speaking, principles of learning, structuring the informative speech, types of informative speeches, and ethics and informative speaking. This chapter is full of useful information and terrific examples.

NOTHSTINE, WILLIAM L., CAROLE BLAIR, AND GARY A. COPELAND. *Critical Questions: Invention, Creativity, and the Criticism of Discourse and Media.* New York: St. Martin's Press, 1994. This is an anthology of essays on the criticism of discourse and media. For the beginning critic, Part I is especially valuable because it discusses basic characteristics of criticism. As people develop their ability as public speakers, they must become effective self-critics—carefully making the right choices. This is a book by experts about how proper choices are made. Reading it will "provoke socially responsible thinking and acting." (p. 7)

OLIU, WALTER, CHARLES T. BRUSAW, AND GERALD J. ALRED. *Writing That Works: Effective Communication in Business,* 4th ed. New York: St. Martin's Press, 1992. Effective speechmaking first requires effective writing. In this textbook the authors begin with a chapter on "Getting Started," and then, in separate chapters with numerous examples, talk about organization, writing drafts, achieving emphasis, creating tables and illustrations, and making an oral presentation. It is a comprehensive and well-written guide.

SHERMAN, THEODORE A., AND SIMON S. JOHNSON. *Modern Technical Writing,* 4th ed. Englewood Cliffs, NJ: Prentice-Hall, 1983. This book is mentioned because of its emphasis on how to present technical information like tables and figures. Also, it includes an excellent chapter, "Oral Presentation of Technical Information." Much useful, practical advice in this textbook.

VERDERBER, RUDOLPH F. *The Challenge of Effective Speaking,* 9th ed. Belmont, CA: Wadsworth, 1994. Verderber includes one of the most extensive sections on informative speaking in any basic textbook. Besides covering the principles and use of visual aids, he has separate chapters on explaining processes, descriptive speeches, speeches of definition, and expository speeches. A complete approach supported with outlines and speeches illustrates the basic types of informative speeches.

15

The Persuasive Speech

CHAPTER OBJECTIVES

After reading this chapter, you should be able to:

1 Explain how persuasion relates to the communication model.

2 Define persuasion and describe its purpose.

3 Distinguish between values, beliefs, and attitudes, and explain the purpose of each.

4 Explain what makes persuasion difficult.

5 Describe each of the strategies persuaders can use.

6 Briefly outline the seven ethical standards persuaders should follow.

Chris works for the Greek Life office. Basically, the job involves presenting speeches about the importance of Greek letter organizations. Although it sounds like Chris gives informative speeches, the speeches have a twofold persuasive purpose: to refute Greek stereotypes and to get students to attend rush information night. Chris stresses that people who belong to Greek letter organizations are more likely to remain in college to receive a bachelor's degree. Also, he says, fraternity and sorority membership has a substantial positive effect on persistence in studies, satisfaction with instruction and social life, and overall satisfaction with college. After Chris finishes talking and answers questions, he circulates a sign-up sheet to get commitments for rush information night. Chris's speeches have proved to be a successful recruitment device for the Greek Life office, and the office has already recruited other speakers because of Chris's success.

Rhonda gives a speech to her speech communication class about the need to donate blood. After having classmates visualize a potential accident, she offers the statistic that 275 donors are needed daily to meet the patient blood needs of local hospitals. Rhonda tells exactly how the blood is used and that a single donation can save from one to four lives. To demystify the process for her classmates she explains exactly what donors go through. She refutes the most common arguments against donating, and near the end of the speech she shows the tiny bandage she is wearing as a result of her own donation. Because the Bloodmobile is on campus, she gives the hours they will be set up in the student union, and she ends her speech with an American Red Cross quotation: "When you give blood, you give another birthday, another anniversary, another laugh, another hug, another chance."[1]

Both Chris and Rhonda are engaged in the act of **persuasion**—the process of trying to get others to change their attitudes or behavior. Most of you are involved in some sort of persuasion every day of your life. You try to persuade someone to join you for lunch or to join your study group. Others are involved in trying to persuade *you*: radio commercials exhort you to buy, telephone salespeople offer bargains on a variety of goods and services, professors try to persuade you to turn in your papers on time, and candidates for student government try to persuade you to vote for them.

Since persuasion runs through every aspect of our society, you need to study how it works. Understanding persuasion will help you evaluate the persuasive techniques of others. Studying persuasion also will help you develop your own persuasive messages in the most effective way possible.[2]

HOW DOES PERSUASION RELATE TO THE COMMUNICATION MODEL?

Often when we think of persuasion, we think of a communicator having an influence on a listener or on many listeners, such as a salesperson on a purchaser or a politician on a group of potential voters. This places an emphasis on the source of the communication as the main influence in the persuasion process. However, sometimes when we think of persuasion, we think of people buying products ("Okay, I'll buy the larger TV with the clearer picture"), changing attitudes ("Maybe Paula is the better candidate"), or altering their beliefs ("All right, maybe student demonstrations can make a difference"). This places an emphasis on the receivers of persuasive messages as the main part of the persuasion process.

When we emphasize the message in a persuasive situation, we might say, "That is a powerful statement" or "What a great speech!" And yet the focus of persuasion should not be on the sender, the receiver, *or* the message. All share in the persuasive process, even though one may play a more important role than the other two. You might not have purchased the product if the salesperson hadn't been terrific. The salesperson might not have sold the product if the receiver hadn't been ready, willing, and able to purchase it. Or the persuasive message might just have been *the* right message at *the* right time.

The point of this discussion is that what happens in the sender as he or she delivers the message and adjusts to feedback is often just as important as what happens in the receiver. To be an effective persuader means that you need to be concerned about all three elements, not concentrate on one to the exclusion of the others. It is only when all three combine with each other successfully that effective persuasion occurs.

Persuasion takes many forms. What are some of the persuasive messages the salesperson might be giving to the customer?

Listing all the persuasive messages that have affected you over the past 12 hours is really a difficult task. Advertisers have tried to get you to buy their products; you may have turned down a telemarketer offering a new credit card or a person selling magazine subscriptions; a friend may have asked for a loan of $5; your family may have tried to get you to come home for the weekend; a newspaper editorial may have convinced you to attend this weekend's athletic contest to show your school spirit; your dormitory friends may have persuaded you to go downtown with them; an instructor may have told you to keep up with your reading; a speaker in your class may have tried to get you to donate blood.

Notice that it is impossible to escape persuasive speaking, and persuasion has consequences. Change can occur when persuasion takes place. **Persuasion** is the process that occurs when a communicator (sender) influences the values, beliefs, attitudes, or behaviors of another person (receiver).

The key to understanding persuasion is influence. **Influence** refers to the power of a person or thing to affect others—to produce effects without the presence of physical force. Influence causes effects. For example, lending a friend $5 could cause a change in your character—making you realize that lending money is not so painful and thus making you more understanding or charitable in the future. The newspaper editorial on this weekend's athletic contest could have changed your thoughts about school spirit and your role in it. Your dormitory friends could have changed your mood for the day and given you something to look forward to tonight. An instructor could have changed your action by getting you to read regularly rather than put it off until exam time. Influence implies a degree of control over the thinking, emotions, and actions of others. Social influence is what occurs when a person's values, beliefs, attitudes, or behaviors are changed because of the behavior or presence of another person.

To fully understand persuasion, we need to understand influence and motivation. Persuasion involves influence, but you are unlikely to do something *just because* someone else affects you in some way. That is where motivation comes in. **Motivation** is the stimulation or inducement that causes you to act. For example, let's say that you decide to go downtown with your dormitory friends to avoid being annoyed and irritated by their pestering if you don't go. Maybe, too, you agree because that way you have someone to go out with. Let's say you decide to keep up with your reading because it will help you do better in that course. In these hypothetical instances alone, it becomes clear *why* we are motivated to do what we do— in other words, these are reasons and outcomes that are desirable.

Persuasion, influence, and motivation are closely linked. As persuaders, if we can relate *our* goals to things that persuade, influence, or motivate our listeners (or things that have all these effects), we are far more likely to be successful. But if it were truly this simple, people would be pulled and pushed so often that a numbing effect might eventually block out persuasive efforts. Brent, for example, was called so often by telemarketers that he responded to those who called, often acting like they knew him, with "Is this a sales call?" and (if the answer was "yes") "We don't accept solicitation by phone." Elvin contacted his post office so he would receive no junk mail.

It should be clear that any persuasive effort involves ethics. Sometimes ethical choices are clear from common knowledge and good judgment alone. Sometimes ethical choices are not clear. When involved in making decisions that may be questionable, you should consult other people when possible. If students in your class are planning something new, thinking about taking an unusual risk, or attempting to push the frontiers of acceptability, they are well advised to clear their decision or choice with their instructor first.

There is no doubt that persuasion plays a significant role in people's lives, and it does have consequences. Before we discuss specific strategies that persuaders can use to influence and motivate others, we need to look at values, beliefs, and attitudes because these are precisely what persuaders are trying to influence.

■ WHAT ARE VALUES, BELIEFS, AND ATTITUDES?

When a persuasive message taps into our values, beliefs, and attitudes, we are not only more responsive to the message, but we are more likely to like or accept the sender. When persuasive messages do not tap into our values, beliefs, and attitudes, we are less responsive to them. For example, we tend to respond positively to people who share our values. If you believe in the importance of recycling, you will be more likely to be receptive to a speaker who advocates recycling. Thus, persuaders who have investigated audience values, beliefs, and attitudes are more likely to be effective if—and this is the big "if"—they can adapt to them and use them effectively in their presentation.

Marcus, as he was considering subjects for a persuasive speech, thought about talking to his class on the topics of welfare, Medicare, and the graduated income tax. As he used the information he gained from his own classroom audience analysis, he came up with an entirely different set of subjects; topics more closely tied to students' values, beliefs, and attitudes included suicide and racism.

Values

Values are our beliefs about how we should behave or about some final goal that may or may not be worth attaining.[3] This definition divides values into two types: (1) *instrumental values* that guide people's day-to-day behavior, and (2) *terminal values* (some final goal that is or is not worth attaining).

Instrumental and terminal values are fairly easy to distinguish. Values that guide day-to-day behavior might be similar to those learned in scouting organizations—loyalty, honesty, friendliness, courage, kindness, cleanliness, thrift, and responsibility. Terminal values may vary, but some are shared by all human beings: freedom, the value of world peace, or family security. Other enduring values include inner harmony, happiness, safety, personal security, achievement, a progressive value system ("Every year things are getting better and better"), enlightenment (the value of the scientific method and rationality), and patriotism.

There are two points to think about when considering these terminal values. First, they are not likely to be changed because of one brief, persuasive speech; they change only over time. Second, the degree to which you can tie your approach or appeal into these terminal, widely accepted values may help you achieve your goals. That is, if you can show your approach is consistent with, supports, or reinforces the values your audience holds, then listeners are more likely to accept the new approach as a natural outgrowth of the values they already support. Marcus chose racism as his topic, for example, because he could relate it to so many terminal values his classmates support: freedom, equality, friendship, inner harmony, and happiness.

Beliefs

Often, it is values that determine beliefs. Also they may anchor beliefs. For example, if one of our values is patriotism, this value might result in a variety of beliefs. We might believe in a capitalistic economy, a democratic form of government, a public education system, a highly productive agricultural system, and the Judeo-Christian religious tradition.

Beliefs are statements of knowledge, opinion, and faith. A statement of knowledge might be "I believe [know] that if I let go of this book, it will drop to the floor." A statement of opinion might be "I believe [opinion] that vitamin supplements help keep us healthy." A statement of faith might be "I believe [have faith] that there is a God."

Where do we get our beliefs? Beliefs can come to us from a variety of sources. Besides our own observations, we depend on the observations of our parents, teachers, religious leaders, and friends—especially as we grow up. As adults, we depend more on professionals, scientists, and journalists. The point here is that we seldom develop beliefs in isolation from other people. Our interactions have much to do with what we observe, how we observe it, and the conclusions we draw from our observations.

If you compare values with beliefs, you realize that beliefs are, in general, easier to change than values. Values are central; they are more securely anchored. The fact that beliefs are easier to change does not necessarily mean they can and will be changed. Beliefs, for example, can be changed with more or better knowledge: examples, statistics, or testimony. Statements of opinion can be changed in the same way. Statements of faith are less likely to be changed—at least by a brief persuasive speech.

TRY THIS

Stop for a moment and list on a sheet of paper all the persuasive messages designed to influence you that you have read, heard, or seen during the past 12 hours. Remember to include messages you have heard from instructors, friends, family members, roommates, boyfriends or girlfriends, advertisers, TV commentators, newspaper or magazine columnists, religious leaders, and politicians. List as many as you can remember.

Attitudes

Attitudes are groups of beliefs that cause us to respond in some way to a particular object or situation. Let's say that you have a group of beliefs regarding honesty that are connected to educational experiences—test taking, paper writing, and doing your own work. This might result in the negative beliefs "I don't believe in cheating," or "I don't believe in presenting someone else's work as my own." According to our definition of *attitude,* this group of beliefs would cause us to respond in some way: to speak out in favor of honesty, to discourage friends or classmates from being dishonest or depending on the strength of the beliefs or attitude, to report cheating or plagiarism that you observe.

■ WHAT MAKES PERSUASION DIFFICULT?

The purpose of this section is threefold: first, it is designed to help you have realistic expectations. Persuaders, especially beginning persuaders, often become too optimistic about what they can accomplish in persuasive speeches. Second, it is designed to motivate you. If you know before you begin putting together your persuasive speech how difficult the process of change can be, you will be more likely to put in the time and effort to make the process work. Third, this section is designed to offer some specific difficulties persuaders may face so that you can try to prepare in advance to overcome these hurdles.

One obvious difficulty is the sheer amount of persuasion that occurs. To say that we are besieged by persuasive messages is an understatement. Your persuasive message is likely to be just another persuasive message unless you take special care to make it stand out or to make it different from others.

A second difficulty is that persuasion tends to work slowly, over time. For example, how often have you gone out and bought a product after hearing or seeing just one advertisement for it? How often are we prompted to do anything as a result of just one message? Effective persuasion often works over time. We rarely take action after seeing just one advertisement. Usually we have to see the advertisement over and over. Or, perhaps, see different versions of the advertisement that focus on various aspects of the product until all our questions have been answered and our objections overcome. Persuasive speakers, however, do not ordinarily have the luxury of repeated efforts.

A third difficulty is that the value, belief, or attitude we are trying to change may be deeply entrenched. Many values, beliefs, and attitudes are tied into others. Some of these are based on family and religious traditions, others on deep personal commitments made early in life or personal experiences we have had. Many early experiences are etched in our memory. Henrik grew up eating fast food; he's not going to change to a nutritional eating plan because of one speech. Letty's family was prejudiced against Catholics; a single persuasive message about ecumenism probably will have little effect. Shocking circumstances, fearful activities, or events that evoke strong emotional reactions often make such imprints. It's unusual for a single speech to shake or change our strongest feelings.

A fourth difficulty is that some people we hope to persuade have structured their lives around some basic "truth," and their habits and beliefs are entrenched. For example, some people still believe that you can catch a cold by going outside in the cold without wearing a coat. This belief runs counter to everything we know about viruses and how colds are communicated. But to try to change someone's belief in this "truth" would be difficult, perhaps impossible.

A fifth difficulty is laziness. People, in general, are not easily aroused to action or activity. Getting people to do something, sometimes anything, can be difficult, let alone asking them to change an established way of doing things, or even thinking. It might better be said that people are inclined to follow familiar, traditional, well-traveled routes. The routine is easier, well known, more comfortable, and perhaps more rewarding—at least, it's predictable to do things the way they've always been done.

A sixth difficulty is that people want freedom of action. A threat to that freedom, like a persuasive appeal—"Do things my way"—causes people to react, maybe even to reject the appeal. People might respond in an opposite direction: "I'll show you!" "I don't want to be told how to do it!". Freedom of action is so strong that some people respond negatively to a persuasive appeal even when the point of view expressed is similar to their own.

Many other factors can affect the receptiveness of your audience. Time of day may affect how awake or responsive people feel. Your audience's educational level could affect how much your listeners understand, how complex your argument can get, or how technical your language can be. Socioeconomic level might affect the kinds of subjects you select. For example, you might speak to an audience of young people about how to get a job or how to impress an employer, or talk to a group of retirees about investments and exotic travel opportunities.

Is this bullhorn likely to be a barrier between the speaker and the audience? Would the speaker be better served by a microphone?

Gender can be a difficulty as well. Some men have trouble dealing with women who show tendencies to dominate and control; these men lose energy and initiative.[4] Sometimes when speakers are trying to persuade others, they are perceived as dominating or controlling. How do males respond to female persuaders? Diana Ivy and Phil Backlund, writers on gender, raise the question "Wouldn't it be great if women could act assertively (even aggressively) without the risk of being perceived as a threat, without being called masculine, or worse?"[5] Ivy and Backlund raise another interesting question: "Wouldn't it be great . . . for a guy to be able to communicate in a nurturing, caring fashion to women and men alike, without risking rejection or embarrassment for being unmasculine?"[6] How might women respond to a male speaker who gets excessively emotional? How about the man who does not conform to the traditional male stereotypes of dominance, power, and control? The answers are not clear.

A speaker can turn these difficulties into strengths by carefully analyzing the audience. They must use information about their audience in their research and in their other preparation—selecting their organization scheme, choosing their language, and presenting their message. Our discussion of the difficulties of persuasion points out what we mentioned earlier: persuasion involves all three elements—sender, message, and receiver—working together.

Effective persuasion requires rigorous audience analysis, careful limiting of the persuasive focus or intent, much time in thorough preparation, great care in selecting the proper argument and evidence, detailed attention to the way the message is constructed, and much practice in effective delivery. Information about the audience can affect the choices you make in each

What symbol is helping to give credibility to this Texas speaker?

area, and it may not be easy to apply all your information about your audience to each area. But nothing worthwhile in life comes easily; effective persuasion is no exception.

WHAT STRATEGIES CAN PERSUADERS USE?

Now you have a good idea of how persuasion relates to our model of communication; you understand what persuasion is and what its purpose is; you have an idea of how values, beliefs, and attitudes are involved in the process; and you have some indication of how difficult persuasion is likely to be. You now have a foundation for examining strategies. In persuasion, just as in any other form of communication, there are no guarantees. No strategy is foolproof. The best approach is to use all the available strategies to meet the demands of the audience. Obviously, different audiences will require different approaches, so the more strategies you can use, the better.

Determine Your Purpose

Determining your purpose at the outset will provide a focal point for the entire effort. Subtracting a purpose from a persuasive effort is like pulling out the main rod of an umbrella. Without the rod, the whole umbrella collapses. Your purpose should be a highly specific and attainable persuasive goal.

TRY THIS

Let's be realistic. Assume you will hear or have already heard a persuasive speech in this class. What is it that prevents *you* from changing your beliefs or taking action based on what the speaker said? We mentioned several reasons: the sheer amount of persuasion that occurs; how persuasion tends to work; deeply entrenched values, beliefs, and attitudes; the truisms on which many of us base our lives; laziness; and our desire for freedom of action. Can you think of other difficulties that affect *you* directly? Why were you not persuaded? If you were, why were you persuaded? What made you more receptive?

We overheard one student say, "These are classroom speeches. They are simply done to satisfy a classroom assignment. They aren't to be taken seriously." And yet, a student is a real speaker, with real ideas, who *can* have a real effect. Classmates are real audience members with hearts and minds, who *can* respond in a real way. Some students look at college as preparation for life, not as life itself. It could be that all that is necessary is a change of attitude.

When you begin planning a persuasive speech, one of the first questions you should ask yourself is what you want your audience to think or do. As we have noted in previous chapters, this is called your specific purpose. Here are some specific purpose statements for persuasive speeches:

To Get Audience Members to Believe a Certain Way

- To persuade audience members that state lotteries exploit poor people
- To persuade audience members that their college theatre program is worthwhile
- To persuade audience members that sex education at the elementary school level needs to be expanded

To Get Audience Members to Act

- To persuade audience members to attend church
- To persuade audience members to stop eating red meat
- To persuade audience members to write their congressional representatives in support of stronger gun-control legislation

If you keep your specific purpose in mind, it will be easier to generate main points for support. As you find support for your purpose, remember that you will want your audience to respond in one or more of the five following ways:

1. *To change their ideas.* A speaker wants to persuade the audience to change a belief or way of thinking or to reinforce a belief and take action. For example, a speaker who wants to convince listeners that state lotteries exploit the poor will provide evidence that poor people are the most likely to spend money on lotteries and that lotteries serve no constructive purpose.
2. *To take action.* For example, a speaker who wants the audience to attend church, stop eating red meat, or write to congressional representatives will try to motivate listeners to do certain things.
3. *To continue doing what they are already doing.* Some audience members might already be doing what you are asking them to do. For example, if several members of the class are taking theatre classes, they might find the speech on supporting the college theatre program interesting because it *reinforces* what they already believe.
4. *To avoid doing something.* The speaker might want audience members to stop eating red meat, to stop buying a particular product or service, or to get their legislators to prohibit personal firearms or abolish capital punishment.
5. *To continue not doing something.* This goal is slightly different from goal 2. It works best if audience members are considering taking action you're against. For example, if they're thinking about playing the lottery (because the payoff has become so large) or not going to church, you might be able to persuade them not to do so. Your speech might persuade listeners who don't eat red meat not to give in to peer pressure if they're out with a crowd of friends at a fast-food place.

Any audience is likely to include listeners who represent every possible point of view on your subject. When you're planning your speech, you should consider all of them.

Analyze Your Audience

Whether you use your own observations, surveys, interviews, or research, you need to get good information about your audience—as we discussed in Chapter 10, "Getting Started." We mention this again here to remind you to appeal to the values, beliefs, and attitudes whenever possible.

The second reason to analyze your audience is to predict its response to your persuasive effort. Many audiences reveal wide diversity. For example, even when speaking about day care to a group of working mothers—women who share a common desire to find good day care for their children—you will find big differences in age, socioeconomic background, and even marital status. Because of the problems of appealing to a diverse, or heterogeneous, audience, it might be helpful to select a target audience.

Your **target audience** is a subgroup of the whole audience that you must persuade to reach your goal. You aim your speech mostly at these individuals, knowing that some members of your audience are opposed to your message, some agree with it, some are uncommitted or undecided, and to some, it's irrelevant.

Politicians always go after a target audience. A legislator may speak at a school and target those who will vote for a specific issue or use the occasion to refute comments made by an opponent. A candidate may speak in a factory and target those people who will support a local zoning ordinance that would create more factories and, thus, further employment. Politicians have to do this because their success often depends on how many different constituencies they can appeal to. When uncommitted or undecided individuals are targeted, it is because they are most likely to be influenced by persuasion.

Appeal to Your Audience Using Logic

A **logical appeal** is one that addresses listeners' reasoning ability. Evidence in the form of statistics or any other supporting material will help to persuade the audience. Chapter 12 explains in detail the kinds of supporting material you can use in a logical appeal.

A logical appeal may be argued in several ways: through deductive reasoning, inductive reasoning, causal reasoning, or reasoning by analogy.

DEDUCTIVE REASONING

Deductive reasoning moves from the general to the specific. Here is a deductive argument used by one student:

> *Acid rain is a problem throughout the entire northeastern United States.*
> *Pennsylvania is a northeastern state.*
> *Pennsylvania has a problem with acid rain.*

Care is needed, however, with this pattern of reasoning. Have you ever heard someone say, "It's dangerous to generalize"? A faulty generalization really is faulty deductive thinking—as in this example:

> *All college students procrastinate.*
> *Mary is a college student.*
> *Therefore, Mary procrastinates.*

INDUCTIVE REASONING

Another logical technique is **inductive reasoning**—reasoning from the specific to the general. Usually when we use inductive reasoning we move from a number of facts to a conclusion. Here is how a student used inductive reasoning to persuade her audience that the college should require everyone to take a foreign language:

In some parts of the United States, you need to understand Spanish to get by.

Americans are traveling more and more to countries where a language other than English is spoken.

The mark of an educated person is that he or she can speak, write, and read at least one other language.

Conclusion: Everyone should learn another language.

When you use evidence in a speech, you can organize it in the way that best suits your material. Sometimes it will work best to give the facts and then draw the conclusion (induction); in other cases you might want to start with the conclusion and then support it with facts (deduction).

CAUSAL REASONING

Another way to reason is causally. **Causal reasoning** always uses "because"—either implied or explicitly stated: "I failed the class because I didn't complete the assignments" or "The basketball team is losing because it has an incompetent coach." This latter example points out some of the problems of causal reasoning. That the coach is incompetent may be a matter of opinion. The team might be losing because it doesn't have good players or because the other teams have taller players or because there is no way of recruiting good players. The causal pattern can be used for presenting evidence as well as for organizing an entire speech. The cause-and-effect pattern is one of the ways to organize a speech discussed in Chapter 13.

REASONING BY ANALOGY

Finally, you can reason by **analogy**. In this case you compare two similar cases and conclude that if something is true for one, it must also be true for the other. Casey used analogy to try to get his listeners to understand the value of new electronic gadgets and gizmos. He said, "Think of these as tools to make your life easier. These are just like the tools you've been using all along. The only difference is that these electronic tools are faster and more adaptable to your specific needs."

Often speeches of policy use analogy. Advocates of a policy look to see if the policy has succeeded elsewhere. For example, Katrina was trying to get her listeners to understand the new "information superhighway" since her goal was to get her listeners to take an active part in the information explosion:

The information age is upon us, and it is in full swing. It is a digital revolution, but it needn't be scary. It is just like what we have been seeing splashed across the business pages of our newspapers. Think of the information superhighway as a massive electronic merger. Just as telephone, cable, computer, and media Goliaths have merged, separate databases have

TRY THIS

Consider the following topics, and see if you can frame an argument for each side. Are there subjects where you are so firmly committed to one side that you can't even think of an opposing argument?

abortion	*gays in the*	*prayer in schools*
baseball salaries	*military*	*racism*
capital punishment	*grades*	*recycling*
cigarette smoking	*gun control*	*rock lyrics*
control of the	*legislation*	*seat belts*
Gaza Strip	*health reform*	*violence on*
environmental	*industrial*	*television*
pollution	*pollution*	*year-round*
feminism	*organ transplant*	*school*
freedom of speech		

been linked together through networking to give consumers—us—access to huge electronic storehouses of information now housed in far-flung and inaccessible libraries around the planet. To take an active part will give us—at our fingertips—a wealth of information that has never been available before.

Appeal to Your Audience Using Emotion

An **emotional appeal** focuses on listeners' needs, wants, desires, and wishes. Recent research shows that the people who are most successful at persuasion are those who can understand others' motives and desires—even when these motives and desires are not stated. To do this, researchers found, the persuader must be able to understand someone else's feelings without letting his or her own feelings get in the way.[7]

In a public speaking situation it is impossible to appeal to each person's motives and desires, so it helps to know that there are some basic needs that we all have.

APPEALING TO NEEDS

Psychologist Abraham Maslow proposed a model that arranges people's needs from relatively low-level physical needs to higher-level psychological ones.[8] This model, referred to as a **hierarchy of needs,** is shown in Figure 15-1. Let's take a look at the needs in the hierarchy and see how they can help you decide what emotional appeals to put in your persuasive speech.

As you can see at the bottom of Figure 15-1, the first needs all human beings have are *physiological needs.* Starving people do not care about freedom; their need for food is so great that it outweighs all other needs. Therefore, physiological needs must be taken care of before other needs can be met. Since we usually assume that basic needs are taken care of, they are generally not a basis for a persuasive speech.

Safety needs are next in the hierarchy. The whole area of safety needs can be useful in persuasion, since all of us have these needs in varying degrees. Notice how this speaker appeals to the student audience's need for safety:

> In the last three months there have been six assaults on this campus. Where have they occurred? All in parking lots with no lights. When? At night, after evening classes. Does this mean that you can't take any more evening classes without fearing for your life? Should you leave your car at home so you can avoid the campus parking lots?

Belongingness and love needs, the next level, also have a potent appeal. If you doubt this, turn on your television set and note how many commercials make a direct pitch to the need to be loved.

Here is how one student used the need to belong to urge new students to join "The Way"—a religious group on campus:

> The first year is the hardest year of college. You are in a new environment and are faced with a bewildering array of choices. I felt this way when I was a freshman. Then I met someone from "The Way" who invited me to one of its meetings. The minute I walked in the door several people met me and made me feel welcome. Today some of these people are my best friends.

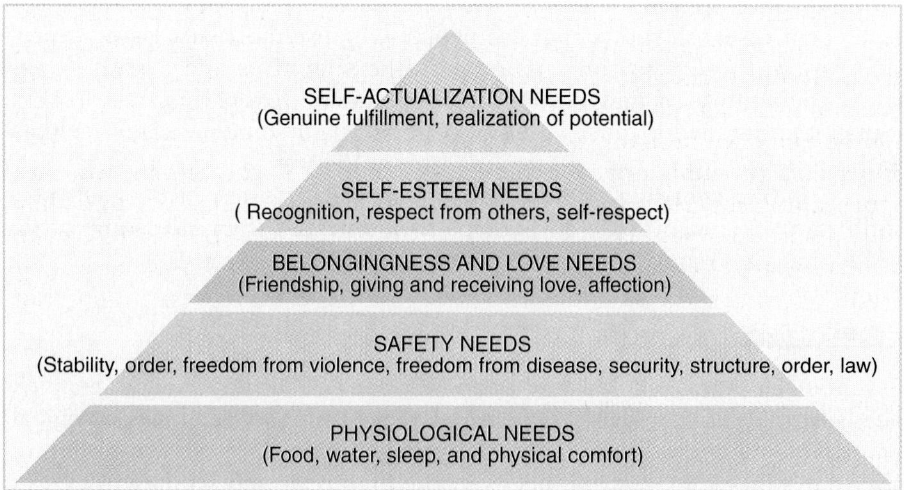

FIGURE 15.1

Maslow's Hierarchy of Needs

SELF-ACTUALIZATION NEEDS
(Genuine fulfillment, realization of potential)

SELF-ESTEEM NEEDS
(Recognition, respect from others, self-respect)

BELONGINGNESS AND LOVE NEEDS
(Friendship, giving and receiving love, affection)

SAFETY NEEDS
(Stability, order, freedom from violence, freedom from disease, security, structure, order, law)

PHYSIOLOGICAL NEEDS
(Food, water, sleep, and physical comfort)

Self-esteem needs stem from our need to feel good about ourselves. We see a lot of persuasion based on these needs in self-help books. Typical themes are that you'll feel good about yourself if you change your fashion style, learn how to climb mountains, practice meditation, and so on. One student appealed to self-esteem needs when she gave a speech called "Try Something New":

> *I have a friend who, at the age of 35, decided to learn how to play the flute. She had never played an instrument before, but she loved music and thought it would be interesting to give it a try. Now that she has been studying for two years, she told me, "I will never be a great player but this has been a wonderful experience. I enjoy my recordings even more because I know what the musicians are doing. I understand so much more about music. It's wonderful to try something new." I am here today to urge you to try something new yourself. To see what you can discover about yourself.*

At the top of his hierarchy, Maslow puts *self-actualization needs*—the need to recognize one's potential. This need involves our desire to do our best with what we have. An admissions director for a community college gave this speech when she talked to a group of older women in an attempt to persuade them to go to college:

> *I'm sure that many of you look back at your high school days and think "I was a pretty good writer. I wonder if I still could write" or "I really liked my business courses. I would like to try my hand at bookkeeping again." I believe one of the saddest things that can happen to us is not to be able to try out things that we are good at, things that we have always wanted to do. Our new college program for returning adults will give you a chance to do just that—try out the things you are good at.*

You have the best chance of choosing the right emotional appeal if you have done a thorough job of researching your audience. For instance, safety needs tend to be important to families—especially those with young children. On the other hand, younger audiences, such as college students, generally focus more on belonging, love, and self-esteem needs. If you were going to focus on safety needs to encourage the buying of savings bonds, a college audience probably wouldn't find it very interesting. Self-actualization needs probably appeal most to an older audience. Adults who are approaching midlife are the most likely to ask themselves whether they have made the right choices for their lives or whether they should make some changes. Age, of course, is only one factor to consider in assessing needs. The more information you have about your audience, the better the chance of selecting the right emotional appeals.

APPEALING TO OTHER EMOTIONS

Appeals can also be made to other emotions that all of us feel. In each of the examples that follow, the speaker is appealing to a common emotion.

In persuading her audience to be more aggressive in protecting themselves against street crime, this speaker used the emotion of fear:

> *Nearly 35 million personal and household crimes are committed in the United States each year. A personal theft occurs every 2.5 seconds, and a violent crime every 5 seconds. There is an attack on a woman every 13 seconds. No wonder people are scared. I am not here to tell you there is nothing to fear; I am here to tell you that you can reduce your fear by doing three things that will make you a tougher target: first, always be alert; second, have a plan; and third, protect privacy.*

In the next example, the speaker wanted audience members to consider taking a foster child. She used compassion as a way of getting them to feel sympathetic to the children:

> *What happens when a child has no home? When the child is shunted around to five different foster homes in four years? This happens to thousands of American children every year. There is no place they can call home.*

In this speech, the speaker used the emotion of anger to get her classmates excited about food-stamp fraud:

> *Did you know there are wealthy people out there making millions of dollars off food stamps? Did you know that the food-stamp program costs taxpayers $24 billion a year? Did you know that after Medicaid, the food-stamp program is the most expensive in the federal welfare system, and one of the most poorly run? Radical reform is needed. I am fed up with the waste, and you should be too. If you support my ideas that we need to tighten eligibility, cut excesses, and crack down on criminals, then will you sign these petitions? If you sign them, I will send them to our legislators. I'm angry, and I hope you are, too.*

Sometimes you can appeal to a collective emotion. This student urged students to attend an honors convocation by appealing to their pride:

> *The most unsung heroes and heroines of this campus are those who have academic achievements. Do you know that 15 students from this school have scholarships to medical school next year? That for the past six semesters students from this campus have gone on highly competitive federal internships? That we are ranked as number four in the nation for our writing program?*

When you are going to give a persuasive speech, think about the emotions you can appeal to. Emotions are powerful tools in persuasion. If you can find a good way to use them, they will add strength and power to your speech.

CONSIDER THIS

Here we give you an opportunity to make some ethical judgments. Sometimes the line blurs between what is proper and what is not. Often, we are left to make the judgment ourselves. Ask yourself, as you read this, "Did Lisa do the right thing?"

Lisa presented a persuasive speech on the need for recycling paper, plastic, and aluminum products. To illustrate the many types of recyclables and how overpackaged many grocery products are, she used as an effective visual aid a paper grocery bag filled with empty cans, paper products, and a variety of plastic bottles and containers. After listening to her well-researched, well-delivered speech, with its impassioned final appeal for us to help save the planet by recycling, the class watched in amazement as she put the empty containers back in the bag, walked to the corner of the room, and dropped the bag in the trash can! After a few seconds that seemed like minutes, someone finally asked the question that had to be asked: "You mean you're not going to take those home to recycle them?" "Nah," said Lisa. "I'm tired of lugging them around. I've done my job."

Source: George L. Grice and John F. Skinner, *Mastering Public Speaking* (Englewood Cliffs, NJ: Prentice-Hall, 1993), pp. 24–25.

QUESTIONS

1. Did Lisa's actions affect the message of her speech? Should the two be related?

2. Did Lisa's actions cause her to lose credibility?

3. If you consider Lisa's action careless or thoughtless, what could you have done in this situation to let Lisa know *your* feelings? Is it appropriate to let others know your feelings in such situations?

STRUCTURE YOUR MATERIAL EFFECTIVELY

How you decide to structure your material may depend on the material itself; it may depend on your own interests or intentions; or it may depend on the situation or assignment. The most important consideration, however, is your listeners' attitude, or how you expect your audience to react. Let's review the organizational schemes most commonly used in persuasive speeches: cause-and-effect order, problem-solution order, and motivated sequence. (We covered these and other organizational formats in Chapter 12, "Organizing and Outlining the Speech.") Here we will discuss several topics related to persuasive speaking: questions of fact, value, and policy; one-sided versus two-sided arguments; and order of presentation.

Questions of Fact, Value, and Policy

Chapter 9 discussed using questions of fact, value, and policy in group discussion. Now let's see how these questions can be used for persuasive speeches.

QUESTIONS OF FACT

A *question of fact* deals with what is true or false. One student used a question of fact when he spoke on the question "Do Unidentified Flying Objects Really Exist?" The purpose of his speech was to persuade the audience that they did.

QUESTIONS OF VALUE

A *question of value* is concerned with some aspect of a moral issue: whether something is good or bad, right or wrong, beneficial or detrimental, and so on. Note how a student used a question of value to discuss the topic of plagiarism:

Specific Purpose: To persuade my audience that plagiarism of any kind is unacceptable.

Central Idea: Plagiarism may have short-term gains, but it does long-term harm.

Main Points: I. People's professional careers have been ruined when it was revealed that they had cheated in college.
II. People who plagiarize deny themselves the opportunity to learn new skills.
III. Plagiarism is theft; rather than take someone's possessions, you steal his or her ideas and work.

QUESTIONS OF POLICY

Questions of policy deal with specific courses of action and usually contain such words as *should, ought,* or *must.* Here are the main points for a speech based on a question of policy:

Specific Purpose: To persuade my audience that all students should be granted a one-term work experience opportunity during their four-year education.

Central Idea: A work experience will give students a realistic understanding of the workplace before they graduate.

Main Points:
I. Work experiences are an effective way to give students real-world experience.
II. Work experiences provide students with useful contacts outside of education.
III. Work experiences offer students a better base for understanding their education.
IV. Work experiences develop skills that cannot be developed in education.

One-Sided versus Two-Sided Arguments

Should persuaders present one side or both sides of an issue? When you know your listeners basically support your ideas, one side may be sufficient. For example, a student knew that she didn't have to persuade her audience of the pros and cons of being quiet in the library. Instead, she came up with some ideas for what her listeners could do to make the library quieter.

There are occasions, however, when speakers should present both sides of the picture. Often the presentation of both sides will boost credibility: the speaker is likely to be perceived as fairer and more rational. When an issue of public importance is controversial, it's a good idea to present both sides, since most people will probably have heard something about each side. When a student spoke on gun control, he presented both sides because he knew there were strong feelings for and against. Another speaker chose to present both sides of the sex education issue. She thought sex education should be taught at home, but she wanted to let her audience know that others preferred it to be handled in the schools.

There has been extensive research comparing the one-sided versus two-sided speech. The results seem to indicate that (1) a two-sided speech is more effective when the listeners have completed at least a high school education; (2) the two-sided speech is especially effective if the evidence clearly supports the thesis; and (3) the two-sided presentation is more effective when listeners oppose the speaker's position, but the one-sided approach is more effective when listeners already support the thesis.[9]

Order of Presentation

Certain ways of organizing speeches seem to be especially effective for a persuasive speech. As we discussed in detail in Chapter 12, the *problem-solution order* works well for persuasion. It lets the speaker build tension by describing the problem and getting listeners involved in it; then the speaker can relieve the tension by providing a solution.

Another organizational pattern that works well for persuasion is the **comparative advantage order.** When using this pattern, a speaker looks at some proposed solutions to a problem and then persuades the audience to choose a particular one by emphasizing its advantages. For example:

If you follow the newspapers, magazines, and books, you know there are many solutions about how to live a better life. One is to follow a better diet. Another is to get more sleep. A third is to exercise more. A fourth is to develop better time-management skills. But I have a solution that draws strengths from each of these, and that is self-discipline. I favor this last solution because . . .

The *motivated sequence*[10] was discussed in some detail in Chapter 12, but because of its popularity and usefulness for persuasion, we will review it here. The five steps of the motivated sequence, which is based on the problem-solution form, suggest five specific main points for developing a speech. Any problem-solving speech can be adapted to this form.

1. The *attention* step's purpose is to gain the attention of the audience. You do this by following the suggestions in the section "The Speech Introduction" in Chapter 12.
2. The *need* step points out a problem that affects audience members. In this step you create a sense of urgency about the problem.
3. The *satisfaction* step gives relief to the audience by providing a solution to the problem.
4. The *visualization* step lets the audience see how much better things would be if this solution were put into effect.
5. The *action* step urges the audience to go out and take some action that will help solve the problem.

Since the motivated sequence follows the human thought process, it is extremely easy to use. In fact, you might be using it without even knowing it. Here's how Maria tries to persuade her roommate Carlotta to move from the dorm to an off-campus apartment:

Attention: Do you realize how small this room is? We don't have any-place to store our clothes—let alone our books and CDs.

Need: We really need a space where we can spread out a little and invite our friends in without sitting nose to nose.

Satisfaction: See all the ads for off-campus housing? We can get an apartment in town for a little bit less than we are paying for the dorm.

Visualization: Just imagine—if we had our own apartment we could each have a separate room. We could have all our friends over at one time.

Action: Here's the list of apartments that are for rent. Let's start making some appointments to go and see them.

Now see how one student speaker developed a persuasive speech using the motivated sequence:

CONSIDER THIS

Effective persuasion is difficult without the added difficulty of persuasion between members of different cultures. The following is one of the conclusions Anderson, a writer on intercultural communication, reaches in her article, "A Comparison of Arab and American Conceptions of 'Effective' Persuasion":

Given the vastly different assumptions about the role of persuasion in society, it is not surprising that misunderstandings occur between Americans and Arabs, even when the same "language" is used. Communicating across a cultural gap requires more than just a knowledge of respective vocabularies. It also requires an understanding of the different cultural rules for what constitutes "reasonable" political debate.

Source: Janice Walker Anderson, "A Comparison of Arab and American Conceptions of 'Effective' Persuasion." In Larry A. Samovar and Richard E. Porter (Eds.), *Intercultural Communication: A Reader*, 6th ed. (Belmont, CA: Wadsworth, 1991), pp. 96–105.

QUESTIONS

1. Have you ever thought about the differences between persuading an audience made up of members of your own culture and persuading an audience made up of members of another culture? What are some of the differences you would encounter?

2. What can be done to resolve the misunderstandings that occur when Americans talk to people of other cultures?

3. What might some of the "cultural rules" for Americans be that are referred to in the last sentence of the quotation?

Specific Purpose: To persuade my audience that the campus newspaper should be funded directly by the activity fee rather than by student government.

Central Idea: When student government funds the newspaper, it often tries to control the news.

Main Points: I. *Attention:* This week the student government says it will stop funding the newspaper unless the newspaper stops criticizing the government.

II. *Need:* This has been a problem for a long time. Whenever the government doesn't like what the paper says, it closes the paper down.

III. *Satisfaction:* The only way to solve this problem is to fund the paper directly with money from the student activity fee. If government doesn't control the funding, it can't control the newspaper.

IV. *Visualization:* The newspaper will be able to play its proper role as watchdog of government, and all of you will no longer find that the paper has not come out because the government has closed it down again.

V. *Action:* I have a petition addressed to the president of this university. I hope all of you will sign it.

Select Your Language Carefully

Whether you support a question of fact, value, or policy, how the audience responds to your message is likely to depend on your ability to motivate them. Remember the difficulty we pointed out—people are not inclined to think or act the way you want them to unless you motivate them. In Chapter 4, "Verbal Communication," we discussed the importance of language; here, we simply want to underscore the importance of language for appealing to listeners' emotions.

Try to keep your mind on language while you select supporting material. You will want to find emotion-arousing material for both your introduction and conclusion. You will want to stimulate the emotions of your listeners with special words. And you will want to find emotional pictures that will create the appropriate response.

Charles W. Colson, founder of Prison Fellowship, used this powerful introduction to begin a speech titled "Can We Be Good Without God?":

> *Last December, newspapers ran a striking photograph of a group of people held at bay by armed guards. They were not rioters or protestors; they were Christmas carolers. The town of Vienna, Virginia, had outlawed the singing of religious songs on public property. So these men, women and children were forced to sing "Silent Night" behind barricades, just as if this were Eastern Europe under communist rule instead of Christmas in America in 1992.*[11]

Look at this powerful conclusion by Antonia C. Novello, Surgeon General of the United States, in her speech "Alcohol and Tobacco Advertising: Prevention Indeed Works":

> *We must work even harder to let the industry know that as long as we are around, the industry will not decide who the next smokers will be and who the next drinkers will be.*
>
> *As long as I am your Surgeon General, I will work for all these things. But remember, no one individual alone should be responsible for the*

*health and welfare of our children. The pulpit has infinite space to ac-
commodate those who care enough to make a difference.*

   *As we continue to work together in the years ahead, I know that our
collaboration will lead to even greater success.*

   *My friends, the time to act is NOW: our next generation is counting on
us, and we have precious little time to rehearse.*

   Thank you, and may God bless. [12]

Her emotion-arousing words include "no one individual alone should be
responsible," "The pulpit has infinite space," and "the time to act is *now.*"
She engages her audience deeply through emotion.

   In addition to finding emotion-arousing material for introductions and
conclusions, consider using language that stimulates the emotions of listeners. Notice how William J. Madia, senior vice president of Battelle, chose
effective language in getting his listeners at Ohio State University to be concerned about their environment. In "Making the Right Choices: Risk
Assessment and Environmental Ethics," Madia said:

> *When it comes to the environment, we can't ignore the legacy that we leave
> behind. I'm sure many of us would like to have the opportunity to go back
> in time and pay our ancestors not to wipe out some extinct species, or not
> to deplete the whale population, or not to dump chemical soup into the
> Ohio River.* [13]

Notice in this brief excerpt the use of words like "wipe out," "deplete," and
"dump." But even the choice of "extinct species" and "dump chemical soup"
serve Madia's purpose in arousing listeners' concern over the environment.

   Finally, select language that evokes images—emotion-filled pictures in
listeners' minds. Look at the image-producing language Dr. Joan E. Aitken
selected in this part of her speech at a parents' workshop titled "Light the
Fire: Communicate with Your Child." Dr. Aitken had just passed around a
basket of shells and told each audience member to select one. Then she
said:

> *That shell is all that is left of life. Some are broken. I'm told that the species
> I'm holding dates back to the age of the dinosaurs. Look at the thickness
> of protection this kind of shell has offered its species over the last million
> years. For every one of these shells found on the beach, billions more have
> been crushed into sand. There is nothing left of those shells, no structure
> for us to examine. I want you to think about the protective shell you are
> building around your child's life.* [14]

Aitken used "broken," "thickness," and "crushed," which are specific words
designed to help listeners create images. She took listeners back to the time
of the dinosaurs, into the effect of billions of years of wave action, and then
moved them into the present and how parents deal with their children. Her
speech evokes powerful images.

The likelihood of our being persuaded depends greatly on the person doing the persuading. You can probably think of people in your own life who are particularly persuasive. Why are some people more persuasive than others? Research on persuasion says we are more likely to be effective as persuaders if listeners consider us to be credible. **Credibility**, or believability, consists of four qualities: expertise, dynamism, trustworthiness, and ethics. Let's look at each of them.[15]

Expertise

Someone who has **expertise** possesses special ability, skill, or knowledge. That is, he or she is an expert. A speaker who is perceived as an expert on his or her subject gains much credibility. For example, let's say that on the news one night you see a woman talking about the effects of long-term exercise on health. The anchorperson introduces her by saying that she is a medical doctor from Johns Hopkins Medical School who has been studying the effects of exercise. Since the results of her study are interesting, you listen closely. The next day you hear a student give a persuasive speech about the value of exercise. Some of his comments, however, contradict some of what you heard on the evening news. Which speaker do you believe? In this case there isn't much doubt. You believe the physician because she is an expert.

EXPERTISE BASED ON PERSONAL EXPERIENCE

When you are a speaker trying to persuade an audience, it will help your credibility if you can show some expertise about your subject. Expertise does not depend only on book learning or specialized training; you can be an expert because of your personal experience. Nancy, for example, speaks of her own experience with alcoholism:

> One night I went to a party. I remember the early part of the evening but that's about all. The next thing I remember was waking up in my own bed. I have no recollection of the end of the party or how I got home. When I woke up that morning and realized I didn't remember anything, I knew I was in serious trouble.

You don't always have to relate such a dramatic experience as Nancy's. One student who had done volunteer work with the Red Cross persuaded classmates to serve as volunteers. Another student persuaded several classmates to petition the dean of students for better food in the cafeteria. She knew that the food was poor, as did many members of her audience. Thus she used both her experience and the experience of audience members to make her point.

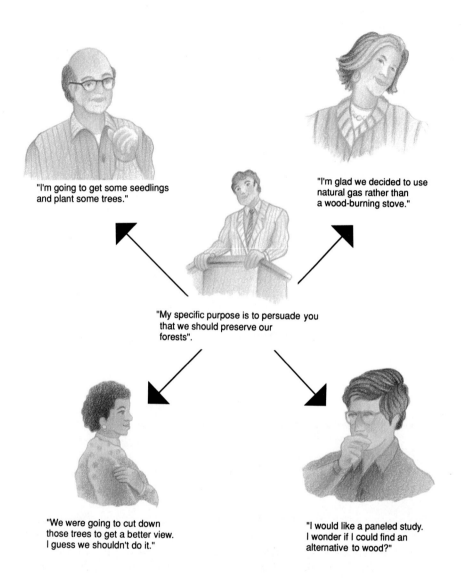

"I'm going to get some seedlings and plant some trees."

"I'm glad we decided to use natural gas rather than a wood-burning stove."

"My specific purpose is to persuade you that we should preserve our forests".

"We were going to cut down those trees to get a better view. I guess we shouldn't do it."

"I would like a paneled study. I wonder if I could find an alternative to wood?"

EXPERTISE BASED ON COMMITMENT

Another way to show expertise is by establishing your commitment to your topic. Listeners are more inclined to believe speakers who have taken actions that support their position. If you can show that you have contributed to charity, you are more likely to persuade others to contribute. If you are trying to persuade people to become scout leaders and can point out that you have been a scout or have worked with scouts for many years, people are more likely to take you seriously.

EXPERTISE THROUGH RESEARCH

Expertise can also be built through research. By interviewing and reading articles and books, you can quote acknowledged experts, thereby making your speech more credible. When you are using information derived from experts, make that clear in your speech with such references as:

> *According to Dr. John Smith, a noted authority in this area . . .*
>
> *From an article in last week's* U.S. News & World Report *. . .*
>
> *David McCullough's best-selling book . . .*

Dynamism

Speakers with **dynamism**, another aspect of credibility, show a great deal of enthusiasm and energy for their subject. For example, when a student tried to get his classmates to become more politically active, he spoke of his own work in a local politician's primary campaign as one of the most exciting times of his life. He described his experience so vividly that the audience was able to feel his excitement.

How does this speaker's dress make him more credible to the audience? Is he aided by the presence of Miss Laredo?

It's easy to be dynamic about a subject you're enthusiastic about. When Hanna spoke about the Australian exchange program, she started this way:

> When your classmates are fighting snow and ice, you will be on the sunny beaches of Australia. When it's winter here, it's summer there. You'll have a chance to talk with people who speak your language. You'll have a chance to see how a different political system works, and you'll have a chance to visit spaces that are more wide-open than you've ever dreamed of. A semester in Australia will change your life.

Much of the dynamism in a speech will be created nonverbally. A speaker who stands up straight, projects his or her voice to the back of the room, and doesn't hesitate will be seen by the audience as more dynamic than one who doesn't do these things. Watch for the most dynamic speakers in your class and make some mental notes on how they convey their energy and enthusiasm nonverbally.

Trustworthiness

A speaker with **trustworthiness** is perceived as reliable and dependable. Sometimes we have no way of knowing whether a speaker is trustworthy unless he or she does something unreliable, like showing up an hour late for a speech. In a speech communication class, however, after a month or so, most students can identify classmates who are reliable and dependable. These are people who come on time for class, give their speeches on time, pull their weight in a group, and give evidence that they have spent time preparing for a speech. Because of their previous behavior in class, they are perceived as trustworthy and therefore worth listening to.

Be Ethical

Ethics are a matter of conforming to acceptable and fair standards of conduct. Ethics are particularly important to persuasion because you are trying to change people—often in a significant way. If your audience doesn't perceive you as ethical, your speech will fail. Here are some ethical principles that are particularly useful in persuasive speaking:

1. Treat your audience with respect. Assume that audience members are intelligent and mature and will respond to a well-reasoned and well-organized appeal.
2. Take care not to distort or exaggerate your facts. Find the best facts you can, and let them stand on their own.
3. Avoid lying or name-calling. Even if you think that the opposing side is stupid or vicious, it's unacceptable to say so.
4. Avoid suppressing key information. If you discover important information that doesn't support your view, include it but find a way of refuting it.

These questions are designed to challenge you with respect to what is ethical. Apply the ethical principles you have just read to each of the following situations:

1. Is it ethical to give a speech advocating a position with which you disagree?
2. Is it ethical to present a speech just to fulfill an assignment—a speech that you feel no commitment to or responsibility for?
3. Are student speakers under obligation to provide listeners with ideas that are logically developed and well supported?
4. Are student speakers responsible for being fully knowledgeable about their topics?
5. Should student speakers concern themselves with the consequences of their speaking?

5. If you have something to gain personally from your persuasive speech, tell your audience what it is.
6. Show respect for your opponent or the opposing side. Do not dismiss ideas from the opposition: show how your ideas are better.
7. Take the time to develop and organize the best possible speech you can. Make it worth the audience's time to listen to you.

SUMMARY

Persuasion is the process that occurs when a communicator influences the values, beliefs, attitudes, or behaviors of another person. The focus of persuasion should be on the sender, the receiver, *and* the message, because all three share in the persuasive process. It is only when all three combine with each other, successfully, that effective persuasion occurs.

The key to understanding persuasion is influence, the power of a person or thing to affect others—to produce effects without the presence of physical force. Persuasion involves motivation as well. Motivation is the stimulation or inducement that causes you to act. We are motivated to do what we do in order to reduce tension, meet needs, or achieve goals, or because we want personal growth, mastery of the environment, and self-understanding. These are useful motivators for persuaders to keep in mind.

We are more likely to respond to persuasive messages that tap into our values, beliefs, and attitudes. Values are types of belief, centrally located within one's total belief system, about how one ought or ought not to behave, or about some end state of existence that is or is not worth attaining. Instrumental values guide people's day-to-day behavior, and terminal values are central to our culture. Beliefs are simple propositions, conscious or unconscious, inferred from what people say or do. People often begin statements of belief with the phrase "I believe that. . . ." Attitudes are relatively enduring sets of beliefs around an object or situation that predispose people to respond in some preferential manner. Persuaders who are sensitive and responsive to the values, beliefs, and attitudes of listeners are more likely to be successful.

Effective persuasion, even though it happens on a daily basis, is difficult. Speakers who understand why it is difficult to change values, beliefs, and attitudes can put the process in perspective and create the proper mental attitude. Difficulties include the sheer amount of persuasion that occurs; how slowly persuasion tends to work; how deeply entrenched values, beliefs, and attitudes may be; the truisms that may guide listeners; laziness; and the desire for freedom of action. These difficulties should increase persuaders' willingness to invest time, effort, and care in their preparation for speeches.

There are specific strategies persuaders can use to be effective. When you prepare a speech, you must determine your purpose, analyze your audience, appeal to your audience using logic, appeal to your audience using emotion, structure your material effectively, select your language carefully, build your credibility, and be ethical.

SAMPLE PERSUASIVE SPEECH

Here is a persuasive speech by Michelle Lynn Meyers, Bowling Green State University. In her speech, "A View to a Kill," Michelle follows the motivated sequence order. The full transcript of the speech is given at the left, and a commentary is on the right. (The numbers in the outline refer to Meyers's notes listed at the end of her outline.)

Title

A View to a Kill

Specific Purpose

To persuade my audience that too much violence on television has a negative effect on children.

Central Idea

Television violence is a contributing cause of violence and aggressive behavior in our society.

Experts estimate that by the time children reach the age of eighteen, they will have spent more time watching television than any other activity besides sleeping.[1] Eleven-year-olds, these experts say, watch an average of four hours a day, with much of it depicting violence.[2] Many young people who wind up in hospitals having been shot, according to the *Los Angeles Times*, say that they are surprised that it hurts because it doesn't hurt on television. Too much violence is shown to children and a feel for reality is not being presented to these children. Should television be screened for the safety of our children?[3]

Does too much violence on television affect children? The National Association for the Education of Young Children points out that preschoolers are vulnerable to the negative influence of media because they are not yet able to distinguish fantasy from reality, and their underlying motives for behavior and understanding of the subtleties of moral conflicts are not yet developed.[4]

Morris Freeman, writing in a recent issue of *The Washington Post*, says television is robbing children of their most short-lived gift: innocence.[5] Television, the experts of *TV Guide* say, is a contributing cause of violence in our society. Years of research have gone into establishing television violence as a contributing cause—and the word *cause* is not used lightly by scientists.[6] Let me make it very clear: scientific opinion, according to Neil Hickey, writing in *TV Guide*, holds that televised violence is, indeed, responsible for a percentage of the real violence in our society.

What is new is that psychologists, child experts, and the medical community are beginning to treat televised violence as a serious public health issue—like smoking and drunk driving—and they feel the public needs to be educated for its own safety and well-being.[7]

Television violence, according to *The Wall Street Journal*, is at an all-time high. A total of 1846 individual acts of violence were recorded during 18 hours of television on April 2, 1992, from 6 A.M. to midnight.[8]

According to the Center for Media and Public Affairs, a nonprofit monitoring com-

Meyers begins with a powerful authoritative statement for her attention step. She establishes her credibility by depending on experts at the outset.

Here, Meyers lets listeners know exactly what her topic is.

Meyers begins her need step with a clear statement of the problem.

Meyers uses her sources effectively.

Here, Meyers makes her need real for her listeners.

She wastes no time in clarifying the need and driving her point home.

Meyers has a strong case, and she gains support from additional experts here.

Meyers cites a reputable source for her statistic.

Notice once again how Meyers builds her credi-

pany, of ten channels analyzed, WTBS, a Ted Turner Broadcasting System station, clocked the most violent acts at 18 an hour and 471 scenes of violence over 18 hours.[9]

Children's television programming on the weekends is saturated with violence. Violent acts per hour in cartoons have risen from 25.5 in 1988 to 32 last year—an all-time high![10]

Dr. Lenord Eron, of the University of Illinois stated, "There is no longer any doubt that heavy exposure to televised violence is one of the causes of aggressive behavior, crime, and violence in society." Eron estimates that fully 10 percent of the actual violence in our society is attributable to viewing violence on television.[11]

Now that I've explained the problem, let me show you how violence works on children.

Children simply mimic the behavior observed during a program. If they are average, they witness at least 8000 TV murders by the time they leave elementary school. According to *U.S. News & World Report*, after viewing a violent cartoon, they will run over to a nearby child and start to do the things they just saw.[12]

My roommate told me that her 5-year-old cousin was going to crawl into a sewer drainpipe to look for the Teenage Mutant Ninja Turtles—proof that cartoons are influential. Her mother caught her just in time.

I know that most of you have viewed cartoons, but many of you probably haven't thought much about the effects they can have on children. If you have brothers or sisters, nieces or nephews, cousins, or even children of your own, realize the kinds of shows they watch. The *TV Guide* task force studied males at the ages of 8, 18, and 30 and found that viewing violence at age 8 predicted aggression at 18 and serious criminal behavior at 30.[13]

No longer can there be any doubt that heavy exposure to televised violence causes aggressive behavior, crime, and violence in society. "Television violence," according to

bility by using excellent sources.

Meyers depends on statistics to explain the extent of the problem.

Here, Meyers adds strength to her statistics with her use of testimony. She has a great deal of useful evidence.

This is a transition.

Meyers injects her sources whenever she can to boost her credibility.

Here, Meyers adds some personal experience to her speech. This piece of information is added for interest.

Meyers relates her problem directly to her audience here.

This is Meyers's transition between her need step and her satisfaction step.

Judy Mann, writing in *The Washington Post*, "affects youngsters of all ages, both genders, all socioeconomic levels, and people at all levels of intelligence."[14] But what can be done about it?

It is obvious something needs to be done to prevent an increase in violence. The younger we start to educate children, the better they will understand.

The first way to start to educate children is to restrict what they can view. Children get up early in the morning and turn anything on. There are uncut movies on at any time during the day. Parents are not always aware of what their children are viewing. We need to promote passage of a law requiring all new televisions to be manufactured with built-in circuitry that will allow parents to "lock out" channels and programs during times they contain high levels of violence.[15]

Peggy Charren, former president of Action for Children's Television, suggested a media-literacy merit badge for both Boy Scouts and Girl Scouts. This would be designed to teach kids that the violence seen on television is not the solution to problems.[16]

The American Psychological Association suggests parental guidance in helping children. They want parents to watch an episode with children to know what their children are viewing, to discuss the violence with them—why it happened and how painful it is. Parents, according to the APA, should explain how the violence is faked and not real, and finally, encourage children to watch programs with characters who cooperate, help, and care for each other.[17]

That is the plan: restriction, children's education, and parental guidance. What is the effect that such a plan can have?

If we do not regulate what children are viewing, many children will view violence as a means to solve problems. An effect of violent television is the direct imitating of the aggression seen on television. Children accept aggressive acts in programs or movies as an accurate portrayal of life rather than mere entertainment.[18]

With the acceptance of my three-part plan,

Once again, Meyers uses her sources effectively.

Here, Meyers begins the satisfaction step by previewing her solution.

Notice how Meyers constructs this paragraph deductively by beginning with her generalization.

This is the first part of Meyers's plan for solving the problem: restriction.

The second part of Meyers's plan has to do with education.

The third part of Meyers's plan is parental guidance, and she offers four ways that parents can help.

Here is Meyers's transition from her satisfaction step to her visualization step.

In this part of her visualiza-

we will begin to see networks pull cartoons and other shows high in violence—especially during periods when children are watching. For example, Ted Turner's WTBS pulled a *Popeye* cartoon because it showed a child attempting suicide. Nickelodeon refused to run a cartoon in which Bugs Bunny plays Russian roulette with Yosemite Sam. Out of Nickelodeon's package of 300 *Looney Tune* cartoons, the network threw out 20 cartoons and made edits in many more.[19]

All right, you may now be asking what *you* can do about all this. What part can *you* play in helping to control the amount of violence depicted on television?

There is proof that televised violence is directly linked to violence in our society. Television is a contributing cause of violence and aggressive behavior. Nearly all heavy viewers behave more aggressively than light viewers.

Dr. Carole Liberman, chairperson of the National Coalition on Television Violence, pointed out that since everybody agrees that *Sesame Street* can teach children the alphabet, TV people should admit that children can learn the ABC's of violence from violent entertainment.[20]

The next time you sit down to watch a cartoon or any shows that children watch, pay particular attention to all the violence in the program or programs. As a viewer, you should become aware of the violence on television. Call or write the station that ran the cartoon or show, asking those responsible for the program to either edit it or cut it altogether. They *do* listen. Violence is having an effect, and it will affect our generation, too. *You* can and you should make a difference!

SOURCE: This speech was given by Michelle Lynn Meyers in a basic speech class at Bowling Green State University, Bowling Green, Ohio, November 23, 1992.

tion step, Meyers offers some specific evidence of what can happen by telling what has already happened. Most audience members can identify with her examples here.

Here is Meyers's transition from her visualization step to her action step.

First, Meyers repeats some of the proof offered earlier in her speech for the cause-effect relationship.

Meyers uses a strong bit of testimony here in her close.

Finally, Meyers ends by making a strong plea to her listeners not to sit idly by but to take some direct action.

Notes

1. Sandra Weber, "How to React to Graphic Violence on TV, Real and Fake," *The New York Times*, Feb. 10, 1991, p. LI2.

2. Terry Pristin, "Soul-Searching on Violence by the Industry," *The Los Angeles Times*, May 18, 1992, p. F12.

3. Pristin, p. F12.

4. Lilian G. Katz, "How TV Violence Affects Kids," *Parents* (January 1991), p. 111.

5. Morris Freeman, "Sordid Entertainment—Does It Steal Children's Innocence?" *The Washington Post*, Sep. 26, 1992, p. A21.

6. "The Experts Speak Out," *TV Guide* (Aug. 22, 1992), p. 12.

7. Neil Hickey, "How Much Violence?" *TV Guide* (Aug. 22, 1992), p. 10.

8. "TV Violence Measured," *The Wall Street Journal*, Aug. 17, 1992, p. B4.

9. Hickey, p. 10.

10. "The Experts," p. 13.

11. "The Experts," p. 13.

12. David Whitman, "The War Over Family Values," *U.S. News & World Report* (June 8, 1992), p. 38.

13. Hickey, p. 11.

14. Judy Mann, "Beyond Murphy Brown," *The Washington Post*, May 27, 1991, p. B11.

15. Hickey, p. 11.

16. "The Experts," p. 19.

17. Hickey, p. 11.

18. "The Experts," p. 20.

19. Richard Turner, "Censors Scissor Frames to Sanitize Some Classic Cartoons," *The Wall Street Journal*, July 29, 1992, p. B5.

20. "The Experts," p. 16.

■ NOTES

[1] From "Give Another Chance," an American Red Cross flyer, June, 1992.

[2] See Mary John Smith, *Persuasion and Human Action: A Review and Critique of Social Influence Theories* (Belmont, CA: Wadsworth, 1982) for a comprehensive overview of persuasion. Also see Erwin P. Bettinghaus and Michael J. Cody, *Persuasive Communication*, 5th ed. (New York: Holt, Rinehart and Winston, 1994), Charles U. Larson, *Persuasion: Reception and Responsibility*, 6th ed. (Belmont, CA: Wadsworth, 1992), Roxane Salyer Lulofs, *Persuasion: Contexts, People, and Messages* (Scottsdale, AZ: Gorsuch Scarisbrick, 1991), and Herbert W. Simons, *Persuasion: Understanding, Practice, and Analysis*, 2d ed. (New York: Random House, 1986).

[3] Milton Rokeach, *Beliefs, Attitudes, and Values: A Theory of Organization and Change* (San Francisco: Jossey-Bass, 1968), p. 124.

[4] Mary Monedas, "Men Communicating with Women: Self-Esteem and Power," in Linda A. M. Perry, Lynn H. Turner, and Helen M. Sterk (Eds.) *Constructing and Reconstructing Gender: The Links among Communication, Language, and Gender* (Albany, NY: State University of New York Press, 1992), p. 197–208.

[5] Diana K. Ivy and Phil Backlund, *Exploring Gender Speak: Personal Effectiveness in Gender Communication* (New York: McGraw-Hill, 1994), p. 61.

[6] Ibid.

[7] Daniel Goleman, "Influencing Others: Skills Are Identified," *The New York Times*, February 18, 1986, pp. C1, C15.

[8] Abraham H. Maslow, *Motivation and Personality*, 2d ed. (New York: Harper & Row, 1970), pp. 80–92.

[9] Wayne N. Thompson, *Responsible and Effective Communication* (Boston: Houghton Mifflin, 1978), p. 209. According to Thompson, research supporting these generalizations has been extensive. The original study was by Carl I. Hovland, Arthur Lumsdaine, and Fred Sheffield, *Experiments on Mass Communication*, vol. 3 of *Studies in Social Psychology in World War II* (Princeton, NJ: Princeton University Press, 1949), pp. 213–214.

[10] Bruce E. Gronbeck, Raymie E. McKerrow, Douglas Ehninger, and Alan H. Monroe, *Principles and Types of Speech Communication*, 12th ed. (New York: HarperCollins, 1994), pp. 193–223.

[11] Charles W. Colson, "Can We Be Good without God? Subjective Standards without Transcendent Moral Truths," *Vital Speeches of the Day* (May 15, 1993), p. 463.

[12] Antonia C. Novello, "Alcohol and Tobacco Advertising: Prevention Indeed Works," *Vital Speeches of the Day* (May 15, 1993), p. 458.

[13] William J. Madia, "Making the Right Choices: Risk Assessment and Environmental Ethics," *Vital Speeches of the Day* (May 15, 1993), p. 461.

[14] Joan E. Aitken, "Light the Fire: Communicate with Your Child," *Vital Speeches of the Day* (May 15, 1993), p. 474.

[15] See Ruth Ann Clark, *Persuasive Messages* (New York: Harper & Row, 1984) for a review of credibility in persuasion through 1983. Also see James M. Kouzes and Barry Z. Posner, *Credibility: How Leaders Gain and Lose It, Why People Demand It* (San Francisco: Jossey-Bass, 1993). Kouzes and Posner include over 25 pages of notes on pp. 289–315.

■ FURTHER READING

BETTINGHAUS, ERWIN P., AND MICHAEL J. CODY. *Persuasive Communication*, 5th ed. New York: Holt, Rinehart and Winston, 1994.   This excellent, research-based textbook includes sections relevant to this chapter on developing attitudes and beliefs, predicting individual response, the influence of the communicator, and structuring messages and appeals. A thorough examination of persuasion.

HOUZES, JAMES M., AND BARRY Z. POSNER. *Credibility: How Leaders Gain and Lose It, Why People Demand It*. San Francisco: Jossey-Bass, 1994.   On the basis of surveys of more than 15,000 people, 400 case studies, and 40 in-depth interviews, the authors provide a guide for readers interested in building personal and organizational success. In addition to specific chapters on leadership and credibility, there are chapters on discovering yourself, appreciating constituents and their diversity, affirming shared values, developing capacity, serving a purpose, sustaining hope, and struggling to be human. A great book.

JAKSA, JAMES A., AND MICHAEL S. PRITCHARD. *Communication Ethics: Methods of Analysis*. Belmont, CA: Wadsworth, 1988.   Jaksa and Pritchard begin by clarifying the need for ethics. They address several questions: What are the ethics of persuasion? How are methods of reasoning in ethics developed? How should ethics be applied in everyday communication? Full of numerous examples, this is a useful approach with challenging discussion questions.

JOHANNESEN, RICHARD L. *Ethics in Human Communication,* 3d ed. Prospect Heights, IL: Waveland Press, 1990. Johannesen begins with a consideration of ethical responsibility in human communication. Then, in separate chapters, he discusses political, psychological, dialogical, situational, religious, utilitarian, and legal perspectives. His chapter "Some Basic Issues" is especially practical and insightful. This book has become the standard in the speech communication field. It is thorough and well researched.

KAHANE, HOWARD. *Logic and Contemporary Rhetoric,* 6th ed. Belmont, CA: Wadsworth, 1992. The strength of this book is in the guidelines Kahane offers for using and developing logical argument. More than most other available sources, Kahane helps readers both identify and eliminate fallacies of reasoning. An outstanding resource.

LARSON, CHARLES U. *Persuasion: Reception and Responsibility,* 6th ed. Belmont, CA: Wadsworth, 1992. This book emphasizes students' need to become skillful consumers or receivers of persuasion. The secondary focus is on symbolic behavior—the language central to every persuasive act. The book also discusses the impact of the media, especially electronic media, on persuasion. In Chapter 2, "Perspectives on Ethics in Persuasion," Richard Johannesen explains the six major ethical perspectives in the most complete and well-researched discussion of the topic in any persuasion textbook.

LULOFS, ROXANE SALYER. *Persuasion: Contexts, People, and Messages.* Scottsdale, AZ: Gorsuch Scarisbrick, 1991. This introductory textbook depends on a four-element communication model—culture, context, people, messages—as its organizing device. Lulofs provides a solid understanding of persuasion, and the book is well-researched practical, well-written with numerous examples.

PAULSON, LYNDA R. (WITH TOM WATSON). *The Executive Persuader: How to Be a Powerful Speaker.* Napa, CA: SSI (Success Strategies Inc.), 1991. Paulson is the founder of the Executive Speaking Experience and a veteran of twenty-five years of helping business people to become better communicators. This how-to book takes readers step by step from preparation to presentation. Chapters cover topics such as personal positioning, power, strategic focus, orchestration, dynamic delivery, and impact and retention.

RUSK, TOM (WITH D. PATRICK MILLER). *The Power of Ethical Persuasion.* New York: Viking (Penguin Books), 1993. Rusk is an associate clinical professor of psychiatry at the University of California, San Diego. He divides this book into three parts: "The Roots of Ethical Persuasion," "How Does Ethical Persuasion Work?" and "Applying Ethical Persuasion." Rusk discusses a practical method for persuading others in difficult and emotionally charged situations. Following his method can promote respect, understanding, caring, and fairness.

TRENHOLM, SARAH. *Persuasion and Social Influence.* Englewood Cliffs, NJ: Prentice-Hall, 1989. Trenholm uses examples from law, politics, religion, education, counseling, sales, and advertising as she demonstrates the power of persuasion in our everyday lives. In addition to explaining theories of persuasion and principles of persuasive message construction, Trenholm analyzes tactics used by professionals. Complete, in-depth, well-researched coverage that includes key concepts, questions for discussion, and exercises and projects.

ACKNOWLEDGMENTS

p. 208: Two adaptations from *Overcoming Relationship Impasses* by Barry L. Duncan and Joseph W. Rock. Copyright © 1991. Reprinted by permission of Plenum Publishing Corporation.

p. 246: "Men Communicating with Women: Self-Esteem and Power" from *Constructing and Reconsidering Gender*, edited by Linda Perry et al. Reprinted by permission of State University of New York Press.

pp. 248, 258: Excerpt from "Communication in the Multicultural Group" by Richard E. Porter and Larry A. Samovar from *Small Group Communication*, edited by Robert S. Cathcart and Larry A. Samover, 6th ed. Copyright © 1992 Wm. C. Brown Communications, Inc., Dubuque, Iowa.

p. 259: Excerpt from *The Eight Essential Steps to Conflict Resolution: Preserving Relationships at Work, at Home, and in the Community* by Dudley Weeks. Copyright © 1992 by Dudley Weeks. Reprinted by permission of the Putnam Publishing Group.

pp. 271–272: Excerpt from *How to Make a Speech* by Steven Allen. Reprinted by permission of the author.

pp. 333, 369, 411, 414: Enclosed excerpts pp. 17–18, 45, 71, and 106–107 from *Well Said and Worth Saying*, C. Barry McCarty (Nashville: Broadman Press 1991). All rights reserved. Used by permission.

p. 348: Excerpts from *You've Got to be Believed to Be Heard* by Bert Decker. Copyright © 1992 by Bert Decker. Reprinted by permission of St. Martin's Press.

p. 370: Excerpts from *The Sir Winston Method: The Five Secrets of Speaking the Language of Leadership* by James C. Humes. Copyright © 1991 by James C. Humes. Reprinted by permission of William Morrow & Co. Inc.

p. 376: Table from *Developing Your Speaking Voice*, 2d ed., by John P. Moncur and Harrison M. Karr. Copyright © 1972 by John P. Moncur and Harrison M. Karr. Reprinted by permission of HarperCollins Publishers.

p. 381: Chart, "One Cavern's Size," from *The New York Times*, May 6, 1991. Copyright © 1991 by The New York Times Company. Reprinted by permission.

p. 383: USA Snapshot "Nearly half of the nation doesn't buy books" 6/24/93. Copyright 1993, *USA Today*. Reprinted with permission.

p. 384: Graph, "Comparing Resident and Commuter Student Populations," by Louis J. Fabian, Assistant to the President & Director, Planning & Evaluation, Lock Haven University. Reprinted by permission.

p. 388: Excerpt from "Consider This" by Ruth Olscamp from *At BG*, Spring 1993. Reprinted by permission of Bowling Green State University.

pp. 404, 445: Excerpts from *Mastering Public Speaking* by George L. Grice and John F. Skinner. Copyright © 1993 by Allyn and Bacon. Reprinted by permission.

p. 405: "Communications in the Future" by Richard Kostyra from *Vital Speeches of the Day*, October 15, 1990. Reprinted by permission of the publisher and the author.

p. 406: "Equity by 2000" by Sarah Harder from *Vital Speeches of the Day*, December 1, 1986. Reprinted by permission of the publisher and the author.

p. 408: "The Art of Waste Minimization" by Douglas E. Olesen from *Vital Speeches of the Day*, August 15, 1990. Reprinted by permission of the publisher and Douglas E. Olesen.

p. 416: "Opportunities for Hispanic Women" by Janice Payan from *Vital Speeches of the Day*, September 1990. Reprinted by permission of the publisher and the author.

p. 418: "Establishing High Standards for the Teaching Profession" by James A. Kelley from *Vital Speeches of the Day*, April 1, 1991. Reprinted by permission of the publisher and the author.

p. 442: "Hierarchy of Needs" from *Motivation and Personality* by Abraham H. Maslow. Copyright 1954 by Harper & Row, Publishers, Inc. Copyright © 1970 by Abraham H. Maslow. Reprinted by permission of HarperCollins Publishers.

p. 450: "Can We Be Good without God? Subjective Standards without Transcendent Moral Truths" by Charles W. Colson, from *Vital Speeches of the Day*, May 15, 1993. Reprinted by permission of the publisher and *Imprimis*, the monthly journal of Hillsdale College, Hillsdale, MI.

p. 450: "Alcohol and Tobacco Advertising: Prevention Indeed Works" by Antonia C. Novello, from *Vital Speeches of the Day*, May 15, 1993. Reprinted by permission of the publisher and Antonia C. Novello.

p. 451: "Light the Fire: Communicate with Your Child" by Joan E. Aitken, from *Vital Speeches of the Day*, May 15, 1993. Reprinted by permission of the publisher and Joan E. Aitken.

PHOTOGRAPHS
Contents
p. v: Skjold/PhotoEdit; p. v: Michael Newman/PhotoEdit; p. vii: Bob Daemmrich/Image Works; p. viii: Amy C. Etra/PhotoEdit; p. xi: Lawrence Migdale/Stock, Boston; p. xiii: Terry Wild Studio; p. xiv: John Coletti/Stock, Boston; opposite page 1: Richard Pasley/Stock, Boston.

Chapter 1
p. 2: Comstock; p. 9: Tony Freeman/PhotoEdit; p. 10: Comstock; p. 11: Billy E. Barnes/Stock, Boston; p. 14: David R. Austen/Stock, Boston; p. 20: Collins/Monkmeyer.

Chapter 2
p. 28: Chester Higgins Jr./Photo Researchers; p. 35: Comstock; p. 39: Terry Wild Studio; p. 45: Tom Levy/Photo 20-20.

Chapter 3
p. 54: Terry Wild Studio; p. 57: MacDonald Photography/Unicorn Stock Photos; p. 63: Tony Freeman/PhotoEdit; p. 66: David Lissy/Picture Cube; p. 69: Robert Brenner/Photo Edit.

Chapter 4
p. 82: Stephen Frisch/Photo 20-20; p. 86: Brady/Monkmeyer; p. 95: Ilene Perlman/Stock, Boston; p. 99: Bob Daemmrich/Stock, Boston; p. 101: Bohdan Hrynewych/Stock, Boston.

Chapter 5
p. 114: T. Michaels/Image Works; p. 118: Russell D. Curtis/Photo Researchers; p. 122: Terry Wild Studio; p. 131: Terry Wild Studio; p. 139: Bonnie Kamin/Comstock; p. 146: Terry Wild Studio.

ACKNOWLEDGEMENTS

Chapter 6
p. 148: Terry Wild Studio; p. 154: Michael Newman/PhotoEdit; p. 164: Mary Kate Denny/PhotoEdit; p. 172: Shackman/Monkmeyer.

Chapter 7
p. 182: Steve Bourgeois/Unicorn Stock Photos; p. 191: Jeff Isaac Greenberg/Photo Researchers; p. 193: Alan Oddie/PhotoEdit; p. 198: Bob Daemmrich/Stock, Boston; p. 212; Blair Seitz/Photo Researchers.

Chapter 8
p. 214: Gary Conner/PhotoEdit; p. 221: Rogers/Monkmeyer; p. 225: Elizabeth Crews/Image Works; p. 228: Byron/Monkmeyer.

Chapter 9
p. 238: Tim Brown/Tony Stone; p. 243: Comstock; p. 249: Comstock; p. 254: Bruce Ayres/Tony Stone; p. 225: L. Goodsmith/Image Works; p. 266: Hasegawa/Monkmeyer.

Chapter 10
p. 268: David Joel/Tony Stone; p. 273: Susan McCartney/Photo Researchers; p. 292: Jim Pickerell/Stock, Boston.

Chapter 11
p. 302: Griffin/Image Works; p. 310: Bob Daemmrich/Image Works; p. 311: R. Sidney/Image Works.

Chapter 12
p. 330: Joyce Wilson/Photo Researchers; p. 339: Terry Wild Studio; p. 345: Charles Gupton/Stock, Boston.

Chapter 13
p. 362: Bob Daemmrich/Image Works; p. 379: Sarah Putnam/Picture Cube; p. 387: Frank Siteman/Stock, Boston.

Chapter 14
p. 398: Frank Siteman/Stock Boston; p. 402: Bob Daemmrich/Image Works; p. 406: Jeffrey Muir Hamilton/Stock, Boston; p. 409: Shackman/Monkmeyer; p. 412: Seth Resnick/Stock, Boston.

Chapter 15
p. 426: Art Gingert/Comstock; p. 429: Michael Newman/PhotoEdit; p. 435: Mary Kate Denny/PhotoEdit; p. 436: Bob Daemmrich/Stock, Boston; p. 454: Bob Daemmrich/Stock, Boston.

GLOSSARY

Abstract(s)   Summaries of articles. Abstracts will tell you enough about an article for you to decide whether it is worthwhile to locate the entire thing.

Abstract symbol   A symbol which represents an idea.

Accommodation   Something that occurs in groups when people on one side of an issue give in to the other side.

Active listener   A listener who makes a mental outline of important points and thinks up questions or challenges to those points.

Adaptors   Nonverbal ways of adjusting to a communication situation.

Affection   A feeling of warm, emotional attachment we have for people we appreciate and care for.

Agenda   A list of all the items that will be discussed during a meeting.

Aggression   A physical or verbal show of force.

Analogy   In reasoning, comparing two similar cases and concluding that if something is true for one, it must also be true for the other.

Anecdote   A short, interesting story based on an experience.

Articulation   The ability to pronounce the letters in a word correctly.

Assertiveness   Taking the responsibility of expressing needs, thoughts, and feelings in a direct, clear manner.

Assessment   The evaluation of what took place during communication.

Attitudes   Deeply felt beliefs that govern how one behaves; also, a group of beliefs connected to an object or situation that causes us to respond in some way.

Audience analysis   Finding out what one's audience members know about a subject, what they might be interested in, and what their attitudes and beliefs are.

Authoritarian leader   One who holds the greatest control over a group.

Avoidance   A refusal to deal with conflict or painful issues.

Beliefs   One's own convictions; what one thinks is right and wrong, true and false; also, they are classified as statements of knowledge, opinion, and faith.

Bibliography   A list of sources (books, magazines, interviews, newspapers) used to prepare a speech or report.

Bilingualism   The ability to speak two languages.

Body   The main part of the speech.

Body movement (kinesics) Describes a phenomenon responsible for much of our nonverbal communication.

Brainstorming A technique of free association; in groups, when all members spontaneously contribute ideas in a group without judgments being made. The goal of brainstorming is for the group to be as creative as possible.

Card catalog Entries in the library's card catalog are organized in three ways: by author, by title, and by subject.

Catalog The library catalog consists of information about all the material in the library; it identifies where that material can be found.

Causal reasoning Reasoning that uses the word *because*—either implicitly or explicitly stated.

Cause-and-effect order Organization of a speech around why something is happening (*cause*) and what impact it is having (*effect*).

Central idea The main idea of a speech.

Channel The route traveled by a message; the means it uses to reach the sender-receivers.

Coercive power In an organization, the ability of a leader to punish followers (e.g., by criticizing them, refusing to pay attention to them, using power to demote them, refusing to raise their pay, or firing them).

Cognitive dissonance A psychological theory, applied to communication, which states that people seek information that will support their beliefs and ignore information that does not.

Cohesiveness The feeling of attraction that group members have toward one another. It is the group's ability to stick together, to work together as a group, and to help one another as group members.

Collaboration When people in conflict try to work together to meet the other person's needs as well as their own.

Commitment A strong desire by both parties for the relationship to continue. In groups, it is the willingness of members to work together to complete the group's task.

Communication Any process in which people share information, ideas, and feelings.

Comparison Pointing out the similarities between two or more things.

Comparative advantage order A method of arranging a speech that enables the speaker to compare the advantages of one solution over another.

Compatibility Similar attitudes, personality, and a liking for the same activities

Competition Something that occurs in groups when one side cares more about winning than it does about other member's feelings.

Complaint Expression of dissatisfaction with the behavior, attitude, belief, or characteristic of a partner or of someone else.

Composition The makeup of a thing.

Compromise When each side in a conflict has to give up something in order to get what it wants.

Computer catalog A catalog that duplicates the library's card catalog by having call numbers and entries arranged by author, subject, and title. The main difference between the computer catalog and the card catalog is that the former almost always gives you information about the book's availability.

Conclusion In a speech, the closing remarks that tie a speech together and give listeners the feeling that the speech is complete.

Concrete symbol A symbol that represents an object.

Conflict Expressed struggle between at least two individuals who perceive incompatible goals or interference from others in achieving their goals.

Conflict resolution Negotiation to find a solution to the conflict.

Connotative meaning The feelings or associations that each individual has about a particular word.

Consensus The point at which all members of a group agree.

Contrast Pointing out the differences between two or more things.

Control Attitude that one is always right and that no other opinion or fact is worth listening to; getting people to do what you want them to do.

Costs and rewards Problems and pleasures of a relationship.

Credibility The believability of a speaker based on the speaker's expertise, dynamism, trustworthiness, and ethics.

Critical listening Evaluating and questioning what has been heard.

Criticism A negative evaluation of a person for something he or she has done or the way he or she is.

Critics-analyzers Group members who look at the good and bad points in the information the group has gathered. These members see the points that need more elaboration, and they discover information that has been left out.

Data base A collection of information that can be read on a computer screen.

Deductive reasoning Reasoning from the general to the specific.

Defensive communication When one partner tries to defend himself or herself against the remarks or behavior of the other.

Definition A brief explanation of what a word or phrase means.

Democratic leader One who lets all points of view be heard and lets group members participate in the decision-making process.

Demographic analysis Data about characteristics of a group of people, including such things as age; sex; education; occupation; race, nationality, ethnic origin; geographic location; and group affiliation.

Denotative meaning The dictionary definition of a particular word.

Diagram May range from a simple organizational chart to a complex rendering of a three-dimensional object. It is particularly valuable in showing how something works.

Dialect The habitual language of a community.

Displays of feelings Face and body movements that show how intensely we are feeling.

Doublespeak A term that refers to euphemisms created by an institution, such as government, to cover up the truth.

Dynamism For speakers, a great deal of enthusiasm and energy for their subject.

Emblems Body movements that have a direct translation into words.

Emotional appeal An appeal that focuses on listeners' needs, wants, desires, and wishes.

Empathic listening Listening for feelings, in contrast to listening for main points or listening to criticize ideas.

Empathy The ability to recognize and identify with someone's feelings.

Encouragers These group members praise and commend contributions and group achievements.

Enunciation How one pronounces and articulates words.

Ethics The moral values brought to a communication experience; also, conforming to acceptable and fair standards of conduct.

Ethnicity A shared history, tradition, and culture.

Ethnocentrism A term implying that one's own ethnic group is so special that it occupies the center of the world.

Etymology The study of the origin and development of words.

Euphemisms Inoffensive words or phrases which are substituted for words that might be perceived as unpleasant.

Evaluative statements Statements involving a judgment.

Example A short illustration that clarifies a point.

Expertise Having the experience or knowledge of an expert.

Expert power The influence and power that an expert has because he or she knows more than anyone else.

Extemporaneous speaking Speaking from notes.

Family Two or more individuals who are joined together at a particular point in time through the biological or sociological means of genetics, marriage, or adoption.

Flip chart A series of pictures, words, diagrams, and so forth. It is made up of several pages that speakers "flip" through.

Full-sentence outline A complete map of what a speech will look like.

Function How things perform or how they can be used.

General purpose The intention of the speaker to inform or persuade.

Graph Statistical material presented in a visual form that helps viewers see similarities, differences, relationships, or trends.

Groupthink A group dysfunction in which the preservation of harmony becomes more important than the critical examination of ideas.

Harmonizers-compromisers Group members who help to resolve conflict in the group, settle arguments and disagreements through mediation, and attempt to discover solutions acceptable to everyone.

Hidden agenda Unannounced goals, subjects, or issues of individual group members or subgroups that differ from the group's public or stated agenda.

Hierarchy of needs The relative order of the physical and psychological needs of all human beings.

Hypothetical example An example that is made up to illustrate a point.

Illustrators Gestures or other nonverbal signals which accent, emphasize, or reinforce words.

Impromptu speaking   Speaking on the spur of the moment with little time to prepare.

Inclusion   Involvement with others.

Inductive reasoning   Reasoning from the specific to the general.

Inference   A logical conclusion drawn from a set of data.

Inflection   A change in pitch used to emphasize certain words and phrases.

Influence   The power of a person or things to affect others—to produce effects without the presence of physical force.

Information givers and seekers   Members of groups who either give information or seek it.

Informative speech   A speech that concentrates on explaining, defining, clarifying, and instructing.

Initiators-expediters   Members of groups who suggest new ideas, goals, solutions, and approaches.

Instrumental values   Those values that guide people's day-to-day behavior (how one should or should not behave).

Interactionist approach   When leaders of groups arise because of the combination of their personality traits and the situations in which they find themselves.

Intercultural communication   Communication that occurs whenever two or more people from different cultures interact.

Interpersonal communication   One person interacting with another on a one-to-one basis, often in an informal, unstructured setting.

Intimacy   Quality of interpersonal relationships characterized by spontaneity, self-disclosure, motivation, interdependence, and tension and balance.

Intrapersonal communication   Communication that occurs within a person.

Introduction   In a speech, the opening remarks that aim to get attention and build interest in the subject.

Johari Window   A model of the process of disclosure in interpersonal relationships, developed by Joseph Luft and Harry Ingham.

Key-word outline   An outline containing only the important words or phrases of a speech that help to remind speakers of the ideas they are presenting.

Laissez-faire leader   One who does very little actual leading. This leader suggests no direction for and imposes no order on a group.

Language environment   The environment in which language takes place, e.g., in a classroom.

Leader   A person who influences the behavior of one or more people.

Leadership style   The amount of control a leader exerts over a group.

Listening   Hearing and responding to given information, both intellectually and emotionally.

Logical appeal   The use of reasoning and evidence to advance an argument or point of view.

Main idea   The central thought in a passage, speech, or lecture.

Maintenance roles   Group members who play these roles focus on the emotional tone of the meeting.

Manuscript speaking   Writing out an entire speech and reading it to the audience from the prepared script.

Message   Comprised of the ideas and feelings that a sender-receiver wants to share.

Metamessages   The meaning, apart from the words, in a message.

Minor points   The specific ideas and information that support the main points.

Mixed messages   Messages that occur when verbal and nonverbal communication conflict.

Monotone   Little variety of pitch in a speech.

Motivated sequence   Organization of a speech that involves five steps: attention, need, satisfaction, visualization, and action.

Motivation   The stimulation or inducement that causes people to act.

Multimedia   Refers to various media (e.g., text, graphics, animation, and audio) used to deliver information.

Noise   Interference that keeps a message from being understood or accurately interpreted.

Nonverbal communication   Information we communicate without using words.

Nonverbal symbol   Anything communicated without words, e.g., facial expressions or hand gestures.

Norms   Expectations that group members have of how other members will behave, think, and participate.

Observers   Group members who aid in the group's cohesiveness by being sensitive to the needs of each member.

Organizational chart   A chart that shows the relationships among the elements of an organization, such as the departments of a company, the branches of federal or state government, or the committees of student government.

Organizational power   The ability of a leader to be influential because of his or her place in the organizational hierarchy (e.g., as a boss or supervisor).

Pace   How quickly or slowly one speaks.

Paralanguage   The way we say something.

Passive listener   A listener who records but does not evaluate what is heard.

Perception   How people look at themselves and the world around them.

Periodicals   The inclusive name for magazines, journals, and newspapers.

Personal inventory   Appraising your own resources.

Persuasion   The process of trying to get others to change their attitudes or behavior; also, the process that occurs when a communicator (*sender*) influences the values, beliefs, attitudes, or behaviors of another person (*receiver*).

Persuasive speech   A speech in which the speaker takes a particular position and tries to get the audience to accept and support that position.

Pitch   Highness or lowness of the voice.

Polls   Surveys taken of people's attitudes, feelings, or knowledge.

Prediction   From past experience with a person, a listener tries to predict what he or she will say next.

Problem-solution order   Organization of a speech into two sections: one dealing with the problem and the other dealing with the solution.

Pronunciation   The ability to pronounce a word correctly.

Proxemics   The study of how people and animals use space.

Proximity   Close contact that occurs between people who share an experience such as work, play, or school.

Psychological risk   Taking a chance on something new, e.g., on a new person or place.

Psychological safety   Approval and support obtained from familiar people, ideas, and situations.

Public communication   The sender-receiver (*speaker*) sends a message (*the speech*) to an audience.

Quality (of voice)   Comprised of all voice characteristics: tempo, resonance, rhythm, pitch, and articulation.

Questions of fact   Questions that deal with what is true and what is false.

Questions of policy   Questions that are about actions that might be taken in the future.

Questions of value   Questions of whether something is good or bad, desirable or undesirable.

Race   Biological characteristics, such as color of skin, eyes, hair, and so forth.

Racism   A term implying that one's race is superior to all others.

Rapport-talk   Type of language women use in conversation, designed to lead to intimacy with others, match experiences, and to establish relationships.

Rate (of speech)   Speed at which one speaks.

Referent power   When leaders enjoy influence because of their personality.

Reflected appraisals   Messages a person gets from others.

Regrettable talk   Saying something embarrassing, hurtful, or private to or about another person.

Regulators   (1) Group members who play this role help regulate group discussion by gently reminding members of the agenda or of the point they were discussing when they digressed. (2) Nonverbal signals which control the back-and-forth flow of speaking and listening, such as head nods, hand gestures, and other body movements.

Report-talk   Type of language men use in conversation, designed to maintain status, to demonstrate knowledge and skills, and to keep center-stage position.

Reward power   A leader can have an influence if he or she can reward the followers (e.g., through promotions, pay raises, or praise).

Rhetorical question   A question that audience members answer mentally rather than aloud.

Ritual language   Communication that takes place when we are in an environment in which a conventionalized response is expected of us.

Roles   Parts we play, or ways we behave with others.

Rules   Formal and structured directions for behavior.

Scripts   Lines given to people to speak that are tailored to fit a specific situation.

Selective attention   The ability to focus perception.

Self-concept   How a person thinks about and values himself or herself.

Self-disclosure   Process by which one person tells another something he or she would not tell just anyone.

Self-esteem   See *self-concept*.

Self-fulfilling prophecies   Events or actions that occur because a person and those around her or him expected them.

Self-perception   The way in which one sees oneself.

Sender-receiver   In communication situations, people who simultaneously send and receive messages.

Setting   Where the communication occurs.

Small-group communication   Gatherings of three to thirteen members who meet to do a job or solve a problem.

Small talk   Social conversation about unimportant topics that allows a person to maintain contact with a lot of people without making a deep commitment.

Social comparison   Comparing and contrasting oneself with others.

Spatial order   Organization of a speech by something's location in space (e.g., left to right, top to bottom).

Specific purpose   A statement for a speech that tells precisely what the speaker wants to accomplish.

Statistics   Facts in numerical form.

Stereotypes   Oversimplified or distorted views of another race, ethnic group, or even a culture.

Study   An in-depth investigation of a subject.

Style   The result of the way we select and arrange words and sentences.

Substantive conflict   Conflict that arises when people have different reactions to an idea. Substantive conflict is likely to occur when any important and controversial idea is being discussed.

Supporting material   Information that backs up your main points and provides the main content of the speech.

Supporting points   Materials that reinforce the main idea in a passage, speech, or lecture.

Symbol   Something that stands for something else.

Systems theory of family   This theory describes a family as a dynamic whole composed of constantly shifting interrelationships but still bounded and rule-governed.

Tables   Columns of figures arranged in an order that enables the viewer to easily pick out the needed information.

Target audience   A subgroup of the whole audience that you must persuade to reach your goal.

Task roles   Roles that help get the job done. Persons who play these roles help groups come up with new ideas, aid in collecting and organizing information, and assist in analyzing the information that exists.

Terminal values   Some final goal that is worth or not worth attaining.

Territory   Space we consider as belonging to us, either temporarily or permanently.

Testimony   Another person's statements or actions used to give authority to what the speaker is saying.

Time order   Organization of a speech by chronology or historical occurrence.

Topical order   Organization of a speech used when the subject can be grouped logically into subtopics.

Transactional communication   Communication as a transaction between two or more people.

Transitions   Comments that lead from one point to another to tell listeners where the speaker has been and where the speaker is going.

Trustworthiness   In the giving of a speech, one's being perceived as reliable and dependable.

Values   A type of belief about how we should behave or about some final goal that may or may not be worth attaining.

Verbal symbol   A word that stands for a particular thing or idea.

Vertical file   A file that contains pamphlets and booklets written by various groups; generally filed by subject in the library.

Visual aids   Visual material that helps illustrate key points in a speech or presentation. They are devices such as charts, graphs, and slides.

Vocal fillers   Words we use to fill out our sentences or to cover up when we are searching for words.

Volume (of vocal sound   How loudly we speak.

INDEX

Johari Window, 163 (illus.), 171
Johnson, Bonnie, 204

Katz, Lillian G., 40
Karr, Harrison M., 376
Keeshan, Bob, 415
Keillor, Garrison, 33
Kellerman, Kathy, 159
Kelley, Win, 278
Kevorkian, Dr. Jack, 260
Key-word outline, 352–353
Kilpatrick, James J., 411
Kinesics, 126
  (*See also* Body movement)
Klass, Perri, 120
Knapp, Mark L., 160–162, 184,
  190

Laissez-faire leader, 249–250
Lakoff, Robin Tolmach, 89
Language:
  appropriate vs. inappropriate,
    91–92
  clarity in, 104–105
  and dialect, 97–98
  and environment, 90–94
  and gender, 95–97
  moral choices in, 106–107
  powerful talk in, 105
  as a ritual, 91
  speaking in, 98–101
  and specialization, 92–94
  and style, 94–101
  understanding, 90
  vividness in, 106
  and words, 86–90
  writing in, 98–101
  (*See also* Words)
Leaders:
  authoritarian, 247–248
  characteristics of, 245
  definition of, 243
  democratic, 248–249
  and influence, 243–245 (illus.)
  and interactionist approach,
    246–247
  laissez-faire, 249–250
  and personality, 245
  and power types, 244
  responsibilities of, 252–254
  and roles, 250–254
  types of, 247–250
Leadership style, 247
Legitimate power, 244
Leisure clothing, 132

Library:
  catalog, 306–307
  staff, 316
  use of, 306–316
Line graphs, 382, 384 (illus.)
Listening:
  active, 64–65
  and anxiety, 57–58
  assessment in, 61–62
  attitudes, 64–65
  and cognitive dissonance, 57
  critical, 69–72
  definition of, 56
  empathic, 72–77
  for enjoyment, 77–78
  for feelings, 73
  importance of, 60–61
  for information, 65–69
  and involvement, 417–422
  passive, 64–65
  and predictions, 61, 68
  and problems in, 56–61
  process of, 61–64, 65 (illus.)
  reasons for, 56–60
  reflective, 192
  and relating, 68
  the skill of, 60–61
  time devoted to, 61 (illus.)
  types of, 58–60, 65–78
Logical appeal, 439
Love-intimacy touch, 138
Luft, Joseph, 163

Madia, William J., 451
Main idea:
  definition of, 66
  identification of, 66–67
  points of, 334–336
  (*See also* Central idea)
Main points, 334
Maintenance roles, 256–258
Management, floor, 161
Maslow, Abraham, 37, 441–443
McCarty, Barry, 333, 368–369, 411,
  414
McCaw, Craig, 413
McLuhan, Marshall, 20
Meanings:
  connotative, 87
  denotative, 87
Mehrabian, Albert, 8, 125, 140–141
Mental outline, of speeches, 67–68
Messages, 8
  control, 174
  mixed, 122
  support, 174

Metamessages, 103–104
Metzger, Annie, 354–358
Meyers, Michelle Lynn, 456–461
Microfiche, 311
Microfilm, 311
Minatoya, Lydia, 34, 137
Minor points, 334
Mixed messages, 122
Moncur, John P., 376
Monedas, Mary, 246–247
Monotone, 377
Monroe, Alan H., 340
Moore, Monica M., 130
Motivated sequence, 340–341,
  448–450
Motivation, 430
Mouton, Jane, 260
Muehlenhard, Charlene L., 124
  (illus.)
Multimedia, 386

Nader, Ralph, 296
Needs:
  belongingness and love, 442
  safety, 442
  self-actualization, 443
  self-esteem, 443
  physiological, 442
Negative listening responses, 73–74
Nervousness:
  controlling, 388–391
  (*See also* Speaker anxiety)
Newspapers, 311–312
Noise, 10–11
  external, 10
  internal, 10
  semantic, 10
Noller, Patricia, 166, 170–171
Nonverbal communication:
  attitudes in, 125
  cues in, 124 (illus.)
  definition of, 116
  feelings in, 125
  functions of, 119–121
  importance of, 116–121
  improving, 139–142
  mixed messages in, 122–123
  principles of, 121–125
  and symbols, 8
  time in, 138–139
  touch in, 136–138
  as a transaction, 116–117
  types of, 125–132
  verbal and, 117–119
Nonverbal symbols, 8
Norms, 219